Minutes Of Proceedings Of The Institution Of Civil Engineers, Volumes 21-30

MINUTES OF PROCEEDINGS

OF THE

INSTITUTION

OF

CIVIL ENGINEERS.

GENERAL INDEX,
VOLUMES XXI. TO XXX.

• SESSIONS 1861–62 to 1869–70.

LONDON:
Published by the Institution,
25, GREAT GEORGE STREET, WESTMINSTER, S.W.
1871.

WILLIAM CLOWES AND SONS, STAMFORD STREET AND CHARING CROSS.

PREFACE.

THIS GENERAL INDEX of Volumes XXI. to XXX. (inclusive)
forms a continuation of the previous Index of Volumes I. to
XX., and has been compiled upon the same plan. In its
preparation the first step taken was to make out a list of
the subjects forming the contents of these volumes; next to
indicate, between inverted commas, the exact titles of the
different "Papers," under their leading subject-heading, and
then to append to these the analysis of each communication,
as previously given, with, in addition, an Alphabetical List
of the various speakers. It will also be found that, with a
view to facilitate consultation, as many cross-references and
subordinate entries have been introduced as possible. In
every case the name of the author appears as part of each
subject-entry. The name-entries were afterwards proceeded
with, and in regard to these, it will be observed that they had
to be entirely remodelled. Thus, there is first given, after
each name, within brackets, what may be termed the personal
history in the Institution of every individual—his election.

the awards he has received, the positions he has filled, etc. Then, alphabetically arranged under each name, are the subjects upon which he has written or spoken at the meetings, corresponding with the main subject-entries throughout the work.

The principal subject and name entries have been printed in capital letters, while the cross-references and minor entries are in ordinary type. It is believed that by the system adopted, it will be an easy task to find what has been communicated in writing to the Institution, or has been spoken at the meetings, on any question, or by any individual, during the period to which this General Index relates. At the same time, the members of all classes are earnestly desired to point out any omissions, or errors, they may find, with a view to a corrected copy of the Index being preserved in the Institution.

THE INSTITUTION OF CIVIL ENGINEERS,
25, *Great George Street, Westminster, S.W.*
August 3, 1871.

MINUTES OF PROCEEDINGS

OF

THE INSTITUTION OF CIVIL ENGINEERS.

GENERAL INDEX.

VOLUMES TWENTY-ONE TO THIRTY.

The Roman Letters refer to the Volume; the Arabic Numerals to the Page.

A.

ABBATT.

ABBATT, E. A. [Admission, xxix. 98.]

ABBEY, J. H. [Election, xxviii. 518.]

ABBOTT, J. H. [Election, xxvii. 55.]

ABERNETHY, G. [Memoir, xxv. 522.]

ABERNETHY, J. [Telford medal, xxii. 120, 130; Member of Council, xxv. 161; xxvi. 119; xxvii. 122; xxviii. 158; xxix. 208.]

Canal, Suez, xxvi. 449.—State of works in February, 1867, 449.—Alteration of the slopes, 449.—Jetties at Port Saïd, 450.—Dredging operations in Lake Menzaleh, 450.—Cost of excavating, 454.

Canals. Non-existence of canals specially adapted for the application of steam-power, xxvi. 32.—Aire and Calder Navigation, 32.—Freshwater canal of Darius Hystaspes, 449.—Cavour Canal carried under Alpine torrents, xxix. 124.

Cement, Portland, use of, for the foundations of marine works, xxv. 113.—Employment of, in situations exposed to currents of water, 113.

Docks, graving. Cost of the hydraulic lift graving dock, xxv. 310, 319.—Cost of graving docks at Birkenhead and

ABERNETHY.

·Falmouth, 320.—Advantages claimed for hydraulic lifts, 320.—Floating docks, 321.—Economical working of stone graving docks, 322.—Cost of working the hydraulic lift graving dock, 340.—Practicability of lengthening a vessel on a pontoon, 340.—Cost of the Falmouth graving docks, 352.

Drainage of fen districts bordering the Witham, xxviii. 101.

Hydraulic apparatus. Cost of, as applied to the lock-gates at Silloth, xxi. 343. — Proposed at Aberdeen Docks, 344.

Locomotive engines used on the Giovi incline, xxvi. 72.

Low-water basin at Birkenhead, xxix. 5.—Sluicing operations at ditto, 6.

Ports of Swansea, Blyth, and Silloth. "Description of works at the ports of Swansea, Blyth, and Silloth," xxi. 309. — Remarks, 342.—Non-existence of a bar at Aberdeen Harbour, 342.—Cost of dock at Silloth, 343, 344.—Proposed hydraulic machinery at Aberdeen Docks, 344.

Railway, Mont Cenis, xxvi. 370.—Great depth of snow on the Mont Cenis during winter, and the necessity of

B

ABERNETHY.

protecting the railway by a covered way, 370.

Rivers and estuaries. Erroneous opinion that the non-existence of a bar at Aberdeen Harbour is due to freshes of the Dee, xxi. 342.—Treatment of tidal rivers, and of rivers dependent on the volume of fresh water delivered to the sea, 343.—Effect of jetties and training-walls on tidal rivers, xxiv. 77.—Piers at the mouth of the Tyne, xxvi. 438. Effect of the enclosure of Jarrow Slake, 438.—Improvements in the Dee at Aberdeen Harbour, 439.—Causes of the changes in the navigable channel of the Humber, xxviii. 497.—Embanking the shore between Sunk Island and Spurn Point, 497.—Improvement of the Tyne, 497.

ABERNETHY, J. [Election, xxvi. 79.]

ABERNETHY, J., Jun. [Admission, xxvii. 53; Election, xxix. 98.]

Abstracts of receipts and expenditure, xxi. 150; xxii. 127; xxiii. 124; xxiv. 121; xxv. 178; xxvi. 133; xxvii. 137; xxviii. 174; xxix. 233.

Accidents in mines, vide COAL MINES; upon railways, vide RAILWAY ACCIDENTS.

ADAMS, H. [Admission, xxvii. 180.]

ADAMS, W. [Election, xxviii. 439.]

Locomotive engine, radial axle, trials of the, xxiii. 438.

Permanent way. Wear of steel rails, xxvii. 380.

Railway, North London, working expenses of the, xxx. 200.

ADAMS, W. A. [Election, xxiv. 144.]

Railway rolling stock. Cost and maintenance of, xxiv. 496.—Construction and upholding of freighters' wagons, 497.—Coal wagon stock on the North Eastern Railway, 497.—Experience of the Midland Wagon Company, 497.—American locomotives and rolling stock, xxviii. 397.—Success of bogie carriages on the Sirhowy railway, 397.—Cast-iron wheels for railway rolling stock, 397.—Bogie system of carriages for road traffic, 397.

ADAMS, W. B. [Watt medal, xxiv. 109, 124.]

ADAMS.

Locomotive engines. Locomotive engines for traversing sharp curves, xxvi. 74.—Double locomotive engines, 75.—Adapting the tenders of engines as a means of increased traction, 75.—Most suitable position of the cylinders of locomotives, 75.

Permanent way. Question of rail manufacture, xxvii. 396.—Wear of rails by the grinding action of the rolling stock, 397.

Radial axle locomotive engine, xxiii. 438.

Railway breaks. Self-acting gravitation lever breaks, xxviii. 260, et seq.—Common system of breaks, 262.

Railway gradients and curves, xxviii. 264.

Railway locomotion. "On the impedimental friction between wheel tire and rails, with plans for improvement," xxiii. 411.—Remarks, 438.—Results of the trial of the radial axle engine on the North London railway, 438.—Performance of a radial axle engine on the St. Helens railway, 438.—Suitability of ditto for express trains, 439.—Adhesion of elastic wheel-tires, 439.—Radiation of the axles, 439.—Mr. Buck's invention of an elastic permanent way, 439.—Elastic permanent way laid down on the North London railway, 439—Difference between iron rails and steel rails, 440.—Details of the system of elastic permanent way, 441.

Railway rolling stock. Spring tires, xxvi. 76.—Breakage of tires, 76.—Wheels loose on the axle, 76.—Means for reducing the friction of rolling stock, xxvii. 397.—Bogie trucks, xxviii. 386, 391, et seq.—Oil axle-boxes and the rolling friction of railway carriages, 388.—Bogie wagons and caster wagons, 389.—American railway carriages, 390.—Width of railway carriages, 390.—Four-wheel railway stock, 390.—Locomotives with inside and outside cylinders, 391, 402.—Coal trains, 392.

Railways. Light railways and cost of

ADDRESSES.

gauge, xxiv. 380; comparative cost of light and heavy railways, xxvi. 74.

ADDRESSES of Presidents:—
Fowler, J., xxv. 203.
Gregory, C. H., xxvii. 180.
Hawkshaw, J., xxi. 173.
M'Clean, J. R., xxiii. 151.
Vignoles, C. B., xxix. 272.

ADDY, J. [Admission, xxviii. 216.]

ADIE, P. [Election, xxiv. 458.]
Surveying. Measuring distances by the telescope, and description of a tele-meter, xxi. 40.

ADLEY, C. C. [Election, xxi. 345.]
Railway accidents, relative number of, on Indian and English railways, xxii. 227.
Railway telegraph, efficiency of, in working single lines of railway in India, xxii. 227.—Mechanical arrange-ment of, 227.

AGNEW, J. A. [Resignation, xxviii. 167.]
Agricultural conditions of Great Britain, and other countries, xxiii. 152; xxvii. 519.

AGUILAR, J. V. [Admission, xxix. 98.]

AIRD, A. [Election, xxiv. 511.]

AIRD, J., Jun. [Associate of Council, xxiv. 106.]
Cements, influence of water on, xxv. 128.
Concrete under water, use of, xxv. 128.
Drainage of towns. Drainage of Lon-don south of the Thames, xxiv. 344, et seq.—System of subways in Paris, 345.—Cost of construction of the me-tropolitan sewers, 346.

AIRY, G. B. [Telford medal, xxvii.124,142.]
Beams, deflection of loaded, xxvi. 286.
Bridges. "On the use of the suspension-bridge with stiffened roadway, for railway and other bridges of great span," xxvi. 258.—Remarks, 266.—Supporting suspension bridges, 267.—Britannia Bridge, 267.—Angles formed by the chains over the top of the piers of suspension bridges, 273.—Fall of a bridge over the Seine, from too great steepness in the land-side chains, 273.—Lower brace rods of suspension bridges, 273.—Sectional area of girders for suspension bridges, 274.—Deflec-

AIRY.

tion of loaded beams, 286.—Quantity of iron required in a tubular bridge and in a suspension bridge of the same length, 287.—Advantages of crossing wide spans by suspension rather than by tubular bridges, 288.—Amount of drop in any given suspension arch from the effects of expansion by tempera-ture, 307.

Canal, Suez. Relative level of the Mediterranean and the Red Sea, xxvi. 468.—Evaporation of water from the Bitter Lakes, 468.—Intention of the ancient canal at Suez, 468.—Western pier at Port Saïd, 469.

Coasts, formation of, xxiii. 226.—Origin of the pebbles of the Chesil bank, 226.—Effect of tidal currents in Wexford harbour and at Liverpool, in ploughing up the bottom, 228.—Cause of the deterioration of Harwich harbour, 228.—Formation of shingle banks, 237.—Inland cliffs between Landguard Common and the Deben, 238.—Origin of Landguard Common, 238.—Use-lessness of constructing piers to stop the accumulation of shingle if it is raised from the bottom of the sea, 238.—Tendency of pebbles to travel from the horns of a bay to its centre, 239.—Backwater behind the Chesil Bank and Slapton Sands, 239.—'Etangs' between Narbonne and Perpignan, 239

Lighthouses, optical apparatus of, xxvi. 507.—Originally defective arrange-ment of the optical apparatus in the Whitby Lighthouses, 507.—Shape of the lenses for a dioptric apparatus, 508.—Testing the adjustment of diop-tric lights, 509. — South Foreland dioptric light and parabolic reflector, 509.

Railway accidents. Apparatus for ef-fecting communication between the guard and the engine-driver on rail-way trains, xxi. 383.

Railway locomotion. Behaviour of light and heavy engines respectively on firm and yielding rails, xxi. 411.

Tides. Elevation of mean water in pro-gressing up the Shannon estuary

AIRY.

xxviii. 512.—Tides in the Humber, 513.—Effect of the Dogger and the Wells banks on the tides of the east coast of England, 513.

AIRY, W. [Election, xxvi. 544; Telford premium, xxviii. 161, 179.]

Girders. "On the experimental determination of the strains on the suspension ties of a bowstring girder." xxvii. 443.—Remarks, 448.—Results to be obtained from models, 448, 449.

Lighthouses, optical apparatus of, xxviii. 35.—Difference in quality between the glass made by French and English manufacturers for lenses for lighthouses, 35.—Grinding lenses, 35.

AITCHISON, G. [Memoir, xxi. 569.]

AITKEN, R.

Permanent way. Rigidity of 'pot' sleepers, xxiv. 30.

ALBERGA, C. A. [Admission, xxvii. 180.]

ALBERT, HIS ROYAL HIGHNESS PRINCE. [Decease, xxxii. 615.]

Albert harbour, Greenock. Vide STRUCTURES IN THE SEA.

ALEXANDER, A.

Locomotive engines for the Mont Cenis Railway, xxvi. 329.

ALEXANDER, C. D. [Election, xxvii. 553.]

ALEXANDER, T. [Election, xxiv. 458.]

ALFRED, HIS ROYAL HIGHNESS PRINCE (Duke of Edinburgh). [Election, xxv. 508]

ALLAN, G. [Election, xxix. 322.]

ALLAN, T.

Telegraphic communication between Great Britain and India, and its extension to Australia and China, xxv. 57.

ALLCARD, W. [Memoir, xxi. 550.]

ALLEN, E. [Election, xxiv. 184.]

ALLEN, E. E.

Canals, steam-power on, xxvi. 22.—Results of working paddle-wheel steam-tugs on the river Thames, 22.

ALLISON, J. [Election, xxiii. 320.]

ALLPORT, J. J. [Election, xxiv. 257.]

Railway stations. Best mode of laying out, xxv. 284.—Station to be erected by the Midland Railway Company

ANDREW.

in the Euston Road, 284.—St. Pancras goods station of ditto, 285.—Inadvisability of placing engine-sheds close to passenger and goods stations where the ground is valuable, 285.—Turntables and traversers, 285.—Height of platform adopted by the Midland Railway Company, 286.—General arrangement of the St. Pancras station of the Midland railway, xxx. 94.—Colouring of the roof of ditto, 95. —Income derived from advertising-boards at the St Pancras station, 99.

Railway trains, communication in, xxvi. 94. Electrical system, 94.—No satisfactory system yet devised,95.—Failure of the rope-and-bell system, 96.

Railways, gauge of, particularly as affecting the facility of working the traffic, xxiv. 385.

Alpine roadway passes, table of, xxvi. 333.

AMERICAN iron bridges, vide BRIDGES, IRON; timber bridges, vide BRIDGES, TIMBER; locomotive and rolling stock, vide LOCOMOTIVE ENGINES AND ROLLING STOCK.

ANDERSON, A. G.

Gas, illuminating power of coal, xxviii. 468.—Rate of consumption of sperm candles when burning, 468.—Illuminating value of candles, 469.—Standard gas as a test of illuminating power, 469.

ANDERSON, B. [Election, xxiv. 144.]

ANDERSON, J. [Election, xxi. 257.]

ANDERSON, H. [Election, xxv. 352.]

ANDERSON, H. G. [Election, xxvii. 443; Memoir, xxviii. 618.]

ANDERSON, H. J. C. [Election, xxvi. 544.]

ANDERSON, W. [Election, xxviii. 216.]

ANDREW, W. P.

Port of Kurrachee, xxii. 482.—Capabilities, 482.—Position as compared with the port of Bombay, 483.—Improvement of the harbour, 484.

Railway, Scinde, xxii. 480.—Length, 480.—Chief object the substitution of railway communication for creek

ANDREWS.

navigation, 480.—Proposed extension to the Bolan Pass, and its probable advantages, 480.—Circumstances that enhanced the cost, 481.
Railway sleepers. Best material for sleepers in India, xxii. 482.—Wood liable to vibration not much affected by the white ant, 482.
ANDREWS, C. [Election, xxiii. 320.]
ANDREWS, J. O. [Election, xxiii. 110.]
ANDREWS, T. [Election, xxvi. 79.]
ANDROS, A. C. [Election, xxvi. 310.]
ANLEY, J. L. [Election, xxi. 48.]
ANNUAL GENERAL MEETINGS, xxi. 132; xxii. 111; xxiii. 111; xxiv. 105; xxv. 160; xxvi. 118; xxvii. 121; xxviii. 157; xxix. 207.
ANNUAL REPORTS OF COUNCIL, xxi. 134; xxii. 113; xxiii. 113; xxiv. 108; xxv. 163; xxvi. 120; xxvii. 123; xxviii. 160; xxix. 209.
ANSTED, Prof. D. T. [Telford medal and premium, xxix. 211.]
Lagoons and marshes. "On the lagoons and marshes of certain parts of the shores of the Mediterranean," xxviii. 287.— Remarks, 307.— Engineering details of the works carried out, 307.—Estimated cost of the works of reclamation beyond the delta of the Rhone, 322.—Origin of the lagoons near the mouth of the Rhone, 323.
Rivers, freshwater floods of, xxvii. 230.—Tabulated comparisons of rivers, 230.—Flood regulators of rivers, 230.—Inundations of the Nile, 231.—Glaciers as flood regulators, 231.—Geological formation of the soil as a flood regulator, 232.—Drainage areas of England, 232.
Water supply. Purification of water in Nature, xxvii. 24.—Mineral springs, 24.—Various sources of water supply, 25.
ANSTIE, J. [Election, xxx. 106.]
APPLEBY, C. J. [Election, xxiii. 257.]
Canals, steam traffic on, in Sweden and in Holland, xxvi. 40.
APPLETON, E. [Election, xxii. 540.]
APPOLD, J. G. [Memoir, xxv. 523.]
ARCHER, F. E. [Election, xxvii. 55.]

ARROW.

ARCHIBALD, C. W. [Election, xxiii. 110.]
ARCHIBALD, W. F. A. [Admission, xxix. 272.]
ARDAGH, J. C., Lieutenant, R.E. [Election, xxvi. 79.]
ARMITAGE, E. [Election, xxix. 98.]
Armour-plated ships. Vide SHIPS OF WAR.
ARMSTRONG, G. F. [Election, xxix. 98.]
ARMSTRONG, R.
Ships and steam-vessels. Resistance to bodies passing through water, xxiii. 342.—Whether the mechanical effect of forces, or a pressure of steam, is a constant or a variable quantity, 342.—Trials of the 'Flying Fish,' 'Victor,' and 'Pioneer,' 342.—Diminution of the coefficient in proportion to the increase of the velocity of the piston, 343.—Conservation of the mechanical effects of force, 343.—Theoretical amount of pressure in pounds required in the cylinder of a steam-engine, 343.—Mechanical equivalent of a unit pressure of steam, 344.—Dynamometer experiments made on board the 'Rattler,' 344.
ARMSTRONG, T. W. [Election, xxv. 429.]
ARMSTRONG, Sir W. G. [Member of Council, xxi. 133; xxii. 112; xxiii. 112; xxiv. 106.]
Hydraulic apparatus for the dock gates at Swansea, xxi. 338.—Machinery for shipping coal at Swansea, 339.
Injector, Giffard's, xxiv. 222, 240.
ARROW, Captain Sir F.
Lighthouses. Superiority of cut glass to moulded lenses for the lighting apparatus of lighthouses, xxiii. 27.—Superiority of the dioptric to the catoptric system of lighthouse illumination, xxvi. 516.—Gibraltar Light, 517.—Dartmouth Light, 517.—Revolving catoptric light at Beachy Head, 518.—South Foreland Lights, 519.—Necessity of caution in effecting changes in the method of lighthouse illumination, 519.—Royal Commission on Lights, Buoys, and Beacons, 520.—Lighthouse authorities and their officers, 525.—Wolf Rock lighthouse, xxx. 17.

ARTERIAL CHANNELS.

Arterial channels and outfalls of the country, on the discharge from under-drainage, and its effect on the (Denton, J. B.), xxi. 48.—*Vide* also DRAINAGE.

ARTESIAN WELLS.

" On the machinery employed in sinking artesian wells on the Continent." By G. R. Burnell, xxiii. 459.—Changes in boring machinery necessitated by the increased depths of wells, 459.— The Grenelle well, 459.—Many deep wells subsequently sunk on the Continent, 459.—Euyenhausen's inventions, 460.—Well at Passy projected by the Municipal Council at Paris, 460.— Operations undertaken by M. Kind, 460.—Collapse of the upper portion of the boring, 460—Details of well when completed, 460.—Water supply and cost, 461.—Additional wells projected by the Municipal Council of Paris, 461.—Fauvelle's system of well-boring, 462.—The ordinary system of well-boring, 462.—Kind's system of well-boring, 463.—Details of the trepan used by M. Kind, 464.—Euyenhausen's sliding joint as adopted by M. Kind, 465.—Wooden rods used for the suspension of the trepan, 465.—Spoon used for withdrawing the products of the working of the comminutor at Passy, 466. — Tools for removing broken parts of machinery from the excavation, 466.—Method of working the machinery at Passy, 468.—Rate of progress of the work at Passy, 468. —Proportions of time usually employed in the various details of well-boring by Kind's system, 468.—Essential difference between the systems of M. Kind and those of the ordinary well-borers, 469.—Faults of the lining of the Passy well, 469.—Escape of the water through the joints of the wooden tubing into the basement beds of the Paris basin, 470.—Subterranean disturbances at times render the water unfit for human consumption, 470.— Advantages of the free falling tool of Euyenhausen as applied by M. Dru, 470.—Boring operations to commence

at the chalk in the wells to be sunk in the Paris basin, 471.

Discussion.—Beardmore, N., 477.—Burnell, G. R., 477.—Homersham, S. C., 474.—Mather, W., 475, 477.—Vignoles, C. B., 473, 477.

Artillery and projectiles, xxi. 180, 255; xxvii. 192; xxviii. 407; xxix. 293, *et seq.* *Vide* also SHIPS OF WAR.

ASHBURY, J. [Decease, xxvi. 129.]

ASHBURY, J. L. [Election, xxv. 429.]

ASHCROFT, P. [Election, xxvi. 79.]

Permanent way. Wear of rails on the South Eastern Railway, xxvii. 378, 405.—South Eastern Railway Company's specification for rails, 379.

ASHHURST, F. H. [Admission, xxvii 53.]

ASHMEAD, F. [Election, xxiv. 358.]

ASHWELL, W. H. [Election, xxvi. 242.]

Astronomer Royal, the. *Vide* AIRY, G. B.

ATHERTON, C.

Ships and steam-vessels. Generally-received law by which present practice is regulated in determining the amount of power by which steamers of any given size may be expected to be propelled at any given speed, xxiii. 350.—Theoretical principles upon which that law is based, 350.—Possibility of vessels of different types of form producing the same coefficent, 351.—Precision with which the capabilities of a new ship may be predetermined, 352.—Performances of the 'Great Eastern,' 352.— Superior capabilities of large vessels as compared with smaller vessels, 352. —Considerations by which the sizes of ships, with reference to their profitable employment, must be limited, 352.

ATKINSON, C. R. [Election, xxv. 262.]

ATKINSON, J. S. [Memoir, xxv. 525.]

ATKINSON, W.

Bridges. Set taken by lattice girder bridges after a severe test, xxv. 254.— Maximum load per foot run to be provided for in iron bridges, 258.

Canals. Gradients of the canal of Isabel II. and of the Canal de Marseille, xxv. 499.

Gas, illuminating power of coal, xxviii.

AUBERTIN.

464.—Film of platinum as an adjunct to a gas-burner, 464.—Parliamentary standard of candles for attesting the illuminating power of gas, 465.

Railway locomotion. Relative commercial value of the engines employed on the Mont Cenis and on the Mauritius railways, xxviii. 267.—Resistance of curves determined from experiments on the New York and Erie railroad, 267.—Experimental trip on the Erie railroad, 404.—Origin of the cast-iron chilled wheels, bogie frame, and one-compartment carriage adopted for American rolling-stock, 404.—Comparative cost of cast-iron and wrought-iron wheels, 405.—Sources of supply of iron for cast-iron wheels in America, 405.—Bogie trucks, 406.—Superiority of oil to grease for lubricating rolling stock, 406.—Weight of rolling-stock, 406.—American sleeping-cars, 406.

Water supply. As to supplying towns with soft water, xxv. 499.—Effect of soft water in dissolving lead, 500.

Weirs. Principal dimensions and circumstances of the most remarkable weirs constructed in Spain, xxvii. 552.

AUBERTIN, J. J.

Railway, São Paulo (Brazil), xxx 58.—

AYRTON.

Finances, 59.—Government control exercised during its construction, 59.—Physical characteristics and climate of the Serra do Mar, 60.—Serra do Mar inclines, 60.—Incline surmounting the Serra traversed by the Dom Pedro Segundo railway, 61.—Question of working the Serra do Mar incline on the rope system or as a locomotive line, 61.

AUSTIN, C. E.

Water supply. Strainer erected at St. Petersburg for purifying the water of the River Neva, xxvii. 46.—Effect produced upon the water, 47.—Purification of water by filtration due to mechanical action, 47.

AVERN, F. M. [Election, xxx. 215.]

AYLMER, R. [Election, xxiv. 184.]

AYRTON, A. S.

River Hooghly and the Mutla, xxi. 31.—Supposed advantages of removing the emporium for trade from Calcutta to the head of the Mutla, 31.

Telegraphic communication. Telegraph system in India, xxv. 20.—Extension to China, 21.—Suggested telegraph route from the head of the Persian Gulf to Beyrout, 21.

8

B.

BABBAGE.

BABBAGE, C.
Lighthouses, optical apparatus of, xxvi. 525.—Practicability of establishing occulting signals in connection with the lights of lighthouses, 525.
Railway accidents, xxi. 385.—Resulting from mechanical causes, 385.
Railway trains. Contrivances he employed on the Great Western railway for obtaining an autographic record of, the times of starting and stopping, the velocity at every instant, the tractive force employed, and the curve of progression, xxi. 385.

BABINGTON, J. H. [Election, xxiv. 98.]
BADDELEY, J. F. L., Major R.A. [Memoir, xxii. 634.]
BADGLEY, W. F., Capt., B.S.C. [Election, xxviii. 439.]
BAGE, W. [Election, xxvii. 553.]
BAGNALL, W. [Memoir, xxiv. 538.]
BAGNELL, J. J. [Resignation, xxviii. 167.]
BAILEY, J. [Election, xxx. 106]
BAILLIE, R. D. [Admission, xxix. 98.]
BAINBRIDGE, E. [Admission, xxix. 98.]
Coal-mining. "On coal-mining in deep workings," xxx. 340.—Remarks, 407.—Safety lamps, 407.
BAIRD, F. [Memoir, xxx. 428.]
BAIRD, N. [Decease, xxvii. 131.]
BAKER, B. [Election, xxvii. 55.]
Bridges. Arched ribs of the Victoria bridges, Pimlico, xxvii. 94.—Distribution of the load, 94.—Strains, 95.
Permanent way. Testing iron and steel rails, xxvii. 386.—Comparative strength of ditto, 386.—Effect of drilling and punching holes in rails on their strength, 386.—Effect of the position of holes in the flanges of rails, 387.
BAKER, C. B. [Election, xxvi. 242.]
BAKER, W. J.
Railway trains, safety-cage for traversing, xxvi. 101.

BARLOW.

BALDRY, J. D. [Election, xxv. 64; Auditor, xxvi. 118; xxvii. 121.]
Bridges. Cast-iron bridges over the river Severn, on the Severn Valley and the Coalbrookdale railways, xxvii. 108.—Proper material for bridges, 110.
Foundations. Use of Milroy's Excavator in sinking cylinders at the bridge over the River Clyde for the Glasgow (City) Union railway, xxviii. 356.—Ditto, at the Hutchesontown-street bridge over the Clyde at Glasgow, 358.
BALFOUR, General.
Irrigation in India, xxvii. 525.
BALFOUR, J. M. [Election, xxv. 508.]
BANISTER, F. D.
Permanent way. Wear of rails on the Brighton railway, xxvii. 394.
BARCLAY, C. [Election, xxiv. 184.]
BARLOW, P. [Memoir, xxii. 615.]
BARLOW, P. W.
Bridges. Different forms of truss for iron girder bridges, xxiv. 449.
—— Suspension, xxvi. 278.—Propriety of making the platforms of suspension bridges of wrought iron, 278.—Pont de Cubsac, 278.—Lambeth suspension bridge, 278.
Railways. Gauge of, xxiv. 388.—Whether an exceptionally narrow gauge is desirable, 388.
BARLOW, W. H. [Member of Council, xxiii. 112; xxiv. 106; xxv. 161; xxvi. 119; xxvii. 122; xxviii. 158; xxix. 208.]
Bridges. Cast-iron, xxvii. 111.—Victoria bridges, Pimlico, 111.—Determination of strains on bowstring-girder bridges, 448.
—— Suspension. "Description of the Clifton Suspension bridge," xxvi. 243.—Remarks, 265.—Death of Captain Huish, chairman of the Clifton

BARLOW.

Bridge company, 265.—Angles at which the chains leave the piers in suspension bridges, 308.—Capability of the Clifton suspension bridge to bear a heavy load, 308.—Inexpediency of land ties to prevent oscillation, 309. —Superiority of stiffened suspension bridges to girders for crossing wide spans for railway purposes, 309.

Gas, illumnating power of coal, xxviii. 456.

Girders, xxiv. 445.

Iron plates, experiments upon, when strained in lines not passing through their centres of gravity, xxiv. 445, 446.

Light. Difference of colour in light produced from various sources, xxviii. 456.

Materials, durability of, xxvii. 570.— Rails in sidings decay sooner than in the main lines of railways, 570.— Resistance of materials, xxix. 48.— Theoretical ratios which exist between tensile, compressive, and transverse resistance, 48.

Permanent way. Usual mode of constructing, xxiii. 434.—Adams's elastic road almost identical with Buck's, 434. —Motion of carriages having wheels on one side larger than those on the other, 434.—Life of iron rails on the Midland railway, xxv. 408.—Destruction of permanent way caused by the imperfect fitting of the parts, 408.

Railway income and expenditure, xxviii. 271.—Working expenses of the Mauritius railways compared with those of the Brighton railway, 271.—Returns of the Board of Trade relative to railways, xxix. 336.—Relation of the receipts to the capital cost of railways, 337.

Railway stations. Roof of Cannon Street station, Charing Cross railway, compared with the roof of the Midland Railway station at St. Pancras, xxvii. 431.

——— " Description of the St. Pancras station and roof, Midland railway," xxx. 78.—Remarks, 104.—Pressures and strains, 104.—Colouring of the

BARRY.

station, 105.—' Underpinning ' of ditto, 105.

Railway trains, communication in, xxvi. 117.—Statement of Mr. Allport as to the rope-and-bell system of communicating in trains, 117.

Steel, strength of, xxv. 409.

Viaducts, choice of material for, xxii. 56.

BARNABY, N.

Ships of war. Vessels of the ' Monitor ' type not seagoing vessels, xxvi. 185.— Suitability of ditto for coast defences, 186.—Defenceless condition of the bottoms of monitors, 187.

BARNARD, C. [Election, xxviii. 325.]

BARNES, J. H. [Election, xxiv. 184.]

Barometer, long tube (Howson, B.), xxi. 32.

BARRON, F. C. [Election, xxvii. 443.]

BARROSO, le Chev. Z. [Election, xxvii. 553.]

BARRY, E. M. [Associate of Council, xxix. 208.]

BARRY, J. D.

Agricultural conditions of Great Britain, Spain, and some other countries, statistics of, xxvii. 519.

Irrigation in Spain, xxvii. 517.—Legislation on waters in Spain, 517—Tamarite canal, 518.—Quantity of water used by various canals, 519.—Agricultural conditions of Great Britain, Spain, and some other countries, 519. —Irrigation channels cut by ploughs, 519.—Growth of the ' Eucalyptus globulus ' renders districts healthy, 520.—Cost of some recently executed canals in Spain, 520.—Dam and tunnel of the Laguna del Rey, 520.

BARRY, J. W. [Election, xxvii. 218; Telford medal and premium, xxviii. 161, 178.]

Cellarage in London, value of, xxx. 96.

Land, value of, in London, xxx. 95.

Railway arches, rental to be derived from, xxvii. 441.

Railway station roofs. Cost of, xxvii. 431.—Advantages of station roofs of large span where land is valuable, 440.—Cost per square of station roofs, 440.—Economy of roofs of large span where land is expensive, illustrated in

the case of the Cannon Street and Charing Cross stations, xxx. 96.

Railways. " The City Terminus Extension of the Charing Cross railway," xxvii. 410.—Remarks, 431.—Cost of City Terminus extension, 431.— Charing Cross and Cannon Street stations, 440 ; xxx. 96.

———— Mauritius, xxviii. 269.—Capital cost, 269.—Engines used, 269.— Working expenses per train mile, compared with those of the Cape railway and the London and Brighton railway, 270.

BARRY, T. D. [Election, xxiii. 257.]

BARTHOLOMEW, E. G.

Railway telegraphs, xxii. 218.—Inexpediency of using a train-signalling telegraph for other purposes, 218.— Number of pivots in Preece's semaphore system objectionable, 218.— Question of signalling trains by telegraph, 219. — Wheatstone's magnetic signals, 220.—Caution signal as generally given on railways, 220.— Expediency of telegraph signals at level crossings, 220.—Numerous railway accidents avoided by the use of the telegraph, 220.

BARTHOLOMEW, W. H.

Canals, steam-power on, xxvi. 25.— Paddle tugs first adopted on the Aire and Calder navigation, 25.— Character of the navigation, 25.— Two classes of steam-tugs introduced on ditto, 26.—Train of boats for carrying minerals, 27.

River Humber, xxviii. 509.

BARTLETT, T. [Memoir, xxiv. 524.]

Boring machine designed by him for facilitating the progress of the Mont Cenis tunnel, xxiii. 288.—Results obtained by ditto when worked with compressed air, 289.—Colonel Menabrea's comparison of ditto with a machine made by M. Sommeiller, 289. —Failure of M. Sommeiller's machine on first trial, 290.—Greater amount of work done by his own machine, 290.

BARTON, J. [Election, xxiv. 511.]

BARTON, J. G. [Admission, xxviii. 325.]

BARTON, W. C. [Election, xxvii. 443.]

BASEVI, Captain G. H. [Resignation, xxviii. 167.]

BASEVI, J. P., Captain R.E. [Election, xxiii. 310; Resignation, xxix. 217.]

BASSETT, A.

Drainage of towns. Works at Newport, xxii. 284.

BATEMAN, J. F. [Member of Council, xxv. 161; xxvi. 119; xxvii. 122; xxviii. 158; xxix. 208.]

Aqueducts. Gradients of the Loch Katrine aqueduct of the Glasgow waterworks, xxv. 502.

Canals, steam-power on, xxvi. 28.— Screw propulsion on the Aire and Calder canal, 28.—Results obtained by canal boats on the Forth and Clyde canal, 28.—Cost of working by steam on ditto, 39.

Concrete, consolidation of, under water, xxii. 440.—Construction, with Portland cement concrete, of the quay walls at Dublin harbour, xxv. 142.

Drainage of towns, xxiv. 340.—Flow of sewage in pipes, 340.

Groynes for the protection of Spurn Point, xxviii. 499.

Irrigation in Spain, xxvii. 512.—Henares canal, 512.—Rainfall at Madrid, 512. —Value of irrigation in Majorca and Spain, 512.—Distribution of water in Spain for irrigation purposes, 513.— Cost of irrigating land in the most effectual way in Majorca and Spain, 514.—Weir across the river Henares, 515.

Lagoons and deltas of rivers on the shores of the Mediterranean, xxviii. 307.

Rivers. Perennial and flood discharge of, xxii. 362.— Upper Thames, 362.— Quantity of water flowing off the ground, in a given time, by the river Medlock at Manchester, 362.—Quantity of flood-water flowing into the Woodhead reservoir in a given time, 363.—Regulating effects of large lakes, 363.—Discharge of the river Clyde at Carstairs in the winter of 1856-57, 363. —Discharge of the Shannon in flood

BATEMAN.

at Killaloe, 364.—Inapplicability of formulæ and coefficients in the case of the floods of rivers, xxvii. 253.

Rivers and estuaries. River Tyne, xxvi. 424.—Effect of the construction of the North Bull Wall on the bar at Dublin harbour, 424.—Increase in the capacity of the estuary of the river Mersey, 425.—Estuary of the Humber and the effect produced on it by Spurn Point, xxviii. 498.—Capacity of the estuary of the Mersey as affected by the Liverpool and Birkenhead docks and the Wallasey Pool enclosure, 499.

Tunnels. Comparison of boring operations by machines and manual labour, xxiii. 317.—Time occupied in boring operations in constructing the aqueduct between Loch Katrine and Glasgow, 318.—Application of machinery for large tunnels, 318.

Viaducts. Reconstruction of the Dinting and Mottram viaducts without interruption to the traffic, xxii. 334.

Water, filtration of. Speed of filtration of water through a good sand-filter, xxvii. 10.—Confervoid growth in uncovered shallow reservoirs of pure water, 38.—Filtration of water through animal charcoal, 38.—Decanting water from the top of reservoirs in lieu of filtration, 39.—Manchester water supply, 39.—Bleaching powers of the atmosphere on water exposed in reservoirs and lakes, 39.—Ditto, as exemplified in Loch Katrine, 39.—Ditto, in the Lake of Geneva, 40.—Constituents of sand filter-beds, 40.—The several methods of purifying water, 41.

Water, flow of. Calculations of the flow of water off the ground in the Woodburn district, xxv. 472.—Mill power in the Woodburn district, 473.—Geological features of ditto, 473.

Water supply. Physical characteristics of the inhabitants of hard and soft water districts, xxv. 500.—Action of the Loch Katrine and Loch Ness water on lead pipes, 500.—Tendency of hard water to produce gravel and

BAZALGETTE.

stone, 501.—Destruction and absorption of mussels in water-pipes, by the introduction of soft water, 501.—Lead-poisoning by the use of soft water at Manchester, 501.—Saving effected in domestic establishments in Glasgow by the introduction of the Loch Katrine water, 501.—Causes which give water freshness for drinking purposes, 502.—Reduction of the death-rate consequent on the introduction of the Ennerdale Lake water into White-haven, 506.

BATTEN, J. B. [Election, xxiv. 458.]

BATTERSBY, J. [Election, xxix. 98.]

BAUMANN, J. [Admission, xxviii. 216.]

BAXTER, R. D. [Election, xxvi. 79.]

BAYLIS, E. W. [Admission, xxvii. 54]

BAYLIS, H. [Election, xxvi. 242.]

BAYLISS, J.

Railways. São Paulo railway, Brazil, xxx. 71.—Objection to the use of rope-traction on the Serra do Mar incline, 71.—Inexpediency of adopting the atmospheric system for a railway in such countries as Brazil, 71.—Cost of working the Serra do Mar inclines, 71.—Iron permanent way for railways in Brazil, 72.—Formation of embankments on the São Paulo railway, 72.—Loss of life among Europeans employed, 72.—Cost per mile, 73.

BAYLISS, S. [Election, xxiii. 257.]

BAYLISS, W. P. [Election, xxiv. 358.]

BAYLY, W. C. [Election, xxv. 64.]

BAYNES, C.

Cement, breaking weight of, xxv. 122.—Qualities of cements of different specific weights, 122.—Conditions of cement generally required, 123.—Manipulation, 123.—Slow-setting qualities of heavy cement, 123.

Public works, Canterbury, New Zealand, xxix. 123.—Bridging torrential rivers, 123.—Probability of the Christchurch river changing its course, 124.

BAZALGETTE, E. [Admission, xxvii. 54; Miller prize, xxix. 212.]

BAZALGETTE, J. V. N. [Auditor, xxii. 111; xxiii. 111.]

BAZALGETTE, J. W. [Telford medal and

BEACONS.

premium, xxv. 164, 180; Member of Council, xxvii. 122; xxviii. 158; xxix. 208.]

Cement, Portland, xxv. 124.—Strength, 124.—Setting of, in running water, 125.

Drainage of towns. "On the main-drainage of London and the inter-ception of the sewage from the river Thames," xxiv. 280.—Remarks, 315. —System of drainage of Paris, com-pared with that of London, 315.—Separation of sewage from rainfall, 353.—Reservoirs at the outlets of the main sewers of the metropolis, 353.—Distribution of the metropolitan sewage for manure, 354.—Cause of deposit in London sewers in former times, 355.—Velocity of flow in pipe-sewers, 355.—Idea that the inter-cepting sewers of London would be likely to lead to pestilence in dry weather, 356.—Comparative pumping power at Deptford and Crossness, 357. —Subway in the Thames Embank-ment, 357.—Purification of the river Thames, 357.—Effect on Woolwich of the discharge of the sewage at Cross-ness, 357.—Scheme for utilizing the London sewage, 358.

Foundations. Best mode of sinking cylinders through different kinds of soil, xxviii. 347.

Materials. Use of cast iron for struc-tures liable to decay, xxvii. 572.

Piers and landing-stages, xxviii. 227.—Points of resemblance between the New Ferry and New Brighton landing-stages and those of the Thames Em-bankment, 227.

Railway arches, rental to be derived from, in London, xxvii. 438.

Railway trains, communication in, xxvi. 105. — Protection proposed to be afforded to passengers by electrical communication, 105. — Insufficiency of the signals at present provided, 112.

Beacons on the Wolf Rock. Vide LIGHT-HOUSES, Wolf Rock.

BEAMISH, G. H. T. [Admission, xxix. 98.]

BEARDMORE.

Beams, deflection of loaded, xxvi. 286. Vide also MATERIALS, strength and resistance of.

BEARDMORE, N. [Member of Council, xxii. 112; xxiii. 112; xxiv. 106; xxv. 161; xxvi. 119; xxvii. 122; xxviii. 158; xxix. 208.]

Beacons on the Wolf Rock, cause of the destruction of the, xxx. 25.

Canals, steam-power on, xxvi. 35.—General character of inland canals, 35. —Failure of steam trains on ditto, 35. —Retarding effect of a narrow channel on the speed of boats, 36, 43.—Propor-tions of various river navigations and inland canals, 36.—Screw steam-barge used on the river Lee, 37.—Engines of ditto, 39.—Cost of steam haulage on canals, 37, 38.—Vertical retaining-walls on the river Lee, 38. — Growth of weeds in canals, 39.—Cargo trains. 39. — Boilers of engines for use on, 42.

Coal-breaking by machinery, xxviii. 129. —Hydraulic machine for breaking down coal, invented by Mr. C. J. Chubb, 129.

Commercial success of engineering works, xxvii. 537.

Concrete, mixing, xxii. 441.—Strength of a wall of Kentish ragstone backed by, 442.—Advantages of using, in large masses, 443.

Harbours. Albert harbour, Greenock, xxii. 440.—Situation and character of the works of the Albert harbour, 440, et seq.—Rise and fall of the tide at Greenock, 441.—Question of the solidity of the Greenock pier, 441.

Iron, deterioration of, in fresh and salt water, xxii. 442; xxviii. 228.

Irrigation in India, xxvii. 537.—Advan-tages of irrigation and canal works in India, 538.—Ganges canal, 538.—Distinction between the Madras irri-gation works and those of Upper India, 539.

Low-water basin at Birkenhead, xxix. 21. —Destruction of granite masonry by the rapid descent of water, 21.—Low-water or tidal basins in the Mersey

BEARDMORE.

considered in connection with the size of steam-vessels, 22.

Materials, durability of, xxvii. 569.—Decay depending on damp, 569.—Cause of damp, 569.—Slow decay of iron and wood in the interior of continents where the climate is dry, 569.—Durability of iron plates for roofing in Russia, 570.—Decay of iron in water, xxviii. 228.

Piers and landing-stages, xxviii. 228.—Pontoons of the New Ferry and New Brighton landing-stages, 228.—Landing-stages on the Thames Embankment, 228.

Railway trains, communication in, xxvi. 97.—Electrical system, 97, 106

River Lee, erosion of the bed of the river below the weirs, xxix. 21.

Rivers, gauging the flow of, xxv. 474; xxvii. 235.—Gauging the river Lee and the Saône, 236.—Flood on the river Lee in 1852, 237.—Best way of gauging streams of limited dimensions, 238.

Rivers and estuaries. Use of jetties for deepening rivers, xxiv. 85.—Estuary of the Tees, 85.—Improvement of ditto, 86.—Dredging operations in the river Tyne, xxvi. 432, et seq.—Piers at the mouth of the river Tyne, 432.—Deepening of the river Clyde, 433.—Bar of the river Mersey, 434.

Sluice, Middle Level, disaster at the, xxvii. 538.

Steam-engines. Performance of the Fowey Consols pumping engine, xxiii. 83.—Suitability of the Cornish engine for mine-pumping, 84.—Formation of holes round the foot-valves of pumping engines, xxix. 22.

Water, flow of, off the ground, xxv. 474.—Difficulty of gauging floods, 474.—Mill power in the Woodburn district. 474.—Geological features of ditto, 474.—Lignaca swallow, 475.—Proportion of rainfall at Belfast and in the Woodburn district, 475.—Flow of water off the ground in the winter months, 475.

Wells, boring, xxiii. 477.

BELCHER.

BEARDMORE, N. St. B. [Admission, xxvii. 54.]

BEATTIE, A. [Election, xxiv. 184.]

BEATTIE, W. G.
Injector, Giffard's, xxiv. 251.—Greater economy in the use of pumps with feed-water heaters than in the use of, 251.

BEAZELEY, A.
Lighthouse lanterns. Amount of opacity caused by the framing of, xxviii. 44.—Erection of the Trinity House lanterns, 44.

Piles. M'Alpine's, Weisbach's, Rankine's and Sanders' formulæ for determining the resisting power of, xxvii. 306.—Supporting power of, as estimated by various formulæ, for the Cudgegong bridge, Mudgee, 307.

BEAZELEY, M. [Election, xxvi. 242.]
Lighthouses. Superiority of the mode of dovetailing together the stones of the Wolf Rock lighthouse to that adopted at the Eddystone lighthouse, xxx. 25.—Terms 'Wolf' and 'Gulf' rock, 26.

BECKETT, W. H. B., Captain, B.I. [Election, xxix. 322.]

BEDLINGTON, R.
Coal-breaking by machinery. Remarks as to Mr. C. J. Chubb's drilling apparatus (Chubb, C. J.), xxviii. 150.

BEHR, F. B. [Election, xxvii. 218.]

BELCHER, Admiral Sir E.
Docks. Swansea, xxi. 339.—Great Grimsby, xxiv. 54.—Danger apprehended from the removal of Spurn Island, 54.

Drainage of towns, xxiv. 321.—Burning noxious gases evolved from sewers, 321.

Materials. Ravages of the teredo and of white ants, xxiii. 29.

Rivers and estuaries. Deep water wherever a curvature is exposed to the action of the ebb-tide, xxi. 298.—Upper stratum of fresh and under-stratum of salt water in the Thames at Woolwich at the first quarter of flood-tide, 339.—Effect of the salt-water in disturbing the silt, 340.—

BELL.

Velocity of streams and currents less than generally supposed, 340.—Changes in the Humber, xxiv. 54.—Probable effect of the removal or breach of Spurn Island, 54, 56.

Ships of war. Requisite degree of protection by armour for, xxi. 214.—Facilities for replacing armour-plates, 215.—Method of armour-plating the sides of vessels, 215.—Portholes for giving a greater angular range for guns, 217.—Sinking vessels by concussion, 217.—Qualities necessary for fighting ships, xxvi. 223.—Speed essential for a line-of-battle ship, 223.—Sinking monitors by ramming, 224.—Ships of the line, 224.

Steam navigation. Relative performance of sailing-vessels and steam-vessels, xxix. 175.—Turbines for the propulsion of vessels, 176.—Forms of ships, 177.

BELL, C. N. [Election, xxvi. 398.]

BELL, H. [Election, xxvi. 310.]

BELL, H. P. [Election, xxv. 262.]

BELL, H. M. [Admission, xxviii. 325.]

BELL, I. [Election, xxvi. 544 ; Telford premium, xxix. 211.]

Foundations. "On sinking wells for the foundations of the piers of the bridge over the river Jumna, Delhi railway," xxviii. 325.—Remarks, 350. Comparative merits of Milroy's Excavator and Kennard's Sand Pump, 350.—Sinking wells, or cylinders, through sand under water, 351.

BELL, I. L. [Election, xxvi. 544.]

Iron and steel. Manufacture of Bessemer steel, xxvii. 349.—Supplies of iron available for the manufacture of ditto, 349.—Production of fibrous and tough iron from the same pig, 351.

Permanent way. Comparative cost of manufacture of steel and of iron rails, xxvii. 350.—Specifications prepared by engineers for the manufacture of iron rails, 350.—Analyses of iron rails on the North Eastern railway, 351.—Presence of phosphorus in rails, 352.

BELL, R. B. [Election, xxiii. 375.]

BELL, V. G. [Election, xxviii. 517.]

BERKLEY.

Railway inclines. Probable expense of working the Serra do Mar inclines with locomotives, xxx. 69.—Cost of locomotive power on the Mont Cenis railway, 70.

BELL, W. [Election, xxiii. 110.]

Bridges. Strains of the Victoria bridges, Pimlico, xxvii. 103.

BENSON, Sir J. [Election, xxi. 258.]

BERGHEIM, J. S. [Admission, xxvii. 54.]

BERKLEY, G.

Bridges. Construction of, in India, xxiv. 194.—English railway bridges, xxv. 260.—Supervision of the officers of the Board of Trade in testing, 260.—Undesirableness of laying down fixed rules relating to the strain on parts of, 260.—Moving loads on, 260.

Gas, tests for ascertaining the illuminating power of coal, xxviii. 464.—Improved Argand burner, 464.

Iron and steel. Superior strength of Bessemer steel to iron, with illustrative tables of experiments, xxv. 385, et seq.—Uniformity in the quality of iron and of steel, 391.—Introduction of Bessemer steel into structures of art, 391.—Tensile strength of iron obtainable in America, xxviii. 395.

——"On the strength of iron and steel, and on the design of parts of structures which consist of those materials," xxx. 215.—Remarks, 256.—Experiments on the strength of iron links, 256.—Method of conducting ditto, 274.

Locomotive engines, xxiii. 434.—Experiments on the 'White Raven' fitted with Adams' radial axles, 434.

Permanent way. Wooden keys in warm climates, xxiv. 18.—Adoption of double-headed rails, or Vignoles rails, xxv. 382.—Comparative strength of steel and iron rails, 382, et seq.—Life of a rail represented by the work done, 383.—Best form of rail for permanent way, 383.—Superior strength of Bessemer steel to iron, with illustrative tables of experiments with steel and iron rails, steel plates, steel cylinders, and steel axles, 385, et seq.

Railway inclines. Working steep in-

BERKLEY.

clines, xxviii. 271, 272.—Power of engines for working ditto, 271.—Break power, 272.—Accident on the Bhore Ghât incline, 272.—Catch-sidings at the foot of railway inclines, 272.—Making up trains for descending inclines, 272.—Engines used on the Giovi, Semmering, and Great Indian Peninsula railway inclines, 273.

Railway locomotion. Injurious effect of the weight of locomotives on permanent way, xxviii. 393.—Adhesion of wheels of locomotives on rails, 393.—American locomotives, 393.—Cast-iron and wrought-iron wheels for railway rolling-stock, 393.—Efficiency of cast-iron wheels on the Grand Trunk railway of Canada, 394.—Tensile strength of iron obtainable in America, 395.—Sleeping-carriages on American railways, 395.

Railway sleepers, xxii. 256.—Kyanised native sleepers on the Great Indian Peninsula railway, 256.—Liability of creosoted sleepers to split when exported to India, 486.

Railway stations. Height of platforms, xxv. 287.—Station arrangements at the Great Western railway, Paddington, and at the Great Northern railway, King's Cross, 288.—Best form of locomotive engine-shed, 288.

Railways and public works in India. Scinde railway, xxii. 456.——Cost of earthwork and block-in-course in Western India, 486.—Importance of securing means for readily shipping or unloading goods at the termini of Indian railways, 486.—Liability of imported creosoted sleepers to split, 486.—Importance of sending out agents and employés of good character, 487.—Sleepers on the Great Indian Peninsula railway, xxiv. 18.—Wooden keys, 18.—Preservation of iron, 18.—Rolling-stock on the Great Indian Peninsula railway, 18.—Piccotah pump, 194.—Construction of bridges in India, 194.

Viaducts, xxv. 260.—Reconstruction of the Mhow-ke-Mullee viaduct, xxix. 399.

BIDDER.

Berkley, J. J. [Memoir, xxii. 618]
Berbell, W. [Admission, xxvii. 55.]
Bessemer, H. [Election, xxv. 479.]
Permanent way. Most advantageous mode of working up old steel rails, xxv. 402.—Necessary weight of steel rails for permanent way, and the economy of their use when compared with iron rails, 402, 414.

Bessemer iron and steel, xxv. 385; xxvii. 393. *Vide* also PERMANENT WAY; and IRON AND STEEL.

Best, S. C. [Election, xxiv. 257.]
Bethell, H. S. [Election, xxvi. 477.]
Timber, creosoted and uncreosoted, xxvii. 294.—Table of experiments upon ditto made by M. Forestier for the Paris Exhibition of 1867, 294.—Superior vertical resistance and elasticity of creosoted over uncreosoted timber, 294.—Decay of ligneous fibre and dry-rot originating in the sap, 570.—Preservation of wood, 571.

Bethell, J. [Memoir, xxvii. 597.]
Timber. Similarity of Palmyra timber to creosoted wood, xxii. 62.—Effect of nature and situation on the durability of wood, xxiv. 30.—Difficulty of creosoting heartwood sleepers, 31.—Great strength of creosoted half-round sleepers, 32.

Bevan, T.
Cement, Portland, xxv. 130.—Strength, 130.—Effect of a greater or less amount of chalk in the manufacture, 131.—Breaking test, 131.—Method of testing for over-limed cement, 132.

Bewick, T. J. [Election, xxiv. 257.]
Beyer, C. F.
Duplicate machinery, manufacture of, xxii. 612.
Locomotive engines, adhesion of the wheels of, on railways, xxvi. 352.

Bidder, E. [Election, xxvii. 553.]
Bidder, G. P. [Past-President, xxi. 172; xxii. 166; xxiii. 150; xxiv. 143; xxv. 202; xxvi. 164; xxvii. 179; xxviii. 215; xxix. 271.]
Bridges and viaducts. Hownes Gill viaduct, xxii. 52.—Cost of, and materials for, viaducts, 52.—Ironwork

BIDDER.

used in railway bridges to keep down
the level, 55.
Coal-mines. Coal-getting machinery as
a substitute for gunpowder, xxviii.
143.—Danger of employing gunpowder
in mines subject to fiery gas, 143.—
Mr. C. J. Chubb's hydraulic coal-
getting apparatus, 144, 145.—Principles on which machines for breaking
down coal should be designed, 144.—
Similarity of principle between
Mr. C. J. Chubb's and Mr. Grafton
Jones' coal-getting apparatus, 145.—
Ventilation of coal-mines, 146.
Docks, graving. Hydraulic lift graving
dock, xxv. 341.—Application of ditto,
341.—Cost of ditto, 341, et seq.—
Accidents asserted to have occurred
to vessels lifted by ditto, 342.—Origin
of ditto, 342. — Suitability of the
hydraulic lift to the Victoria Docks,
343.—Time occupied in lifting vessels
by the hydraulic lift, 344.
Drainage of land, xxi. 83.—Discharge
from under-drainage, 83.—Method of
gauging the discharge, 85. 107.—Discharge from drained land at Mitcham,
108.—Evaporative power of the soil,
109.
Drainage of towns. Main-drainage of
London, xxiv. 346.—Past and present
condition of the river Thames, 348.
Locomotive engines, disturbing forces of,
xxii. 102.—Numerous causes which
tend to produce oscillation in, 102.—
Adhesion of driving-wheels of, xxiii.
404.—Question of locomotive power
and economy, 441.
Permanent way, xxv. 450.—Wear of
rolling stock and rails, 450.—Repairs
and renewals of permanent way, 450.
—Use of iron or steel rails, 450.—Life
of sleepers, 451.—Manufacture and
wear of rails, xxvii. 384.—Specifications and tenders for iron rails, 384.—
Wear of rails by locomotives, 384.—
Bessemer rails, 385.—Effect of charg-
ing the extra cost of steel rails to
capital account, 385.
Ports of India, necessity for perfecting,
xxii. 489.

BIDDER.

Railway accidents, xxi. 389.—Relative proportion of accidents in England and upon the Continent, 390.
—Use of continuous breaks un-
likely to diminish the number of
accidents, 390.—Operation of Lord
Campbell's Act not beneficial for any
interest, 390.—Case in point in an
accident on the Great Northern
railway, 390.—Cases at Hatfield and
Tottenham, 391.—Juries generally
biassed against railway companies,
391.—Unfavourable effect upon the
railway interest produced by the
reports made on accidents by inspectors
appointed by the Board of Trade,
391.—Little use of submitting scientific
evidence to an ordinary jury, illustrated in the case of a railway accident
at Merton, 392.—Objections taken to
the conduct of the South-Western
Railway Company for not abandoning
certain plans they had adopted, 393.—
Details of the accident at Merton,
393.—Propriety of limiting the liability of railway companies, 395.—
Proposed railway companies' insurance
society, 395.—Constitution and working of such a society, 395.—Objections
to the manner in which the Board of
Trade inspectors discharged their
duties, 396.
Railway locomotion. Resistance of a
curve to a train a function of the
velocity, xxiii. 404.—Adhesion of the
driving wheels of locomotives to the
rails, 404.—Question of locomotive
power and economy, particularly as regards improvements in locomotives, 441.
Railway locomotives and rolling-stock,
xxiv. 501.—Actual cost and maintenance of railway rolling-stock, 501.—
Terms of a contract for the maintenance and working of the rolling-
stock of the North Staffordshire
railway, 503.—Results of experience
in regard to large systems, 504.—Life
of an engine, 506, 508.—Railway
accounts, 506.—Average cost of maintaining engines, carriages, and wagons,
on various railways, 509.

BIDDER.

Railways, disadvantages of minute directorial interference in the management of, xxi. 389.—Continental system of railway traffic management, though safer, unsuited to English habits, 389.—Narrow-gauge railways, xxiv. 377.—Asserted economy of working ditto, 377.—Standing Orders of Parliament, with respect to the limits of deviation, in line and level, permitted to be made in the construction of railways, 378.—Level crossings, 379.—Prussian railways, xxv. 450.—Speed on ditto, 450.—Percentage of earnings of railways, xxviii. 280.—Railway gradients in England, 281.—Parliamentary proceedings in the case of the original London and Brighton railway and a proposed rival line, 281.—Closing the capital accounts of railways, 282.—Propriety of making the Mauritius railways, 283.

Railways and public works in India, xxii. 489.—Scinde railway, 489.—Plan adopted for the passage of flood-water over the Scinde railway, 489.—Railway sleepers for India, 489.—Necessity of perfecting the ports of India, 489.—Mode in which Indian railways ought, in future, to be carried out and worked, 489, et seq.

Reclaiming land from the sea, xxi. 485.—Formation of the marshes in Holstein and Denmark, 485.—Instances of land reclamation by the Netherlands Land Company, 485.—Destruction of the Middle Level Sluice, 486.—Reclamation of land by pumping, and by the regulation of the water in excess, 486.—Effect of reclamations upon the régime of estuaries and tidal rivers, 487.—Closing of reclamation banks, xxiii. 182, 183.—Proper area for enclosure, 183.—Extent of depression of the enclosed area below the level of highwater, with instances, 183.

Rivers, freshwater floods of, xxvii. 248.—Formulæ for defining the flood-producing capabilities of a district, 248.—Flood moderators, 249.—Devastating flood on the Scinde railway

BIDDER.

in 1866, 249.—Inapplicability of any formula to ditto, 249.—Report to the Directors of the Scinde Railway Company with regard to the flood of 1866, 250.

Rivers and estuaries, xxi. 32.—The Hooghly and the Mutla, 32.—Relatively small mechanical effect of land water, as compared with tidal water, from the examples of the Danube and the Thames, 299.—Effect of reclamations and embankments upon the régime of estuaries and tidal rivers, 487.

Ships and steam-vessels, 'line of least resistance' in, xxiii. 358.—Surface resistance, 358.—Theory of the 'wave line, 358.—Resistance of the 'Great Eastern,' 359.

Ships of war. Iron-plated ships, xxi. 245.—Free discussion upon these and similar subjects attended with public benefit, 245.—Reluctance of the Admiralty to introduce improvements in the Navy, 246.—Duties required from vessels of war, 247.—Incapacity of vessels to cope with modern forts, 247.—The 'Warrior' failing in everything but speed, 247.—Impossibility of constructing ironclad ships combining every desirable element, 247.—Resistance of armour-plates and force of impact of projectiles, 248.—Speed essential in naval warfare, 248.

Sluice, Middle Level, destruction of, xxi 486.

Tunnels, xxiii. 308.—Mont Cenis tunnel, 308.—High cost of boring ditto, 308.—Suitability of Mr. Bartlett's machine for perforating ditto, 309.

BIDDER, G. P., Jun. [Election, xxi. 48; Telford medal and Manby premium, 135, 152; Auditor, xxv. 160; xxvi. 118.]

Bridges, suspension, xxvi. 285.—Deflection of, 285, 286.

Injector, Giffard's, xxiv. 241, 244.

BIDDER, S. P., Jun. [Election, xxxvii. 59; Telford premium, xxix. 211.]

Coal-mining. "On machines employed in working and breaking coal, so as to avoid the use of gunpowder," xxviii.

BIDDER.

113.—Remarks, 122.—Further explanations of the machine devised by him, 122, 128, 153.—Undercutting coal, 134, 154.

BIDDER, W. H. [Election, xxiii. 257.]
Girders, lattice, xxiv. 448.—Attachment of lattice-bars to the vertical plates of the flanges, 448.

BIGG, H. H. [Election, xxi. 258.]

BIGSBY, G., Lieutenant, R.E. [Election, xxvii. 55.]

BILLSON, O. [Election, xxi. 48; Decease, xxix. 217.]

BINNIE, A. R. [Election, xxiv. 184.]

BIRCH, J. B. [Memoir, xxii. 640.]

BIRCH, R. W. P. [Admission, xxvii. 180.]

BIRCKEL, J. J.
Railways, American, xxviii. 430.—Unsubstantial character of permanent way on ditto, 430.—Adaptation of bogie trucks to railroad carriages, 430.—Unsteadiness of locomotives with radiating axle-boxes on straight lines of railway, 431.—American railway cars, 431.—Train resistances, 431.—Coefficient of friction of driving-wheels on rails, 431.—Locomotive engineering in the United States, 432.

BIRD, J. B. [Election, xxvii. 320.]

Birkenhead, low-water basin and sluicing operations at. Vide LOW-WATER BASIN AT BIRKENHEAD.

BIRKINSHAW, J. C. [Decease, xxvii. 131.]

BLACK, G. [Election, xxiv. 458.]

BLACKBURN, J. [Election, xxvi. 79.]

BLACKBURNE, J. W. [Election, xxix. 98.]

BLACKLOCK, W. T. [Election, xxvii. 443.]

BLACKWELL, T. E. [Memoir, xxiii. 481.]

BLAIR, J. F. [Election, xxi. 258.]
Railways, cost of construction of, in poor districts, xxvi. 66.—Cost of construction of the Great Northern and Western (of Ireland) railway, 66.
River Clyde. Low-water of spring-tides at Glasgow, xxix. 19.

BLAKE, H. W.
Steam-engines, xxiii. 101.—Single-acting and rotary, 101.—Objections against the single-acting Cornish engine, 101.—Disadvantages of the double-cylinder engine, 102.—Ulti-

BOUCH.

mate economy in working of the simple high-pressure, single-cylinder, expansive and rotative engine, 102.—Saving in first cost of raising the same quantity of water, by adopting the single-cylinder rotary engine, instead of the Cornish engine, 103.

BLAKE, James Hills. [Admission, xxx. 106.]

BLAKE, John Hopwood. [Admission, xxvii. 218; Election, xxviii. 325.]

BLANDY, A. F. [Election, xxvi. 165.]

Blasting, xxiii. 229; advantages of gun-cotton for, 318. Vide also COAL-MINING; and TUNNELS.

BLATCHLEY, C. G. [Election, xxviii. 59.]

BLAXLAND, G., Jun. [Election, xxix. 98.]

BLOM, Colonel F. [Decease, xxv. 531.]

BLOUNT, J. [Election, xxii. 540.]

Blyth, Swansea, and Silloth, description of works at the ports of (Abernethy, J.), xxi. 309. Vide also PORTS.

BLYTH, B. H. [Memoir, xxvi. 556.]

BLYTH, B. H. [Admission, xxvii. 320.]

BLYTH, E. L. I.
Viaduct. "Description of the Loch Ken viaduct, Portpatrick railway," xxi. 258.

BODMER, J. G. [Memoir, xxviii. 573.]

BOHN, G. [Election, xxv. 429.]

BOLCKOW, H. W. F. [Election, xxii. 451.]

BOLDEN, H. [Election, xxii. 451.]

BOLLAND, J. [Election, xxvi. 242.]

BOLTON, Captain F. J. [Election, xxii. 540.]

BONNIN, W. W. [Election, xxvi. 79.]

Boring and boring-machines. Vide ARTESIAN WELLS; COAL-MINING; and TUNNELS.

BORRADAILE, J.
Ports in India. Superior situation of the port of the Mutla to that of Calcutta, xxi. 31.

BOTFIELD, B. [Memoir, xxiii. 503.]

BOUCH, T.
Viaducts. Considerations which governed the choice of materials for the Hownes Gill, Deepdale, and Beelah viaducts, xxii. 52.—Lateral spread of the piers in the Hownes Gill viaduct, to secure a greater area for the foundations, 56.

BOULNOIS.

BOULNOIS, H. P. [Admission, xxvii. 54.]
BOULTON, S. B.
 Timber. Value of creosoting timber as
  a preservative against the attacks of
  marine insects in the case of piles in
  Holland and Belgium, xxvii. 564.—
  Preparation of timber for creosoting by
  the French and Belgian Governments, 565.
BOUQUIÉ, A. [Election, xxvi. 477.]
BOUBNE, J. [Watt medal and Telford
  premium, xxvii. 124, 142.]
 Gunpowder, relative dynamic value of,
  burnt in American and English guns,
  xxvi. 235.
 "Ships of war," xxvi. 166.—Remarks,
  180, et seq.—Monitor system of vessels,
  228.—Expediency of thick armour-
  plating, 230.—Means of propulsion of
  monitors, 230.—Ventilation of ditto,
  231.—Bulkheads in ditto, 232.—Impracticability of ramming the 'Dictator,'
  232.—Depth of the armour of the
  'Dictator' below water, 233.—Question
  of the penetrability of the armour-
  plating of the 'Dictator' and of the
  'Bellerophon,' 234.—Penetration of
  solid and laminated armour, 234.—
  Effect of heavy shot at low velocities,
  236.—Limit to the power of guns, 236.
  —Seaworthiness of monitors, 237.—
  Captain Fox's Report on the perform-
  ance of the 'Miantonomah' in the
  Atlantic, 238.—Mr. Reed's improved
  designs for monitors, 239.—Efficiency
  of the monitor system as tested in
  practice, 240.—Propriety of introduc-
  ing the monitor system into the Royal
  Navy, 241.
BOURNE, J. F. [Election, xxvi. 398.]
 Lighthouse. "The Roman Rock Light-
  house, Simon's Bay. Cape of Good
  Hope," xxviii. 49.—Remarks, 58.
Bow, R. H.
 Materials, resistance of, xxix. 76.
BOWDEN, J. [Election, xxviii. 232.]
BOWEN, O. [Election, xxii. 451.]
BOWER, James. [Election, xxvii. 443.]
BOWER, John. [Election, xxx. 323.]
BOWER, J.
 Lighthouses, Red Sea, xxiii. 28.—Intro-

BRAMWELL.

duction of diagonals in their construc-
 tion, 28.
BOYD, J.
 Iron. Analysis of West Cumberland
  hæmatite Bessemer pig iron, xxvii.
  393.
 Permanent way. Mixture of iron for
  the manufacture of rails, xxvii. 392.—
  Specifications and tests for rails, 392.
BOYD, J. E. [Election, xxvi. 398.]
BOYS, J. C. [Election, xxx. 106.]
BRADBURY, A. B. [Election, xxix. 98.]
BRADY, F. [Election, xxvii. 553.]
BRAGGE, W.
 Permanent way. Wear of steel and iron
  rails on the Erie railway, xxvii. 381.
  —Progress of steel railmaking in
  seven years, 381.
BRAHAM, C. B. [Admission, xxvii. 120.]
BRAHAM, F. S. [Admission, xxvii. 120.]
BRAIDWOOD, J. [Memoir, xxi. 571.]
BRAITHWAITE, F. [Council Premium, xxi.
  135, 152; Memoir, xxvi. 560.]
 Evaporation, spontaneous, xxii. 364.
 Rain-gauge, Dickinson's, xxii. 365.
 River Thames, xxii. 364.—Large quan-
  tity of water abstracted from the river
  above Teddington Lock, 364.
BRAMWELL, F. J. [Auditor, xxi. 132;
  xxii. 111; Member of Council, xxvii.
  122; xxviii. 158; xxix. 208.]
 Bridges, American iron, xxii. 558.—
  Principles involved in the construction
  of the trusses, 560.—Fink truss, 561,
  et seq.—Compression bar of the Fink
  truss compared with that of an ordinary
  diagonal truss, 563.—Bollman truss,
  567.—Cause of the waste of metal in
  the Fink and Bollman trusses, 567.—
  Murphy-Whipple truss, 567; xxiv.
  437.
 ———, suspension, xxvi. 290.—Over
  the Niagara river between Queenstown and Lewistown, 290.—Fribourg,
  290.—Temporary, over the Niagara
  river, 290.—True use of the principle
  of suspension, 291.—Varying width
  apart of the suspension ropes of the
  Queenstown and Lewistown bridge,
  291.—A suspension bridge more or
  less 'lively' in the inverse ratio of

BRAMWELL.

the quantity of material in the rope or chain, 291.—Inexpediency of complicating the works of suspension bridges, 292.

Cement. Tests of quality, xxv. 136.—Fallacy of the test by weight, 137.—Method adopted at Woolwich for ascertaining the specific gravity of gunpowder, 138.—Similar method for ascertaining the specific gravity of cement, 138.—Limit to the specific gravity of good cement, 139.—Effects of gauging cement with different quantities of water, 139.—Mixtures of cement with different kinds of sand, 140.—Behaviour of Portland cement concrete in contact with iron, 141.—Substitution of cement bricks for ordinary bricks, 141.

Coal-mining, xxviii. 134.—Undercutting, 134.—Coal-getting machinery invented by Mr. Bartholomew, Mr. Grafton Jones, Mr. C. J. Chubb, and Mr. S. P. Bidder, 135.

Docks, graving. History of floating docks, xxv. 313.—Screw dock, 314.—Supporting the bilges of vessels in docks upon the keel taking the blocks, 315.—Rigidity in floating docks, 315.—Injurious effect of using hydraulic presses for keel blocks in a stone dock, 316.—Operations taking place in the hydraulic lift dock, 317.—Means of preventing an undue lifting of one press as compared with another, 317.—Failure of the American sectional dock, 317.—St. Thomas floating dock, 318.

Drainage of towns. London and Paris, xxiv. 326.—Pumping engines for raising the sewage at Crossness and Abbey Mills, 326.—Real offices sewers are required to fulfil, 328.

Foundations. Cylinder foundations, xxviii. 351.—Kennard's Sand Pump and Milroy's Excavator, 352.—Use of hydraulic digging, or water currents, in sinking cylinders, 352.—Plenum and vacuum processes for sinking cylinders, 353.—System of outward currents, 354.—Sinking cylinders for the foundations of Rochester, Saltash,

BRAMWELL.

and Kehl bridges, 355.—Method of sinking cylinders by compressed air due to the Earl of Dundonald, 355.

Gas, pressure for getting the best effect out of coal, xxviii. 456.

Girders. Uniform stress in girder-work, xxiv. 436.—Allusion to Murphy-Whipple truss, 437.—Effect upon material, either in compression or extension, due to putting the load, or strain, out of the centre of gravity of that material, 439, 446.—Inverted queen truss without the top member, xxvi. 292.—Deflection of a girder in accordance with the cube of its length, 292.

Gunpowder, method of testing specific gravity of, at Woolwich Arsenal, xxv. 138.

Injector, Giffard's, xxiv. 219.—Hydraulic apparatus for illustrating ditto, 228, et seq.—Application of injectors to locomotives, 236.

Iron and steel. Effect of sea-water on cast iron, xxii. 440.—Advantage of drilling instead of punching rivet-holes, 530.—Strength of cast iron, and result of experiments to ascertain the same, 558.—Toughness of iron increased by melting, 560.—Welding Bessemer steel, xxv. 426.—Strength of iron bars, xxx. 267.

Materials. Cement in contact with iron, xxv. 141.—Substitution of cement bricks for ordinary bricks, 141.

———, strength and resistance of, xxiv. 439.—Effect upon material, either in compression or extension, due to putting the load, or strain, out of the centre of gravity of that material, 439, 446.—Relation of form to the strength of materials, xxix. 76.

Permanent way, maintenance and renewal of, xxv. 407.—Wear of rails by trains at high speeds, 407.—Superiority of suspended joints to joints upon a chair on railways, 408.—Blenkinsop rail, xxvi. 361.

Piers and landing stages, xxviii. 226.—Accident to the New Brighton pier, 226.

BRAMWELL.

Railway curves and inclines. Resistance on the curves of railways, xxvi. 358, 380.—Reasons why engines on Mr. Fell's construction traverse curves more easily than ordinary engines, 360.—Average gradients on the Mauritius and the Mont Cenis railways, xxviii. 258.—Working steep railway inclines with locomotive engines and stationary engines, xxx. 67.—Break-van in use on the Serra do Mar inclines, 68.

Railway locomotives and rolling stock. Oscillatory movements of locomotive engines, xxii. 85.—Inexpediency of single-cylinder locomotive engines, 92.—Plan for insuring the accurate boring of tires, 612.—Railway wheel-making, xxv. 451.—Disc-wheels, 451.—Superiority of ditto to spoke-wheels, 452.—Grinding steel tires, 453.—Manufacture of compound steel and iron wheels, 453.—Manufacture of metal spoke-wheels, 453.—Injurious effects of breaks, 455.—Superiority of construction of breaks in America, 456.—Compound locomotive engines, xxvi. 72.—Sledge breaks, 361.—System of breaking by reversing the engines, 361.—Contrivance for getting the cranks of the vertical axles over the centres in the engines used on the Mont Cenis railway, 362.—Use of steel for wheel tires and axles, 364.—Depreciation of locomotives, xxx. 202.—Fund to meet the cost of renewals, 203.

Railway telegraphs. Resemblance between Clark's and Spagnoletti's system, xxii. 229.

Railway trains, communication in, xxvi. 96.—Opposing system and the equilibrium system of electrical currents, 96.

Rotary fans, xxx. 303.—Form of blades, 303.—Cases, 303.—Fans working tandem-fashion, 303.

Ships and steam-vessels. Resistance of plane surfaces drawn through water at right angles to themselves, xxiii. 364.—Natural flow of water in the case of a flat surface moving in water, 365.—

BRAMWELL.

Resistance to the bows of vessels, 365.—Power put forth by rudders, 366.—Skin resistance of a vessel different to that inside a pipe, 366.—Apparent slight differences between the friction of a rough and a polished surface moving through the water, as shown by a Griffiths screw, 367.—Real work of a screw done by the leading edge of the blade, 367.

Ships of war, xxvi. 197.—Penetration of shot in experiments against armour-plates, 197.—Liability of monitors to be pooped, 198.

Steam-engines. Duty of Cornish pumping engines, xxiii. 54.—Equivalent of milions of duty represented by consumption of coal per H.P., 54.—Proposed plans for inducing the owners of mines to work their engines more economically, 54.—Fuel, 54 —Indicator diagrams, 55.—Amount of expansion, 55.—How far economy is due to the engine, and how far to the boiler, in Cornish pumping engines, 55.—Contrivances adopted from the Cornish engine, 56.—Waste of fuel in ditto, 56.—Most beneficial use of ditto, 56.—Conversion of a Boulton and Watt into a Cornish engine. 57.—Great cost of Cornish pumping engines, 57.—Details of the working not favourable for obtaining economy, 58.—Economy from slow rate of combustion, 59.—Comparison between the duty of the Cornish engine in its best days, and that of. other engines, 60.—Erroneous opinion that one cause of the falling-off of the duty of the Cornish engines is due to excessive loading, 73.—Statement that low duty results from diagonal drawing, 74.—Loss resulting from the use of single-cylinder instead of double-cylinder engines, 74.—Pumping engines for raising the metropolitan sewage at Crossness and Abbey Mills, xxiv. 326.—Inexpediency and wastefulness of working non-condensing engines at low pressures, xxvi. 33.

Steam navigation, xxix. 168.—Perform

BRAND.

ance of marine engines, 168.—Relation of speed to the expenditure of fuel in steam-vessels, 187.—Auxiliary propulsion of vessels, 187.—Improvements in steam navigation, 188.—Surface condensation in marine engines, 188.—Duty and H.P. of marine engines, 189. — Screw-propellers, 190. — Griffiths' feathering screw-propeller, 190.

Tunnels, machinery for boring, xxiii. 301.—Air-compressing machines of M. Sommeiller used at the Mont Cenis tunnel, 301.—Air-compressing pump used at the Modane end alone, 301.—Pumps used by the Portable Gas Company, 302.—Air-compressing pump in which water was introduced to get rid of the clearance, 302.—Clearance in an air-compressing pump, 302.—Horizontal boring bar propelled by air, 303. —Force required to propel the boring bars at the Mont Cenis tunnel, 303.—Proposed increase of the pressure of air for working the boring machine, 303.—Superiority of Mr. Bartlett's boring machine, 304.—Machine invented by M. Leschot for boring by rotary motion by means of a diamond cutter, 305.

BRAND, J. [Election, xxiv. 184.]

BRANFILL, J. A. C. [Election, xxiii. 459.]

BRASSEY, T.
Portrait of, by S. B. Halle, bequeathed by H. P. Burt, xxvi. 126.
Tunnels, machinery for boring, xxiii. 295.—M. Sommeiller's machinery for boring the Mont Cenis tunnel, 295.—Perforating machine by Chevalier Maus, 296.

BRASSEY, T., jun. [Election, xxvi. 79.]

BRASSINGTON, J. W. [Election, xxii. 167.]

BRAY, W. B.
Surveying and levelling. "On measuring distances by the telescope," xxi. 34.

Brazil, public works in Pernambuco, in the Empire of (Peniston, W. M.), xxii. 385. *Vide* also PUBLIC WORKS, Brazil.
———, climate of, xxiv. 1. *Vide* also MATERIALS, durability of.
———, description of the line and works of the São Paulo railway, in the

BRERETON.

Empire of (Fox, D. M.). *Vide* also RAILWAYS.

Breaks. *Vide* RAILWAY BREAKS.

Breakwaters, construction of, xxii. 443, *et seq.*; xxiv 168, *et seq.*; xxv. 112, *et seq.* *Vide* also DOCKS, Marseilles; PORTS; and STRUCTURES IN THE SEA.

Brebner's (A.) refraction protractor (Henderson, D. M.), xxviii. 34.

BREMNER, A. [Memoir, xxiii. 505.]

BRERETON, R. M. [Election, xxiv. 144.]

BRERETON, R. P.
Bridges : Saltash. "Description of the centre pier of the Saltash bridge, on the Cornwall railway, and of the means employed for its construction," xxi. 268.—Remarks, 275.—Difficulty of keeping up a constant pressure of 40 lbs. to the inch in the large cylinder, 275.—Effect of great air-pressure on workmen employed in the cylinder, 276.—Weight of the Saltash bridge cylinders, 276.
———, Victoria, Pimlico, xxvii. 92.—Effect of changes of temperature, 93.—Wrought-iron arches of large span, 94.—Dimensions of the pier, 99.
———, suspension. Original designs for the Clifton suspension bridge, xxvi. 266.—One of the piers lower than the other, 266.—Strains on the piers of suspension bridges, 271.—Permanent set of iron suspension links, for bridges under strain, xxx. 270.—Proportions of the Hungerford bridge and the Clifton bridge links, 270.—Object of the swelled-out shoulder of ditto, 271.—Proportions of the links of the Chepstow and the Saltash bridges, 271.—Steel arches of the bridge over the river Missouri, at St. Louis, 272.—Testing the links of the Saltash bridge, 272.

Canals, steam-power on, xxvi. 27.—Disturbance to the soft bottoms of canals occasioned by screw-propellers, 27.—Effect of the 'Great Eastern' steamship working her screw in shoal-water, 28.

Cements. Use of Portland cement for foundations under water, xxv. 143,

BRERETON,

144, 146.—Setting properties of Portland cement and lias mortar when used with sea-sand or sea-water, 143.

Gas. Difficulty of testing the illuminating power of coal, xxviii. 461.—Sperm candles as at present manufactured an imperfect standard, 461.

Irrigation in India, results of, xxvii. 537.

Lighthouse apparatus, xxvi. 521.—Excellence of the dioptric light at Kingsweare, Dartmouth, 521.

Materials, resistance of, xxix. 63.—Elastic change of form of, 64.—Cases of unforeseen failures of girder-bridges, 64.—Molecular adhesion in the case of bolts, 65.—Friction of shroud-laid and hawser-laid rope, 65.—A paper of pins bent by the vibrations in constant travelling by railway, 66.—Resistance of materials to compression, 66.—Shearing rivets and punching plates, 67.—Failure from torsion of the paddle-shaft and rudder-shaft of the 'Great Eastern' steamship, 67.—Continuous girder-bridges, 68.—Destruction of the entrance-gates of the Plymouth docks, 69.—Accident to the sea-gate of the dock at Briton Ferry, 69.

Mathematical books and papers, value of, lessened by frequently containing material errors from want of due revision, xxix. 64.

Permanent way. Durability of iron rails made in 1849 for the South Wales railway, xxvii. 375.

Piles. Vacuum and plenum processes of pile-driving, xxvii. 303.—Driving piles in diluvial clay and mud to carry railway viaducts in Cornwall and Devonshire, 303.—M'Alpine's formula for determining the resisting power of piles, 303.

Railway curves and inclines, xxvi. 378.—Cause of the increased resistance on sharp curves, 378.—Ascent of inclines by heavy locomotive engines, 378; xxviii. 274.

Railway income and expenditure, xxvii.

BRIDGES.

485.—Percentage of the receipts on the cost of the Charing Cross railway, 435.

Railway locomotives and rolling stock. Working steep inclines, xxviii. 274.—Ordinary and weighted lever-breaks, 275.—Performance of the locomotives on the Mauritius railways, 275.—Locomotive repairs and renewals on American railways, 396.—Accident from a bogie engine leaving the line, 397.

Railway stations, xxv. 286.—Use of railway-station platforms on the Continent, 286.—Changes in the height of the platforms at stations of the Great Western railway, 287.—Size of roofs for railway stations, xxvii. 434.

River Witham, xxviii. 82.—Drainage through the Grand Sluice, and navigation by the river to Boston, 82.

Rivers, freshwater floods of, xxvii. 241.—Colonel O'Connell's formula for classifying rivers as flood-producers, 241.—Gauging the fall of rain, 242.—Lakes as flood moderators, 242.—Removal of forests from mountainous districts augments floods, 242.

Ships of war, xxi. 209.—Method of attaching armour-plates to the sides of vessels, 209.

Steam navigation. Abandonment of the superheating apparatus in the Kingstown and Holyhead steam-packets, xxii. 597.

Tunnels, machinery for boring, xxiii. 296.—Perforating machine invented by Chevalier Maus, 296.

BRESSE, M.

Materials, resistance of. Letters relative to the history of the 'Theorem of the Three Moments' (Heppel, J. M.), xxix. 42, 46.

BREWSTER, Sir D. [Decease, xxviii. 167.]

BRIDGES.

Britannia. Preservation of the iron-work, xxvii. 559.

Cannon Street, Charing Cross railway, xxvii. 411.

Charing Cross. "The Charing Cross bridge." By H. Hayter, xxii. 512.—

BRIDGES.

General description, 512.—Cylinders
for the openings, 154 feet span, 513. —
Sinking the cylinders, 514.—Filling the
cylinders and weighting, 515.—Each
pair of cylinders connected together
transversely by a wrought-iron box-
girder, 516.—Superstructure of the
openings, 154 feet span, 516.—Main
girders spanning the 154-feet openings,
516.—Rivet-holes drilled, 517. — Results of testing a girder, 519.—Question as to the propriety of continuity
of girders, 520.—Cross-girders for the
openings, 154 feet span, 521.—Method
of suspension, 521.—Fan end, 522.—
Roadway and footpath platforms, 524.
Causes that retarded the completion
of the bridge, 524.—Cost, 525.—Table
of results of experiments on plate iron,
of the kind used in the construction of
the Charing Cross bridge, 527.

Discussion. — Bramwell, F. J., 530.—
Cochrane, J., 530.— Cowper, E. A.,
531. — Hawkshaw, J., 533, 538.—
Hayter, H., 532.—Hemans, G. W.,
529.—Heppel, J. M., 529.— Mallet, R.,
532. — Phipps, G. H., 528, 535.—
Russell, J. S., 530, 534. — Sheilds,
F. W., 532.

Chey-Air. "The Chey-Air bridge,
Madras railway." By E. Johnston,
xxiv. 184.—Features of the Chey-Air
river, 184.—Site of the bridge, 184.—
The piers, 185, 186.—Process of excavating for the foundations, 185.—
The Piccotah pump, 186. — Timber
platforms on which the masonry was
constructed, 186. — Stability of the
piling and timber round the dams,
186.—Stone used for the foundations
and piers, 187.—Cost of preparing
a single dam, with timber platform,
ready to receive the masonry, 187.—
Workpeople employed, and wages,
187.—Quantities of materials, cost,
and time occupied in completion, 187.
—Character of the work remaining
to be done, 188.—Iron superstructure
of the bridge over the river Cavery,
188. — Mode of bridging the wide
rivers on the Madras railway, 189.

BRIDGES.

Discussion.—Berkley, G., 194. — Giles,
A., 195.—Hawkshaw, J., 195.—Hep-
pel, J. M., 190.—Rennie, Sir. J., 196.
—Walker, J., 194.

Pennair. "Description of the Pennair
bridge, Madras railway, N.W. Line."
By E. Stoney, xxix. 382. *Vide* also
RAILWAY BRIDGES AND VIADUCTS.

Saltash. "Description of the centre pier
of the Saltash bridge on the Cornwall
railway, and of the means employed
for its construction." By R. P. Brereton, xxi. 263. — Locality described,
268.—Bridge of seven openings first
proposed objected to by the Admiralty,
268.—Powers obtained in 1847 for a
bridge with four spans over the river,
268.—Bed of the river examined by
means of a wrought-iron cylinder, 268.
—Final determination on two main
spans of 455 feet each, 269.—Dimensions of the bridge and central pier,
269.—Cylinder for the construction of
the masonry pier, 270.—Constructed so
as to admit of the application of air-
pressure in the inside, 270. — Two
smaller cylinders and dome to effect
this, 270.—Cylinder commenced on the
beach in 1853, 271.—Floated to position
and sunk in 1854, 271.—In final position in February, 1855, 272.—Progress
of the work interruptions from leakage
and bad nature of the trap-rock, 272.
—Additional cylinder for applying air-
pressure, 273. — Loading the new
cylinder, 273.—Progress of the masonry interrupted by leakage, 273. —
Masonry to the cap of the pier completed, 274.—Final completion of the
bridge, 274.

Discussion. -- Brereton, R. P., 275.—
Cochrane, J., 275. — Hawkshaw, J.,
276. -- Lawrence, F., 275.

Sarine, on the Lausanne and Fribourg
railway, xxv. 252.

Victoria, Pimlico. "Description of the
Victoria bridge on the line of the
Victoria station and Pimlico railway."
By W. Wilson, xxvii. 55.—Extension
of the railway from Battersea Fields
to Victoria, 55.—Site of the Victoria

BRIDGES.

bridge, 56.—Position of the piers, 56. — The foundations, 56. — The masonry, 58.—The superstructure, 59. —The roadway and approaches, 63. —The quantities of the materials, 65. —Cost, 65.—The engineers and contractors, 65.—Mode of execution of the work, 65. — Results of testing the bridge, 66. — Extreme strains produced by the most unfavourable combination of circumstances, 67.—Appendix : summary of quantities of wrought iron, 67.

————, " On the widening of the Victoria bridge and approaches to the Victoria station, and on new railways at Battersea." By C. D. Fox, xxvii. 68.—Enumeration of the works, 68.—Widening of the Victoria station and Pimlico railway, 68.—Widening of the Victoria bridge, 69.—The abutments, 70.—The piers, 71.—The superstructure, 72.— The platforms, 73.—Results of testing the bridge, 73.—The ironwork, 74.— The quantities of the materials, 74.— Cost, 74.—High-level line of the London, Brighton, and South Coast Railway Company, 75.—Branch line from the Wandsworth Road, 75.—The bridges, 76.—The brick arches, 77.— Stations, 78.—Diversion and raising of the West End and Crystal Palace and West London Extension railways, 78. — High-level line of the London, Chatham, and Dover railway, 78.—Longhedge Junction railway, 79.—Connecting link to Clapham Junction, 79. —Low-level lines from Victoria bridge, 80.—Permanent way, 80.—Cost, 80.— The engineers and contractors, 80.— Appendix: widening of Victoria bridge, Pimlico ; particulars of loading, 81.

Discussion. — Baker, B., 94. — Baldry, J. D., 108.—Barlow, W. H., 111.— Bell, W., 103.—Brereton, R. P., 92, 99.—Cowper, E. A., 99, 107.—Fogerty, J., 112.—Fox, Sir C., 113, 119.—Fox, C. D., 82. — Gregory, C. H., 87.— Hemans, G. W., 98.—Heppel, J. M., 98.—Lloyd, J. H., 112.—Longridge,

BRIDGES.

J. A., 108.—Phipps, G. H., 88, 108.— Reilly, C., 84.—Sheilds, F. W., 97, 98. —Taylor, J., 111.— Tyler, Capt. H. W., 110.—Vignoles, C. B., 112.—Wilson, W., 82, 116.—Young, F. W., 105, 107, 108.

Vide also BRIDGES, IRON ; BRIDGES, SUSPENSION ; BRIDGES, TIMBER ; FOUNDATIONS ; GIRDERS ; RAILWAY BRIDGES AND VIADUCTS ; and VIADUCTS.

BRIDGES, IRON.

American. '' American iron bridges.'' By Z. Colburn, xxii. 540.—Advantages of iron over timber bridges, 540.— Earliest iron bridges erected in that country, 540. — Major Delafield's arched bridges, 540.—Captain Meigs' aqueduct bridge at Washington, 540. —Iron arched bridge over the Schuylkill river at Philadelphia, 541.— Plate-girder bridge over the Carroll's Run stream, on the Baltimore and Susquehannah railroad, 542. — Strength of American cast-iron, 543· —Ditto of American wrought-iron, 544.—Extent of working strains allowed, 545.—Peculiarities of the iron-trussed bridges as distinguished from trussed bridges in England, 546.— Rider's trellised bridge, 547. — The Whipple bridge as improved by J. W. Murphy, 547.—The tension rods, 549. —Cost of American bridges, 549.—The Pennsylvania Central railroad bridge across the Schuylkill at Philadelphia, 549.—Cost of ditto, 550.—Wrought-iron rolled beams employed for the top and bottom chords of the pivot span of ditto, 550.—Pivot upon which the turning span of the bridge is made to revolve, 551.—Bollman's truss bridge, 552.—Bridge at Harper's Ferry, 552. —Bridge designed by A. Fink, 553.— Bridge on the Baltimore and Ohio railroad over the Monongahela river, 554. — The Barren River and Erie River bridges, 555.—Cost per lineal foot of the Bollman and Fink trusses for a single line, 555.—Great range of temperature in America unfavourable to the use of cast iron for railway

BRIDGES.

bridges, 555.—Cost of wrought-iron plate girders in Canada, 555.

Discussion.—Bramwell, F. J., 558. -Colburn, Z., 557, 573.—Cowper, E. A., 569.—Hawkshaw, J., 573.—Jenkin, F., 567.—Phipps, G. H., 571. —Sheilds, F. W., 572.

Coalbrookdale, railway, xxvii. 112.— Cost, 112.—Castings of the ironwork, 112.

Girder. "Studies of iron girder-bridges recently executed, illustrating some applications of the modern theory of the elastic resistance of materials." By C. Reilly, xxix. 403.—Introduction, 403. — BRIDGE No. 1, 405.— Principal peculiar features, 406.— Experience of the system, 406.—Sufficiency of foundation, 406.—Resistance of a pier; its construction, 406.—Construction of the superstructure, 408.— Loads supported by the girders, 409. —Load upon one pier, 409.—Greatest intensities of stress, 409.—Girders, 410.—Quality of the work; quantities and weights of materials in the viaduct, and its cost, 410.—Precautions to be observed in fixing screw-piles, 412.—THE PIERS: analysis of the stress and deformation of an intermediate pier, when one span is loaded and the next unloaded, by the greatest moving load, 412.—To find the greatest intensity of stress on any normal cross-section, the angle of inclination of any normal with the axis of x, and the deflection or value of y corresponding, 417.—Intensity and distribution of stress on any normal cross-section, 419.—Joint, 423.—Point of inflection, 424.—Inclination of any normal cross-section with axis of y, 424.—Position of place of greatest deflection of the deformed mean fibre from the axis of x, that is, from the mean fibre in its primitive state, 425.—The magnitude of the deflection of the deformed mean fibre at any point x, 425.—Greatest pressure of the screw-flanges of the pier upon the earth foundations, 425. —Re⬛⬛⬛⬛⬛⬛sidering the dynamic

BRIDGES.

effect of the moving load, 426.—Conclusions from the preceding analysis, 426.—THE GIRDERS: moving load on one girder, 426.—Fixed load estimated to be carried by one girder, 427.— Weight and intensity of total load uniformly distributed, 428.—Depth of girder: maxima of intensities of stress permitted: position of the mean fibre: origin of co-ordinates: considerations fixing the thickness of web-plate, 428. —Mode of computing the longitudinal bending stress at any section whose abscissa = x, 429. —Distribution of material in the lower boom, 430.— Distribution of material in the top boom, 432.—Deviation, if any, of the actual rotation-axis from its assumed position, O z, 434. — Distribution of material in the top boom, continued, 435.—Greatest shearing stress upon a section of the girder: its effects: resistance of the web to buckling, 435. —Shearing force and stress at the bearing: resistance of the end pillars, 439.—Resistance of the rivets: rivets in end pillars: rivets connecting the web with the booms: rivets fixing the horizontal plates of the booms, 440.— Deflection of the girders: dynamic effect of the moving load travelling at a high velocity, 442.—Appendix to Bridge No. 1, Note A, 444.—Ditto, Note B,—BRIDGE No. 2: motives: uniform stress, 451. - General conditions of construction requisite for uniform stress, 453.—Conditions of economy of construction, 455.—General remarks on this bridge: conditions assigned: standards of minimum strength: span, 458.—Comparison of strength, weight, and cost of the ironwork, 458.—RAIL GIRDERS: distribution of loads on one rail-girder, 460.— Longitudinal bending stresses, 460.— Subsequent alteration of section; resulting deviation of rotation-axis from O z; consequences of that deviation. 463.—Shearing force and stress upon web: resistance of the web to buckling, 464.--Resistance of rivets: rivets

BRIDGES.

connecting the web with the booms: rivets fixing the horizontal plates of the booms, 466.—RAIL GIRDER FASTENINGS : the moment of resistance of the two jaw-plates, 468.—Resistance of the group of rivets fixing the jaw-plates to the end of the rail-girder, 468.—Greatest intensity of shearing stress on the section of the jaw-plates, 470.—Greatest stress on the pin of the articulation, 470. — CROSS-GIRDER : general construction: fixed load : greatest moving load, 472.—Stresses, 473.—Riveting, 474.— Unequal loading, 474.—CROSS-GIRDER FASTENINGS : resistance to bearing pressure, 474.— Intensity of shearing stress on a section of the pin, 475. — Resistance of the pin to flexure, 475.—Resistance of the short beams of plate iron, extending across the width of the truss, and supporting the pin of the articulation, 476.—MAIN GIRDERS : form, span, and depth, 478.—Moving load, fixed load, total load, 480.—Stresses upon the bars of the truss, 478.—Joints of the truss, 480.—Remarks on some of the other joints, 486.—Web, 487.— Booms, 491.—Top saddle, 492.—Pressure on the articulated bearing of the two saddles, 495. — Bottom saddle, 495. — Appendix to Bridge No. 2 : investigation of least radius of gyration of section of equal-sided angle-iron, 497.

Trent, at Gainsborough, xxv. 261.— Launching on rollers the girders of ditto, 261.

BRIDGES, SUSPENSION.

Caxanga, xxiv. 29.

Cincinnati, U. S. Over the river Ohio, by Mr. Roebling, xxvi. 267.

Clifton. "Description of the Clifton suspension bridge." By W. H. Barlow, xxvi. 243.—History and origin of the undertaking, 243.—Mr. I. K. Brunel's design, 243.—Appropriation of the chains of the Hungerford suspension bridge, 243.—Rearrangement of Mr. Brunel's design, 244.—Principal dimensions of the bridge, 244.—

BRIDGES.

The chains, 244, 247.—The links, 245. —The roadway, 245.—Erection of the chains, 245, et seq.—Attachment of the suspension-rods and cross-girders, 247. —Variation of the curve of the chain during construction, 247.—Strain at the centre of the chains, 248.—The piers, 248. — Suspension-rods, 248.— Brickwork, 248.—Stiffening girders, 249.—Provision for the effects of expansion and contraction, 249.—Cost of ironwork, 249.—Result of testing the bridge, 249.—Table showing the deflections produced by the test-load of 500 tons evenly distributed, 250. — Deflections produced by high winds, 251.—Suitability of suspension bridges for the passage of railway trains, 251. —The Lambeth suspension bridge, 252.—Design for stiffening suspension bridges by Messrs. Ordish and Le Feuvre, 252.—Stiffening suspension bridges with the least quantity of metal, 252. — Form of continuous girder approaching in economy of materials to a stiffened suspension bridge, 252.—Table of experiments on cast-iron beams, showing the weight on the centre span at the time of fracture, 254.—Table showing the deflections with 100lbs. uniformly distributed over centre span, 255.—Best mode of connnection for the chains of suspension bridges, 256.—Proposed introduction of steel for the chains of suspension bridges, 256. — Contribution of funds for the construction of the Clifton suspension bridge, 257.

Of great span. "On the use of the suspension bridge with stiffened roadway for railway and other bridges of great span." By G. B. Airy, xxvi. 258.— Better methods available for wide crossings than simple tubular bridges, 258.—Mathematical investigation of the subject proposed, 258.—How the stiffening principle forms an integral part of the plan of the bridge, 258.— Curvatures produced by a weight placed on the stiffened roadway of a bridge when connected with, and when

BRIDGES.

unconnected with, a suspension chain, 259, 260.—Crucial experiments on the subject, 260, et seq.—Investigation of the results of ditto, 262, et seq.—Rule for planning a strengthening tube or girder of a suspension bridge, 263.—Consideration of the limit to the width which can be safely crossed by a suspension bridge with strengthened roadway, 263.—Plan proposed for constructing a girder for stiffening the roadway of a suspension bridge, 264.

Discussion. — Airy, G. B., 266, 273, 274, 286, 307.—Barlow, P. W., 278.—Barlow, W. H., 265, 307.—Bergue, C. L. A. de, 269.—Bidder, G. P., Jun., 285, 286. — Bramwell, F. J., 290.—Brereton, R. P., 266, 271.—Claxton, Capt. C., 265.—Cochrane, J., 269.—Cowper, E. A., 279, 283. — Fowler, J., 266, 297.—Gregory, C. H., 268.—Hawkshaw, J., 274, 283. — Hemans, G. W., 265.—Heppel, J. M., 304, 306.—Johnson, T. M., 294.—Kinipple, W. R., 293.—Lane, C. B., 289.—Law, H., 268.—Le Feuvre, W. H., 273.—Longridge, J. A., 270, 272.—Phipps, G. H., 301.—Porter, J. H., 284.—Radford, G. K., 267.—Richardson, R., 268, 273.—Reilly, C., 272, 274. — Sheilds, F. W., 282, 284.—Tyler, Capt. H. W., 297, 306.—Vignoles, C. B., 270, 272.—Whiting, J. E., 306. — Williams, R. P., 295.—Young, E. W., 299.

Links of, xxx. 270, et seq. Vide also IRON AND STEEL ; and MATERIALS, durability of..

BRIDGES, TIMBER.

American. "American timber bridges." By J. R. Mosse, xxii. 305.—The only works available in new and poor countries where timber is abundant and cheap, 305.—The lattice bridge not suitable for heavy traffic, 305.—The Howe bridge, 306. — Description of an ordinary Howe bridge over the James river at Richmond, 307.—Weight of bridge per lineal foot, and calculation of strains, assuming a load of 3000 lbs. per lineal foot uniformly distributed, 307. —

BRIDGES.

Ordinary dimensions for a span of 150 feet, without arches, on the Portland railway, 308. — Strains, assuming a weight of 3000 lbs. per lineal foot, 308.—The improved Howe truss as constructed on the Philadelphia and Reading railway, 308.—Reference to its supporting loaded coal-wagons after several of the main trusses had been broken, 309.—Subject to very heavy loads, 309.—Limit of safe compression on timber framing, 310.—Approximate quantities of materials in this bridge, 310.—Deflection at first small, but rapidly increasing with the decay of the bridge, which soon occurs through the use of unseasoned timber, 310.—Disadvantages from the combination of the arch and truss, 311.—Piers generally built of granite masonry, sometimes of brickwork, 311.—Great height of the piers of a truss bridge built over the Genesee river, 312. — McCallum's inflexible arched truss, 312.—Dimensions for a 200-feet span railway bridge for a single line, 312.—Distribution of strains, 313.—Deflection when loaded, 313.—Effect of the arch and arch-braces in sustaining a train on the occasion of an accident or injury to a bridge, 314.—Results of testing a bridge over the Susquehannah river, showing a very small deflection, 314.—Durability and economy of the bridge referred to by Mr. Post, 314.—Aggregate length of bridges on different railways, 314. — Design for a railway swingbridge over the Mississippi river at Clinton, Ohio, 315.—Calculations in reference to the tension on the available sectional area of the bottom chord, 315.—Mr. McCallum's experience of the deflection of railway timber bridges after several years' use, 316.—Dimensions of a McCallum common road bridge of 150 feet span, 316.—Adaptation of the Howe truss to roofs of considerable span as carried out at the Dunkirk station of the New York and Erie railway, 316.—Accuracy of the designs

BRIERLEY.

in proportion to the strains coming on the timbers, 317.

Discussion.—Colburn, Z., 318.—Curtis, J. G. C., 323.—Giles, A., 324.—Gregory, C. H., 321.—Mallet, R., 325.—Moorsom, Capt. W. S., 324.—Ormsby, A. S., 323.—Sheilds, F. W., 323.

Palmyra palm. "On the use of the timber of the Palmyra palm in the construction of bridges." By H. Byrne, xxii. 58. – But little other timber in Southern India and Ceylon, 58.—Used for bridges in the northern part of Ceylon, 58.—General description, 59.—Beams for roadway bearers, 59—Durability of the bridges, 60.—Tabular statement of the cost of a bridge of Palmyra timber, 61.—Practical value of Palmyra timber from its great cheapness, 61.

Discussion. — Bethell, J., 62. — Doyne, W. T., 63. — Gregory, C. H., 63.—Pole, Prof. W., 63.—Russell, J. S., 62.

BRIERLEY, J. [Election, xxv. 65.]

BRIGGS, R.

Fans. "On the conditions and the limits which govern the proportions of rotary fans," xxx. 276.—Remarks, 297.—Uses of rotary fans, 297.—Fans with spiral casing, 306.—Ascertaining the useful effect of fans, 307.—Fans of repeated effort, 308.

BRIGHT, Sir C. T. [Election, xxi. 257; Telford medal, xxvi. 121, 138.]

Telegraph cables. Construction of the Malta and Alexandria submarine telegraph cable, xxi. 531.—Core of the Atlantic telegraph cable, 531.—Speed of working submarine telegraphs, 532.—Unsuitable character of the outer covering of the Malta and Alexandria cable, 532.—Red Sea and the Sardinia and Cape Bona telegraphs, 533.—Probability of the Malta and Alexandria telegraph requiring repairs before long, 534. — Successful mechanical operation of laying the Malta and Alexandria telegraph, 534. — Endurance of gutta-percha at moderate temperatures, 534.

Telegraphic communication. "The tele-

BROOKS.

graph to India, and its extension to Australia and China," xxv. 1.—Remarks, 16.—Commercial success of the telegraph to India, 16.—Defective working of the Turkish and Indian lines, 16, 63.—Hooper's india-rubber core for electric cables, 17.—Telegraph route to India passing from Beyrout to Bagdad, 63.—Deep-sea telegraph line from Muscat to Bombay, and from Ceylon to Australia, 63.—Insulating material of submarine cables, 63.—Outer covering of submarine cables, 64.

BRINE, F., Major R.E. [Election, xxix. 98.]

BRISTOW, E. J. [Election, xxix. 98.]

BROAD, R. [Election, xxv. 262.]

Viaducts. Launching girders over piers, xxv. 250.

BROADBRIDGE, J. [Election, xxiv. 511.]

Broadlands, tabular statement of experiments on drainage and rainfall at (Denton, J. B.), xxi. 127.

BROADRICK, G. [Election, xxviii. 59.]

Railway breaks in use on the Serra do Mar inclines, xxx. 69.

BROCK, W. [Election, xxiv. 184.]

Steam navigation. Results obtained from the trials of the steamships 'Europe' and 'Afrique,' xxix. 197.

BROGDEN, A. [Election, xxiv. 144.]

BROMLEY, M. [Admission, xxx. 106.]

BROOKE, C.

Iron and steel, determination of specific gravities of, xxix. 75.

Materials, resistance of, xxix. 53, 75.—Flexures of beams under strain, 53.—Provinces of statics and dynamics, 53.

BROOKES, A. G. [Admission, xxvii. 320.]

BROOKES, W. [Election, xxv. 479.]

BROOKS, W. A. [Telford premium, xxvii. 124, 142.]

Breakwaters and harbours, errors in construction of recent, xxii. 444.—Kurrachee harbour, 487, 489.—Lieut. Taylor's plan for improvement of ditto, 488.

Canal, Suez, xxvi. 458.—Difficulty of keeping the canal clear of sand deposits, 458.—Ship-canal proposed to be supplied from the waters of the Nile, 458.—Western pier at Port Saïd,

BROOKS.

459.—Recent deposits produced by the western currents from the Nile, 459.—Result of borings through Lake Menzaleh, 460.—Probable result of the tidal action at Suez, 460.—Deposit of salt in the Bitter Lakes, 461.—Dredging operations, 462.—Mr. R. Stephenson's opinion, 462, *et seq.*—Difference of rainfall in India and in Egypt, 472.

Coasts, &c. East coast of England, xxiii. 248.—Cause of the change in direction of Landguard Spit, 249.—Suggestions for driving away Landguard Spit, 249.—Possibility of the shingle found between Hunstanton and Woolverton being ships' ballast, 251.

Reclaiming land from the sea, xxiii. 184.—Enclosures from the sea easy where there is a considerable foreshore, 184.—Closing of reclamation banks, 185.—Necessity of leaving sluices in reclamation banks for the future drainage of the enclosed lands, 185.

River Tees, xxiv. 72.—Works executed by the Tees Navigation Company, 72.—Navigation of the Tees not injured by the groynes or jetties, 72.—Depth of water on the bar, 73.—Injurious effects likely to arise from the construction of the slag pier on the South Gare and Bran Sands, 73.—Supposed abstraction of tidal water, 73.—Constancy of the depth of water on the bar, in whatever direction the sea-reach debouches, 73.—Inexpediency of dredging the Tees, 74.—Evils to be anticipated from the slag-work at the mouth of the river, 74.—Formation of a ship-canal from Cargo Fleet to Redcar, 76.—Height of the tides in the river Tees, 96.—Cost of the improvements, 97.—Transverse jetties, 97.

River Tyne. "Memoir on the river Tyne," xxvi. 398.—Remarks, 421.—Dredging Shields Harbour and the bar, 421, 424, 439.—Mr. J. Walker's opinion of the cause of the bar, 421, 440.—Probable effect of prolonging the piers at the entrance, 434.—Probable shoaling of the bar on the cessation of dredging operations, 439.

BROWN.

Rivers and estuaries. The Hooghly and the Mutla, xxi. 30.—Improvements of Dublin Harbour mainly due to tidal water, 296.—The debouching waters and littoral current set along the concave face of the pier at Swinemunde, maintaining a permanent deep-water channel, 296.—Depth of water over the bar at Kurrachee, xxii. 487.—Contraction of the tidal flow caused by works in progress at Kurrachee injurious, 487, 489.—Difference in the high-water levels often found on the seacoast and the inland portions of an estuary, xxiii. 184.—Increase of the sandbanks below the entrance of the tidal basin of the Great Grimsby docks, xxiv. 56.—Supposed advantages of dredging the beds of rivers by steam, 97.—A river with a tortuous course liable to shoal, 98.—Cause of the formation of bars at the mouths of rivers, xxvi. 422.—Utility of jetties as contrasted with parallel walls in removing shoals from rivers, 440.—Depth of water on the bar of the river Mersey, 440.—Tidal phenomena in spacious and restricted channels, 461.

Ships and steam-vessels, xxi. 232.—Lieutenant R. Wall's system of diagonal frames, 232.—Applicable to ships of war, 232.

Waves, motion of, in deep seas, xxii. 444.

BROOME, R. [Election, xxvii. 218.]

BROTHERHOOD, P. [Election, xxvii. 553.]

BROTHERHOOD, R. [Election, xxv. 479.]
   Timber, creosoted, not liable to attack by white ants, xxv. 416.

BROTHERS, H. [Election, xxx. 1.]

BROUGHAM AND VAUX, Lord. [Memoir, xxviii. 167, 168; xxx. 418.]

BROUNGER, R. E. [Admission, xxvii. 320.]

BROWN, E. P. [Admission, xxvii. 54.]

BROWN, F. D. M., Captain, B.S.C. [Election, xxx. 215.]

BROWN, Sir J. [Election, xxii. 65.]

BROWN, J., Jun. [Election, xxv. 262.]

BROWN, S. [Election, xxiii. 320.]

BROWN, T. F. [Election, xxviii. 59.]

BROWNE.

BROWNE, B. C. [Election, xxiv. 62.]
BROWNE, V. [Election, xxviii. 517.]
BROWNE, W. R. [Election, xxvii. 443.]
BROWNING, A. G. [Election, xxiii. 257.]
BROWNING, H. B. [Election, xxvii. 55.]
BROWNING, T. G. [Election, xxii. 65.]
BRUCE, G. B.

Girders, xxiv. 21.—Suspension of cross-girders, 21.

Iron and steel, strength of, xxx. 266.—Strength of iron bars and sleepers, 266.—Effects of a sudden reduction in the section of a bar of iron on its strength, 267.

Permanent way, xxi. 407.—Sleepers, 407.—Suspended fishjoint, 407.—Supply of sleepers for tropical climates, xxiv. 21.—Specifications and tests for rails, xxvii. 374.—Results of testing steel rails with holes punched in the bottom flange, 375.

Piles, resisting power of, xxvii. 314.—Formulæ for determining ditto, 314.

Railway accidents, xxi. 407.

Railway locomotives and rolling stock. Increasing the weight and size of engines, xxi. 408.—Expediency of supplying locomotive engines with 'bogies,' as on the American railways, 408.—Use of the bogie engine, xxiv. 22.

Railway trains, communication in, xxi. 408.—Value of the bell used on American railways for communicating between guards and drivers, 408.

Railways and public works in India, xxii. 484.—Scinde railway, 484.—High cost of labour on ditto, 484.—Question of dispensing with contractors in India, 485.—Training young people in India to different trades, 485.—Expediency of using iron instead of wooden sleepers in India, 485.—Question of allowing flood-water to run under or over the Scinde railway, 485.—Necessity of sending mechanics of good character to foreign countries, 486.

Railways, light narrow-gauge, xxvi. 65.—Inexpediency of introducing in England, 65.

BRUNLEES.

BRUFF, P.

Coasts, &c. East coast of England, xxiii. 242.—Movement of shingle in the neighbourhood of Harwich, 242.—Prolongation of Landguard Point, 243.—Projects for restoring the entrance of the rivers Ore and Alde, 244.—Destruction of the ancient city of Dunwich, 244—Submarine ridges of shingle at some miles from the shore the source of the pebbles on the Suffolk coast, 245.

Railways, narrow-gauge, Norwegian, between Throndhjein and Storen, and between Hamar and Eleverum, the character of the lines, the details of the works upon them, especially the bridges and viaducts, and their economy of construction, with particulars of the rolling stock, xxiv. 371, 375.

BRUFF, W. F. G. [Election, xxiv. 62.]
BRUNDELL, B. S. [Election, xxviii. 517.]
BRUNDELL, R. S. [Election, xxviii. 59.]
BRUNLEES, J. [Council premium, xxii. 120, 130; Member of Council, xxv. 161; xxvi. 119; xxvii. 122; xxviii. 158; xxix. 208.]

Boring machine invented by Mr. E. J. J. Dixon, xxiii. 319.

Breakwater and pier at Point de Galle, design for a, xxii. 446.

Britannia bridge, durability of the, xxvii. 575.

Drainage. Views entertained in the middle of the seventeenth century, xxi. 119.—Benefits vegetation derives from deep drainage, 119.—Height of floods increased by drainage operations in rivers which, like the Thames, have a low rate of fall, but diminished where the fall is rapid, as in the Tweed, 120.

Iron, preservation of, xxiv. 21.—Boiled in a preparation of tar and asphalte, 21; xxvii. 575; xxviii. 230.—Decay of, in salt-water, 230.

Iron and steel, strength and resistance of, xxi. 240.—Strength of puddled steel greater than best Staffordshire iron plates, 240.

BRUNLEES.

Permanent way. Greater durability of iron sleepers to wooden sleepers on the São Paulo railway, xxiv. 21.—Preparation of tar and asphalte for preserving iron rails, 21.—Saving to be effected by the adoption of wider-topped rails for main lines, xxvii. 402.

Piers and landing stages. Cost of the New Ferry and New Brighton piers, xxviii. 226.—Pontoons of ditto, 228, 230.

Piles, M'Alpine's and Rankine's formulæ for determining the resisting power of, xxvii. 309.—Clusters of screw-piles used in the Eau Brink viaduct near Lynn, 310.—Sinking disc-piles for the Morecambe Bay viaducts and Southport pier, 310.—Corkscrew-piles for hard gravel shale in the piers on the river Mersey, 310.—Screw-piles for alluvial deposits, 310.—Piling in the Solway viaduct, 310.—Sinking timber piles in sand, 311.—Bearing power of the Morecambe Bay sands, 311.—Mitchell's screw-pile, 311.

Railway accidents. "Railway accidents,—their causes and means of prevention," xxi. 345.—Remarks, 418.—Data from which he had deduced his averages of railway accidents, 418.—Education of engine-drivers and points-men, 419.—Weight of locomotives, 419.—Utility of danger-whistles, 419.—Argument that a cessation of accidents would lead to carelessness, 419.—Return of railway accidents during 1861, 420.—Consequences of the penalties devolving upon railway companies as carriers, 420.

Railway inclines, xxvi. 342, 343.—Clip break employed on the Serra do Mar incline, xxx. 57, 77.

Railways. Festiniog railway, and narrow gauge line from Portmadoc to Gorsedda, xxiv. 386.—Mont Cenis railway, xxvi. 341.—Level crossings for ditto, 341.—Snow-plough for ditto, 341.—Available power derived from the various engines found most effective in working inclines, 342, 343.—Com-

BRUNTON.

parative cost of the various plans for protecting the Mont Cenis railway, 394.—Damage by floods to ditto, 394.—Advantage of Mr. Fell's locomotive in getting rid of deadweight, 394.—São Paulo railway, xxx. 57.—Cubatão viaduct, 57.—Working the Serra do Mar inclines with fixed engines and ropes, 57, 77.—Clip-break employed on the Serra do Mar incline, 57, 77.—Construction of the Mugi viaduct, 58.—Difficulty of traversing the Serra do Mar, 58.—Gradients of the Serra do Mar inclines, 76.—Inapplicability of the atmospheric system for the Serra do Mar inclines, 77.

Reclaiming land from seas and estuaries, xxi. 481.—Slope of the outer face of sea-walls, 481.—Materials for construction, 481.

River Witham, Grand Sluice and the outfall of the, xxviii. 98.

Rivers and estuaries. Action of the piers at the mouth of the River Tyne, xxvi. 438.—Half-tide weirs in sandy bays, 438.

Ships of war, xxi. 241.—Suggestion as to fitting armour-plates to merchant vessels, 241.

BRUNLEES, John. [Admission, xxviii. 216.]

BRUNTON, G. [Election, xxii. 65.]

BRUNTON, J. [Telford medal and premium, xxiii. 114, 126.]

Permanent way. Burnettising process of saturating sleepers with chloride of zinc, xxii. 495.

Railway switches, improvements in the mode of actuating and locking, and of interlocking the points and signals on railways, xxix. 24.

Railways. "Description of the line and works of the Scinde railway,' xxii. 451.—Remarks, 494.—Prices paid for labour, 494.—The cost per mile not excessive, 495.—Waterway, 496.—Lowering of the line to allow of the passage of floods, 496 ; xxvii. 256.

Rivers, freshwater floods of, xxvii. 256.—Rainfall and floods in Scinde, 256.—Lowering the line of the Scinde railway, to allow of the passage of floods,

BRUNTON

256.—Rise and fall of the River Indus, 256.

Timber. Preservative effect against white ants, of the immersion of timber in chloride of zinc, xxii. 496.

BRUNTON, R. H. [Election, xxvii. 443.]

BRUNTON, W. A. [Election, xxiv. 511.]

BRYCE, A. [Election, xxii. 396.]

Permanent way. Supply and cost of sleepers in the Madras Presidency, xxii. 258.

BUCHANAN, G. [Election, xxx. 323.]

BUCHANAN, W. C. [Election, xxiii. 442.]

BUCK, J. H. W. [Election, xxviii. 232.]

BUCKHAM, T. [Election, xxv. 65.]

BUDD, G. O. [Election, xxii. 336.]

BULLMORE, F. C. [Election, xxix. 59.]

BUNTEN, J. C. [Election, xxviii. 517.]

BURDER, W. C. [Admission, xxvii. 54.]

BURGE, C. O. [Election, xxv. 352.]

BURKE, C. T. [Admission, xxviii. 2.]

BURKE, F. E. [Admission, xxix. 98.]

BURNELL, G. R. [Telford premium, xxiv. 110, 125; Election, xxv. 262; Telford premium, xxvi. 121, 138; Decease, xxviii. 168.]

Artesian wells. "On the machinery employed in sinking Artesian wells on the Continent," xxiii. 459.—Remarks, 477.

Drainage of towns. Paris, xxiv. 316.—London, 316.

Water supply. "On the water supply of the city of Paris," xxv. 480.—Remarks, 506.—Physical characteristics of men not dependent on the use of hard or soft water, 507.—Greater wholesomeness of hard than of soft water, 507.—Water yielded by the wells of Passy and of Grenelle, 507.

BURNETT, R. H. [Election, xxv. 262.]

BURSTAL, E., Captain R.N.

Coasts, &c. River Thames and East Coast of England, xxiii. 233.—Changes in the channels of the estuary of the Thames, 233.—Encroachments of the coast between the Blackwater and

BYRNE.

entrance of the Thames, 234.—Inexpediency of attempting to prevent the degradation of the cliffs at Clacton, Great Holland, and the Naze, 234.—Shingle travelling with the prevailing sea, 235.—Landguard Point, 235.—Travel of shingle at Dungeness and Orfordness, 235.—Occurrence of shingle at the bottom of the sea off Hastings, 235.

BURT, H. P. [Decease, xxvi. 129.]

Timber, creosoting, xxii. 255.—Creosoted sleepers sent out to India, 255.—Creosoting operations not carried out with success in India, 255.—Australian woods difficult of creosoting, 256.—Preparation of creosoted sleepers, xxiv. 22.

BUTLER, J. T. [Election, xxx. 215.]

BUTTERTON, W. [Election, xxiii. 257.]

BYRNE, E. [Telford medal and premium, xxvii. 124, 142.]

Water, filtration of. "Experiments on the removal of organic and inorganic substances in water," xxvi. 544.—Supplement, xxvii. 1.—Remarks, 6.—Determination of the quantity of organic matter in water by the process of incineration, 6.—Rate of filtration of water, 7.—Different methods of analysing impurities in water, 48.—Purification of water by animal charcoal, 48, et seq.—Removal of organic matter from water by sand, 49.—Time of contact necessary between charcoal and water in the process of filtration, 50.—Action of charcoal in sugar refining, 50.—Behaviour of permanganate of potash with different kinds of organic matter, 50.—Magnetic carbide, 52.—Substitution of a pure for a contaminated supply of water, 53.

BYRNE, H.

Bridges. "On the use of the timber of the Palmyra palm in the construction of bridges," xxii. 58.

C.

CADIAT.

CADIAT.
Port Saïd, renseignements sur les jetées de, **xxv.** 133.
Calcutta, relative cost of the transport of merchandise to, from various places in the interior, by railway and by water, in 1857, **xxi.** 5.
CALEY, J. A. [Election, **xxv.** 64.]
CALVER, E. K., Staff-Captain, R.N. [Election, **xxv.** 429.]
Rivers and estuaries. The Humber as a harbour of refuge, **xxviii.** 499.—Exclusion of water by enclosures in tidal estuaries not followed by an elevation of the highwater level, 500.—Increase of sands at the mouth of the Humber, 500.—Dredging in the river Tyne, 500.—Datum of Captain Hewett's levels of the Humber, 501.—Importance of preserving tidal volume in rivers, 501.
CALVERT, Dr. C.
Coke, advantages of making, in circular ovens, **xxiii.** 454.
CALVERT, J. [Election, **xxiv.** 458.]
Materials, decay of, in tropical climates, **xxiv.** 34.—Preservation of railway sleepers, 34.—Ravages of black ants and white ants, 34.—Preservation of stone and bricks in the tropics, 35.— Telegraph posts of stone and iron in India, 35.
CAMPBELL, E. L. [Admission, **xxvii.** 54.]
CAMPBELL, J. F.
Lighthouses, optical apparatus of, **xxvi.** 532.—Adjustment of the dioptric light at the South Foreland, 532.
CAMPBELL, T. P. [Election, **xxviii.** 59.]
CAMPION, J. M. [Admission, **xxvii.** 180.]
CANALS.
Amsterdam sea, **xxix.** 287.
Ancient and modern, **xxix.** 275.
Steam-power on. " Results of the employment of steam-power in towing vessels on the Gloucester and Berkeley

CANALS.

canal." By W. B. Clegram, **xxvi.** 1.—Description of the canal, 1.— Classification of vessels navigating the canal and horse-power employed, 1, 2.—Introduction of steam-tugs, 2. —Saving thereby effected, 3.—Capabilities of the steam-tugs, 3.——Advantages of the employment of steam as a towing power, 3.——Prejudicial effects on the banks from the increased wash, 4.—Precautionary measures, 4.— Increase of traffic, 5.—Effect of the employment of tugs on the mud deposits, 5. —— " On the employment of steam-power upon the Grand Canal, Ireland." By S. Healy, . **xxvi.** 6.—Description of the canal, 6.—Methods of applying steam-power to canal navigation, 6.—Steam-boats designed to carry cargo proved unremunerative, 6.—Failure in propelling by chain-haulage, 7.—System of hauling boats in trains by small towing steamers, 7.—Details of the screws, 7.—Capabilities of the towing steamers, 7.—Cargo-carrying steamers on the river Shannon, 8.—Appendix I. Grand Canal Company, Ireland.— Specification of machinery of tug steamers, 9.—Appendix II. Specification of a pair of engines for the canal towing steamers, 9.
Discussion.—Abernethy, J., 32.—Allen, E. E., 22.—Appleby, C. J., 40.— Bartholomew, W. H., 25.—Bateman, J. F., 28, 39.—Beardmore, N., 35, 39. 42.—Bramwell, F. J., 33.—Brereton, R. P., 27.—Clegram, W. B., 16.— Cowper, E. A., 34.—Delany, J. F., 40. —Mallet, R., 28, 32, 33.—Milne, J., 10.—Phipps, G. H., 22.—Pole, W., 17. —Scott, M., 28.—Thomas, E., 14.— Thomas, H., 24.—Ure, J. F., 20.— Vignoles, C. B., 32, 33.—Williams, E. L., 16.—Williams, E. L., Jun., 23.
Suez, **xxiii.** 160.—International commis-

CANTERBURY.

sion, 160, 167.—Comparative advantages of the two systems proposed for constructing a direct canal between the Mediterranean and Red seas, 161,164.
—— "The Suez Canal." By Colonel Sir W. T. Denison, R.E., xxvi. 442.—Inspection of the works, 442.—Two distinct undertakings, 442.—Fresh-water canal, 443.—Dry-dock and basin at Suez, 443.—Intended course of the salt-water canal at Suez, 443 —Cutting at Chalouf, 444 —Bitter Lakes, 444.—Termination of branch from the fresh-water canal at Ismaïlia, 444.—Progress of the works through a sandbank east of Ismaïlia, 444.—Works between the deep sand-cutting and Lake Menzaleh, 445.—Dredging machines, 445.—Western breakwater at Port Saïd, 445.—Concrete blocks for ditto, 446.—Accumulation of sand on the western face, 446.—Dredging required at Port Saïd, 446.—Great cost of the 'plant' for the canal, 446.—Adopted slope of the canal bank too steep to be maintained, 447.—Effects produced by the wash from a boat on the banks, 447.—Probable ultimate slope of banks, 447.—Practicability of keeping the canal open on a level between the Red Sea and the Mediterranean, 447.—Mr. Hawkshaw's report, 447.
Discussion.—Abernethy, J., 449, 454, 460.—Airy, G. B., 468.—Brooks, W. A., 458, 460, 472.—Curtis, J. G. C., 472.—Denison, Sir W. T., 449, 451, 468, 472.—Hawkshaw, J., 451, 454, 476.—Hawksley, T., 471, 472.—Hemans, G. W., 470.—Heppel, J. M., 464.—Lange, D. A., 455.—Murray, J., 454, 465.—Rawlinson, R., 454.—Redman, J. B., 469, 470.
——Works executed and required, xxix. 303.—Probable success as a financial speculation, 304.
Vide also STEAM NAVIGATION.
Canterbury, New Zealand, memoir on the public works of the province of, (Dobson, E.), xxix. 99. *Vide* also PUBLIC WORKS.
CAPPEL, A. J. L. [Election, xxvi. 79.]

CEMENTS.

CAPPER, C. [Election, xxiv. 62; Memoir, xxx. 465.]
Dock, graving, hydraulic lift, xxv. 310.—Commercial success of the Thames Graving Dock Company, 310
CARBUTT, E. H. [Election, xxiii. 110.]
CAREY, J. S. [Admission, xxvii. 553.]
CARFRAE, J. A. [Admission, xxvii. 443.]
CARGILL, T. [Election, xxx. 106.]
CARLILE, H. [Election, xxv. 352.]
CARPMAEL, A. [Election, xxviii. 439.]
CARPMAEL, W. [Memoir, xxx. 430.]
CARR, D. A. [Admission, xxvii. 54.]
CARRINGTON, T. C., Jun. [Election, xxx. 215.]
CARROLL, E. B. [Election, xxviii. 518.]
CARRUTHERS, J. [Election, xxv. 203.]
CARTER, H. [Admission, xxviii. 439.]
CARTMELL, F. [Admission, xxix. 98.]
CASEBOURNE, C. T. [Election, xxvii. 443.]
CASEBOURNE, T. [Memoir, xxiv. 527.]
CASH, J. [Admission, xxvii. 218.]
CASTLE, E. J., Lieutenant R.E. [Election, xxvi. 544.]
CATO, A. [Election, xxviii. 59.]
CATO, C. J. [Election, xxii. 65; Memoir, xxvii. 599.]
CAWKWELL, W. [Election, xxiv. 511.]
Railway stations, xxv. 289.—Arrangement of platforms, offices, and warehouses on the London and North Western railway, 289.
CAWLEY, C. E.
Water supply, xxv. 477.—Storing flood-water for the supply of a town, 477.—Utilisation of ditto by mills, 477.
CAY, W. D. [Election, xxiii. 320.]
CEMENTS.
Strength of: "Experiments on the strength of cement, chiefly in reference to the Portland cement used in the southern main-drainage works." By J. Grant, xxv. 66.—Portland cement scarcely used before 1859, 66. — Large harbour and dock works constructed with Portland cement in France, 66.—Samples of cement obtained for the purpose of experiment, 66.—Specifi-

CEMENTS.

cation for cement for the southern high-level sewer, 67. — Machine devised for testing the cement, 67.— Adhesion between the bricks and cement, 67. — Standard of breaking weight on an area of 2¼ square inches, 67.—Price, 68.—Increased use of Portland cement, 68.—Superiority of Portland to Roman cement, 68.— Manufacture of Portland cement, 68. —Value of tests, 69, 78.—Precautions necessary in the use of the cement, 69.—Description of tables of results of experiments on Portland and other cements, 70, *et seq.*—Importance of having the cement finely ground, 70. —Results of the tests and experiments, 77, *et seq.* — Further experiments desirable, 78.—Appendix: abstract of experiments with Portland cement, mixed neat, and immersed in water, for seven and fourteen days, 80.—Ditto, for seven days, 80, 81.— Ditto, mixed with an equal proportion of sand, 81. — Summary of seven days' tests for the metropolitan main-drainage contracts on the south side, 82.—Ditto, southern high-level sewer, 83.—Ditto, St. George's wharf contract, 83.— Ditto, southern outfall sewer, 84.— Ditto, Deptford pumping station and gasworks, 84.—Ditto, Southwark and Westminster communication, 85. — Ditto, southern high-level extensions, 85. — Ditto, low-level sewer, 85.— Ditto, southern outfall works, 86.— Ditto, southern low-level sewer, 86.— Results of breaking weights of Portland cement, gauged neat, and with different proportions of sand, 87, *et seq.* —Ditto, mixed with fresh and salt water, 90.—Ditto, of Roman cement, mixed neat, and with different proportions of sand, 91, *et seq.*— Ditto, with Keene's cement, and Parian cement, 96. — Ditto, with Medina cement and sand, 96.—Table of experiments on the compression of Portland cement bricks, 97.—Ditto on the compression of bricks, 98, 99.

CEMENTS.

—Abstract of experiments on the strength of various kinds of bricks, 100.—Experiments on Gisborne's Exbury bricks, 101. — Ditto on small blocks of stone, 101.—Quantities used in making brickwork blocks, in compo composed of Portland cement and river sand, 102.— Experiments as to the quantities of Portland cement, sand, and water used in making compo, or cement mortar, 102.—Experiments with neat Portland cement immersed in water immediately on setting, to illustrate increase of strength, 103. — Tensile strains of cements of different specific gravities at different periods, 103.—Summary of Portland cement tests at the southern outfall works, Crossness, showing increase of strength with increased specific gravity, 104.—Experiments with neat Portland cement, showing strength after setting from one to seven days, 105.— Experiments in crushing blocks of granite, York, Portland, and Bramley Fall stones; and neat Portland, Roman, Parian, Medina, and Keene's cements, 106, *et seq.*—Clause as to Portland cement in earlier specifications, 111. — Ditto as first amended, 111.—Ditto as last amended, 111.—Form of register of Portland cement, 111.

Discussion.—Abernethy, J., 113.—Aird, J., Jun., 128.—Bateman, J. F., 142.— Baynes, C., 122.—Bazalgette, J. W., 124. — Bevan, T., 130. — Bramwell, F. J., 136.—Brereton, R. P., 143, 144, 146.—Coode, J., 144.—Curtis, J. G. C., 134.—Dines, G., 129.—Druce, E. R. N., 113, 148.—Fowler, J., 144, 158.—Fox, Sir C., 128.—Francis, C. L., 123.— Grant J., 153.—Hartley, Sir C., 150.— Hawkshaw, J., 146.—Hemans, G. W., 112, 113.—Jennings, J., 130.— Kinipple, W. R., 125.—Lane, C. B., 135.—Longridge, J. A., 133.—Maudslay, H., 129.—Rawlinson, R., 114.— Redman, J. B., 141.—Ridley, T. D., 153.—Russell, J. S., 129, 130, 134.—

CERERO.

Vignoles, C. B., 135.—White, G. F., 117.

Theil limeused in the works at Marseilles, Algiers, and Cherbourg, xxiv. 169.

Zumaya cement, xxx. 24.

Vide also Docks, Marseilles; and STRUCTURES IN THE SEA.

CERERO, Captain R. [Election, xxiv. 184.]

CHADWICK, E.

Drainage of land, xxi. 93.—Desirability of keeping statistics of the results of under-drainage, 93.

—— of towns, xxiv. 331. — Main-drainage of London, 331.—Flow of sewage in pipe sewers, 333.—Application of sewage-manure to the soil, 335.—Value of fresh sewage for agricultural purposes, 336.—Schemes for separating rain-water from town sewage, 337. — Proper outfalls for the metropolitan sewers, 338.

Railway income and expenditure, xxix. 349.—Tramways as feeders to railways, 349.—Value of railways independently of their earning a dividend, 350.—Saving to be effected by the unity of management of railways, 351.

Water supply, xxvii. 32.—Various methods of water supply for towns, 32.—Hard and soft water, 33, 34.—Sources of contamination of water, 33.—Selection of water for domestic animals, 34.—Effect of tainted springs on cholera, in epidemic conditions, 34.—Inadequacy of common filters, 34.—Filtration through strata occupied by vegetation, 34.—Capability of various soils for filtration, 35.

CHAMBERS, C. [Election, xxiii. 151.]

CHAMPAIN, J. U., Major, R.E. [Election, xxv. 203.]

Telegraphic communication to India and China, xxiv. 22.—Working of the Indo-European telegraph, 22.—Mismanagement of the Turks in working ditto, 22.—Telegraph routes from England to the head of the Persian Gulf through Turkish territory and Russian territory, 23.—Delays in transmitting telegraphic messages from England to India through

CHEFFINS.

Russia, 23.—Route from Bagdad to Beyrout impracticable for a line of telegraph, 24. — Telegraphic mismanagement in India, 24.—Extension of the telegraphic system to India and China, 25.

CHANCE, J. T. [Election, xxvi. 544; Telford medal and premium, xxvii. 123, 142.]

Lighthouses. "On optical apparatus used in lighthouses," xxvi. 477.—Remarks, 507.—Glass used for ditto, 535.—Optical apparatus of the Start lighthouse, 535.—Inferiority of the dioptric light at the South Foreland, 536. — Proposed improvements in catoptric apparatus, 537.—Distinction between the effects of quantity of light and intensity of light, 538.—Catoptric revolving light at Beachy Head, 539. — Photometrical experiments on lights, 539.—Results of experiments by French optical engineers on the quantity of light emitted respectively by dioptric and catoptric lights, 539.

CHAPMAN, C. W. R. [Election, xxii. 451.]

CHAPMAN, E. T.

Water supply. Mechanical removal of organic matter from water by animal charcoal, xxvii. 14.—Dr. Clark's process of softening water, 14.—Putrefaction of nitrogenous organic matter, 15.

CHAPMAN, R. [Election, xxiii. 151.]

Charcoal, tables of the effect of the filtration of Thames water through (Shield, H.), xxvii. 27–29. Vide also WATER, FILTRATION OF.

Charing Cross bridge, the (Hayter, H.), xxii. 512. Vide also BRIDGES.

Charing Cross railway, the city terminus extension of the (Barry, J. W.), xxvii. 410. Vide also RAILWAYS.

CHARLTON, F. [Election, xxix. 98.]

CHATTERTON, J.

Telegraph cables. Electrical resistance of the Malta and Alexandria submarine telegraph cable, xxi. 536.

CHEESMAN, F. [Admission, xxvii. 54.]

CHEFFINS, C. F. [Memoir, xxi. 578.]

CHESIL BANK.

Chesil Bank, arrangement and origin of, xxiii. 226, *et seq.*

CHUBB, C. J. [Telford premium, xxix. 211.] Coal-mining. "On coal-getting machinery as a substitute for the use of gunpowder," xxviii. 118.—Remarks, 122. —Results of getting coal with his hydraulic apparatus, 122, 149, *et seq.* —Boring tool, 122, 150. — Undercutting coal, 134.—Mr. Grafton Jones' coal-getting machine, 153.

CHUBB, H. [Election, xxviii. 325.]

CHUBB, J. [Resignation, xxix. 217.]

CHURCH, J.
Coke for locomotives, xxiii. 455.—Difference in quality between coke made in close ovens and in open ovens, 455.—Carbon produced by coke under the best circumstances, 455.
Gas, illuminating power of coal, xxviii. 462. — Gas-burners, 462.—Imperfections of the present methods of ascertaining the illuminating power, 462.

CHURCH, J., Jun. [Admission, xxvii. 55.]

Civil Engineers (Hawkshaw, J.), xxi. 173, 184.—Great moral and social benefits resulting from the labours of, 186.—Education of, xxii. 35, *et seq.*—Knowledge required by a Civil Engineer, (Fowler, J.), xxv. 203, 212.—Competition by foreign engineers, 204.—Engineering problems of the present time, 205.—Definition of a Civil Engineer, 207.—Classification of the works intrusted to a Civil Engineer, 208.—Railway engineering, 213.—Dock and harbour engineering, 214.—Waterworks and drainage engineering, 215.—Mechanical engineering, 217.—Mining engineering, 218.—Artillery engineering, 218.—Preparation required by a Civil Engineer, 219.—Description of a Civil Engineer, by Thomas Tredgold, xxvii. 181.—Question of commercial success, 537, *et seq.* —Early progress of engineering (Vignoles, C. B.), xxix. 274.—French and English engineers, 279, 285, 316. Proper aims of Civil Engineers, 317.—Dr. Whewell on theoretical and prac-

CLARK.

tical work, 317.—Honourable ambition in the minds of engineers to have their names associated with works with which they have been connected, 318. —Technical qualifications, xxx. 21.

Civil Engineers in India : correspondence with the Government of India respecting a notification addressed by that government to engineers employed in the Department of Public Works, xxix. 224.

CLARK, D. K.
Locomotives and rolling stock, xxx. 197. —Depreciation of locomotives, 197.

CLARK, E. [Telford medal and premium, xxvi. 121, 138 ; Watt medal, xxviii. 161, 178.]
Docks, graving. "The hydraulic lift graving dock," xxv. 292.—Remarks, 310.—Cost of the hydraulic lift graving dock, 310, 312, 347, 351.—Means of access for repairing vessels, 349.—Cost of manipulation, 349.—Difference between the system of raising with hydraulic power and emptying pontoons of water, 350.—Hydraulic lift graving dock not of universal application, 351.—Stiffness of pontoons, 351.—Commercial aspect of the hydraulic lift graving dock, 351. — Rapidity of construction, 352.
Materials, durability of. "On engineering philosophy : the durability of materials," xxvii. 554.—Remarks, 564. —Extraordinary difference in the durability of materials, 564.—Cause of rust in iron rails and plates not in use, 577.—Paint as a preservative of iron, 578.—Galvanised iron, 578.

CLARK, E. H. [Telford medal and premium, xxv. 164, 180 ; Election, 203.]
Docks. "Description of the Great Grimsby (Royal) docks," xxiv. 38.—Remarks, 54.—Cost, 54.—Scour of the tides, 60.—Supply of fresh water, 60.—Extent of silting-up, 60.—Formation of timber ponds, 60.—Mud banks in the tidal basin, 61.
Estuary of the Humber. Probable effect of constructing a channel between the Spurn Point and Kilnsea, xxiv.

CLARK.

59.—Excellence of the harbour formed by the Spurn promontory, 59.

Timber, value of creosoting, xxiv. 54.

CLARK, John. [Election, xxvi. 165; Memoir, xxx. 431.]

CLARK, John.

Railway rolling stock, xxvi. 385.—Retarding force to the passage of railway vehicles round sharp curves, 385.

CLARK, L.

Telegraph cables, xxv. 45.—Deep-sea telegraph cables and shallow-water cables, 45. — Improvements in telegraphy, 46.—Segmental conductor of the Persian Gulf cable, 46.—Improvements in the manufacture of gutta-percha, 46.—Use of hemp saturated with water or tar-liquor in the manufacture of telegraph cables, 47.—Hooper's telegraph core, 47.—Electrical measurements of resistance in a submarine cable, 47.—Outer coverings for submarine cables, 48.—Profitable nature of submarine cables, 48.

Telegraphy, practicability of improvements in, by a system of abbreviation, xxv. 49.—Practicability of the Red Sea telegraph route to India, 49.

CLARK, W. [Election, xxiii. 257.]

CLARKE, A., Lieut.-Col., R.E. [Election, xxiv. 358; Associate of Council, xxix. 208.]

CLARKE, C. J. [Election, xxviii. 216.]

CLARKE, G.

Ships of war, xxi. 243.—Buckling of iron armour-plates from the impact of shot, 243.—Backing of armour-plates in iron vessels, 243.—Cellular system of backing the best, 245.

CLARKE, S. [Election, xxv. 65.]

Railway accidents, xxi. 389.

Railway stations, etc., xxv. 280.—Railway offices at the side of the platform, best adapted for long traffic, and at the end of the platform for short traffic, 281.—King's Cross and Leeds stations, 281.—Great Northern Railway goods station at King's Cross, 282, 288.—Growing requirements of railway companies for space in the neighbourhood of London, 282.—Com-

CLUTTERBUCK.

parative utility of turntables and traversers at passenger and at goods stations, 282.—Goods traffic, 283.—Accommodation for shunting carriages after the arrival of a train at the King's Cross station, 288.—Cambridge station, 289.

CLARKE, T. C. [Election, xxvi. 398.]

CLARKE, William. [Election, xxv. 65.]

CLARKE, William. [Election, xxv. 508.]

CLARKE, W. W. [Election, xxvii. 443.]

CLAXTON, C., Captain, R.N. [Resignation, xxi. 148.]

Bridge, Clifton suspension, xxvi. 265.—Shares of the Clifton Bridge Company taken up by the leading London engineers, 265.—Mr. Brunel's original design for the bridge, 265.

CLAYTON, A. [Election, xxiv. 458.]

CLAYTON, R. S. [Election, xxvii. 443.]

CLEGG, S. [Memoir, xxi. 552.]

CLEGRAM, W. [Memoir, xxiii. 485.]

CLEGRAM, W. B.

Canals, steam-power on. "Results of the employment of steam-power in towing vessels on the Gloucester and Berkeley canal," xxvi. 1.—Remarks, 16.

CLIFTON, E. N. [Election, xxviii. 216.]

CLOWES, C. [Admission, xxvii. 54.]

CLUTTERBUCK, C. C. [Admission, xxvii. 120.]

CLUTTERBUCK, Rev. J. C.

River Thames. Perennial and flood waters of the, xxi. 84.—Influence of drainage on the flow of the Thames, 84.—Effect of the direction of the wind during rain in producing floods in the Thames, 85.

——"The perennial and flood waters of the Upper Thames," xxii. 336.—Remarks, 353.—Antagonism in the interests of the mills and the navigation, 353.—Winter floods diminished by agricultural drainage, 353.—Water at Thames Head issuing from the oolite, 357.—Difficulty in getting accurate statistics of the Upper Thames, 368.—Capacity of the river for the discharge of flood-water, 369.—Small amount of evaporation from a surface

CLUTTON.

of water, exemplified in the case of dew-ponds, 369.—Dalton's gauge, 369. —Water supply to be obtained from the chalk, 369.—Influence of the chalk formation on the Thames, xxvii. 229.— Floods of the Thames, 229.

Rivers, freshwater floods of, xxvii. 229.— Inapplicability of any formula to rivers in general, 229.

Water supply. Want of sufficient knowledge of the geological condition of strata whence water can be procured, xxii. 353.—Supply to be obtained from the chalk, 369.—Supply from the artesian wells in the Paris basin, xxv. 496.—Supply from the lower greensand in England, 497.—Danger of tampering with underground sources of water, 497.

CLUTTON, R. G. [Election, xxvii. 443.]

COAL.

Amount of coal raised annually in Great Britain equivalent to the annual production of timber on an area equal to that of France, xxiii. 156.—Development of coal the main cause of increase of wealth, 156.—Question as to the permanence of coal supply, 156.—Theory of central heat, 157.— Equivalent in horse-power of daily consumption of coal, 157.—Coal may be drawn profitably from almost any depth, 158.

Distillation of. "On the distillation of coal, the utilization of the resulting products, and the manufacture of coke." By M. Pernolet, xxiii. 443.—Recent improvements on the Continent, 443.—Economy of the improved method of charring pursued in Belgium and France, 443.—Reduction in the price of coke from its employment, 443.—Increase in the yield of coke, 444.—Proportion of tar and ammoniacal liquors collected, 444.— Ditto of gas, 444.—Gas sometimes used in maintaining the necessary temperature for distillation, 445.—Quantity of coke burnt and amount of heat required for the ovens of the Paris Gas Lighting Company, 445.—Products of

COAL-MINING.

1000 tons of pit-coal, 445.—Net value of the supplementary products which the improved ovens extract, 445.—Saving that might be effected at Newcastle and Wigan, 446.—Economy to be effected by the utilization of the gas produced by the improved ovens, 446. —Various purposes to which the gas might be applied, 446.—Use of gas in blast furnaces for the manufacture of cast iron, 447.—Improved ovens may be used for the anthracites if some richer coals be mixed with them, 447. —Saving that might be effected in this way at the works of the Shelton Bar Iron Company, 447.—Tar or dry pitch may be used with non-bituminous coals, 447.—Description of the improved coke oven, 448.—Cost of altering an oven, 450.—Profit resulting from the alteration, 451.

Discussion.—Calvert, Dr. C., 454.— Church, J., 455.—Cowper, E. A., 454. —Lambert, T., 455.—Penny, A., 456. —Pernolet, M., 457.—Siemens, C. W., 452.—Stephenson, H. P., 457.

Coal-gas, experiments on the standards of comparison employed for testing the illuminating power of (Kirkham, T. N.), xxviii. 440. Vide also GAS.

Coal-mines, ventilation of, by fans, .xxx. 304.—Coefficient of friction of air in mines, 304. Vide also FANS, ROTARY.

COAL-MINING.

Machinery. "On machines employed in working and breaking coal, so as to avoid the use of gunpowder." By S. P. Bidder, xxviii. 113.—Satisfactory results obtained by Mr. Bidder's machine at the Harecastle colliery, 113, 115.—Inventions previously brought forward, 113.—Their defects, 114. — Description of the machine devised by Mr. S. P. Bidder, 115.—Reasons for the abolition of the use of gunpowder in mines, 117.

"On coal-getting machinery as a substitute for the use of gunpowder." By C. J. Chubb, xxviii. 118.—Increasing difficulties attending the working of coal-mines, 118.—Accidents, and injury

COAL-MINING.

to the coal, caused by the explosion of gunpowder, 118.—Objections to the use of wedges for getting coal, 119. —Description of the apparatus devised by Mr. C. J. Chubb, 119.— Results obtained, 120.—Experiment at Harecastle, 120.—Economical results of working with the apparatus, 120. Discussion. — Beardmore, N., 129. — Bidder, G. P., 143.—Bidder, S. P., 122, 128, 134, 153.—Bramwell, F. J., 134, 135.—Coe, J., 148.—Chubb, C. J., 122, 134, 149.—Craig, W. Y., 123. —Gregory, C. H., 155.—Grissell, H., 142.—Johnson, H., 131.—Jones, G., 128, 129.—Lupton, A., 131, 134.— Mallet, R., 129, 136.—Phipps, G. H., 147.—Siemens, C. W., 141.—Smyth, W. W., 129.—Steel, T. D., 148.— Williams, R. P., 146.—Woodhouse, J. T., 127.

Methods of working. "On the relative safety of different modes of working coal." By G. Fowler, xxx. 323.— Analogy between accidents from colliery explosions and boiler explosions, 323.—Classification of accidents adopted by inspectors, 324. —Accidents by falls, 324.—Principal methods of working coal, 324.—Pillar work, 324.—Long-wall work, 325.—Safety of workmen engaged affected by diversity of principles of working, 325.— Accidents by falls of roof, 326.—Accidents from falls fewer in long-wall working than in pillar working, 327. —Reason for ditto, 328.—Iil-effect of undersized pillars, 328.—Settlement in long-wall mines, 329.—Ventilation, 329.—Importance of clearing gas from cavities in the roof, 330.—Large explosions of rare occurrence in well-ventilated mines, 330.—Effect of barometrical changes on the safety of a mine, 330.—General reasonings as to the effect which the mode of getting coal may have upon the safety of mines from explosion, 331.—Discharge of gas from coal-seams, 331.—Amount of gas liberated from solid coal in workings, 332.—More gas liberated in

COAL-MINING.

pillar than in long-wall mines, 333.— Relative area of coal-surface exposed in pillar and in long-wall mines. 333. —Long-wall mines easy of ventilation, and therefore less liable to explosions, 334.—Ventilation in pillar mines in the North of England, 334.—Goaf in long-wall mines, 335.—Ditto in pillar mines. 335.—Goaf ventilation, 336.—Extension of long-wall working, 337.— Recapitulation, 337.— Appendix : Table of circumstances connected with different explosions in the years 1866, 1867, and 1868, 338.

"On coal-mining in deep workings." By E. Bainbridge, xxx. 340.—Question as to the resources of the coalfields of the British Islands, 340.—Royal Commission, 340.—Rate of production of coal in the United Kingdom, 340. —Causes affecting the duration of the English coalfields, 340. — Object of the Paper, 341.—Enumeration of the different divisions of the subject, 341. —Extension of the coal-measures : Introduction, 342.—Notice of previous Papers bearing on the subject of the extension of the coal-measures, 343.— Description of the map, 344.—Estimate of the resources of the present and future coalfields, 345.—Extent to which coal-mining has been prosecuted up to the present time : Introduction, 346.—Data respecting the depth of the chief English and foreign deep coal-mines, 347.—Sinking pits, 348. — Raising coals, 349.— Underground conveyance of coals, 349.— Ventilation, 350.—Mode of working, 350.—Consideration of the difficulties of deep mining—Introduction, 351.— Enumeration of difficulties expected to be met with in working coal at a depth of 7000 feet. 351.—Temperature : scope of the inquiry as to temperature, 352.—Account of experiments relating to the internal temperature of the earth, 353.—Account of experiments relating to the temperature of the air in mines, and the cooling effect of ventilation, 359.—Causes of high

COASTS.

temperature in mines, 370.—Consideration of the difficulties of deep mining beyond that of temperature: Pressure of superincumbent strata, 376.—Working the coal, 377.—Ventilation, 377.—Raising the coal, 395.—Cost of sinking, 395.—Increased cost of production, 395.—Explosive gas, 396.—Health of miners, 396.—Summary, 396.—Appendix: List of authorities consulted, 402.—Observations undertaken to show the increase in temperature of air-currents, with distance from the shafts, at several Belgian pits, 403.—Observation made at No. 2 pit, Charbonnage de l'Agrappe, 404.

Discussion.— Bainbridge, E., 407.—Knowles, J., 406.—Stephenson, G. R., 405.

COASTS.

England. "The East Coast between the Thames and the Wash estuaries." By J. B. Redman, xxiii. 186.—Leeward progression of the shingle up-channel on the south coast; on the east coast, southwards; and on the north coast of Norfolk, westward, 186.—Effect of the increased scour of the Thames in progressive removal of shoals in the upper reaches, 186.—Dredging required to a greater extent than formerly, 186.—The Halfway and Erith reaches encumbered with débris caused by breaches that formerly occurred in the river-walls, 186.—Changes in the sandbanks of the Thames delta, 187.—The Blyth sand, and Maplin and Foulness sands, 187.—Low cliffs about Southend, and in the Isle of Sheppey, subject to falls, 187.—Degradation of the coast about St. Osyth's, 187.—Groyne at Eastness indicates an encroachment of the sea, 187.—Waste of Clacton cliff, 187.—Recession of the land at Holland, 188.—Holland haven, 188.—Groynes at the foot of Frinton cliff have not arrested the decay, 188.—Cliffs about Walton-le-Soken have fallen coincident with record, 188.—Large slips of London clay at the Naze, 188.—Re-

COASTS.

semblance to those at Warden point in the Isle of Sheppey, 188. — Attempts, by drainage and staking, to render a slip permanent, 189.—Earthen sea-walls, for protecting Walton and Stone marshes, 190. —Handford water, 190.—Constant struggle to maintain the frontage between Handford water and Harwich, 191.—Regular sea-defences about Dovercourt, 191.—Removal of cement stones from Beacon cliff and Landguard, 192.—Artificial paving of Beacon cliff, 192.—Changes in Landguard Point, 192.—Alteration of Admiralty lights consequent on the modern overlap of the point, 193.—Distribution of the sand and shingle on the point, 193.—Westerly increase of the spit, 194.—Easterly decrease of ditto, 195.—Harwich lapsing to the condition of a bar harbour due to the waste of ditto, 195.—Manner in which the point has been formed, 195.—Local action produces changes in the spit, 196.—Pier proposed under the Harwich Harbour Bill, 196.—Bull cliff, 196.—Sand dunes at the entrance of Bawdsey haven, 196.—Waste of Bawdsey cliff, 197.—Bawdsey beach, 198.—Largest pebbles on the crest of the beach at Shingle-street, 199.—Description of Orford haven from the 'North Sea Pilot,' 199.—Changes in the position of the entrance, 200.—Bar of shingle across the entrance, 200.—North Weir point, 200.—Progressive march of the shingle in a south-westerly direction, 200.—Orfordness, 200.—Shingle 'fulls' of Orfordness, 201.—Modern projections of the Ness, 202.—Points of resemblance between Dungeness, Langley point, and Orfordness, 202.—High-light and Low-light towers, 203. — South-westward progression of the Orford haven in three centuries, 203.—Thorpeness, 203.—Dimensions of the beaches between Aldborough and Landguard Point, 204.—Minsmere level, 204.—Degradation of crag at Dunwich heath, 205.—Shore fronting Dunwich bay,

COASTS.

205.—Southwold harbour frequently blocked up with shingle, 205.—Proposal to improve the harbour, by extending the north pier, 206.—Early condition of the shore, 206.—Present condition of the haven, 207.—Town of Southwold, 207.—Encroachments of the sea, 207.—Easton Bavent, 207.—Dimensions of Benacre Broad, 208.—Sea Row, 208. — Pakefield, 208. — Lights erected, 208.—Lowestoft an artificial harbour, 209.—Its position in some respects advantageous, 209.—Southward movement of the outlying sands, 209. — Foreshore of Lowestoft Ness, 209.—The 'Denes,' 210.—Southern movement of the point of the Ness, 210.—Degradation of the cliffs at Corton, 210.—Changes consequent on the accumulation of sand at Yarmouth, 211.—Diminution in depth of water over Yarmouth bar, 212.—Sand hillocks from Winterton to Waxham, 212.—Ruins of Eccles church, 212.—The 'Marrams,' 213.—Encroachments of the sea at Happisburgh, 214.—Loss at Walcot, 214.—Waste of cliffs at Mundesley, 215.—Outcrop of the chalk north of Mundesley, 216.—Encroachments of the sea at Cromer, 217.—Foulness rocks, 217.—Artificial defences, 218.—Chalk at Beeston hill, 218. — Weybourn beach, 219. — Movement of shingle towards the Wash west of Cromer, 219. — Blakeney, 219. — 'Marram' sandhills, between Blakeney and Brancaster, 219. — Great extent of sands at Wells beach, 220.—Effect of construction of sea-wall between Wells quay and Holkham, 220. — Wild character of shore in front of Burnham Overy, Burnham Deepdale, and Brancaster, 221.—Crater-like depression in 'Scott Head' sandhill, 221.—Natural advantages of Brancaster, 221.—Red and white chalk at Hunstanton, 222.—Belt of shingle from Hunstanton to Woolverton creek, 222. — Norfolk Estuary works, 223.—Groynes south of Hunstanton, 223.—General features

COFFERDAM AND SYPHONS.

of the lowland between Hunstanton, Woolverton creek, and Castle Rising, 223. — Shingle 'fulls' and saltings between Snettisham and Woolverton, 224.

Discussion.—Airy, G. B., 226, 237. — Brooks, W. A., 248, 251.—Bruff, P., 242.—Burstal, Capt. E., 233.—Coode, J., 239, 252.—Gregory, C. H., 229.—Hawkshaw, J., 235.—Murray, J., 245. —Redman, J. B., 225, 251, 253, 254.—Rennie, Sir J., 231.—Russell, J. S., 236.—Valentine, J. S., 249, 251.—Vignoles, C. B., 230, 254.

Vide also LAGOONS AND MARSHES; and RIVERS AND ESTUARIES.

COBB, G. H. [Election, xxiii. 151.]

COCHRANE, A. B. [Memoir, xxiii. 506.]

COCHRANE, J. [Associate of Council, xxi. 133.]

Bridges. Difficulty of keeping the cylinder at the Saltash bridge free from water, xxi. 275.—Drilling the rivet-holes in the girders of the Charing Cross bridge, xxii. 530.

———, suspension. Erection of the Clifton suspension bridge, xxvi. 269.

Drilling rivet-holes, xxii. 530; xxx. 265, 267.

Iron bars, experiments on the strength of, with drilled holes and punched holes, xxx. 265, 267.

COCK, W. H. [Election, xxvii. 218.]

COCKAYNE, O. [Memoir, xxi. 581.]

CODDINGTON, W. H. [Election, xxiv. 358.]

CODRINGTON, T. [Election, xxv. 262.]

COE, J.

Coal-getting, by wedges, xxviii. 148.

COFFERDAM AND SYPHONS.

"Account of the cofferdam, the syphons, and other works, constructed in consequence of the failure of the St. Germains sluice of the Middle Level drainage." By J. Hawkshaw, xxii. 497. —The Eau Brink Cut as completed in 1857, 497.—Failure of the St. Germains sluice, and bursting of the western bank of the Middle Level drain, 498. —Steps taken by the Middle Level Drainage Commissioners, 498.—Earthwork dam commenced and partially

COGAN.

carried out, 498.— Failure of first attempt to construct a permanent cofferdam, from a barge breaking loose and destroying the piles, 499.— Levels of the water in the River Ouse and in the drain, 499.—Account of the construction of the cofferdam, 500. — Pile-work, 500. — Precautions adopted to obviate the scour of the water, 501.—The panels, 502.—Failure of the first attempt to close the dam, 502.—Dam finally closed, 503.—Further strengthening, 503.—Reasons for adopting syphons for draining off the surplus water, 504.—The syphons, 504.—Works subsidiary to the adjustment of the syphons, 505.—Apparatus for putting the syphons into action, 506.—Reason for adopting two valves instead of one, 506.—Covering of the syphons, 507.—Stopping the breach, 507.—Syphons will probably be found to answer all the purposes of a permanent sluice, 508.—Total quantities of the several kinds of materials used in the construction of the cofferdam and the syphons, 509.—Tables showing the working of the syphons, 509, *et seq.*—Capacity per foot in height above datum of the drain between the syphons and the Outwell sluice, 511.

Cofferdams, xxiv. 57, *et seq. Vide* also Docks, Great Grimsby.

Cogan, D. [Election, xxiv. 511; Decease, xxvi. 129.]

Coghlan, J. [Election, xxiv. 458.]

Cohen, M.

Railway curves and inclines, xxvi. 330. —Working of the steep gradients of the Baltimore and Ohio railway, 330.

Coimbra, A. T. [Election, xxii. 65.]

Coke. *Vide* Coal.

Coke, R. G. [Election, xxi. 345.]

Colbron, J. P. [Election, xxvi. 242].

Colburn, Z. [Telford medal and premium, xxiii. 114, 126; Election, xxiv. 184; Watt medal and Telford premium, xxix. 211.]

Bridges, iron. " American iron bridges," xxii. 540.—Remarks, 557.—Economy

COLBURN.

of American iron bridges, 557.— Small quantity of material in, 557. —Strength of, 558.—Assumed load of bridges of 200 feet span adopted by Messrs. Murphy, Whipple, and Bollman, 558.—American cast iron, 558.—Comparative merits of American iron truss-bridges, 573.

Bridges, American timber, xxii. 318.— Superiority of iron and stone to the best timber bridges, 318.—Duration of timber bridges, 318. — Instances of costly renewals and failures of, 319.— Weakness of the lattice-bridge over the James river at Richmond, Virginia, 320.—Destruction of American timber bridges by fire, 320.—Necessity of watchmen to prevent incendiarism, 320.—Cost of American timber bridges, 321.

Gunpowder used in the American service, dynamic value of the, xxvi. 201.

Injector, Giffard's, xxiv. 243.

Iron, American cast, xxii. 558.

Locomotive engines and rolling stock, xxiv. 386. — Engines for working a temporary line, on a gauge of 3 feet 3 inches, during the construction of the Great Western railway of Canada, 386.

—— " American locomotives and rolling stock," xxviii. 360.—Remarks, 385.— Adoption in Canada of the peculiarities of the railway practice of the United States, 423.—Use of cast-iron wheels for the rolling stock on Canadian railways, 423.—Weight and price of chilled wheels, 427.—Bogie trucks, 427.—American sleeping-cars, 427.— Adhesion of driving-wheels upon American lines, 427.—Working of the locomotive ' Reuben Wells,' 428.

Permanent way, xxvii. 380.—Breakages of iron rails on American railroads, 380.—Adoption of steel rails, 381.

Railway locomotion, xxiii. 403. — Resistance to trains on curves as ascertained by experiments on the New York and Erie railway, 403, 404 ; xxviii. 428.—Proportion between the weight on the driving-wheels of a loco-

COLLET.

motive and the adhesion, as observed on the Brentwood incline of the Great Eastern railway, xxiii. 404.

COLLET, J. [Election, xxv. 508.]

COLLEY, T. L. [Election, xxvii. 55; Memoir, xxx. 466.]

COLLIER, J. [Election, xxx. 323.]

COLLINGE, A. [Resignation, xxviii. 167.]

COLLINGWOOD, Captain C. T. [Decease, xxii. 636.]

COLLINSON, J. [Election, xxviii. 517.]

COLLINSON, Admiral R.
Lighthouse apparatus, xxviii. 36.—Relative advantages of petroleum and colza-oil for lighthouse illumination, 36.—Catoptric system better suited than the dioptric for floating lights, 36.—Importance of distinctive characters for sea-lights, 36.

COLLYER, G. C., Colonel, R.E. [Election, xxii. 336.]
Lighthouses, comparative cost of, in the Red Sea and at Cape Rachadah, xxiii. 34.

COLT, S., Colonel, U.S.A. [Memoir, xxii. 636.]

COLTHURST, J.
Ships and steam-vessels. Experiments on the resistance to motion, due to the form of floating bodies (Phipps, G. H.), xxiii. 339.

COLYER, F. [Election, xxx. 323.]

COMBE, J. [Decease, xxvii. 131.]

Communication between London and Dublin. Vide LONDON and DUBLIN COMMUNICATION.

Concrete, application of, xxii. 419, 439, et seq.; xxiv. 147, 168, et seq ; xxv. 133, et seq. Vide also CEMENTS; DOCKS, Marseilles; and STRUCTURES IN THE SEA.

Conversazione (May 31, 1870): Catalogue of works of art, and of engineering models and instruments, exhibited, xxx. 408.

CONYBEARE, H.
Permanent way, xxvii. 357.—Duration of a rail affected by its section, 357.—Various forms of rails, 357, 366.—Vignoles' rail, 357, et seq.—Vertical stiffness of rails, 357.—Strength of

COODE.

different kinds of permanent way, 358. —Rail-heads, 359.—Bearing surface of rails, 360.—Proper profiles for wheel-tires and the wheel-tread of rails, 360, et seq.—Form of the shoulder of rails, 363.—Fish-planes and the vertical web of rails, 364.—Rail-foot, 366.—Delineation of rails by the siderograph, 368.—Rail-fastenings, 371.—Advantages of the Vignoles' road, 373.—Rolling rails from puddled bars, 374.

Railway curves and inclines, xxvi. 334. —Working of the steep gradients on the Brecon and Merthyr railway, 334.—Results of the working of the engine 'Cymbeline,' 335.—Effective adhesion of locomotive engines, 336.—Apparent paradox of an effective adhesion being obtained exceeding that due to the coefficient of friction, 337.—Flattening the gradients on the curves of mountain railways, 337.—Mr. Latrobe's table of resistances due to curves, 337.—Amount of relief given on the curves of the Mont Cenis railway, 338.—'Cymbeline' class of engine, 338.—Instances of sharp railway curves, 339.—Disadvantages of the plan of two engines coupled together, 339.—Traversing Alpine passes by railway zigzags, 339.

Timber, necessity of thoroughly drying, before creosoting, xxvii. 566.

COODE, J.
Cements, xxv. 144.—Tests of the strength of cement, 144.—Construction of sea-walls and piers with Portland cement concrete blocks, 145.—Quality possessed by Portland cement of resisting the action of attrition or abrasion, 145.—Relative amount of adhesion of granite and Portland stone cemented together by Portland cement, 145.—Failure of Portland cement in an open tideway, 146.—Best mode of exporting Portland cement, 146.—Zumaya cement, xxx. 24.

Coasts. East coast of England, xxiii. 239.—Growth of Landguard Point, 239.—Travel of the shingle at ditto,

COODE.

239.—Origin of the Chesil Bank, 240. —Theory of the movement of shingle in deep water untenable, 241.—Passage of the shingle at the Chesil Bank along the beach and not from the deep water towards the shore, 242.— Travel of shingle from the quarter whence the heaviest seas proceed, 252. —Relative distribution of flint shingle and oolitic shingle in the Chesil bank and Weymouth bay, 252:—Condition of the Shambles shoal in Weymouth bay proves that there is no tearing action along the bottom of the sea, 253.

Estuary of the Humber, xxiv. 54.— Construction of groynes for the protection of Spurn Point, 54.—Maintenance of ditto, xxviii. 501.—Effect of groynes on ditto, 501, et seq.—Injurious effect of stopping a breach in the Spurn by a bank of chalk, 502.— Condition of the tides at the Humber entrance, 502.—Policy of enclosing the indent on the Humber side of Spurn Point, 502.—Protection of Spurn Neck by mat-grass, 503.—Acts of Parliament relating to mat-grass, 504.

Lighthouses. Daboll's fog-signal, xxx. 24.—Volume of sea thrown over the Edystone in stormy weather, 24.

Railway inclines, xxx. 74.—Rowe's clip-break as used at the Botallack copper-mine, 74.—Durability of the ropes used in working the traffic on the Serra do Mar inclines, 74.—Destructive agencies to which ropes used for working railway inclines are subjected, 75.

Timber, creosoting, xxii. 258.—Difficulty of impregnating the denser woods of India, 258.

COODE, J. C. [Admission, xxvii. 54.]

COOKE, A. C., Major, R.E. [Election, xxi. 492.]

COOKE, J. G. [Election, xxv. 479.]

COOKE, W. F. [Election, xxvi. 544.]

COOPER, E. [Election, xxvii. 55.]

COOPER, J. [Memoir, xxii. 624.]

COOPER, J. B. [Election, xxix. 98.]

COOPER, R. E. [Election, xxx. 215.]

COWPER.

COOPER, S. T. [Election, xxvi. 544.]

Copper, durability of, in sea-water, xxi. 434, 439.

COPPER ORES.

Sizing, xxx. 131.

Smelting. "On the smelting of refractory copper ores with wood as fuel in Australia." By J. L. Morgan, xxvi. 44.—The Ophir Copper Mining Company, 44.—Failure of the ordinary melting furnaces, 44.— New arrangement of furnace proved successful, 44.—Quartz bricks used in construction of furnaces, 45.—Inexpediency of throttling reverberatory furnaces, 46.— Provision for neutralizing any excess of carbonic acid, 46.

Discussion.—Forbes, D., 47.—Morgan, J. L., 48.—Siemens, C. W., 47.

Cornish pumping engines, on the duty of the (Morshead, W.), xxiii. 45. Vide also STEAM-ENGINES.

COTTAM, G. H. [Election, xxiii. 110.]

COTTERILL, J. H. [Election, xxv. 508.]

COTTON, Sir A.

Irrigation in India, xxvii. 511.—Increase of government revenue and profit to the State from works properly constructed, 511.—Further financial results of irrigation works in India, 533. —Cost of water on the Godavery, on the Ganges canal, and as raised from wells, 534.—Irrigation in Orissa, 535, 536.—Cost of masonry weirs across the rivers in the Madras Presidency, 535.—Objections urged against the construction of irrigation works by private enterprise in India, 535.— Revenue of various districts in India, 536.

COULTHARD, W. [Memoir, xxiii. 506.]

COULTHARD, W. R. [Memoir, xxviii. 618.]

Council, Annual Reports of. Vide ANNUAL REPORTS OF COUNCIL.

Council premiums. Vide PREMIUMS AND PRIZES.

COUSENS, C. B. [Election, xxvi. 544.]

COVENTRY, H. H. [Election, xxvi. 544.]

COWEN, R. [Memoir, xxii. 638.]

COWPER, C. [Memoir, xxi. 581.]

COWPER.

COWPER, C. E. [Admission, xxvii. 54.]
COWPER, E. A.

Boilers, marine, decay of, xxvii. 576.

Bridges. Charing Cross, xxii. 531.—
Testing, 531. — Weight per square
foot of a crowd of men, 531.—
Strains upon cast-iron arches, 569.—
Principles of the construction of the
Victoria bridges, Pimlico, xxvii. 99.
—Calculation of the stability of the
arches of bridges, 100.—Cast-iron
arched bridges, 102.—Stiffness of the
piers of the Victoria bridge, 107.—
Putting in piers for bridges over
torrential rivers, xxix. 125.

—— suspension, xxvi. 279. — Means of
keeping the chain of a suspension
bridge in shape, 279.—Girders or stiff
platforms for strengthening suspension
bridges, 280.—Use of diagonal ties and
struts between the chain and the roadway, 280.—Inverted arch bridge, 281.
—Strains in ditto and in an ordinary arched bridge when loaded, 281,
283.—Light side-chains for preventing
side-motion caused by the wind, 282.
—Economy of carrying a load by a
chain entirely in tension, 283.

Canals, steam-power on, xxvi. 34.—
Haulage of boats through canals, 34.
—Banking-up of water in front of
boats, 34.—Supplying propellers acting by the emission of water through
a pipe leading from the bows of canal
boats, 34.

Coal, distillation of, xxiii. 454.—Eaton's
coke ovens, 454.—Wasteful system of
the old plan of coking in ovens, 454.
—Illuminating power of gas obtained
from one of Siemens' coke ovens,
454.

Fans, rotary, xxx. 297.—Cases, 297.—
Useful effect obtainable, 298, 301.—
Fans for foundry purposes, 301.

Foundations. Dr. Potts' vacuum process
and 'elephant's trunk,' for sinking
piles, xxviii. 348.

Girders, continuous, xxix. 71.—Testing
iron or steel in, 73.

Iron and steel. Operations in each of
the various processes for making, xxvii.

COWPER.

398, et seq.—Old process for making
steel, 398. — 'Marshall' process of
making iron, 400.—Krupp's process of
making steel, 400.—Bessemer process,
400.—Siemens' processes for making
steel, 400. — Testing iron or steel,
xxix. 73.

Lighthouses. Necessity of iron diagonals
in lighthouses constructed of iron piles,
xxiii. 28.

Locomotive engines. Objections to be
urged against single-cylinder locomotive engines, xxii. 94. — Balancing
locomotive engines, 95.—Uniformity of
the rotative power in single-cylinder
and double-cylinder engines, 96.

Railway inclines, xxvi. 376.—Adhesion
of metal upon metal, 376.—Experiments on ditto on steep inclinations,
377.

Railway locomotion. Friction of axle-
boxes fed with oil on the London and
South Western railway, xxviii. 406.
—Friction of trains 407, 409.—Adhesion of wheels, 411.

Railway telegraphs, xxii. 227.—Importance of vigilance on the part of guards
and engine-drivers, 226.—Practice of
working railways in Germany by
telegraph, 226.—Invention of fog-
signals, 226.

Roofs. Curvature of the roof of the St.
Pancras station of the Midland railway, xxx. 102.—New Street station
roof, Birmingham, 103.—Cost of ditto,
103.—Mode of obtaining the proper
dimensions for the Tithebarn Street
station roof, Liverpool, 104. — Proving one of the principals of the roof
of ditto, 104.

Ships and steam-vessels. Possibility of
the 'conoid' curve being found useful in forming the lines of a vessel,
xxiii. 361.—Result of an experiment
to ascertain what curve a waterline
should be, to exert an equal pressure
against the water throughout every
square inch of surface in its length,
361.—Method of ascertaining in what
path the water moves round a s^{1}
363.

COX.

Ships of war, xxi. 207.—Experiments on the effect of shot upon iron plates made at Woolwich in 1846, 207.—Armour-plating the sides of vessels, 208.—Turrets of Swedish monitors, xxvi. 227.—Ventilation of ditto, 227, 228.—Engines of ditto, 227.

Steam-engines. Application of steam-jackets to cylinders and cylinder covers of steam-engines, xxii. 97.—Cornish engines in many respects unsuited for waterworks pumping purposes, xxiii. 61.—Moderate variation of pressure and great expansion in Cornish engines by the application of steam-jacketing in an extended manner, 63.—Two indicator figures from a steam-jacketed engine, 64.—Extracts from report as to the performance of the pumping engines at the Chelsea Waterworks Company at Kingston, 71.—Steam-jacketed reservoirs between high-pressure and low-pressure engines, xxix. 170.—Results of a trial of steam-jacketed engines at the Lambeth waterworks, 171.

Steam navigation. Engines, &c. of the Kingstown and Holyhead steam-packets, xxii. 597. — Engines of Swedish monitors, xxvi. 227.

Stoves. "On recent improvements in regenerative hot-blast stoves for blast furnaces," xxx. 309.—Remarks, 319. —Application of a pair of stoves to one blast-furnace, 319.—Saving of coke effected by using very hot blast, 319. —Economy of large furnaces, 320.—Theory of hot blast compared with cold blast, 320.—Prevention of loss of heat, in hot-blast stoves, by radiation and conduction, 320.—Successive improvements in hot-blast stoves, 321.

Tunnels. Mont Cenis tunnel, xxiii. 296. —Boring tools, 296.—M. Sommeiller's and Mr. Bartlett's perforators, 296.

Water, filtration of, xxvii. 35.—Cost of reburning animal charcoal, 35.

Weight, per square foot, of a crowd of men, xxii. 531 ; xxvi. 281.

Cox, J. H. [Admission, xxvii. 54.]

Cox, W. G. [Election, xxiv. 184.]

CROSSLEY.

CRACKNELL, E. C. [Election, xxv. 352.]

CRAIG, J. [Election, xxvii. 218.]

CRAIG, W. Y. [Election, xxv. 429.]

Coal-mining. Harecastle colliery, xxviii. 123.—Results of experiments on getting coal with machines invented by Mr. Bidder and Mr. Chubb, 123, et seq.—Danger of firing gunpowder in coal-mines, 124.

CRAMPTON, J. G. [Election, xxx. 1.]

CRAMPTON, T. R.

Railway inclines. Temporary steep incline on the Ottoman railway, xxvi. 382.—Cost of working, 384.

Stoves. Superiority of brick stoves to iron stoves for withstanding high temperatures, xxx. 318.—Siemens-Cowper regenerative hot-blast stove, 319.

CRAVEN, A. W. [Election, xxix. 322.]

CRAVEN, J. C. [Election, 79.]

Injector, Giffard's, xxiv. 238.

CRAVEN, W. [Election, xxiv. 62.]

CRAWFORD, R. [Telford premium, xxiii. 115, 126.]

Railways. "The railway system of Germany," xxii. 2.—Remarks, 43.

CRAWFORD, R. W.

Telegraphic communication with India, xxv. 26.—Defective working of the Anglo-Indian telegraph, 26.—Inexpediency of the Government having the control of telegraphs in India, 26.

CRAWFORD, W. F. [Election, xxx. 215.]

CREAMER, W. G.

Railway break, xxii. 240.

CROKER, B. W. [Resignation, xxix. 217.]

CROMPTON, E. [Admission, xxvii. 55.]

CROSS, J. [Watt medal, xxiv. 109, 124 ; Election, xxv. 64.]

Railway locomotion. "On the structure of locomotive engines for ascending steep inclines, with sharp curves on railways," xxiii. 406.—Remarks, 438. —Radial axle engines run steadily on straight lines, 438.

CROSSLEY, J. S.

Permanent way, xxv. 414.—Average duration of rails on the Midland railway, 415.—Relative cost of iron and steel rails, 415.—Inexpediency

CROSTHWAIT.

of creosoting railway sleepers, 415, 417.—Value of old steel rails, 416.

CROSTHWAIT, T. P. S. [Election, xxvii. 180.]

CROUCHER, J. S. [Election, xxiii. 110.]

CROUDACE, C. H. [Election, xxvii. 443.]

CROWLEY, J. S. [Election, xxii. 167.]

CROZIER, W. [Election, xxvi. 242.]

CUBITT, J. [Member of Council, xxi. 133; xxii. 112; xxiii. 112; xxiv. 106. Vice-President, xxv. 161; xxvi. 119; xxvii. 122; xxviii. 158; xxix. 208.]

Bridges, iron. Board of Trade requirements of the maximum load per foot run to be provided for in iron bridges, xxv. 258.

Permanent way. Breakage of turned iron rails on the Great Northern railway, xxv. 410.

Rivers and estuaries. Formation of bars at the mouths of rivers, xxvi. 431.— Water in times of drought retained above the Grand Sluice on the river Witham, for purposes of navigation and irrigation, xxviii. 82.

CUBITT, C. [Election, xxiii. 320.]

CUBITT, W. [Memoir, xxiii. 507.]

CUBITT, Sir W. [Memoir, xxi. 1, 554.]

CUDWORTH, W. [Telford premium, xxiii. 115, 126.]

Viaducts. "The Hownes Gill viaduct on the Stockton and Darlington railway," xxii. 44.—Remarks, 52, 57.

CULLEY, R. S. [Election, xxx. 1.]

Railway telegraphs, xxii. 221.—Permanent system of train signalling by telegraph preferred by signalmen, 221. —Bell system preferable to the system of temporary needle signals, 222.— Possible accidents on railways from errors arising from reversal, demagnetisation, or accident, to the telegraphic signalling wire, and the remedy by the repetition of the signals, 222.—Length of needles employed in telegraph signalling, 223. —System of telegraph signals at the tunnel at the New Street station, Birmingham, 223.

CUNDY, J. [Election, xxv. 479.]

CURTIS.

CURLL, W. H. R. [Memoir, xxv. 526.]

CURRAN, I. [Memoir, xxviii. 619.]

CURREY, E. S. [Election, xxviii. 59.]

CURRIE, G. W.

Railway income and expenditure, xxix. 345.—Financial condition of railway property, 345.—Branch lines of railway, 355.

CURTIS, J. G. Cockburn.

Breakwaters and piers, construction of, xxii. 443.—Importance of considering the 'lead' of sea, and the rise and fall of the tide, 443.

Bridges, timber, xxii. 323.—Great expense incurred in the renewals of timber bridges in Spain, and their liability to be burnt during insurrections, 323.

Cements. Mixture of 'jagghery' with mortar in India, xxiv. 36.—Advantage derived from mixing mortar, cement, or concrete, intended for coast works, in salt or brackish water, xxv. 134.

Civil Engineers, education of, xxii. 41.

Concrete. Use of, in marine structures, xxii. 458.—Desirability of using the materials on the foreshore in making concrete for sea or estuary works, xxv. 135.

Drainage of towns, xxii. 300.—Construction of sewers in New York, 300.— Sewers with a dead level bottom objectionable, 301.

Evaporation in the Madras Presidency, xxvi. 472.

Lighthouses. Nautical difficulties involved in the construction of the Red Sea lighthouses, xxiii. 31.—Suitability of the foundations, 32.— Engineering cost of the lighthouses erected in the Red Sea and at Lobos Cay, 33.

Materials in buildings, decay of, in tropical climates, xxiv. 36.—Germination of seeds in mortar, 36.—Effect of the mixture of 'jagghery' with mortar in India, 36.

Rivers. Flood discharge of, xxvii. 238.

Rivers and estuaries, under and counter-currents at the mouths of, xxi. 340.

E

CUTLER.

Timber. Improbability of the native woods of the Madras Presidency proving suitable for sleepers, xxii. 257.—Superiority of the woods of Singapore, 258.

CUTLER, W. H. [Election, xxii. 65.]
Lighthouses. Magneto-electric light for lighthouse purposes, xxviii. 42.—Foghorns, 42.

Cycloscope, for setting out railway or

CYLINDERS.

other curves (Humphreys, H. T.), xxv. 508.

Cylinders for foundations, xxi. 183, 260, 265, 268, *et seq*.

—— Description of apparatus for excavating under water, and for sinking (Milroy, J.), xxviii. 339. *Vide* also BRIDGES; FOUNDATIONS; PILES; and VIADUCTS.

D.

DAGLISH.

DAGLISH, J. [Election, xxvi. 554.]
DAGLISH, R. [Memoir, xxvi. 561.]
DALE, T. [Election, xxviii. 232.]
DALLAS, H. W. [Admission, xxviii. 325.]
DALRYMPLE, J. [Election, xxiii. 442.]
Danneverke, the Great (Paton, J.), xxi. 448.
DANTAS, J. G. V. [Election, xxviii. 59.]
Danube, description of the Delta of the, and of the works, recently executed, at the Sulina mouth (Hartley, Sir C. A.), xxi. 277. *Vide* also RIVERS.
DANVERS, F. C. [Election, xxvii. 218.]
DARLEY, G. J. [Election, xxiii. 257.]
DAVENPORT, E. G. [Election, xxviii. 517.]
DAVIES, C. [Election, xxvii. 55.]
DAVIES, C. L. [Election, xxiii. 459.]
DAVIS, F. G. [Election, xxviii. 59; Memoir, xxx. 467.]
DAVIS, H. L. A. [Election, xxvii. 55.]
DAVIS, H. W. [Election, xxv. 508.]
DAVIS, J. [Election, xxii. 451.]
DAWSON, G. J. C. [Election, xxvi. 79.]
DAWSON, R. K., Colonel, R.E. [Memoir, xxi. 582.]
DAWSON, W. A. [Admission, xxviii. 439.]
DEAN, C. [Election, xxii. 65; Decease, xxiv. 117.]
DEAS, J. [Election, xxvi 242.]
Permanent way. Wear of steel rails and switches and crossings on the North British railway, xxvii. 352.—Steel-headed and solid steel rails, 352.
DE BERGUE, C. L. A.
Bridges, suspension, xxvi. 269.
Decay of materials in tropical climates, on the, and the methods employed for arresting and preventing it (Mann, G. O., and Heath, W. J. W.), xxiv. 1, 14. *Vide* also MATERIALS.
DELANEY, E. M. J. [Memoir, xxvii. 599.]
DELANO, W. H. [Election, xxvii. 55.]
Irrigation in Egypt, xxvii. 548.—Cost of

DENISON.

the barrage of the Nile, 548.—Produce from irrigated land, 548.
DELANY, J. F. [Election, xxiv. 257.]
Canals, advantages of boats separable into compartments for the navigation of, xxvi. 40.
Ships and steam-vessels. 'Connector' steam-vessel, xxvi. 40.
DE MORNAY, A.
Bridge, suspension, at Caxanga, xxiv. 29.
DE MORNAY, E.
Railways in Brazil on the American principle, advisability of constructing, xxii. 409.
DEMPSEY, W. [Election, xxv. 352.]
DENHAM, C. H. [Election, xxvii. 218.]
DENISON, Major-General Sir W. T. [Watt medal, xxvii. 124, 142; Associate of Council, xxviii. 158.]
Canals. "The Suez canal," xxvi. 442.—Remarks, 449.—Time of completion, 451.—Mean level of the Mediterranean and the Red Sea identical, 468.—Difficulty of making a high-level freshwater canal at the Isthmus of Suez, 472.—Sectional area of the Suez canal, 473.—Financial condition of the Suez Canal Company, 474.—Economy of dredging, 474.—Port Saïd, 475.—Question of drift along shore, 475.—Ancient freshwater canal at Suez, 475.—Tide in the Mediterranean, 476.
Irrigation in India, xxvii. 515.—Distribution of the monsoon rains and water supply, 515.—Diminution of rain from the destruction of forests, 516.—Madras Irrigation and Canal Company, 516.—Irrigation schemes by the intervention of companies, 516.
Rivers, flood discharge of, xxvii. 254.—Relation of the fall of rain to floods, 254.—Effect of forests upon rainfall on the west coast of India, 255, 516.

DENNIS.

DENNIS, W. [Election, xxvi. 398.]

DENNISTON, J. T. [Admission, xxvii. 54.]

DENNYS, F. J. [Election, xxvii. 443.]

DENT, W. D. [Election, xxvii. 451.]

DENTON, J. B. [Telford medal, xxii. 120, 130.]

Drainage. "On the discharge from under-drainage, and its effect on the arterial channels and outfalls of the country," xxi. 48.—Remarks, 83.—Expediency of treating under-drainage in a scientific manner, 83.—Effect of under-drainage on the flow of perennial springs, 84.—Method of gauging the discharge in under-drainage, 86, 121.—Arterial in relation to under-drainage, 121.—Extent of area of drainage experimented on, 122.—Vast expenditure of money incurred from ignorance of the science of drainage, 122.—Necessity of deep under-drainage, 123. — Effect of drying the saturated free soils, 124.—Letter from Lord Palmerston supporting the opinion that under-drainage increased the perennial supply of rivers, 125.—Drainage experiments at Broadlands, 128.—Probable loss of water available for mill-power in former times in the valley of the Test from want of proper drainage, 128.

DERRY, J. D. [Election, xxv. 65.]

DE RUSETT, E. W. [Election, xxvii. 218.]

Ships and steam-vessels. Destruction of marine boilers, xxvii. 575.—Decay of iron plates in steam-vessels, 575.

DESPARD, R. C. [Election, xxi. 257; Memoir, xxiii. 485.]

DEVERELL, G. H. R. [Admission, xxix. 98.]

DIBBLEE, F. L. [Election, xxiv. 62.]

DICKINSON, John. [Resignation, xxiv. 117.]

DICKINSON, John.

Irrigation and navigation works in India, xxvii. 526.—Construction by Government agency, or by private enterprise, 526.

DINES, G.

Cement, Portland, xxv. 129.—Strength, 129.—Trouble frequently given when used for stucco, 129.—Corrosive effect on iron, 129.

DOCKS.

DINNEN, J. [Memoir, xxvi. 563.]

Dinting and the Mottram viaducts, on the reconstruction of the (Fairbairn, W.), xxii. 327. Vide also VIADUCTS.

DITCHBURN, J.

Ships and steam-vessels. Imperfection of the theory of the resistance of vessels, xxiii. 359.—Results of experiments made to ascertain the ratio which the resistance bears to the extent of surface under various given forms and angles, 360.—Reducing the 'plus pressure' in a full-built vessel, by introducing a slight hollow close to the stem, 361.

Ships of war, xxi. 194.—Injurious effects of elaborate fastenings for attaching armour-plates, 194.—Best size of ships, 194.

Divers, xxi. 276.—Relative ability of different men to sustain labour under air-pressure, 276.

DIXON, C. W. [Election, xxvii. 218.]

DIXON, E. J. J.

Boring machine invented by him (Brunlees, J.), xxiii. 319.

DIXON, J. [Election, xxix. 98.]

DOBSON, E.

Public works. "Memoir on the public works of the province of Canterbury, New Zealand," xxix. 99.

DOBSON, J. M. [Admission, xxvii. 54.]

DOCKS.

Birkenhead, xxviii. 518, et seq. Vide also LOW-WATER BASIN AT BIRKENHEAD.

Great Grimsby. "Description of the Great Grimsby (Royal) docks." By E. H. Clark, xxiv. 38. — Dock in existence in 1845, 38.—New dock projected by the Manchester, Sheffield, and Lincolnshire railway company, 38. — The design, 38.—Reclamation from the river, 38.—First stone laid, 39. — Cofferdam, 39. — Piling, 39.— Puddling, 39. — Method of securing the piling, 39.—Temporary sluices, 40. — Floodgates, 40. — Wharf, 40.— Embankment, 41.—Excavation for the foundations, 41. — Locks, 41. — Dock walls, 43. — Quay, 44. — Mortar and concrete, 44.—Limekilns and mortar-

DOCKS.

mills, 44.—Pen-gates and flood-gates for the locks, 44.—Truss-rods for the gate bars, 45.—Gate rollers, 45.—Gudgeons, 46.—Anchor-plates, 46.—Pointing cills, gates, and machinery, 46.—Motive-power for working the gates, 46.—Timber piers and pier-heads, 47.—Creosoting, 47.—Dimensions of the channel, 47.—Drain for the backwater from the country, 47.—Graving dock, 48.—Inverts and gate-tables, 48.—Floor and steps, 48.—Culvert, 49.—Centrifugal pumps, 49.—Engine for working ditto, 49.—Gates of the lock, 49.—Cost of the graving dock, 49.—Accommodation for shipping coal, 49.—Gradients of the railways to the coal spouts, 50.—Hydraulic tower, 50.—Water supply for ditto, 50.—Cornish engine, 51.—Fishing-craft dock, 51.—Pier on the south side of ditto, 51.—Further improvements projected, 52.—Existence of the port dependent on the maintenance of Spurn Point, 52.—Areas of the different docks and basins, and depths of water in the docks and locks belonging to the Manchester, Sheffield, and Lincoln-shire railway, at Grimsby, 53.—Rise and fall of tides in the Humber, 53.—Increase of traffic to Grimsby since the opening of the new docks, 53.
Discussion.—Belcher, Admiral Sir E., 54.—Brooks, W. A., 56.—Clark, E. H., 54, 59, 60.—Coode, J., 54.—Fowler, J., 60.—Hawkshaw, J., 58.—Murray, J., 57.—Rendel, A. M., 57.—Russell, J. S., 59.
Marseilles. "Account of the docks and warehouses at Marseilles." By T. Hawthorn, xxiv. 144.—Old port of Marseilles, 144.—Docks of La Joliette and Napoleon, 145.—Concessions made by Imperial decree to the town of Marseilles, 145.—Reconcession to the dock company, 146.—Materials for construction of moles, 146.—Construction of the breakwater forming the Joliette, Lazaret, Arenc, and Napoleon docks, 147.—Arrangement of classes of natural stone, 147.—Formation of

the artificial blocks of concrete, 147.—Plant used in their manufacture, 148.—Construction of the quay-walls of the docks Lazaret, Arenc, and Napoleon, 148.—Cranes erected on wooden platforms on the quays, 149.—Slipping of the quays of the Mole du Lazaret, 149.—Warehouses surrounding the dock du Lazaret, 149.—Flooring for ditto, 150.—Tunnels for the conveyance of hydraulic and other pipes, 150, 155.—Sheds and buildings on the quay south of the dock d'Arenc, 150.—The bonded warehouses, 150, et seq.—Method of constructing ditto, 152.—Cost of masonry of ditto, 152.—Wrought-iron girders, 153.—Tabular statement of the weight and the cost of the wrought and cast iron used in the floors and columns, 153.—Contract price of the ironwork, 153.—Strength of the floors, 154.—Wrought-iron roofing, 154.—Weight and cost of Λ section of iron for roofing and floor rafters, 154.—Vaulting, 155.—Water-tanks, 155.—Door-locks, 155.—Courts of the warehouses to be covered over with wrought iron and glass, 155.—Graving docks, 156.—Dimensions and cost of ditto, 156.—Pumping engines, 156.—Iron gates, 157.—Floating dry dock, 157.—Faulty construction of ditto, 157.—New graving docks in course of construction, 158.—Hydraulic machines in actual use, 158.—Ditto in course of construction, or about to be ordered, 159.—Prices of machines in use, 159.—General arrangements of the hydraulic engines, 159.—Experiments on the hydraulic machinery of the docks, 159.—Determination of the effective quantity of water given out by the force-pumps, 159.—Principal dimensions of the engines, force-pumps, and accumulators, 160.—The pumps, 160.—Tabular comparison of work given out by engine, pumps, and accumulators, 161.—Hydraulic hoists, 162.—Principal dimensions of ditto, 162.—Comparison of indicated horse-power of engine

DOCKS.

water used, and load lifted by hoists, 163.
—Results of experiments made with
one hydraulic hoist, commencing with
the cradle empty, and then increasing
the load gradually, until in equilibrium,
164.—Indicator for ascertaining the
mean pressure on the ram during its
stroke, 165.—Effective work done by
the hoist, 165.—Results from experiments made with a three-cylinder
direct-acting rotary engine, 166.—Expenditure, 166. — The 'Portefaix' of
Marseilles, 166.

Discussion. — Fowler, J., 168, 182.—
Giles, A., 175. — Grant, J., 182. —
Hawkshaw, J., 168, 170.—Hemans, G.
W., 180. — Hendry, W. T., 181.—
Parkes, W., 169.—Jennings, J., 183.
—Murray, J., 171.—Murton, F., 169.
—Reilly, C., 170.—Rennie, Sir J., 176.
—Redman, J. B., 178. — Vignoles, C.
B., 168, 170.—White, L., 169.

Silloth, xxi. 325. *Vide* also PORTS.
Swansea, xxi. 311. *Vide* also PORTS.

DOCKS, GRAVING.

Hydraulic lift. "The hydraulic lift
graving dock." By E. Clark, xxv. 2 2.
—History of the invention, 292.—Mr.
Stephenson's plan carried out at the
London docks, 292.—Failure of ditto,
293. — Plan for lifting vessels by
hydraulic machinery, 293.—Advantages of ditto, 293.—History of the
graving dock, 293.—Dry docks, 294.
—Dimensions of a large dry dock at
Portsmouth, 294.—Materials used in
the construction of ditto, 295.—Inclined planes or slips, 295.—Objections to ordinary graving docks, 295.
—Floating dock at Marseilles, 296.—
Floating docks of timber in America,
296.—Ditto at Portsmouth and Pensacola, 296.—Dimensions of the dock at
Pensacola, 297. — Floating sectional
docks, 297.—Ditto at Philadelphia,
297.—Limitations to the use of floating docks, 297.—Instances of accidents
to ditto, 298.—The Thames Graving
Dock Company, 298.—Description of
the docks, 298.—The hydraulic lift,
~~~ —Arrangement of the presses and

DORNING.

girders, 299.—Grouping of the presses,
300.—Connection of ditto, 300.—Provisions against accidents from the
bursting of ditto, 300.—Force-pumps,
301. — Pontoons not essential for
raising a single vessel, 301.—Arrangement of pontoons adopted, 301.—
Details of ditto, 302.—Cost of the lift
and other machinery, 303.—Number
of vessels lifted, 303.—Power of the
presses, 303.—Advantages and durability of the pontoon, 303.—Facilities
for blocking vessels, 303.—Strains to
which vessels are liable in stone docks,
304.—Method of docking a vessel in
the Thames graving docks, 305.—
Stiffness of a pontoon, 305.—Stability
of ditto, 306.—Accident resulting from
a storm, 306.—Practicability of en-
larging the system, 306.—No advantage to be gained from the substitution of the pontoon as a partial lifting
power, 307.—Docking large vessels
without horizontal shoring, 307.—
Numerous modifications of the pontoon
suggested, 307.—Financial results of
the undertaking, 308.—Summary of
the principal features of the system,
308.—Other advantages that may be
anticipated, 309.

Discussion. — Abernethy, J., 310, 319,
340, 352.—Bidder, G. P., 341.—Bram-
well, F. J., 313.—Capper, C., 310.—
Clark, E., 310, 312, 347, 352.—Fox,
Sir C., 312.—Giles, A., 311, 325, 344.
—Hawkshaw, J., 337.—Hedger, P.,
311.—Heppel, J., 327.—Kinipple, W.
R., 323, 341. — Murray, J., 332.—
Phipps, G. H., 340.—Redman, J. B.,
330.—Rendel, A. M., 324. — Rennie,
G. B., 333.—Russell, J. S., 311, 345.—
Scamp, W., 334.—Sheilds, F. W., 338.
—Vignoles, C. B., 322.

Vide also DOCKS.

DOERING, F. B.

Surveying and levelling instruments,
xxiv. 104.—Level suspended from a
gimbal joint, 104.

DONALDSON, T. O. [Election, xxiii. 110.]
DONALDSON, W. [Election, xxvi. 398.]
DORNING, E. [Election, xxiv. 62.]

DOUGLASS.

DOUGLASS, J. N.
Lighthouses. Height of waves at the Bishop rock, xxiii. 29.—Excellence of the optical apparatus of the Gibraltar lighthouse, xxvi. 527.—Illuminating apparatus of the South Foreland lights, 527.—Comparative powers of a fixed dioptric light and a revolving dioptric light of the same order, 528.—Lighthouse lanterns, 528.—Electric light as a source of illumination for lighthouses, xxviii. 37.—Petroleum and colza-oil as a source of illumination, 38.—Framing of lighthouse lanterns, and the armature of the optical apparatus, 38.—Cost of Trinity House lanterns, 41.

——— "The Wolf Rock lighthouse," xxx. 1.—Remarks, 26.—Foundation of ditto, and of the Longships lighthouse, 26. —Dovetailing, 26.—Second beacon erected on the Wolf rock, 26.—Daboll's fog-signals and Holmes steam-trumpet, 27.—Cost of various lighthouses in Scotland and in England, 27.
Railway inclines. Rowe's break as used at the Botallack copper-mine, xxx. 76.
DOUGLASS, W. [Election, xxvii. 320.]
DOULL, A.
Railways. Suggested atmospheric motive power for working steep gradients, xxvi. 367.
DOWNES, C. C. [Election, xxv. 263.]
DOYNE, W. T.
Public works in Ceylon, xxii. 63.—Wood of palms and of bamboo, 64.
DRAINAGE OF LAND.
" On the discharge from under-drainage, and its effect on the arterial channels and outfalls of the country." By J. B. Denton, xxi. 48.—Experiments at Hinxworth to determine the relation between the fall of rain and the discharge from under-drainage, 48.—Lands requiring drainage divided into ' surcharged free soils' and ' absorbent retentive soils,' 49.—System of drainage required for each class of soil, 49.—Extent of lands that may be profitably drained in Great Britain, 50.—Description and analyses

DRAINAGE OF LAND.

of the soil on the Hinxworth estate, 50.—Reference to the tables of experiments, 51.—Description of the drains, 51.—Two systems of drainage on an estate near Rugby, 52.—Discharge from under-drainage depends upon the wetness of the preceding seasons, 52.—Rainfall at Hinxworth, 53.—Subterranean water-level of the free soils, 53.—Effect of rains on a clay soil, 54.—Effect of under-draining the free soils, 54.—Absorbent and retentive powers of various clays, 54. —Test-holes, 55.—Quantity of rainfall discharged by the under-drains from the free soil, 55.—Table of monthly rainfall and discharge from the free and mixed soils, reduced to an average daily quantity per acre, 56.—Effect of under-draining the clay-soils, 57.—Quantity of water discharged annually by clays less than that by free soils, 57.—Table of monthly rainfall and discharge from the clays, reduced to an average daily quantity per acre, 58.—Drainage affected by cultivation and the contour of the land, 58.—Assertion that under-drainage increases the flow of perennial springs, 59.—Evaporation from drained and saturated soil compared with rainfall, 59.—Temperature of the soil increased by under-drainage, 60.—Effect of a fall of the barometer on drainage discharge, 60.—Evil of a shallow water-bed, 61.—Results of deep drainage in the Fens, 61.—Drainage operations will diminish evaporation, 61.—Amount of discharge by under-drainage when the soil is saturated calculated for extensive areas, 62.—The "Land Drainage Act, 1861," considered, 63.—Appendix, 65.—Records of water discharged from the Hinxworth drainage, 66.—Summary, 82.
Discussion.—Bidder, G. P., 83, 85, 107.—Brunlees, J., 119.—Chadwick, E., 93.—Clutterbuck, Rev. J.C., 84.—Denton, J. B., 83, 86, 121.—Evans, J., 90.—Field, R., 116.—Gibbs, J., 88, 97.—Grantham, R. B., 92.—Hawkshaw, J., 128.—

DRAINAGE OF TOWNS.

Hawksley, T., 99.—Hemans, G. W., 99.—Lloyd, J. H.,110.—Mallet, R., 114. —Rawlinson, R., 98.—Rennie, Sir J., 97.—Sidney, S., 95.—Simpson, J., 86.

Drainage effected by 'dumb' wells, xxii. 361.

—— in the Fen districts. *Vide* RIVER WITHAM.

—— in the Puttree Valley, xxviii. 85. *Vide* also RIVERS; and RIVERS, FRESH-WATER FLOODS OF.

DRAINAGE OF TOWNS.

"Description of the drainage of the borough of Dundee." By J. Fulton, xxii. 262.—Description of the borough, 262.—Sanitary condition very defective previous to 1851, 262.—Borough under the General Police Act for Scotland in 1851, but sewerage not commenced till 1856, 262.—Cost of works, 262.—Physical features of the town of Dundee, 262.—Account of sewers that existed previous to the commencement of the works, 263.—Sewage discharged at once into deep water, 264.—Proposal to convey the sewage through a cast-iron pipe for irrigating the Barry Sands, 264.—Materials, dimensions, and depth of sewers, 264.—Difficulties met with in excavation, 265.—Gas and water-pipes a source of annoyance and expense, 265.—Deposits of sand prevented by making the intercepting sewers at a greater depth than the lateral sewers, 266.—Manholes, 266.—Junctions for the house-drains and gullies, 266.—Invert blocks, 267.—Gully drains, 267. —Contrivance to prevent the escape of gases, 267.—Branch drains and traps, 267.—Water supply extended, 268.—Sewers rendered self-cleansing by flushing gates, 268.—Description of the process of cleansing the sewers by scrapers, 270.—Cost of cleansing sewers, 270.—Branch drains to underground cellars near the level of high tide, provided with self-acting flap-valves, 270.—No means of ventilation provided, 271.—Proportion of brick sewers to tubular sewers, 272.—Stone

DRAINAGE OF TOWNS.

sewers originally contemplated, 272.—Effect of the drainage on the public health, 272.

"Description of the sewerage and drainage works of Newport, Monmouthshire." By A. Williams, xxii. 273.—Physical and geological features of the locality, 273.—Public works, and rise and fall of the tide, 273.—Waterworks, 273.—Drainage before the construction of the sewers, 274.—Plan of sewerage and drainage carried out, 274.—Arrangement for flushing the lower part of the sewers, 275.—General plan of sewers, 275.—Great rise of the tide neutralizes the ill-effects that might be expected from the numerous outlets into the river, 275.—Description of the outlets and outlet-valves, 276.—Objections to the use of pipe sewers and the comparative cost of brick sewers and pipe sewers, 276.—Table showing the sizes, thickness, and cost of the Newport sewers, 278.—Details of the brickwork, 278.—Difficulties attending the execution of the works from the character of the subsoils, the interference of buildings, and accidental causes, 279.—Ventilators combined with manholes, 280.—Junction-pipes for house drainage, 281.—Gully grates and cess for street drainage, 282.—Cost of the works, 282.—Subsequent works, 282. —Repairs of old sewers, 283.—Improved sanitary condition of Newport, 283.

Discussion.—Bassett, A., 284.—Curtis, J. G. C., 300.—Fulton, J., 284.—Grant, J., 299.—Hawkshaw, J., 304.—Lovegrove, J., 301.—Merry, W., 297.—Newton, J., 295.—Rawlinson, R., 285, 298.—Thorburn, T. C., 284.—Williams, A., 303.

"An account of the drainage of Paris." By H. B. Hederstedt, xxiv. 257.—River Seine made the receptacle of all the sewage, 257.—Brook of Menilmontant, 257.—Principal drains executed between 1808 and 1832, 258.—Survey completed in 1832, 259.—System of drainage subsequently

DRAINAGE OF TOWNS.
carried out, 259.—The five principal divisions of the several drains 259.—Floods of the Seine, 260.—Total length of drains executed at various dates, to 1837, 260.—Position, cost, and special object of the construction of the several drains, 261.—Conversion of the concave surfaces of roads into convex, 262.—Difference between the old and new sewers. 263, 264.—Statement of works executed subsequently to 1855, 263.—Sewers in operation up to the end of 1863, 264.—Old method of cleansing the sewers, 264.—Provision for the discharge of household water and of rain-water, 264.—Nightsoil not admitted to the drains, 265.—Present method of cleansing the drains, 265, et seq.—Cleansing boats, 266.—Truck scrapers, 267.—Travelling circular rake, 268.—Wagons for removing the mud, 268.—Safety chambers for the workmen, 268.—Rise of water at the outfalls during floods, 269.—Section of drains, 269.—Absence of small pipes, 269.—Acts as to the construction of the drains, 269.—Paris waterworks, 270.—Branch drains, 270.—Project for discharging the sewage, of both sides of the city, at Asnières, 270.—Seine cleared of sewage-matter by dredging, 271.—Cost of maintenance, 271.—Nomenclature of the drains similar to that of the streets above, 271.—Entrances to the drains, 271.—Places of rendezvous and store chambers, 271, 272.—Arrangements for discharging the mud into barges in the Seine, 271.—Gas pipes, water pipes, and telegraph lines inclosed in the drains, 273.—Building of the drains, and materials used, 273 274.—Concrete or béton Coignet recently introduced, 274.—Tabular form for recording principal features of each drain or series, 276.—Detailed cost per lineal mètre of drains of different sections in sandstone, rubble masonry, set in cement mortar, 277.—Prices of some of the materials employed in the construction of the drains, 278.—Epitome of

DRAINAGE OF TOWNS.
comparison between the systems of drainage of London and of Paris, 279. " On the main-drainage of London, and the interception of the sewage from the river Thames." By J. W. Bazalgette, xxiv. 280.—Early history of sewerage of London, 281.—The sewers under the management of eight Commissions, 283.—These superseded by 'The Metropolitan Commission of Sewers,' 283.—Various similar commissions, for which ' The Metropolitan Board of Works' was substituted, 284.—Plan prepared under the authority of that board for the main-drainage of London, 286.—The position of the outfalls and the time of discharge, 288.—The velocity of flow and the minimum fall, 289.—Quantity of sewage to be intercepted, 290. — How to dispose of the rainfall, 291.—The sizes of the intercepting sewers, 293. — Description of pumping engines and pumps, 293.—Discharge by gravitation, 294.—The form of the sewers, 294.—Description of the works on the north side of the Thames, 295.— The high-level sewer, 295.—The penstock chamber, 296.—The middle level sewer, 297.—The low-level sewer, 298.—The western division, 298.—The northern outfall sewer, 299.—The Barking reservoir, 302.— The Abbey Mills pumping station, 303.—South side of the Thames, 304.— —The high-level sewer, 304.—The low-level sewer, 306.—The Deptford pumping station, 307.—The southern outfall sewer, 308.—The Crossness reservoir and pumping station, 308.— Tunnels completed, 311.—Method adopted for pumping out the water, 312.—Materials used in the works, 313.—Summary of cost of the works, and of the quantities of materials and of sewage, 314.
Discussion.—Aird, J. Jun., 344.—Bateman, J. F., 340.—Bazalgette, J. W., 315, 352.—Belcher, Admiral Sir E., 321.—Bidder, G. P., 346.—Bramwell, F. J., 326.—Burnell, G. R., 316.—

DREDGING MACHINES.

Chadwick, E., 331.—Grant, J., 341.—Hawkshaw, J., 329.—Haywood, W., 321.—Hemans, G. W., 340, 350.—Lemon, J., 350.—M'Clean, J. R., 358.—Phipps. G. H., 339.—Rawlinson, R., 317.—Vignoles, C. B., 346.

Appendix to discussion, 513.—I. Report from Committee of Metropolitan Commission of Sewers, on plans for drainage of London, 513.—II. Report of Mr. Frank Forster, on the Surrey and Kent drainage, 518.—III. Ditto, on drainage of districts north of the Thames, 521.

Dredging machines, xxvi. 445, 449, *et seq.* *Vide* also CANALS, Suez.

DREW, E. A.

Railway inclines, xxvi. 382.—Temporary steep incline on the Ottoman railway, 382.—Dimensions of the engine used for working ditto, 382.

Drilling rivet-holes, xxii. 530, 534; xxx. 265, 267.

DRUCE, E. R. N. [Election, xxv. 352.]

Cement, Portland, xxv. 113.—Use of, in salt-water, 113.—Testing, 113, 114.—Effect produced by currents, 114.—Strength of, mixed with various

DYNAMITE.

proportions of sand, 148.—Power of Portland cement concrete to resist abrasion, 148.—Superiority of Portland cement of high specific gravity, 149.—Economy in using ditto, 150.

DRYSDALE, C. R. [Resignation, xxi. 148.]

DUCAT, W. M., Captain, R.E. [Election, xxviii. 59.]

DUER, S. [Election, xxi. 48.]

DUNCAN, T. [Memoir, xxx. 431.]

DUNDONALD, Earl of.

Foundations. excavating, under air-pressure (Hawkshaw, J.), xxi. 184.

DUNLOP, W. [Election, xxi. 345; Decease, xxiii. 121.]

DUNN, T. E. [Election, xxii. 241.]

DUNNING, J. [Election, xxv. 65.]

Duplicate machines and engines, on the manufacture of (Fernie, J.), xxii. 604. *Vide* also MACHINES AND ENGINES.

DU PORT, W. J. [Election, xxx. 323.]

DUTTON, F. S. [Election, xxv. 262.]

Railways in Australia, xxix. 353.—Indirect advantages of ditto, 353.—South Australian railways, 354.

DYKE, T. [Election, xxviii. 216.]

Dynamite, superior to powder for blasting operations, xxviii. 142.

E.

EACHUS.

EACHUS, G. E. [Election, xxvi. 79.]

EADS, J. B. [Election, xxviii. 517.]

East coast between the Thames and the Wash estuaries (Redman, J. B.), xxiii. 186. *Vide* also COASTS.

EAST, F. [Election, xxv. 64.]

EASTMAN, T. [Election, xxvii. 55.]

EASTON, J., jun. [Election, xxv. 429.]

EASTON, J. M. [Election, xxvii. 55.]

EBORALL, C. W. [Election, xxv. 65.]

Railway stations, xxv. 277.—Importance of repairing sheds for rolling-stock other than those at the principal works, 277.—Arrangements at the Victoria station, Pimlico, 277.

Railway telegraphs, xxii. 210.—Efficiency and safety of the 'block' system of train-signalling in use on the South Eastern railway, 210.—'Block' system between Wokingham and Reading, 212.

ECKERSLEY, W.

Piles of the viaduct of the Lynn and Sutton Bridge railway at the Eau Brink Cut, xxvii. 317.—Cost, 317.—Constructing piers of screw-piles in clusters, 318.—Driving and screwing piles at the Solway viaduct, 318.—Cost, 318.—Efficient plan of screwing down piles in stiff material at bridges on the Bath and Mangotsfield line of railway over the river Avon, 318.

Tunnels. Mont Cenis, xxiii. 299.—Cost of rock tunnels, 299.—Large number of men employed on the Mont Cenis tunnel, 300.—Superiority of Mr. Bartlett's to M. Sommeiller's perforator, 300.

EDDOWES, E. N. [Admission, xxvii. 54.]

EDGCOME, W. H., Captain, R.E. [Election, xxv. 203.]

EDGEWORTH, D. R. [Election, xxvii. 218.]

EDMISTON, R. [Admission, xxvii. 218.]

ELLIOT.

EDWARDS, G.

Railways, construction of, in Alpine districts, xxvi. 395.—Application of water-power to the traction of trains, 395.—Dangers arising from falls of rock and snow-drift, 395.—Covered ways for railways crossing Alpine passes, 396.

EDWARDS, G. H. [Election, xxiv. 62; Resignation, xxix. 217.]

EDWARDS, G. S. [Admission, xxvii. 120.]

EDWARDS, H. H. [Memoir, xxii. 625.]

EDWARDS, J. H. [Election, xxvii. 55.]

EDWARDS, O. C. [Election, xxiv. 358.]

EGERTON, Hon. A. de T. [Admission, xxvii. 54.]

Electric telegraph, xxi. 178; xxii. 239. *Vide* also RAILWAY ACCIDENTS; RAILWAY TELEGRAPHS; RAILWAY TRAINS, communication in; TELEGRAPH CABLES; and TELEGRAPHIC COMMUNICATION.

ELLACOTT, J. [Election, xxv. 429; Telford medal and premium, xxix. 211.]

Low-water basin. "Description of the low-water basin at Birkenhead," xxviii. 518.

ELLICOMBE, R. R. [Resignation, xxi. 148.]

ELLIOT, Vice-Admiral G. [Election, xxvi. 242.]

Ships of war, xxvi. 202.—Qualifications for a line-of-battle ship, 202; for a frigate, 203; for a corvette, 204.—Increasing the accommodation of monitors, 205.—Turret vessels, 205.—Thickness of armour-plating, 205.—Proposition for an improved monitor by the Chief Constructor to the Admiralty, 206.—Principle of hydraulic propulsion, 206.—Shale oil as a heating agent, 206.—Armour-plated gunboats, 206.—Superiority of turret to broadside ships, 207.—Success of

ELLIOT.

hydraulic motive power exemplified in the ' Waterwitch ' gunboat, 207.

ELLIOT, L. [Decease, xxiv. 217.]

ELLIOT, R. [Election, xxv. 203.]

ELLIOT, W. [Election, xxiii. 110.]

ELLIS, H. S. [Election, xxvii. 580.]

ELLIS, T. C. [Admission, xxvii. 54.]

ELLIS, T. J. [Admission, xxvii. 54; Election, xxix. 98; Miller prize, 213.]

ELLIS, W. I. [Election, xxv. 429.]

Locomotive engines, xxvi. 372.—Adhesion of heavy engines on the Vale of Neath railway, 372.—Tank engines, 373.—Passage of locomotive engines and carriages round curves, 375.

ELSDON, W. [Election, xxx. 106.]

Engineer and Railway Volunteer Staff Corps, xxvii. 201.

Engineering philosophy, on : the durability of materials (Clark, E.), xxvii. 554. *Vide* also MATERIALS.

Engines. *Vide* MACHINES AND ENGINES; LOCOMOTIVE ENGINES ; and STEAM ENGINES.

ENGLAND, G.

Railway, Festiniog, xxiv. 389.—Power of locomotives employed, 389.

ENGLAND, J. [Telford premium, xxv. 164, 180.]

EYKYN.

Injector. " Giffard's injector," xxiv 198.—Remarks, 234.

ERRINGTON, J. E. [Vice-President, xxi. 133 ; Memoir, xxii. 1, 626.]

Estuaries. *Vide* RIVERS AND ESTUARIES.

EVANS, J.

Drainage of land, xxi. 90.—Discharge from under-drainage, 90.—Discharge dependent on the heaviness of the rainfall, 91.—Effect of vegetation in modifying the discharge from under-drainage, 92.

EVANS, J. [Decease, xxii. 123.]

EVANS, J. [Election, xxv. 203.]

Evaporation, xxi. 53, *et seq.*—In the West of England, 105.—Spontaneous, xxii. 364.— In tropical climates, xxvi. 471, 472.

EVERARD, J. B. [Admission, xxvii. 54 ; Election, xxx. 215.]

Excavating under water, description of apparatus for, and for sinking cylinders (Milroy, J.), xxviii. 339. *Vide* also FOUNDATIONS.

Exhibition Building of 1851, testing the girders of the, xxvii. 113.

Explosions in coal-mines. *Vide* COAL-MINING.

EYKYN, J. H. [Admission, xxx. 106.]

F.

FABER.

FABER, Captain C. W. [Election, xxvii. 55.]

FABER, W. C. [Election, xxvii. 180.]

FAIRBAIRN, Sir W.
Iron, comparative value of hot and cold blast, xxx. 321.
Ships of war, xxi. 223.—Strength of iron vessels increased by adopting a cellular system of construction, 223.—Quality of iron for armour-plates, 224.—Mode of fastening armour-plates to the sides of vessels, 224.
Stoves, regenerative hot-blast, xxx. 321.
Viaducts. "On the reconstruction of the Dinting and the Mottram viaducts," xxii. 327.—Remarks, 334.—Works carried on without interruption to the traffic, 334.

FAIRLIE, R. F.
Locomotive engines, xxvi. 367.—Specification of a locomotive engine designed by him, 367.—Double-boiler duplex bogie engine, 367.—Single-boiler duplex-bogie engine, 368.—Performance of engines employed on the Mont Cenis railway and the Copiapo Extension railway, 369.

FAITHFULL, G. E. [Admission, xxviii. 2.]

FALKINER, T. H. [Election, xxiii. 151.]

FANS, ROTARY.
"On the conditions and the limits which govern the proportions of rotary fans." By R. Briggs, xxx. 276.—Writers on the subject, 276.—Ditto on the theory and practice of the turbine water-wheel and the centrifugal pump, 276.—Description and primary function of a rotary fan, 277.—Péclet's reasoning on the theory of fans, 278.—Pressure attainable by rotary fans, 278.—Series of fans, 279.—Action of the rotary fan at work, 279.—Problem of moving a certain quantity of air in a fixed time under some definite resistance, 279.—Effect of the shape of the

FANS.

blades, 280, 283.—Direction of the currents of air, 280.—Opinions of Combes and Rittinger on the condition and forces in a fan, 281.—Proportions and proper number of blades, 282.—Comparison between the flow of water through a pipe and the movement of air in a fan, 282.—Friction of the air a bar to the excess of number of blades, 284.—Practical effects of the adhesion of the air, 284.—Best shape for the blades, 284.—Proportionate number of blades required for a fan having radial blades and blades at an angle of 45°, 284.—Measurement of the real efficiency, 285.—Relative dimensions of sections of fans with different numbers of blades, where the diameter of fans is 10 feet, 285.—Highest velocity of emergence from the periphery of a fan with logarithmic spiral blades of 45°, 286.—Relationship the quantities of air discharged bear to the increased resistances, 286.—Results involved in the assumption that half the quantity of air will be delivered under double the pressure, 287.—Limits of fans of proper proportions brought to definite conclusions, 287.—Caution required in using appliances to remove air from a fan, 287.—General dimensions of a fan 10 feet in diameter, 289, et seq.—Sides used for fans of less diameter than 8 feet, 292.—Construction of fan used at the United States Capitol extension, 292.—Table I. Results of a fan 10 feet in diameter, having an absolute area of discharge of 62·8 square feet, and an effective area of discharge of 50 square feet, 293.—Table II. Ditto, when discharging under double the pressure, 293.—Dimensions of pulleys, 293.—Table III. Fans to be used in ventilation of buildings or mines, 295.—Table IV. Fans to be used for

FARADAY.

supply of air under grates of puddling
or heating furnaces, 296.—Table V.
Fans to be used for supply of air to
tuyeres, as cupolas, smiths' forges,
hollow furnaces, &c., 296.
Discussion.—Bramwell, F. J., 303.—
Briggs, R., 297, 306.—Cowper, E. A.,
297.—Fox, Sir C., 305.—Greenwell,
G. C., 304.—Hawksley, T., 302, 304.
—Unwin, W. C., 305.—Vignoles, C. B.,
308.
FARADAY, Dr. M. [Memoir, xxvii. 582.]
FAREY, B. W. [Election, xxiv. 257.]
FARFAN, J. M. [Election, xxii. 336.]
FARMER, J. S. [Election, xxviii. 59.]
FARRAR, J. [Election, xxviii. 518.]
FARRELL, J. B. [Election, xxx. 323.]
FARREN, G. [Election, xxvii. 180.]
Materials, durability of, xxvii. 567.—
Chemical action on, 567.—Action of
nitric acid on iron, 567.
FAVIELL, W. F. [Election, xxvii. 218.]
FELL, J. B. [Election, xxii. 336.]
Railways. Mont Cenis, xxiii. 313.—
Probable period of construction of the
Mont Cenis tunnel, 313.—Actual
quantity of work done at Bardonnêche,
314.—Actual and estimated cost of
the Mont Cenis tunnel, 315.—Project
of a locomotive railway over the Mont
Cenis pass, 315.—Engines for ditto, 315.
—Whether the proposed railway would
commercially pay, 316.—Respective
heights and lengths of the Mont
Cenis pass and tunnel, 316.—Route
by the pass, 317.—Locomotive en-
gines for working the Mont Cenis
railway, xxvi. 326.—Break system for
ditto, 328.—Modes of dispensing with
the central rail at level crossings, 329.
—Greater economy of the Mont Cenis
summit railway, with the central rail,
compared with the tunnel line, xxviii.
279.
FENNER, H. A. S. [Election, xxvii. 443.]
Fens, drainage of the. Vide RIVER
WITHAM.
FENTON, J. [Memoir, xxiii. 487.]
FENTON, M. [Election, xxv. 203.]
FENWICK, C. R. [Admission, xxvii. 54.]
FENWICK, T. [Election, xxvi. 242.]

FITZROY.

FERNIE, J. [Election, xxii. 65; Watt
medal and Manby premium, xxiii. 115,
127.]
Machines. "On the manufacture of
duplicate machines and engines,"
xxii. 604.—Remarks, 612.—System
founded on the application of Mr.
Whitworth's true plane, 612.—System
of working from known gauges, 613.
FERRAR, W. G. [Election, xxvi. 544.]
FERREIRA, J. N. [Election, xxvii. 553.]
FIELD, A. [Election, xxix. 98.]
FIELD, J. [Past-President, xxi. 172; xxii.
166; Memoir, xxiii. 121, 488.]
Bust of, by Weekes, xxvi. 126.
Waterworks at Thames Ditton and Kingston, extracts from his reports as to the
performance of the pumping-engines
at the (Simpson, J.), xxiii. 70.
FIELD, R. [Election, xxv. 203.]
Drainage of land, xxi. 116.—Evaporation
from constantly saturated free soils,
116.—Heavy rain produces greater
floods from clay soils than from the
chalk formation, 117.—Occasional
drainage of free soils equalises the
discharge of the rainfall, and renders
the flow of rivers more regular, 118.
FIELD, S. [Election, xxiii. 320.]
FILLITER, E. [Election, xxii. 241.]
FINCH, F. G. [Election, xxv. 479.]
FINDLAY, G.
Railway stations, xxv. 283.—Small workshops for the repair of rolling stock
necessary at metropolitan and other
large railway stations, 283.—Arrangement of passenger stations, 283.—
Relative length of station platforms,
283.—Height of platforms adopted on
the London and North Western
railway, 283.—Goods accommodation
at Willesden, 284.—Goods shed and
traffic at Camden, 284.
FISHE, C. C. [Election, xxviii. 517.]
FISHER, A. F. J. [Election, xxvii. 218.]
FISHER, G. [Election, xxviii. 517.]
FISHER, H. A. [Election, xxviii. 59.]
FITZGIBBON, A. C. [Election, xxv. 203.]
FITZROY, Admiral R.
Ships of war, xxi. 219.—Solid and
compounded armour-plates, 219.—

FLACHAT.

Cellular system of construction of iron vessels, 220.—Effect of shot on solid and cellular plating, 221.—Fittings of iron vessels, 222.—Defects of the 'Warrior,' 223.

FLACHAT, E. [Resignation, xxiv. 117.]

FLETCHER, E. [Telford premium, xxv. 164, 180.]
Railway rolling stock. "On the maintenance of railway rolling stock," xxiv. 459.

FLETCHER, H. A. [Memoir, xxi. 585.]

FLETCHER, H. A. [Election, xxiv. 184.]

FLOOD, C. [Admission, xxvii. 54; Election, xxix. 98.]

Floods, on the relation of the freshwater, of rivers to the areas and physical features of their basins; and on a method of classifying rivers and streams, with reference to the magnitude of their floods; proposed as a means of facilitating the investigation of the laws of drainage (O'Connell, Colonel P. P. L.), xxvii. 204.—In the Nerbudda valley, with remarks on monsoon floods in India generally (Howden, A. C.), 218. Vide also RIVERS, FRESHWATER FLOODS OF.

Floods, storm, account of the greatest, on the coast of Denmark, xxi. 449.

Flow of water off the ground, on the results of a series of observations on the, in the Woodburn district, near Carrickfergus, Ireland; with rain-gauge registries in the same locality, for a period of twelve months, ending 30th June, 1865 (Manning, R.), xxv. 458. Vide also WATER, FLOW OF.

FODEN, E. A. [Election, xxiii. 257.]

FOGERTY, J. [Election, xxii. 451.]
Bridge over the river Severn on the Coalbrookdale railway, xxvii. 112.—Cost, 112.—Castings of the ironwork, 112.

FOGG, R. [Election, xxiii. 110.]

Fog-horns, xxviii. 42; xxx. 19.

FOLKARD, A. [Election, xxiv. 458.]

FOOTNER, H. [Election, xxvi. 477.]

FORBES, D.
Furnaces, quantity of fuel used in, xxvi. 47.

FOSTER.

Iron and steel, manufacture of, xxvii. 356.—Bessemer steel, 356.
Permanent way. Homogeneous rails xxvii. 356.

FORBES, J. [Decease, xxvi. 129.]

FORBES, J. S. [Election, xxiv. 257.]
Railway stations, xxv. 278.—Office and platform arrangements at the Victoria station, Pimlico, 278.—Ditto at stations of the London, Chatham, and Dover railway, 278.—Working trains in and out of terminal stations, 279.—Height of platforms, 279.

FORBES, J. S. [Election, xxx. 323.]

FORCHAMMER, Professor.
Marshes in Holstein and Schleswig, formation of, xxi. 483.—Cause of the subsidence of 'unripe' peat-moss, 484.

FORDE, A. W. [Election, xxi. 257.]

FORDE, H. C. [Council premium, xxii· 120, 130.]
Telegraph cables. "The Malta and Alexandria submarine telegraph cable," xxi. 493.—Remarks, 537.—Improvements in telegraphic instruments, 537.—Outer coverings of the Malta and Alexandria and of the Sardinia and Cape Bona telegraph cables, 537.

FORESTIER, —.
Timber, experiments on the relative resistance to crushing weight, and the relative elasticity, of creosoted and uncreosoted (Bethell, H. S.), xxvii. 294.

FORLONG, Major J. G. R. [Election, xxvii. 180.]

FORMAN, J. R. [Election, xxv. 479.]

FORREST, J. [Secretary. xxi. 172; xxii. 166; xxiii. 150; xxiv. 143; xxv. 202; xxvi. 164; xxvii. 179; xxviii. 215; xxix. 271.]

FORREST, W. J. [Election, xxviii. 325.]

FORSTER, F.
Drainage of towns. Report of, on the Surrey and Kent drainage (Hawkshaw, J.), xxiv. 518.—Ditto, on drainage of districts north of the Thames, 521.

FORSTER, G. B. [Election, xxvi. 544.]

FOSTER, W. [Admission, xxvii. 54.]

FOUNDATIONS.

FOUNDATIONS.

Iron cylinders for, xxi. 183.— Mode of sinking ditto by air-pressure, 183. —Patent of the Earl of Dundonald for a similar object, 184. — Four methods of sinking iron cylinders for bridge foundations, 265.—Dr. Potts' system of sinking cylinders by the pneumatic method, 265.—Fascines used for the foundations of the suspension bridge at Kieff, in Russia, 479. — Objections to the several methods of founding works in deep water as at present practised, xxii. 417.—Quay-walls built on piling carried up to the level of low-water have given way at Glasgow, from the decay of the piles, 418.—Great expense and frequent danger in the construction of cofferdams, 418.—System of building by diving-bells very costly, 418.— Vicat's system of founding piers of bridges without cofferdams, 418.— Modification of ditto in the construction of the Westminster and Chelsea bridges, 419.—Concrete encased by wrought-iron cylinders, xxiii. 31.— Method of laying Portland cement concrete at the bottom of the cylinders of the Rochester bridge, xxv. 128.

"On sinking wells for the foundations of the piers of the bridge over the river Jumna, Delhi railway." By I. Bell, xxviii. 325 —Alteration in the apparatus for sinking brick-cylinder foundations, 325.—Original plan of sinking wells for foundations on the banks of rivers, in India, where the soil is sandy, 325.—Method of using the 'jham' adopted in the construction of the railway bridge over the Jumna at Allahabad, 326.—Difficulties experienced in piercing strata of clay, 327.—Number and distribution of wells in the piers, 327.— Average rate of well-sinking, 327.— Rate of payment for ditto, 327.— Situation and features of the site of the bridge, on the Delhi railway, over the Jumna, 328.—Description of the bridge, 328.—Protective works for the

FOWLER.

conservation of the east bank of the river, 329.—Diversion of the river to get the sites of the piers clear of water, 329.—Fixing and sinking the curbs, 330.—Precautions required in well-sinking or cylinder-sinking, 331. —Lime used at the works, 332.— Analysis of calcareous clay, 332.— Preparation of the lime, 333.—The mortar, 333.—Rate of progress of the well-sinking and completing the foundations, 333.—Sand pump, 334.— Mode adopted for working ditto, 334. —Average rate of sinking with ditto, 335.—Superstructure of the bridge, 335.—Girders, 336.—Travellers, 336. —Completion and opening of the bridge, 336.—Various methods adopted for sinking cylinders in Great Britain, 337.—Alterations and adaptations of Mr. Kennard's sand-pump, 337.

"Description of apparatus for excavating under water, and for sinking cylinders." By J. Milroy, xxviii. 339.—Bridge of the Glasgow (City) Union railway across the Clyde at Glasgow, 339.—Determination to sink cylinders for the foundations to a solid stratum, 339.—Weighting the cylinders, 340.—Excavating apparatus, 340.—Mode of working ditto, 341.— Capabilities of ditto, 342.—Effect of the change of level of the tide on the rate of sinking the cylinders, 343.—Advantages of the excavating apparatus, 344.

Discussion.—Baldry, J. D., 356.— Bazalgette, J. W., 347.—Bell, I., 350. —Bramwell, F. J., 351.—Cowper, E. A., 348.—Kennard, H. J., 345.— Milroy, J., 357.—Milroy, J., jun., 349. —Phillips, J., 347.—Redman, J. B., 355.

Vide also BRIDGES; PILES; and STRUCTURES IN THE SEA.

FOWKE, F., Captain, R.E. [Election, xxii. 604; Memoir, xxx. 468.]

FOWLER, A. G. [Admission, xxviii. 216.]

FOWLER, A. M. [Election, xxviii. 232.]

FOWLER, F. [Election, xxv. 262.]

Rivers, freshwater floods of, xxvii. 262. —Valleys of Scinde and the Punjab,

FOWLER.

262.—Line of the Punjab railway, 262.—Rivers of the Punjab flow on self-raised beds, 262.—Floods in the flat country of the Punjab and Scinde caused by artificial embankments, 263.

FOWLER, G.

Coal-mining. "On the relative safety of different modes of working coal," xxx. 323.

FOWLER, J. [Vice-President, xxi. 133; xxii. 112; xxiii. 112; xxiv. 106; President, xxv. 161; xxvi. 119; Past President, xxvii. 179 ; xxviii. 215; xxix 271.]

Address, on taking the chair for the first time after his election as President, xxv. 203.—Activity in the engineering profession, 203.—Competition by foreign engineers, 204.—Former addresses, 204.—The future of the profession, 205.—The engineering problems of the present time, 205.—Definition of a Civil Engineer, 207.—Classification of the works intrusted to a Civil Engineer, 208.—Study of objects and their value, 208.—Choice of materials, 209.—Stone, 209.—Brick, 209.—Mortar and cement, 209.—Iron, 210.—Steel, 211.—Timber, 211.—Knowledge required by a Civil Engineer, 212.—Railway engineering, 213.—Dock and harbour engineering, 214.—Waterworks and drainage engineering, 215.—Mechanical engineering, 217.—Mining engineering, 218.—Artillery engineering, 218.—Preparation required by a Civil Engineer, 219.—The Institution, 223.—Attendance, 225.—Finance, 225.—Library, 226.—Additional facilities, 226.—Lectures, 227.—New building, 227.—Conclusion, 227.

Bridge over the Trent at Gainsborough, xxv. 261.—Launching the girders on rollers, 261.

—— suspension, at Clifton, height of the piers of, xxvi. 266.

Cements and mortars, comparisons of, xxv. 158.

Concrete blocks, xxiv. 168.—Passing concrete through deep water, xxv. 144.

FOX.

Docks, Great Grimsby, xxiv. 60.—Use of fresh water in ditto, 60.

Engineering works, economical construction of, xxix. 347.

Hydraulic machinery at the Marseilles docks, xxiv. 182.

Permanent way. Remaking Bessemer metal into rails, xxv. 379.—Maintenance and renewal of permanent way, 427.—Vignoles rail, 428.—Specifications and tests for iron rails, xxvii. 346.—Use of iron or steel rails, 347.—Relative durability of rails and sleepers, 348.—Best forms of rail, 348.—Combined iron and steel rails, 348.

Railway curves, xxiii. 399.—Junction of reverse curves on the Santiago and Valparaiso railway, 399.

Railway income and expenditure, xxix. 347.—Comparison of railway statistics, 347.—Cost of railway construction and working, 347.—Railway fares, 348.

Railway structures, Board of Trade rules for testing, xxv. 261.

Spurn Point, formation of an opening through, xxiv. 61.

Steel, compressive power of, xxvi. 297.

Telegraph cable, Macintosh's, xxv. 53.

Viaduct, Hownes Gill, spread of the piers of, xxii. 56.

Water, flow of, xxv. 479.

Fox, A. D. [Election, xxviii. 325.]

Fox, Sir C.

Bridges. Erection of the iron girders of the railway bridge over the river Saone at Lyons, xxv. 255.—Load on short girder bridges, 258.—Cast iron for bridges, xxvii. 113.—Southwark bridge, 113.—Why wrought iron should be used for the longitudinal girders of bridges, 114.—Permanent set of iron structures, 114.—Expansion joints of the Victoria bridge, Pimlico, 115.—Lateral instability of piers, 115.—Cast-iron cylinders for the piers of bridges, 115.—Strains on the Victoria bridge, Pimlico, 116.—Barnes and Richmond bridges, 116.—Cost of the railways and bridges at Battersea, 116.

F

FOX.

—Curved ends of the ribs of bridges, 119.

Bridges, suspension, xxx. 272.—Links and pins of chain bridges, 272.—Links of the Kieff bridge over the river Dnieper, 272.

Concrete, deposition of, in running water, xxv. 128.

Docks, graving, xxv. 312.—Lifting apparatus of the hydraulic lift graving dock, 312.—Commercial element of ditto compared with the old form of graving docks, 313.

Fans, best arrangement for, xxx. 305.

Foundations. Method of laying Portland cement concrete at the bottom of the cylinders of the Rochester bridge, xxv. 128.—Parallel and conical piles, xxvii. 299.—Piles in the foundations of London bridge, 299.—Effect of driving piles in a plastic material, 301.—Erection of structures on the alluvial soil of the Clyde valley at Renfrew, 301.—Sinking the cylinders of the railway bridge at Battersea, 301.—Plenum and vacuum methods of sinking cylinders, 301.—Foundations of Rochester bridge, 302. — Chepstow bridge, 302.—Increasing the area of the foundations below the bottom of the cylinders in the Blackfriars railway bridge, 302.—Truncated cones for the cylinder foundations of the South Eastern railway bridge across the Thames, 303.

Girders of the Exhibition Building of 1851, xxvii. 113.

Iron, strength of, xxviii. 418, 419 ; xxx. 272.

Iron structures, permanent set of, xxvii. 114.

Locomotives and rolling stock, xxviii. 415.—Load on the driving-wheels of locomotives, 416.—Rolling stock for light railways, 416, 418.—Wheels of American rolling stock, 417.—Close oil axle-boxes and grease-boxes, 417. —Most economical speed for running trains, 420.

Permanent way, xxv. 381.—Causes of lamination of iron rails, 381.—Supe-

FOX.

riority of rails made by the Bessemer process, 382.—Cause of the greater durability of steel rails as compared with iron rails, xxvii. 342.—Lamination of iron rails from defective welding, 343.—Wear of rails by locomotives, 343.

Pile-driving, xxvii. 298. — Effect of driving piles in a plastic material, 301.

Railway inclines, xxvi. 386.—Working of the Oldham incline of the Lancashire and Yorkshire railway, 386.

Railways, gauge of, xxiv. 369.—Gauge adopted by the Indian Tramway Company, 369.—Gauge of railways generally in India, 369.—Ditto in Queensland, 370.—Causes of failure of the atmospheric system of railway, xxvi. 386.—Pneumatic system of railway for traversing Alpine passes, 387.

Fox, C. D. [Election, xxv. 262; Manby premium, xxvii. 124, 142 ; Telford medal and premium, xxviii. 161, 178.]

Bridges. " On the widening of the Victoria bridge and approaches to the Victoria stations, and on new railways at Battersea," xxvii. 68.—Remarks, 82.—Testing the new Victoria bridge, 82.—Piers of ditto, 82.—Strains on the bridge of the high-level line over the South Western railway, 83.—Rolling into place the girders of the bridge over the low-level lines at Longhedge, 83.—Stability of the Victoria bridge, 84.

Railways. Report on Norwegian Government railways having a gauge of 3 feet 6 inches (Tyler, W. H.), xxiv. 365.

—— " On light railways in Norway, India, and Queensland," xxvi. 49.—Remarks, 61.—Application of Adams's radial axle system to the rolling stock of the Southern and Western railway of Queensland, 61.—Experiments with wheels loose on the axle, 61.—Cost of construction of railways, 62.—Construction of bridges and station buildings on the Queensland line, 62 —Gauge of railways, 63.—Mr. Fairlie's

FOX.

locomotive engine, 78.—Cost and probable returns of the Queensland railway, 78.

Fox, D. M.
Railway, São Paulo. " Description of the line and works of the São Paulo railway, in the Empire of Brazil," xxx. 29.

Fox, F. [Telford medal, xxi. 135, 152.]
Permanent way, statistics of the maintenance and renewal of, xxv. 392.—Relation between the life of a rail and the tonnage carried, 393.—Relative cost of steel and iron rails, 393.—Strength of bridge rails, 394.—Use of steel rails, 394.—Iron permanent way, 394.—Longitudinal system of permanent way, 395.

Fox, W. [Election, xxiv. 458.]
FRANCE, J. R. [Election, xxx. 106.]
FRANCIS, C. L.
Cements, xxv. 123.—Inutility of using Portland cement stronger than the material it has to unite, 123.

FRANCIS, W. [Election, xxvi. 242.]
FRÄNCKEL, E. [Election, xxiv. 62.]
FRANKLAND, Dr. E.
Water, filtration of, xxvii. 8.—Ingredients derived from the oxidation of organic matters in sewage, 8.—Permanganate test, 8.—Effect of animal charcoal on organic matter in water, 8.—Results obtained with animal charcoal as a filtering medium applied to the New River water, 8.—Vegetable charcoal inert in its action on organic matter in water, 9.—Purification of water by filtration through animal charcoal on a large scale, 9, et seq.—Two kinds of organic matter in water, 10.—Amount of organic carbon in New River water before and after filtration, 10.—Rate of filtration of water through a glass tube filled with charcoal, 18.

FRASER, Alexander.
Steam-engines, Cornish, xxiii. 107.—Objection to the use of Cornish pumping engines for the water supply of towns, 107.—Economy obtained in working a Cornish engine of large dimensions, 107.—Risk of accident

FULLER.

not greater with a Cornish engine than with a crank engine, 108.—Recent improvements in Cornish engines, 108.—Duty performed by Cornish engines at the Kew Bridge station of the Grand Junction Water Company, 108.—Method of preventing loss of pressure by wiredrawing, 109.—Space occupied to prevent the piston striking the top or bottom of the cylinder, 109.—Advantage presented in the single-acting Cornish engine, 109.—Cornish pumping engine well adapted for waterworks purposes, 110.

FRASER, Alister. [Election, xxiii. 110.]
FRASER, J. [Election, xxii. 336.]
FRASER, J. G. [Election, xxi. 492; Telford premium, xxiii. 115, 127.]
Tunnels. " Description of the Lydgate and of the Buckhorn Weston railway tunnels,' xxii. 371.—Remarks, 381.—Cost of railway tunnels constructed under the direction of Messrs. Locke and Errington, 381.

FRASER, R. S. [Election, xxiv. 62.]
FREEMAN, J. [Associate of Council, xxv. 161.]
Iron, inconvenience of being guided by set rules in reference to the strain upon, xxv. 260.

FREEMAN, S. T. [Election, xxv. 262.]
FREWER, C. [Election, xxv. 262.]
Friction between wheel-tires and rails, on the impedimental, with plans for improvement (Adams, W. B.), xxiii. 411. Vide also RAILWAY LOCOMOTION.

FROW, C.
Rivers and estuaries, xxviii. 90.—Improvements of the outfalls of the Witham and the Welland, 90.—Geological evidences of changes of level of the Fens, 92.—Levels of the Fens up the Witham and up the Nene, 93.—Low-water tidal levels of the rivers Ouse, Nene, Welland, and Witham, 93.—Rates of fall per mile of ditto, 94.

FRY, T. B. [Admission, xxix. 322.]
FRYER, J. B. [Election, xxvi. 79.]
FULLER, G. [Election, xxiii. 257.]
FULLER, G. W. [Admission, xxix. 98.]

FULTON.

FULTON, J.
  Drainage of towns. " Description of the
  drainage of the borough of Dundee,"
  xxii. 262.—Remarks, 284.—Properly
  constructed drains do not require
  ventilation, 284.

FYSON.

Furnaces. *Vide* COPPER ORES.
FURNESS, G. [Election, xxiii. 257.]
FURNESS, H. D. [Election, xxvi. 310.]
FURNISS, J. R. [Election, xxii. 241.]
FURNIVALL, W. C. [Election, xxii. 65.]
FYSON. A. [Admission, xxx. 106.]

G.

GAERTH.

GAERTH, H. [Election, xxx. 106.]

GAINSFORD, T. R. [Admission, xxvii. 54; Miller prize, xxix. 213.]

GALBRAITH, W. R. [Election, xxiv. 257.] Railways. Necessity for cheaply-constructed railways, with a gauge of 4 feet 8½ inches, in many districts, xxiv. 387.

GALE, H. [Election, xxv. 262.]

GALE, J. M. [Election, xxiii. 257.]

GALE, S. [Election, xxiii. 257.]

GALLEZ, M. [Decease, xxvi. 129.]

GALLOTT, J. L. [Election, xxiv. 62.]

GALTON, D., Captain, R.E. [Council premium, xxii. 120, 130.]

"Railway accidents—showing the bearing which existing legislation has upon them," xxi. 363.—Remarks, 416. —Midland railway worked for several years without any serious accidents, 416.—Importance of an executive head to every railway, 416.—Question of compensation, 416.—Reducing litigation arising from railway accidents by limiting the amount of compensation, 417.—Amounts recoverable as compensation proportionate to the class of carriage in which the passenger was conveyed, 418, 422.

Telegraph cables. Bituminous covering of the Persian Gulf cable, xxv. 19.— Durability of deep-sea cables, 19.

GALTON, H. J. [Election, xxx. 1.]

GAMBLE, J. G. [Election, xxix. 98.]

GAMMON, W. [Election, xxvii. 320.]

GANDON, C. [Election, xxvii. 55.]

GANDY, J. B. H. [Admission, xxvii. 54.]

GARDNER, T. W. [Election, xxvi. 79.]

GARLAND, T. B. [Election, xxvii. 320.]

GARRETT, F. [Election, xxviii. 518.]

GARRETT, H. N. [Election, xxviii. 518.]

GAS.

Illuminating power of coal. "Experiments on the standards of comparison employed for testing the illuminating

GASKELL.

power of coal-gas." By T. N. Kirkham, xxviii. 440.—Want of uniformity in the present standards, 440.—Principles on which the several appliances now in use are constructed, 440.— Means of determining the relative illuminating qualities of two flames, 440, et seq.—Count Rumford's shadow photometer, 440.—Bunsen's method, dependent upon the combination of reflected and transmitted light, 440, et seq.—Apparatus and standards of comparison sanctioned by the municipality of Paris, 441.—Ditto by Act of Parliament in England, 442.—Experiments on the amount of variation in the illuminating power of candles obtained from the principal manufacturers, 443, et seq.—Normal standard candles, 444.—Classification of differences in candles, 444.—Experiments with candles obtained from one manufacturer only, 446.—Experiments for ascertaining whether the French standard of comparison, when used at a photometer on the Bunsen principle, is more reliable than the candle, 447. —Lowe's jet photometer, 449.—Duration test, 451.—Proposed method for determining the correct illuminating power of gas supplied to the public, 452.

Discussion.—Anderson, A. G., 468.— Atkinson, W., 464.—Barlow, W. H., 456.—Berkley, G., 464.—Bramwell, F. J., 456.—Brereton, R. P., 461.— Church, J., 462.—Glover, G., 466.— Gore, H., 458.—Gregory, C. H., 471. —Harrison, T. E., 462.—Hartley, F. W., 457.—Jones, H., 456, 462.— Jones, H. E., 463.—Kirkham, T. N., 453, 470.—Penny, A., 459.—Sugg, W., 454.—Upward, A., 461.—Vignoles, C. B., 465.—Wood, A. H., 465.

GASKELL, T. P. [Election, xxviii. 59.]

GAUDARD.

GAUDARD, J. [Telford medal and premium, xxix. 210.]

  Materials. "On the present state of knowledge as to the strength and resistance of materials," xxviii. 536.—Remarks, xxix. 95.

GAVEY, G. E. [Election, xxiii. 442.]

GEORGE, R. J. [Election, xxx. 215.]

GIBB, A. [Memoir, xxvii. 587.]

GIBB, E. [Election, xxv. 262.]

GIBBONS, C. P. [Admission, xxviii. 517.]

GIBBS, J. [Memoir, xxiv. 528.]

  Drainage of land, xxi. 88.—Evaporation from water exposed to the air, and from a field covered with vegetation, 88.—Capillary attraction, 88.—Experiment bearing on the effect produced by drainage, 88.—Dutch system 88.—Standard depth of draining in Holland, 90.—Systems of agricultural drainage in Holland and England, though different, conduce to the same ends, 97.

  Reclaiming land from the sea, xxi. 479, 480.—Systems of closing reclamation banks in use in Holland, 479.—Destruction of banks by the overtopping of the waves, 480.

  Ships of war, xxi. 210.—Bolting armour-plates to the sides of vessels, 210.—Proposed shield ship, 211.

GIBSON, J.

  Railway rolling stock, maintenance of, xxiv. 499.—Statistics of the maintenance of the rolling stock of the North Eastern Railway Company, 499.

GIBSON, J. M. [Admission, xxvii. 443.]

GIBSON, T. [Election, xxvii. 553.]

Giffard's injector (England, J.), xxiv. 198. *Vide* also INJECTOR.

GILBERT, —.

  Railway telegraphs. Letter, in reference to Mr. Tyer's system (Preece, W. H.), xxii. 234.

GILBERTSON, F. B. [Election, xxvi. 310.]

GILCHRIST, W. G. [Admission, xxx. 106.]

GILES, A.

  Bridges. Interruption to traffic entailed in repairing wooden bridges of large span on single lines of railway, xxii.

GILES.

324.—Cost of the masonry of the Chey-Air bridge, xxiv. 195.

Concrete, liquid, deposition of, in water, xxiv. 176.

Docks. Silloth, xxi. 337.—Unfavourable position of ditto, 337.—Needless expenditure incurred in the hydraulic apparatus applied to the lock-gates at Swansea and Silloth, 337.—Docks and warehouses at Marseilles, xxiv. 175.

—— graving, xxv. 311.—Cost of the hydraulic lift graving dock, 311.—Comparative advantages of ditto, 325.—Shoring ships in dock, 325.—Aggregate tonnage of vessels docked by the Thames Graving Dock Company and the Southampton Dock establishment, 325.—Cost of docking vessels, 325.—Docks at Bow Creek, 326.—Capability of doing work in hydraulic docks compared with ordinary docks, 327.—Time occupied in lifting vessels by the hydraulic lift graving dock, 344.

Low-water basin at Birkenhead, xxix. 18.

Materials, durability of, xxvii. 573.—Creosoted timber attacked by *Limnoria terebrans*, 573.—Vibration inimical to the formation of rust in rails, 573.—Durability of timber, 573.

Ports of Mutla and Calcutta, xxi. 29.—Improbability of the port of Mutla diverting traffic from Calcutta, 29.

Railways. Santiago and Valparaiso railway, xxiii. 402.—Use of ironwork in lieu of stone on ditto, 402 —Gauge of railways, xxiv. 384.—Festiniog railway, 384.

Reclaiming land from the sea, xxi. 481.—Construction of reclamation banks, 481.—Commercial question of the reclamation of the Maplin Sands and Dengie Flats, xxiii. 182.—Probable cost of the works of drainage and reclamation in the delta of the Rhone, xxviii. 322.

Rivers and estuaries. Tidal scour, xxi. 29.—Delta of the Danube, 297.—Deposits from the Kilia branch of the Danube travel southward and tend to

GILPIN.

silt up the Sulina branch 297.—Removal of the deposit of silt below the Grand Sluice on the river Witham, xxviii. 82.

GILPIN, C. [Election, xxv. 262.]

GILROY, G. [Election, xxix. 98.]

GINTY, W. G. [Memoir, xxvii. 589.]

GIRDERS.

Bowstring. "On the experimental determination of the strains on the suspension ties of a bowstring girder." By W. Airy, xxvii. 443.—The principle applicable to other instances of mechanical structures with complex bracing, 443.—Model on which the experiments were made, 443.—Relative stiffnesses of the bow and string, 444.—Process by which the tensions were ascertained, 444.—Expedient to determine the thrusts produced by a travelling load, 444.—Results of the experiments, 445.—Rules by which the strength of ties should be regulated for an evenly-distributed stationary load, 445.—Ditto, for a single moveable load, 445.—Formula deduced from the experiments, 446.—Appendix : Monochord frame for comparison of musical notes, 447.

Discussion.—Airy, W., 448, 449.—Barlow, W. H., 448.—Harrison, J. T., 449.—Tyler, Capt. H. W., 448.

Uniform stress in. "On uniform stress in girder-work, illustrated by reference to two bridges recently built." By C. Reilly, xxiv. 391.—SECTION I. Professor Rankine's definition of uniform stress, 392.—In the two bridges alluded to, one carries the platform on the top, the other has the platform between the main girders, near the bottom, 393.—Details of these bridges, 394.—SECTION II. Forms of truss chosen compared with ordinary forms, 395.—Details of the weight of the truss adopted for No. 1 bridge, discarding all circumstances relating to the stiffening of the parts in compression, and to the practical exigencies of construction, 396.—Ditto of an equivalent ordinary Warren girder-truss,

GISBORNE.

ditto, 397.—Ditto of an equivalent ordinary diagonal truss, ditto, 398.—Weight of stiffening in the struts of No. 1 truss, and comparative weights required for the other two trusses, 398.—Hodgkinson's experiments on long pillars quoted, and conclusion deduced therefrom, 399.—Results of comparison between the three trusses, 402.—Results of a similar comparison between the truss selected for No. 2 bridge, and two equivalent trusses of the character commonly used under the same circumstances, 403.—SECTION III. Peculiarities of detail in the two bridges, with a view to obtain the utmost economy of weight, consistently with moderate economy of workmanship, 409.—Condition of axial symmetry, by which the centres of gravity of the web-joints are made to coincide with the centres of gravity of the booms, 412.—SECTION IV. Comparison of the state of a bar of the top boom of truss No. 2, when under uniform stress, with that condition of unequally distributed stress that would occur if the boom had a suitable trough-shaped section of equal area, 413.—Case 1, stress uniform in intensity, 414.—Case 2, stress unequally distributed, 415.—Conclusion sought to be established by the Paper, 422.—Appendix : Application of the formula employed in the consideration of the last case, 424.

Discussion.—Barlow, W. H., 445, 446, 449.—Bidder, W. H., 448.—Bramwell, F. J., 436, 446.—Gravatt, W., 446.—Heppel, J. M., 431.—Jenkin, F., 446.—Lane, C. B., 449.—Mallet, R., 435.—Phipps, G. H., 427, 447.—Pole, W., 449.—Reilly, C., 426, 450. —Sheilds, F. W., 433.—Woods, E., 433.

Vide also BRIDGES ; BRIDGES, IRON ; BRIDGES, SUSPENSION ; MATERIALS, AND RAILWAY BRIDGES AND VIADUCTS.

GIRDLESTONE, H. J. [Election, xxi. 257.]

GISBORNE, F.

Telegraph cables, xxv. 43.—Distinction between shallow-water and deep-sea

GISBORNE.

telegraph lines, and as to frequent failures of the latter, 43.—Expediency of a general system of submarine coast-lines, laid in shallow water, in short sections, 44.—Telegraph lines projected from Singapore to China and Australia, 45.

GISBORNE, L. [Memoir, xxi. 586.]

GLADSTONE, Dr. J. H.

Lighthouses. Catoptric and dioptric arrangement of lights, xxvi. 521.—Advantages of catoptric lights, 522.—Excellent adjustment of the Cape Grisnez light, 523.—Mr. Campbell's discovery of the method of internal observation, for the purposes of adjustment, of the optical apparatus of lighthouses, 523.—Necessity of care in the erection of lights, as illustrated in the case of a light on the west-coast of Scotland, 524.—Obscuration of light caused by lighthouse lantern framing, xxviii. 43.—Stornoway and the Odessa apparent lights, 43.—Disadvantages of coloured lights for lighthouse purposes, 44.

GLASS, R. A.

Telegraphic communication. xxv. 29.—Traffic through the Malta-Alexandria telegraph cable, 29.—Transmission of telegraphic messages through the Suez and Alexandria line, 30.—Advantages of duplicate or alternative lines of telegraph from England to India, 30.—Red Sea line and the extension of the telegraphic system from India to China and Australia, 30.—Desirability of the European working of the telegraph to India, 31.

GLOVER, G.

Gas, illuminating power of coal, xxviii. 466.—Combustion of sperm-candles, 466.—Gas-burners, 466, et seq.—Boxed photometers, 467.—Precautions to be observed in the measurement of gas, 467.—Superiority of English scientific instruments for practical purposes, 468.

GLYNN, J. [Memoir, xxiii. 492.]

GODSON, G. R. [Election, xxx. 215.]

GODWIN, J. [Memoir, xxx. 434.]

GOING, T. H. [Election, xxv. 65.]

GRAHAM.

GOLLA, L. A. [Election, xxix. 98.]

GOODRICH, S. [Decease, xxvi. 129.]

GOODWYN, H., General, R.E.

Materials, preservation of (Brunton, J.), xxii. 495.—Extract from his report as to the preservative effect of chloride of zinc, 495.

GOOLDEN, C. [Election, xxv. 479.]

GORDON, A. [Memoir, xxx. 435.]

Lighthouses. Foundation of the Red Sea lighthouses, xxiii. 24.—Comparison between the vibration of the lighthouse at Ushruffee and that at Lobos Cay, 24.—Cost of the lighthouses at Lobos Cay and in the Red Sea, 25.—Cost of the illuminating and optical apparatus of ditto, 25.—Revolving cowls for ventilation in lighthouses, 25.—Illuminating apparatus for lighthouses, 25.—Board of Trade and lighthouse engineering, 26.—Use of the Degrand system of lighting apparatus at the Rachadah lighthouse, 26, 28.—Question of using hollow iron piles for the support of lighthouses, 36.

Ships and steam-vessels, determining the speed of, by means of a modified stopwatch, xxi. 44.

GORDON, G. [Election, xxvii. 55.]

GORDON, J. [Election, xxi. 258].

GORDON, L. C., Lieutenant, R.E. [Election, xxvi. 79.]

GORDON, Sir W., Major-General, R.E.

Institution of C. E., connection between the Royal Engineers and the members of the, xxix. 319.

GORE, H.

Gas, illuminating power of coal, xxviii. 458.—Determination of a reliable standard for photometry, 458.

GOSTLING, W. A. K. [Admission, xxvii. 320.]

GOTT, C. [Election, xxii. 451.]

GOTTO, E. [Election, xxii. 167.]

GOWER, C. F. [Election, xxv. 508.]

Gradients, on the working of steep, and sharp curves on railways (Tyler, Capt. H. W.), xxvi. 310. Vide also RAILWAY CURVES AND INCLINES.

GRAHAM, J.

River Tyne, xxvi. 434.—Surveys between

GRAHAM.

1818 and 1860, 435.—Results of works on its banks, 435.

GRAHAM, M. [Admission, xxvii. 218.]

GRAHAM, R. W.

Rivers, freshwater floods of, xxvii. 246. —Extraordinary floods of the rivers Nerbudda and Taptee, 246.—Distribution of rainfall in Western India, 247. —Fissures, produced in the soil by the sun's heat, act as flood moderators in India, 247. — Surface floods on the plains of India, 248.

GRANT, A. [Election, xxv. 203.]

GRANT, J. [Election, xxi. 48; Telford medal and premium, xxvi. 121, 138.]

Cements. Portland cement, xxiv. 182. ——"Experiments on the strength of cement, chiefly in reference to the Portland cement used in the Southern main-drainage works," xxv. 66.—Remarks, 153.—Objections against the use of cement having a high specific gravity, 153, et seq.—Adoption of cement tests, 155.—Water test of Portland cement, 156.—Relative cost of lias lime mortar and of Portland cement mortar, 157. —Portland cement blocks for facing sea-walls, 157.

Docks and warehouses at Marseilles, xxiv. 182.—Walls of the Marseilles docks, 182.

Drainage of towns, xxii. 299.—Method of ventilating the sewers of the metropolis on the south side of the river Thames, 299.—Advantage of a supplementary pipe outlet to discharge at low water, 299.—Question of cleansing sewers, 299.—Means of flushing the sewers of the metropolis, xxiv. 341.— Steam-pumping engines for lifting the sewage at Crossness and at Deptford, 342.—Reservoirs for sewage at ditto, 342.—Ventilation of the metropolitan sewers, 343.—Excellence of the work in ditto, 344.—History of the present system of metropolitan drainage, 344.

GRANT, W. T. [Resignation, xxiv. 117.]

GRANTHAM, J.

Ships of war, xxi. 198.—Experiments on the 'Warrior' target, 198. — Superiority of iron over wooden vessels, 199.

GREAVES.

Steam navigation. "Ocean steam navigation, with a view to its further development," xxix. 126.—Remarks, 161. — Commercial features of the question, 161, 199.—Average speed attained by the Royal West India mail steamers, 200. — Steam-vessels intended for the voyage to Australia, 200, 201.—Performance of the 'Neva,' 200.—Speed of China clippers, 201.— Cleansing the bottoms of vessels, 201. —Expenditure of fuel per indicated H.P. in steamships, 202.—Bearing of the Suez Canal on the question of ocean steam navigation, 203.

GRANTHAM, J., Captain, R.E. [Election, xxii. 241.]

GRANTHAM, R. B.

Drainage of land, xxi. 92.—System of pipe-drainage, 92.

Rivers. Areas of the catchment drainage of the principal rivers in England, xxii. 365. — Valley of the Upper Thames, 365.—Gorges of ditto, the most suitable places for effecting improvements, 365.

GRAVATT, W. [Memoir, xxvi. 565.]

Canals, xxii. 366.

Girder-work, uniform stress in, xxiv. 446.—Effect of suspending a weight, one-sixth of the width of a rectangular column, from the centre, 446.

Locomotive engines, disturbing forces of, xxii. 99.—Question of sinuosity of movement in locomotives when the crank-shaft is perfectly stiff, 99.

Ships and steam-vessels. Best form for a vessel's bows, xxiii. 363.

Surveying and levelling, xxi. 38.— Measuring distances by the telescope, 38.—Theory of ditto, 38.—Personal equation, 46.

GRAVELL, D. [Admission, xxvii. 54; Election, xxx. 106.]

Graving docks. Vide DOCKS, GRAVING.

GREAVES, C.

Evaporation, amount of, xxv. 476.

Steam-engines, xxiii. 67.—Success of the introduction of Cornish practices into waterworks machinery, 67.—Use of high-pressure steam and expansion a

GREAVES.

course of progressive discovery, 67.—Superiority of vertical over inclined shafts for pumping engines, 68.—Duty of engines in Cornwall stated too high, 68.—Danger to machinery from high expansion, 68.—Utility of reporting the duty of the Cornish engines, 69.

Timber. Destructive nature of the climate on wood in India, xxii. 259.

GREAVES, J. H. [Admission, xxx. 106]

GRECK, P. [Election, xxviii. 232.]

GREENE, R. M. [Election, xxviii. 216.]

GREENER, J. H. [Election, xxvii. 218.]

GREENHILL, T. A. [Election, xxiv. 458.]

GREENWELL, G. C. [Election, xxx. 322.] Coal-mines, ventilation of, by fans, xxx. 304.—Coefficient of friction of air in mines, 304.

GREENWOOD, W. [Admission, xxix. 322.]

GREGORY, C. H. [Vice-President, xxi. 133; xxii. 112; xxiii. 112; xxiv. 106; xxv. 161; xxvi. 119; President, xxvii. 122; xxviii. 158; Past President, xxix. 271.]

Address, on taking the chair for the first time after his election as President, xxvii. 180.—Progress of the Institution since its foundation, 181.—Description of a Civil Engineer, by Thomas Tredgold, 181.—Growth of science since the days of Tregold, 183.—Works recorded in the Minutes of Proceedings of the Institution, and that remain to be described, 183.—Expenditure on public works in the Colonies, 183.—Expenditure and results of railway enterprise in Great Britain, 184.—Land drainage, 184.—Branch lines of railway, 184.—Prosecution of public works in India, 185.—Application of engineering to national defence, 185.—Production of small-arms, with interchangeable parts in large quantities, 186.—Small-arms factory at Enfield, 186.—The long Enfield rifle, 187.— Cost of Enfield rifles, 187.—Improvement in rifle-shooting produced by good machinery and ammunition, 187.—Enumeration of rifles made and con-

GREGORY.

verted at Enfield, 187.—Advantages of the Enfield factory, 188.—Impulse to inventions in the material of war and means of defence consequent on the Crimean war, 188.—Iron-cased floating batteries, 189.—Appointment and labours of the Iron Plate Committee, 189.—Progress in the manufacture of iron plates, 192.—Built guns of an early period, 192.—Bronze and cast-iron guns, 192.—The Horsfall gun and Mallet mortar, 193.—The Armstrong and Whitworth guns, 193. — Experiments on ditto by a special mixed committee, 193.—The Royal Gun Factories, 194.—Structure of guns now manufactured for the service, 194.—Dimensions of recently constructed guns and projectiles, 195. —Range of projectiles, 195.—Superiority of rifled guns to smoothbores, 195.—The 'Warrior' and 'Hercules' ships of war contrasted, 196.—The 'Agincourt' class of vessels, 196.—Armament of the 'Invincible,' 197.—Improvements in marine engines, 198. —Strength of the ironclad navy, 198. —Iron armour for land defences, 198. —Important bearing of railways on modern warfare, 198.—Lieutenant Hozier's remarks on the capabilities of railways as tested in the German war of 1866, 199.—Advantage of railways and steamboats in the last American war, 199. — Reports of General Parsons, 199.—Occupation of railways by the United States military authorities, 200.—Labours of the 'Construction Corps,' 200.—Establishment of the 'Engineer and Railway Volunteer Staff Corps,' 201. — Plea for private manufactories, 201. — Dockyards, arsenals, and rivers still unprotected, 202.—Proper size for forts, 202.—Classification of ships of the various services of the navy suggested, 202.—Future of the Institution, 202.

Bridges. Cheap American timber bridges, xxii. 321.—Liability of timber bridges in America to de-

GREGORY.

struction by fire, 322.—Substitution
of wrought-iron girder bridges for
timber bridges on the Grand Trunk
railway of Canada, 322.—Bridges of
wrought iron not of an absolutely
permanent character, 322.—Suspension of cross-girders in iron
bridges, xxiv. 26.—Victoria bridges,
Pimlico, xxvii. 87.

Bridges, suspension, stiffening of, xxvi.
268.

Coal-mining, xxviii. 155.—Machines for
the economical and safe getting of
coal, 155.

Coasts. Movement of shingle in relation to the direction of the prevailing winds, xxiii. 229.—Paper on
'The East Coast between the Thames
and the Wash estuaries,' 229.—Most
appropriate means of preventing the
encroachments of the sea upon the
land, 229.—Economical consideration
of resisting encroachments of the sea,
230.

Engineers, education of, xxii. 42.

—— Correspondence with the Government of India respecting a notification
addressed by that government to engineers employed in the Department
of Public Works in India, xxix. 1.

Gas, illuminating power of coal, xxviii.
471.—Use of the sperm-candle as a
test of the illuminating power of gas,
471.—Chemical tests of the quality
and illuminating power of gas, 471.

Institution of C. E. Authorship of Papers
contributed to the Institution, xxvii.
294, 408.—Increase of members, 580.
—Students of the Institution, 580.—
Completion of the new building,
xxviii. 1.

Lighthouses. Excellency of lighthouse
apparatus exhibited at the Paris
Exhibition of 1867, xxvi. 507; xxx. 19.

Locomotive engines and rolling-stock,
American, xxviii. 430.

Materials, durability of, xxii. 63.—
Decay of creosoted European timber
in tropical climates, and the consequent propriety of using native
timber for railway sleepers, 63.—

GREGORY.

Durability of native woods in Ceylon,
260.—Comparative loss of weight in
iron from oxidation in England and
in Ceylon, xxiv. 25.—Use of timber
in tropical climates, 26.—Deterioration of native and European woods in
the tropics, 26.—Use of coal-tar for
protecting wrought-iron braces, 26.—
Wear observed in rails and tires on
the Pernambuco railway, 27.—Operation of water in the deterioration of
materials, xxvii. 579.—Resistance of,
xxix. 94.

Napoleon III., Emperor of the French,
presentation of the diploma of
honorary member to, xxviii. 518

Physical geography of a district, a
useful study for an engineer, xxviii.
323.

Piers and breakwaters. Use of concrete
as a hearting for, xxii. 439.

Public works of Canterbury, New
Zealand, xxix. 122, 125.

Railway accidents, xxi. 406.—Impossibility of assigning a definite cause to
every railway accident, 406.—Impracticability of keeping certain intervals between trains, so as to insure
a certainty of freedom from collisions,
406.—Possibility of accidents resulting from a too rigid adherence to the
axiom that there should be continuous break-power, and a break-
van at both ends of every train, 406.
—Accidents from too many signals,
407.

Railway gradients, xxviii. 286.

Railway locomotion, xxiii. 428.—Mr.
Adams's invention of the fish-joint,
428.—Introduction of a spring between the tires and the frames of
wheels, 428.—Great value of the
radial axle, especially when applied
to locomotives, 428.—Bogie frames,
429.—Superiority of radiating axles
to bogies, 429.—Results of the trials
of the 'White Raven,' fitted with
Adams's radial axle-boxes, on the
North London railway, 429.—Circumstances preventing lateral oscillation in ditto, 434.—Weight of trains

GRIERSON.

running round curves equal on the two rails, 434.—Wear of the tires of disc-wheels, xxv. 456.—Disadvantages of rails of great weight per yard for permanent way, 456.—American disc-wheels, 457.—Desirability of establishing a balance between the strength of the wheel and rail on railways, 457.—Variations in the estimates of the amount of retardation on railway curves due to differences in the structure of the engines, xxvi. 340.—Local difficulties which would affect the working of a railway over the Mont Cenis, 340.—Rapidity of the starting and stopping of trains on the North London railway, xxx. 206.

Railway stations, xxv. 291.—Workshops in connection with railways, 291.—Cost of station roofs, xxvii. 441.

Railway trains, electrical system of communication in trains, xxvi. 115.—Report of the Sub-Committee of the Railway Clearing-House on ditto, 115.

Railways. Festiniog railway, xxiv. 375, 382.—Impolicy of adopting an exceptionally narrow gauge for all branch lines, 382.—Cost and profit on the outlay of the Charing Cross and Cannon Street railways, xxvii. 441.—Comparative merits and cost of underground and overground railways, 441.—Traffic on the Mont Cenis railway, xxviii. 257.—Mauritius railways, 286.

Rivers, freshwater floods of, xxvii. 229.

Rivers and estuaries, formation of bars at the mouths of, xxvi. 423.

Ships of war, xxvi. 241.—Monitors, 241.

Steam navigation, xxix. 161.

Tunnel, Mont Cenis, xxiii. 300.—Superiority of Mr. Bartlett's to M. Sommeiller's perforator, 300.

Water, experiments on the filtration of, xxvii. 53.

GRIERSON, J. [Election, xxv. 65.]

GRISELL, H.

Coal-mining, xxviii. 142.—Machine for

GWYNNE.

breaking down coal invented by Mr Grafton Jones, 142.

Dynamite, superior to powder for blasting operations, xxviii. 142.

Lighthouses. Construction of the Red Sea lighthouses, xxiii. 35.—Difficulties of constructing the Calf Rock lighthouse from the storminess of the sea, 35.—Cost of the Red Sea lighthouses, 35.

GROSE, D. G. [Election, xxvi. 242; Memoir, xxx. 436.]

GROSVENOR, Lord R. [Election, xxi. 173; Associate of Council, xxvi. 119.]

GROVER, G. E., Lieutenant, R.E. [Election, xxx. 106.]

GROVER, J. W. [Election, xxvi. 242.]

Iron, durability of, in salt water, xxviii. 228.—Decay of iron piles in salt-water, and means of preserving them, 228.

Railway inclines, xxvi. 387.—Obtaining additional friction by the use of V grooves in the driving-wheels of locomotives, 387.

Railway station roofs, xxvii. 437.—Cost of the roof of the New Street station, Birmingham, 437.—Weight to be put on roofs, 437.—Cost of the Worcester station roof, 437.—Point of rupture in the roof of the St. Pancras station of the Midland railway, xxx. 100.—Cost per square of ditto, 101.—Springing of the ribs of ditto, 101.—Weight on ditto compared with that on other structures, 101.—Compressive strain on the metal of the top of ditto, 102.

GUNN, J. C. [Decease, xxvii. 131.]

Gunnery a branch of engineering (Hawkshaw, J.), xxi. 180.

Gunpowder, method of testing specific gravity of, at Woolwich Arsenal, xxv. 138.—Relative dynamic value of, burnt in American and English guns, xxvi. 201, 235.

GUTCH, G. [Resignation, xxix. 217.]

GWYNNE, J. [Election, xxx. 1.]

H

HACKNEY.

HACKNEY, W. [Election, xxviii. 439.]
HADDAN, J. L. [Election, xxx. 323.]
HAKEWILL, H. [Election, xxix. 322.]
HALL, C. [Election, xxx. 323.]
HALL, T. A. F. [Admission, xxvii. 120.]
HALL, W. [Council premium, xxi. 135,152.]
HALSTED, E. P., Captain, R.N.
  Ships of war, xxi. 232.—Effects of projectiles against the 'Trusty,' ironclad, 232.—Use of bolts for fastening
  armour-plates, 234.—Weakness resulting from grooving armour-plates,
  234.—Advantages derived from timber
  backing, 234.—Experiments on the
  'Meteor' and 'Erebus' ironclads,
  235.—Effect of projectiles on screw-
  bolts, 235.—Effect of armour-plates in
  preventing the explosion of shells,
  236.—Defects in the present system of
  proving armour-plates, 236—Relative
  advantages and disadvantages of
  partial and complete protection, exemplified in the cases of the 'Warrior'
  and the 'Gloire,' 237.—Comparison
  of the English and the French armour-
  plated fleets in respect to the principles
  of partial protection, or complete protection, 239.
HAMAND, A. S. [Election, xxx. 323.]
HAMBLETON, F. H. [Election, xxviii. 439.]
HAMBLING, T. C. [Election, xxviii. 439.]
HAMILTON, J. [Memoir, xxx. 470.]
HAMILTON, Captain J. R.
  Artillery. Velocity of 15-inch American
  shot and of Armstrong projectiles,
  xxvi. 218.
  Ships of war, xxvi. 211.—Purposes for
  which monitors were built, 211.—
  Engagement between the 'Monitor'
  and the 'Merrimack' at Hampton
  roads, 212.—Naval attack on Charleston, 213.—Injury sustained by the
  monitors, 214.—Guns employed on
  each side, 214.—Capture of the Confederate ironclad 'Atlanta' by the

HARMAN.

  'Weehawken' and 'Nahant,' 216.—
  Qualities of monitors exemplified in
  the battle of Charleston, 217.—Capture of the Confederate ironclad 'Ten-
  nessee' by Admiral Farragut at Mobile
  achieved by wooden corvettes, 217.
HAMILTON, Admiral W. A. B.
  Lighthouses, xxvi. 524.— Difficulties
  with which the Trinity House has to
  contend in respect of lighthouse
  management, 524.—Proposed visitation of the Trinity House, 525.—
  Services of scientific men in the construction of lighthouses, 525.
HANCOCK, H. J. B. [Election, xxx. 1.]
HANDCOCK, R. [Election, xxx. 1.]
HANNAY, R. [Election, xxiii. 442.]
HANSON, C. A. [Election, xxi. 257.]
HANSON, W. [Election, xxv. 429.]
Harbours, xxi. 185.—Kurrachee, xxii. 487.
  —Recife or Pernambuco, xxii. 385,
  386.—Harbour of refuge contemplated
  at Redcar, xxiv. 76.—Harbours in the
  Gulf of Lyons, 171.—History of Mar-
  seilles, 171.—Present port of ditto,
  171, et seq.—Harbour at Frioul, 172.—
  Harbours on the French and Italian
  coasts, xxv. 150, et seq. Vide also
  DOCKS; LOW-WATER BASIN AT BIRKEN-
  HEAD; PORTS, RIVERS, AND ESTUARIES;
  and STRUCTURES IN THE SEA.
HARCOURT, W. G. G. V. [Election, xxv.
  262.]
HARDCASTLE, W. J. [Election, xxiv. 62.]
HARDING, J. [Admission, xxvii. 120.]
HARDINGE, G. [Election, xxi. 48.]
HARDINGHAM, G. G. M. [Admission, xxix.
  322.]
HARE, H. T. [Admission, xxvii. 54.]
HARGRAVE, C. T. [Election, xxii. 451.]
HARGROVE, J. S. [Election, xxv. 508.]
HARKER, W. [Election, xxiv. 511.]
HARKNESS, J. M. [Election, xxi. 258.]
HARMAN, H. W. [Resignation, xxviii.
  167.]

HARRIS.

HARRIS, C. S. [Admission, xxvii. 443.]

HARRIS, E. [Election, xxii. 336.]

HARRIS, J. C., Major, B E. [Election, xxii. 65; Resignation, xxvii. 131.]

HARRISON, G. [Election, xxviii. 59.]

HARRISON, J. T.

Exhibition Building of 1851, design for, xxvii. 432.

Girders, bowstring, strains on, xxvii. 449.

Irrigation, xxvii. 539.—System of irrigation in the Madras Presidency and in Spain, contrasted with that on the Ganges Canal, 539.—Permanent and temporary weirs in India and in Spain, 540.—Proper inclination to be given to irrigation channels, 541.—Value of water for irrigation, 542.—Volume of water required at different times of the year for different crops in India and Spain, 542.—Irrigation in Madras, Upper India, Spain, and Italy, 542.— Table of statistics of irrigation canals, 543, 544.

Railway income and expenditure. "On the statistics of railway income and expenditure, and their bearing on future railway policy and management," xxix. 322.—Remarks, 322.—Railway income and expenditure an engineering question, 367.— Statistics of railways should be considered separately, 367.—Importance of third-class traffic on railways, 368. —Further development of railways in agricultural districts, 368. — Cheap lines of railway, 369.—Performance of locomotives on the North Eastern railway, 370.—Improvement of railway property, 370.—Charges upon the revenue of a railway company due to the locomotive department, xxx. 194.

Rivers and estuaries. Effect of change of inclination on the bed of the Thames, xxvii. 541. — Ancient and modern deltas of the Rhone, xxviii. 315—Changes in the outlet of the Rhone, and formation of lagoons in its delta, 316.—Tidal action in the Humber, 506.—Spit at Spurn Point, 508.

HARRISON.

Tides. Retardation and progressive increase in height of the tidal wave passing from the north down the east coast of Great Britain, xxviii. 507.

HARRISON, J. W. D. [Admission, xxvii. 54.]

HARRISON, R. [Admission, xxviii. 59.]

HARRISON, T. E. [Member of Council, xxi. 133; xxii. 112; xxiii. 112; xxiv. 106; xxv. 161; xxvi. 119; Vice-President, xxvii. 122; xxviii. 158; xxix. 208.]

Bridges and viaducts, differences in the construction of, on English and German railways, xxii. 32.—Maximum load per foot run to be provided for in iron bridges, xxv. 258.

Docks, Silloth, xxi. 338.—Hydraulic apparatus at, 338.

Gas, illuminating power of coal, xxviii. 462.—Inutility of the parliamentary test, 462.

Locomotive engines, disturbing forces of, xxii. 84.—Balancing of locomotive engines with one or more cylinders, 84.—Cost, earnings, and depreciation, of locomotive engines, xxiv. 509.— Locomotive engines with eight wheels all coupled, xxviii. 264.—Wear of crank-axles in engines working over sharp curves, 265.—Engines with outside cylinders, 401.—Cost of engines on North Eastern railway, xxx. 203.

Permanent way, xxv. 410.—Turned rails, 410.—Weight of steel rails per yard for railways, 411.—Use of steel rails, 411.—Cost of steel and of iron rails, 411.—Form and mode of construction of rails, 412.—Durability of creosoted sleepers, 412.—Causes producing the great wear of the rails of the Great Northern railway on the up-line near London, 413.—Relative amount of work performed by plate-layers in the north of Northumberland and the south of Yorkshire, 414.— Wear of rails on the North Eastern railway, xxvii. 343.—Apparatus for wedging facing-points, xxix. 22.

Railway curves and inclines. Degree of elevation to be given to the outer

HARRISON.

rail on curves, xxiii. 436.—Engines on sharp curves, xxviii. 264.—Question of steepness of gradient in laying out a railway, 265.

Railway income and expenditure, xxii. 30.—Comparative cost of railways and value of statistics as a check on expenditure, 80.—Statistics of the rolling-stock of the North Eastern Railway Company, and the cost of its maintenance, xxiv. 491, 497.—Variation in the circumstances of different portions of the same railway, xxix. 364.—Passenger fares, 364.—Effect of the reduction of fares on the North Eastern railway, 365.—Depreciation of engines, and the inexpediency of establishing depreciation funds, xxx. 204.

Railway locomotion, xxviii. 398.—Adhesion of iron to iron, 398.—Advantage of oil as a lubricator over yellow grease, 400.—Cast-iron disc-wheels, 400.—Wear of wrought-iron tires, 400.—Practical use of the returns, kept by locomotive superintendents, of the consumption of fuel and oil used in working trains, 401.—Power of an engine in shunting a train backwards, 402.

Railway stations, xxv. 280.—Importance of providing accommodation outside railway stations, 280.—Low platforms, 280.—Newcastle central station, 280.—Comparative cost of large or small spans for station roofs, xxvii. 439.

Railway trains, communication in, xxvi. 112.—Efficiency of the rope-and-bell system of communication between guards and drivers in trains, 112.

Railways, English and German, comparison between, xxii. 32.—Festiniog railway, and other exceptionally narrow-gauge lines, xxiv. 383.—Cost of railways, xxvi. 73, 74.—Cost of the line from Thirsk to Malton, 73.—Requirements of the Board of Trade respecting railway crossings, 73.—Mont Cenis railway, xxviii. 264.—Mauritius railways, 265.—Cost, traffic, and working expenses of ditto, 265.—

HARTLEY.

Experiments on the Erie railroad, 397, et seq.—Construction of railways in agricultural districts, xxix. 365.

Rivers and estuaries. River Danube, xxi. 293.—Current setting across from the Crimean shore diverts the deposits from the Danube towards the south, 293.—St. George mouth the best for improvement, 293.—Mr. Hartley's method of improving the Sulina mouth, 293.—Counter-currents during flood-tide at the mouths of rivers, 338.—Effect of freshes in deepening the channels of rivers, 338.—Effect of the enclosure of Jarrow Slake on the River Tyne, xxvi. 428.—Alterations in the range of tide consequent on improvements in the River Tyne, xxviii. 514.

HARRISON, W. [Election, xxiv. 62.]
HARRISON, W., F.G.S. [Election, xxv. 262.]
HARRISON, W. C.

Boring and blasting, xxiii. 317.—Tin tubes for conveying the cartridges to the bottom of the hole in blasting operations, 317.—Boring tools, 317.

Tunnel, Mont Cenis, xxiii. 317.

HART, C. [Election, xxviii. 232.]
HART, J. H. E. [Election, xxx. 215.]
HARTLEY, Sir C. A. [Telford medal, Manby premium, and Stephenson prize, xxii. 120, 130.]

Cements and pozzolana, xxv. 150.—Portland cement blocks of béton used in the Biarritz harbour of refuge, 150.—Ditto at St. Jean de Luz, 151.—Ditto at the Genoa pier, 151.—Pozzolana used at Spezzia docks, 152.—Pozzolana béton blocks in the Leghorn breakwater, 152.—Relative value of cement and pozzolana, 152.

Harbours. Harbour of Swinemunde in the Baltic, xxi. 304.—West pier and east pier, 304.—Harbours on the French and Italian coasts, xxv. 150, et seq.

River Danube. "Description of the Delta of the Danube, and of the works recently executed at the Sulina mouth," xxi. 277.—Remarks, 293.—Depth of the piers, stonework, and piling at the Sulina mouth, 293.—

HARTLEY.

Superiority of the St. George to the Sulina branch of the Danube, 300.— Proposed improvements of the St. George, 300.—Direction and length of the Sulina piers, 301.—South pier, 302.—Want of analogy between the Sulina and Adour, 303.—Probability of the funnel form of piers at river-mouths, in tideless seas, producing shoals, 303.—Necessity for two piers at either the St. George or the Sulina mouth, 304.—Probability of new banks forming beyond the pier-heads at Sulina, 307.—Large volume of water in the St. George channel a disadvantage, from the greater amount of deposit, 307.—Cases of the Danube and the Thames not analogous, 307.

HARTLEY, F. W.
Gas, illuminating power of coal, xxviii. 457.—Candles and lamps for photometric purposes, 457.—Jet photometer, 457.

HARTLEY, J. [Election, xxvii. 553.]
HARTLEY, J. E. [Election, xxii. 65.]
HARTREE, W. [Election, xxvi. 398.]
HARTWRIGHT, J. H. [Election, xxviii. 59; Memoir, xxx. 437.]
HARVEY, N. O. [Memoir, xxi. 558.]
HARWOOD, H. E. [Election, xxv. 352.]
HASLETT, C. [Election, xxiv. 511.]
HASSARD, R. [Election, xxv. 352.]
River Wey, drainage from the basin of the, xxvii. 238.

HAUGHTON, B.
Pier at New Brighton, accident to, xxviii. 226.

HAVERFIELD, J. T., Captain, R.M. [Election, xxvii. 218.]

HAWKES, F. [Election, xxvii. 55.]

HAWKINS, G.
Railway telegraphs, xxii. 212.—System of train-signalling by telegraph on the Brighton line, 212.

HAWKINS, J. I. [Memoir, xxv. 512.]

HAWKSHAW, J. [President, xxi. 133; xxii. 112; Past-President, xxiii. 150; xxiv. 143; xxv. 202; xxvi. 164; xxvii. 179; xxviii. 215; xxix. 271.]
Address, on taking the chair for the first

HAWKSHAW.

time after his election as President, xxi. 173.—Wide range of subjects which the profession of a civil engineer embraces, 173.—Necessity that he should avail himself of the experience of others, 174.—Inventions and discoveries not suddenly made, but the result of a combined and gradual process of investigation, 174. —Progress in civil engineering more apparent than in most other pursuits, 174.—Magnitude and importance of existing railways, 174.—Improvement in steam navigation, 175.—Application of the screw-propeller to steam-ships, 175.—Ships of war, 175.—Displacement, indicated horse-power, and speed, of H.M.S. 'Warrior' and H.M.S. 'Howe,' 175.—Best mode of constructing iron ships of war still an interesting problem, 176.—Speed of steam-vessels and of railway trains a question of cost and relative circumstances, 176.—Present speed of goods and mineral trains inconsistent with due economy, 177.—Passenger traffic also conducted at a greater speed than the state of the road and other matters warrant, 178.—Separation of passenger and goods traffic, 178.—The electric telegraph an agent of intercommunication, 178.—Progress of ditto, 179.—Ocean telegraphy, 179.—Gunnery, 180. —Probability that iron may be used in fortification, 180. — Iron-plated ships of war, 180.—Use of iron extending, 181.—Steel, or homogeneous iron, 181.—Probable results of an improvement in the manufacture of ditto, 182.—Iron cylinders for foundations, 183.—Advantages derived from the use of ditto, 183.—Mode of sinking ditto by air-pressure, 183.—Patent of the Earl of Dundonald for a similar object, 184.—Present age fruitful in mechanical resources, 184.—A motive power in substitution for steam as yet undiscovered, 184.—Limit of improvement of the steam-engine not attained, 185.—Docks and harbours, 185.—Great moral and social benefits

HAWKSHAW.

resulting from the labours of civil engineers, 186.

Artillery. Larger range and greater destructive power of guns, xxi. 180.—Artillery experiments at Shoeburyness, 255.—Possible future weight of projectiles, 256.

Breakwaters, xxiv. 168.—Construction, 168, 170.—Sea slopes, 168.

Bridge, Charing Cross, xxii. 533.—Weight that can be put on London clay, 533.—Loading of the cylinders, 533.—Drilling the rivet-holes in the plates used, 534.—Strains on the girders, 538.

Bridges and viaducts. Reconstruction of the Dinting and the Mottram viaducts, xxii. 335.—Strains in an arched iron bridge, the weight being suspended from the arch, 538.—American iron bridges, 573.—Launching the girders of bridges over the piers, xxv. 256.—Design of the Grand River viaduct, Mauritius railways, 256.—Maximum load per foot run on iron bridges, 257, 258.—Inconvenience of fixed rules in reference to the strain on iron, 259.—Girder and suspension bridges contrasted, xxvi. 284.

Bridges, suspension, of large span, xxvi. 274.—Inapplicability of the suspension principle to railway bridges, 283.—Suspension bridges require the same amount of metal as girder bridges to obtain the same degree of rigidity, 284.—Suspension principle apart from the question of weight of material, 284.

Canal, Suez, xxvi. 451, et seq.—Bitter Lakes, 452.—Cost of the Suez Canal, 453.—Probable causes of currents, 476.

Cements and concrete, xxiv. 168.—Durability of concrete blocks, 168—Practice of passing concrete through water, 170.—Use of Portland cement in a tideway, xxv. 146.—Setting of concrete in water, 146.—Improvement in the manufacture of Portland cement, 147.—Manufacture of concrete with sand and cement, 147.—Experiments

HAWKSHAW.

on Portland cement, 148.—Pozzolana when mixed with lias lime, 148.

Civil Engineers, xxi. 173.—Progress in civil engineering, 174, 184.—Great moral and social benefits resulting from the labours of civil engineers, 186.

Coasts, &c. Origin of the mounds of large stones at the mouths of the rivers running into the Spanish Main, xxiii. 235.—Chesil Bank, 236.—Lagoons on the shores of the Mediterranean, xxviii. 317.

Cofferdam and syphons. "Account of the cofferdam, the syphons, and other works, constructed in consequence of the failure of the St. Germains sluice of the Middle Level Drainage," xxii. 497.

Cofferdams, dimensions and width of, xxiv. 58.—Cofferdam at the Victoria dock at Hull, 59.

Copper, durability of, in sea-water, xxi. 540.

Divers, xxi. 276.—Relative ability of different men to sustain labour under air-pressure, 276.

Docks, xxi. 185.

—— graving, xxv. 337.—Cost of different kinds, 337.—Hydraulic lift graving dock, 338.

Drainage of land, xxi. 128.—Discharge from under-drainage, especially as affecting the 'régime' of rivers, 128.—Effect of agricultural drainage as regards decreasing floods, xxii. 369.

Drainage of towns, xxii. 304.—Necessity for the thorough ventilation of sewers, 304.—Unfitness of earthenware for inverts for sewers, 304.—Impracticability of preventing the fouling of rivers by sewage, 304.—Sizes of sewers, xxiv. 329.—Metropolitan drainage, 330.—Past history, 330.

Dredging machines used in Holland, xxvi. 453.

Electric telegraph, xxi. 178.—Progress of ocean telegraphy, 179.—Saving of time effected by the use of the electric telegraph, xxii. 239.

Fortification, probability of iron being used in, xxi. 180.

HAWKSHAW.

Foundations, iron cylinders for, **xxi.** 183.
—Mode of sinking by air-pressure,
183.—Patent of Earl Dundonald for
a similar object, 184.—Modes of constructing foundations in India, **xxiv.**
195.

Girders. Suspension of cross-girders,
xxiv. 20.—Girders destined for foreign
countries, 195.—Modes of constructing
adopted in India, 195.

Harbours, **xxi.** 185.

Injector, Giffard's, **xxiv.** 238.

Institution of C.E., papers brought before the, **xxii.** 383.—Value of plain
and accurate descriptions of important
works, 383.

Iron and steel, **xxi.** 181.

Locomotive engines, value of heavy,
xxi. 422.—Advantage in giving a cone
to the wheels of a locomotive engine,
437.—Capacity of engines for passing
round curves, 437.—Eight-wheel locomotives on the Mauritius railways,
xxviii. 266.

Materials, durability of, in tropical
climates, **xxiv.** 18.—Decay of timber,
18.—Half-round sleepers, 19.—Preservation of ironwork, 19.—Durability
of iron railway sleepers, 20.—Decay
of creosoted Memel sleepers, 22.

Motive power in substitution for steam
yet undiscovered, **xxi.** 184.

Permanent way, **xxi.** 422.—Importance
of good ballast, 422.—Expediency of
fishjoints being so placed as to give
the greatest possible uniformity of
deflection, 423.—Defects of permanent
way principally arise from too great
economy, **xxiii.** 437; **xxv.** 401.—Use
of steel rails, 405.

Pile-driving in Holland, **xxvii.** 295. —
Overdriving piles, 295.

Portrait, **xxvi.** 126.

Ports of Swansea, Blyth, and Silloth,
xxi. 344.

Railway accidents, **xxi.** 406.—Accident
at Merton, 406.—Legal proceedings
in cases of railway accidents, 420.—
Fixed sum in case of accidents according to the class of carriage in
which the passenger was travelling,

HAWKSHAW.

421.—Use of tires not fastened so as
to remain on the wheel after fracture,
and the liability of a company in such
a case, 422.

Railway curves, **xxiii.** 437 ; **xxviii.** 285.

Railway inclines, **xxvi.** 382.—Cost of
working steep railway gradients, 382.
—Locomotives for ditto, 383.—Gradients and curves of railways should be
adapted to the natural configuration
of a country, **xxviii.** 285.

Railway inspectors of the Board of
Trade, **xxi.** 423.

Railway locomotion. Speed of railway
trains a question of cost and relative
circumstances, **xxi.** 176.—Present
speed of goods and mineral trains
inconsistent with due economy, 177.—
Separation of passenger and goods
traffic, 178, 423.—Passenger traffic
conducted at a greater speed than the
state of the road and other matters
warrant, 178.

Railway rolling stock, **xxi.** 423.—Standard width and height of railway
carriages in India, 423.—Statistics of
the maintenance of railway rolling
stock, **xxiv.** 495.

Railway stations, **xxv.** 289.—Shape of
railway stations generally a matter
of necessity, 289.—Platforms, 290.—
Position of booking-offices, 291.—Station roof springing from the platform
level at Bradford, **xxvii.** 432.—Cost
of station roofs, 432.—Advantages of
station roofs of large span, 440.

Railway telegraphs, **xxii.** 238. — Inapplicability of the train-staff system
of working railways, 238.—Telegraphic arrangements have not in-
duced greater vigilance in engine-
drivers, 239.—Saving of time effected
by the use of the electric telegraph,
239.

Railway traction, **xxx.** 63.—Respective
merits of rope traction and locomotive
traction in a financial point of view,
68.

Railways. Magnitude and importance
of existing railways, **xxi.** 174.—Madras
railway, **xxiv.** 196.—Cost of the

HAWKSHAW.

Charing Cross railway, xxvii. 433.—Cannon Street and Charing Cross railway bridges, 439.—Mauritius railways, xxviii. 266.—Benefits to the colony, 266.—Gradients and curves, 266.—Eight-wheel locomotives 267, 284.—Cost and working expenses, 283.—Advantages obtained by landowners from railways, xxix. 352.—Causes of the depreciation in value of railway property, 352.

Reclaiming land from the sea, xxi. 478.—Reclamation banks, 492.

Rivers and estuaries, xxi. 29.—Maintenance of tidal channels, 29.—Object of constructing piers at the mouths of ditto, 307.—Pier at the mouth of the Düna, 308.—Improvement of the Humber, xxiv. 59.—Maintenance of Spurn Point, 59.—Removal of bars from the mouths of rivers, 100.—Value of fresh water as regards the 'régime' of a river, 101.—Effect of the Grand Sluice on Boston harbour and the river Witham, xxviii. 96.

Ships and steam-vessels, xxi. 175.—Application of the screw-propeller, 175.—Fouling of bottoms, 254.—Strains to which iron vessels are subjected, 255.

Ships of war, xxi. 175.—Displacement, indicated horse-power, and speed of H.M.S. 'Warrior' and H.M.S. 'Howe,' 175.—Best mode of constructing iron ships of war still an interesting problem, 176.—Iron-plated ships of war, 180.—Improbability of rendering ditto effective in every respect, 253.—Best kind of iron plates for resisting projectiles, 255.—Construction of the targets at Shoeburyness, 255.

Sluices. Disaster to the Middle Level Sluice, xxi. 491; xxii. 498; xxvii. 539.—Grand Sluice on the river Witham, xxviii. 96.

Steam-engines, xxi. 185.—Limit of improvement of the steam-engine not yet attained, 185.—Comparative cost of a rotary pumping-engine and a Cornish engine, xxiii. 102.—Improvement of the steam-engine, 110.

HAWKSLEY.

Telegraph cables, xxi. 179.—Ocean telegraphy, 179.—Malta and Alexandria telegraph, 531.—Expense of durable submarine telegraphs, 540.

Tunnels. Mr. Bartlett's perforating machine, xxiii. 308.—Cost and mode of constructing the Mont Cenis tunnel, 308.

Weight per square foot of a crowd of men, xxii. 534.

HAWKSHAW, J. C. [Election, xxvi. 242.]

HAWKSLEY, C. [Election, xxvi. 544; Auditor, xxviii. 157; xxix. 207.]

HAWKSLEY, T. [Member of Council, xxi. 133; xxii. 112; Vice-President, xxiii. 112; xxiv. 106; xxv. 161; xxvi. 119; xxvii. 122; xxviii. 158; xxix. 208.]

Canal, Suez, xxvi. 471.—Levels of the Red Sea, Bitter Lakes, and the Mediterranean, and the currents between them, 471.

Coal-mines, flow of air in, xxx. 304.—Friction of air in ditto, 304.

Drainage of land, xxi. 99.—" The Drainage of Land Act," 99, 102, 106, 108.—Discharge from under-drainage, 100.—Conclusions derived from the Hinxworth experiments inapplicable to three-fourths of England, 100.—Great differences of rainfall in different years, and small proportion of water passing off by springs, 101.—Flow of rivers rendered irregular by under-drainage, and probable injurious consequences, 101.—Proper water-level to be preserved in the Fens, 104.—Mr. Bailey Denton's theory of drainage inapplicable to mountain-land lying on rock, 105.—Drainage by pot-pipes, 105.

Evaporation in the West of England, xxi. 105.—Ditto in tropical climates, xxvi. 471, 472.

Fans, xxx. 302.—Rotary fans and fan cases, 302.—Form of the arms of fans, 302.

Injector, Giffard's, xxiv. 244.

Lighthouse, Wolf Rock, xxx. 28.

Low-water basin at Birkenhead, xxix. 19.

Rainfall at Hinxworth, xxi. 100.—Ditto,

HAWKSLEY.

and evaporation in the West of England during thirteen years, 105.

Rivers and estuaries. River Ouze, above Lynn, xxviii. 83.—Desirability of the removal of the Grand Sluice at Boston, 99.—River Witham changed from a saltwater channel to a 'freshwater channel, 99.—Changes in the relative level of the land in the Fens, and in the Baltic and Russia, 100.—River Mersey, xxix. 19.—Tenacious character of the silt and sand of ditto, 19.

Ships and steam-vessels, xxii. 600.—Speed of the steam-vessels plying between Kingstown and Holyhead, 600.—Skin resistance of vessels, 600.—Similarity between the amount of resistance experienced by water on the external skin of a ship and in the interior of a pipe, xxiii. 353.—Influence of the condition of the surface on the coefficient of friction, 353.—Resistances to a particle of water flowing down the axis of a pipe, 353.—Algebraic expression for ditto, 354.—Resistance to a vessel moving at a high velocity, 354.—Colonel Beaufoy's experiments, 355.—Cases of a very close agreement between the resistances observed in ships and pipes, 355.—Different grades of resistance in a smooth-skinned and rough-skinned ship, 356.—Predetermination of the speed of a vessel, 356.—Ordinary amount of surface resistance per square foot of wetted surface in an iron vessel, 357, 358.—Formula for expressing the velocity of any sharp-built iron steamship, 357.

Sluicing operations at Birkenhead, xxix. 19.

Steam-engines, xxiii. 103. — Cornish engines suitable for raising water from deep shafts, but not for pumping through water-drains, 103.—Other disadvantages of the Cornish engine, 103.—Term 'loose' applied to the Cornish engine, 104.—Relative merits of double-cylinder and single-cylinder engines, 104.—Heavy parts required

HAYTER.

for resisting the great pressure at the commencement of the stroke in the single-cylinder engine, 104.—Light parts required in the double-cylinder engine, 104.—Most appropriate circumstances for employing the Cornish engine, 105.—Loss of power incurred in double-cylinder crank engines, 105.—Results of the duty of engines, 106.—Comparative cost of Cornish engines and crank engines for waterworks, 106.—Best mode of ascertaining the performance of an engine, 106.—Superheated steam, 106.

Water, filtration of, xxvii. 15.—Rate of filtration through charcoal, 15, et seq.—Sand filters, 16.—Carbide filters, 16.—Stone as a filtering medium, 16.—Sand filter-beds of the Leicester waterworks, 19.—Filtration in the London waterworks, 20.

Water supply. Death-rate of Whitehaven not dependent on the water supply from the Ennerdale lake, xxv. 506.—Alleged injurious effects to health of nitrogenous substances in water, xxvii. 17.—Natural soft-water supplies for manufacturing purposes, 20.—Soft water for detergent purposes, 21.—Existence of organic matter in water, 21.—Wholesomeness of ordinary water supply, 21.

HAWTHORN, R. [Memoir, xxvii. 590.]

HAWTHORN, T. [Telford premium, xxv. 164, 180.]

Docks. "Account of the docks and warehouses at Marseilles," xxiv. 144.

HAY, Sir J. D.

Ships of war, xxi. 212.—Best quality of iron for armour-plates, 212.—Most effective thickness, 212.—Fastening by bolts, 213.—Results of experiments upon targets having various kinds of backing, 213.—Experiment to be performed on a target with two iron plates 15 inches apart, 223.

HAYNES, J. W. [Election, xxi. 48.]

HAYTER, H. [Election, xxi. 492; Telford medal and premium, xxiii. 114, 126.]

Bridge. "The Charing Cross bridge," xxii. 512.—Remarks, 532.—Strains on

HAYWOOD.

the girders of the bridge when loaded, 532.

Weight per square foot of a crowd of men, xxi. 532.

HAYWOOD, W.

Drainage of towns. Sewerage of the metropolis, xxiv. 321.—Water-closet system, 321.—Rainfall to be carried off by the intercepting sewers, 322.—Ventilation of sewers, 325.—Large size of the Parisian sewers, 325.—Cleanliness of the sewers of Paris, 326.

HEAD, J. [Election, xxiv. 184.]

HEALY, S.

Canals. "On the employment of steam-power upon the Grand Canal, Ireland," xxvi. 6.

HEATH, A. H. [Admission, xxvii. 320.]

HEATH, L. [Admission, xxvii. 180.]

HEATH, W. J. W. [Election, xxiii. 110; Telford premium, xxv. 165, 180; Memoir, xxx. 472.]

Materials, durability of. "On the decay of materials in tropical climates, and the methods employed for arresting and preventing it," xxiv. 14.

HEBSON, D.

Ships and steam-vessels, improvements in, xxix. 204.—Marine engines and boilers, 204.

HEDERSTEDT, H. B. [Election, xxiii. 151; Manby premium, xxv. 165, 181.]

Drainage of towns. "An account of the drainage of Paris," xxiv. 257.

HEDGER, P.

Docks, graving, Southampton, unremunerative character of, xxv. 311.

HEDGES, K. W. [Admission, xxviii. 59.]

HEDLEY, T. A. [Resignation, xxvi. 129.]

HEINIG, J. [Admission, xxix. 322.]

HEINKE, C. E. [Decease, xxix. 217.]

HEISCH, C.

Water, filtration of, xxvii. 45.—Inefficacy of certain filters fitted to the cisterns at the Middlesex Hospital, 45.—Permanganate test for organic matter unreliable, 45.

HELLYER, G. W. M. [Election, xxi. 257.]

HEMANS, A. W. [Admission, xxvii. 180.]

HEMANS.

HEMANS, G. W. [Member of Council, xxi. 133; xxii. 112; xxiii. 112; xxiv. 106; xxv. 161; xxvi. 119; xxvii. 122; xxviii. 158; Vice-President, xxix. 208.]

Breakwaters and piers, construction of, xxiv. 180; xxv. 112.

Bridges and viaducts. Foundations, xxi. 265.—Deflections of the girders of the Loch Ken viaduct, 266.—Mode of suspending the cross-girders of the Charing Cross bridge by stirrup-irons, xxii. 529.—Foundations of Westminster bridge, xxiii. 31.—Launching the girders of the Grand River viaduct, Mauritius railways, xxv. 248.—Maximum load per foot run to be provided for in iron bridges, 258.—Junction of the arches of the Victoria bridges, Pimlico, xxvii. 98.—Bridging mountain torrents, xxix. 122.

Bridges, suspension, xxvi. 265.—Test-weight of the Clifton bridge, 265.—Suggestion that the oscillation might be prevented by stiffening the structure with diagonal chains, 265.

Canal, Suez, embankments of, xxvi. 470.

Cements and concrete, xxv. 112.—Use of cement for forming piers or walls in water, 112, 113.—Proposed method of depositing Portland cement concrete in deep water, 112.

Drainage of land, xxi. 99.—Effect of, in increasing the volume of the Shannon, 99.

Drainage of towns, xxiv. 340.—Sewerage of London and of Paris, 340.—Utilisation of the sewage of London, 350.

Foundations, xxi. 265.—Four methods of sinking iron cylinders for bridge foundations, 265.—Foundations of concrete encased by wrought-iron cylinders, xxiii. 31.—Dr. Potts' system of sinking cylinders by the pneumatic method, 265; xxvii. 296.

Iron, cohesion of the fibres of, xxix. 74.

Lighthouses, Red Sea, xxiii. 30.—Wooden piles and foundations, 30.

Locomotive engines, xxii. 101.—Greater

HEMANS.

amount of oscillatory motion in out-
side-cylinder than in inside-cylinder
locomotives, 101.—Locomotives for
working railway inclines, xxvi. 72;
xxviii. 256.—Number of locomotives
employed for the train service in
England and America, 385.—Distribution of the weight on the wheels of
a locomotive, 386.
Permanent way, xxiii. 433.—Defects in
Adams's system of elastic permanent
way, 433.—Construction of permanent
way, xxv. 397.—Durability of flat-
footed Vignoles rails on longitudinal bearings on the Midland Great
Western railway of Ireland, 398.—
Advantages of continuous bearings,
414.—Wear and tear of permanent
way, xxvi. 64.
Piers and landing stages, position of
pontoons for, in respect to the current,
xxviii. 229.
Piles, bearing power of, xxvii. 295.—
Accident resulting through driving
piles through a yielding stratum to
a hard base, 295.
Public works, Canterbury, New Zealand,
xxix. 122.—Moorhouse tunnel, 122.—
Bridging over mountain torrents, 122.
—Gauge of railways, 122.
Railway curves. Attempt to equilibrate
the motion of a train on a curve by
raising the outer rail, xxiii. 432.—
Inner rail on a curve generally more
worn than the outer one, 435.
Railway embankments on the seashore,
xxi. 483.
Railway inclines. Obstacles to the
application of the atmospheric system
for Alpine railways, xxvi. 346.—
Pneumatic system for working inclined planes, 387.—Continuous inclines, xxviii. 256.—Catch-sidings at
the foot of inclines, 256.—Resistance
of an experimental train in going up
an incline on the Erie railroad, 385.—
Most economical system of working
steep inclines, xxx. 64.—Serra do Mar
inclines of the São Paulo railway, 64.
Railway income and expenditure, xxix.
343.—Railway fares, 343.—Primary

value of new lines of railway per mile,
343.
Railway locomotion, xxviii. 386.—Distribution of the weight on the wheels
of locomotives, 386.—Coefficient of
adhesion of iron on iron, 411.
Railway station roofs, comparative cost
per square of, xxvii. 435.
Railway telegraphs, xxii. 224.—Failure
of the 'train staff' system of signalling
on Irish railways having a single line,
224.
Railways. Festiniog railway, xxiv. 368.
—Narrow gauge lines, 368.—Cost,
xxvi. 63.—Causes tending to depress
railway enterprise, 64.—Advantage
of light railways, 64.—Introduction
of a light railway in the Isle of
Man, 65.—Gauge of railways in
the province of Canterbury, New
Zealand, xxix. 122.—São Paulo railway, xxx. 64.
Reclaiming land from the sea, xxi. 482.
—Marshes in Denmark and Holland
floating on a surface of water, 482.—
Slope and material for reclamation
banks, 483.—Plan for reclaiming the
Maplin Sands and Dengie Flats, xxiii.
180.—Construction of stone openings
for draining out the water, 180.—Mr.
Heppel's calculations as to the proper-
sized openings, 180.—Mode of closing
the embankments, 181.
River Shannon, xxi. 99.
Rivers and estuaries, piers at the mouth
of, xxi. 296.—Effect of tidal water in
augmenting the scour derived from
the Liffey in Dublin Bay, 296.—
Relative cost of the works of improvement in the rivers Clyde and Tees,
xxiv. 95.—Relative effect of cross-
groynes and longitudinal river-walls,
96.—Dredging operations at the mouth
of the river Liffey, xxvi. 425.—Effect of
sluices on tidal rivers, xxviii. 82.
Ships and steam-vessels, xxi. 240.—
Importance of strengthening the decks
of iron vessels by strong longitudinal
girders on the cellular system, 240.
Ships of war, armour-plated, xxi. 240.—
Ventilation of monitors, xxvi. 226.

HENCHMAN.

Surveying and levelling xxi. 42.—
Measuring distances by the telescope,
42.
Tunnels, xxix. 122.
Water, filtration of, xxvii. 31.—Probable
cost of animal charcoal necessary for
filtering the supply of water to London,
31.
Water supply. Waste of water supplied
to the city of Paris, xxv. 494.—
Condition of water in rivers, xxvii.
32.
HENCHMAN, H. [Admission, xxvii. 553.]
HENDERSON, Captain A. [Memoir, xxx.
472.]
Rivers, Hooghly and Mutla, xxi. 25.
HENDERSON, D. M. [Election, xxv. 352;
Manby premium, xxix. 211.]
Lighthouses. "On lighthouse apparatus
and lanterns," xxviii. 2.—Different
varieties of lanterns in use, 35.—Appli-
cation of the electric light to light-
houses, 46.—Obscuration of light by
the framing of lighthouse lanterns, 46.
—Cost of lighthouse lanterns, 47.—
Lighthouse lantern framing, 47.—
Composition of glass for lenses, 48.
HENDERSON, W. [Election, xxi. 345.]
HENDRY, J. [Election, xxix. 322.]
HENDRY, W. T.
Hydraulic machinery, xxiv. 181.—Cost
of working hydraulic cranes at Cotton's
wharf, 181.
HENNELL, T. [Election, xxviii. 216.]
HENNET, F. C. [Election, xxvi. 242;
Resignation, xxix. 217.]
HENSLOWE, F. B. [Election, xxix. 98.]
HENWOOD, C. F.
Artillery. Charge of powder for 15-inch
guns, xxvi. 185.
Ships of war, xxvi. 185.—Captain Coles'
turret system, 185.
HEPPEL, J. M. [Telford premium, xxiv.
110, 125.]
Bridges and viaducts, xxii. 529.—Adop-
tion of continuous girders for railways
in India, 529.—Deviation of thrust
from the centre of resistance of the
upper member of the main girders of
the Charing Cross bridge, 530.—
Peculiar character of the rivers crossed

HEPPEL.

by the Madras railway, xxiv. 190.—
Best mode of bridging ditto, 191.—
Foundations of the Chey-Air bridge,
191.—Advantages gained by adopting
similar bridges, 192.—Screw-piles for
piers, 192.—Girders of the Chey-Air
bridge, 194.—Principles of construction of iron-girder bridges, 431.—
Launching girders of bridges of the
Madras railway, xxv. 249.—Mechanical condition of the Victoria bridges,
Pimlico, xxvii. 98.—Stability of ditto,
99.—Continuous spans of the Torksey,
Britannia, and Palar bridges, xxix. 44.
—Difficulty of crossing Alpine streams
by bridges, 124.—Sectional area provided for the discharge of the water
under the Pennair and Chey-Air
bridges, 400.—Foundations of ditto,
401.—Rolling girders, 402.
Bridges, suspension, xxvi. 304.—Means
of stiffening suspension bridges so as
to make them applicable to railway
purposes, 304, et seq.
Canal, Suez, xxvi. 464.—Influence of the
Bitter Lakes, 464.
Cements. Use of 'jagherry' in mortar
in India, xxiv. 36.
Docks, graving, xxv. 327.—Hydraulic
lift graving dock, 327.—Flexibility
of the pontoons, 327. — Docking
'hogged' vessels on a flexible pontoon,
328.—Superiority of hydraulic lifts to
ordinary floating docks, 329.—Use of
the hydraulic lift for fixed water-
levels, 330.
Foundations, methods of obtaining, in
India, xxiv. 191.
Materials, decay of, in tropical climates,
xxiv. 36.—Rapid decay of iron rails
stacked at Madras near the sea, 37;
xxvii. 569.
——— resistance of, xxix, 41.—
Equilibrium of continuous beams, 41.
—'Theorem of the Three Moments,'
41.
Permanent way. Experimental method
of testing rails for durability, xxvii.
403.—Tenders and specifications for
rails, 404.
Pile-driving, xxvii. 314. — Amount of

HERAPATH.

pressure to which the head of a pile is exposed during the process of driving, 314.

Railway inclines, xxx. 66.—Working the Serra do Mar inclines of the São Paulo railway, 66.

Railway locomotion, xxiii. 436.—Radiating axles in contradistinction to the bogie frame, 436.—Superiority of locomotives fitted with radial axles for going round curves, 436.

Railway stations, xxx. 99.—Expenditure on the roof of the St. Pancras station, Midland railway, 99.—Mechanical features of ditto, 99.

Railways. Madras railway, xxiv. 190. —São Paulo, xxx. 66.

Reclaiming land from the sea. " On the closing of reclamation banks," xxiii. 168.—Remarks, 185.

Rivers, character of, crossed by the Madras railway, xxiv. 190.—Flood discharge of, xxvii. 259. — Alpine streams falling into the valley of the Rhine, xxix. 124.

Ships and steam-vessels, xxiii. 341.— Difference in the frictional resistance of water through pipes and the motion of a vessel through water, 341.

Ships of war, xxvi. 226.—Opinions of Sir W. Armstrong and Dr. Letheby as to destroying the ventilation of monitors by poisonous gases, 226.

Steam-engines, Cornish, xxiii. 84.

HERAPATH, S. [Election, xxvi. 310.]

HESS, A. J. [Admission, xxix. 272.]

HEWITT, A. S. [Election, xxix. 98.]

HIGGIN, G. [Telford medal and premium, xxviii. 161, 178.]

Irrigation. " Irrigation in Spain : chiefly in reference to the construction of the Henares and the Esla canals in that country," xxvii. 483.

HIGGINS, C. [Election, xxvii. 580.]

HIGGINSON, H. P. [Election, xxvi. 242.]

HILL, F. H.

Railway income and expenditure, xxix. 345.—Cause of the depreciation in value of railway property, 345.

HILL, J. [Election, xxx. 323.]

HILL, R. H. [Election, xxv. 65.]

HOMERSHAM.

HILLS, G. H. [Election, xxv. 352.]

HJORTSBERG, M. [Election, xxvii. 553.]

HOBBS, A. C. [Resignation, xxiii. 120.

HOBBS, W. F. [Memoir, xxvi. 577.]

HODGE, P. R.

Locomotive engines, xxvi. 70.

Railway locomotives and rolling stock, xxviii. 402.—Introduction of chilled wheels in American rolling stock, 402.—Use of oil as a lubricator in place of yellow grease, 403.—History of the construction of locomotive engines in the United States, 403.

Railway locomotion, xxviii. 402.—Coefficient of iron upon iron, 402.

Railways. Light railways in the United States of America, xxvi. 69.

HODGES, R. N. [Admission, xxix. 98.]

HODGKINSON, E. [Memoir, xxi. 542.]

HODGSON, R. S. [Admission, xxix. 98.]

HODSON, G. [Election, xxx. 1.]

HODSON, R. [Election, xxi. 258.]

HOGG, P. [Decease, xxviii. 168.]

HOGGAR, H. E. R. [Admission, xxx. 323.]

HOLGATE, J. T. [Election, xxviii. 59.]

HOLLINGSWORTH, C. E. [Auditor, xxvii. 121 ; xxviii. 157.]

HOLMES, S. F. [Election, xxiv. 511.]

Holstein, sea-dykes of, and of Schleswig, and on reclaiming land from the sea (Paton, J.), xxi. 426. *Vide* also RECLAIMING LAND FROM THE SEA.

HOLT, W. L.

Locomotive engines constructed by Mr. Fairlie, xxvi. 379.

HOLTZAPFFEL, J. J. [Election, xxii. 241.]

HOLTZE, C. G. [Resignation, xxi. 148.]

HOMEM, F. de S. T. [Admission, xxviii. 59.]

HOMERSHAM, S. C.

Drainage of land effected by ' dumb ' wells, xxii. 361.

Rainfall. Results produced by rain falling on different geological formations, xxii. 360.—Difference between the Dickinson and the Dalton percolation gauges, 361.—Comparison of the rainfall in different districts from observations taken at different periods, xxv. 476.—Form of rain-gauge used for the Woodburn experiments, 476.—

HOMFRAY.

Alleged loss of water by evaporation from rain-gauges, 476.

Reservoirs for impounding flood-water, xxv. 475.

Steam-engines, xxiii. 75.—Rotary, expansive acting, flywheel engine the best for waterworks purposes, 75.—Direct-acting Cornish pumping engine ill-adapted for low lifts, 75.—Same amount of water evaporated by the Cornish boiler and Wagon boiler per pound of coal, 82.

Water supply from wells in the chalk, xxii. 362.—Sources of water supply of the city of Paris, xxv. 502.—Comparative qualities of filtered Seine water and of chalk-water, 502.—Action of water upon lead, 503.—Wholesomeness of water dependent on the absence of organic matter, 503.—Lake or river water always more or less impure, 504, 506.

Well-boring, by steam machinery, in the red sandstone at Middlesbrough, xxiii. 474.—Means used for withdrawing the débris, 475. — Mather and Platt's system of well-boring, 475.

HOMFRAY, F. S. [Decease, xxvii. 131.]

HOOD, R. J.

Railway stations, &c., xxv. 277.—Form and arrangement of locomotive sheds, 277. — Lengths of the platforms at the Victoria station, Pimlico, 277. —Requisites of a good station roof, xxvii. 433.—Victoria station roof of the London and Brighton railway, 433.—Charing Cross, Cannon Street, and London, Chatham, and Dover Railway Company's Victoria stations, 434.—Cost of the Paddington station roof, 437.

HOOD, W. [Election, xxiii. 459.]

Hooghly and the Mutla, the (Longridge, J. A.), xxi. 2. *Vide* also RIVERS AND ESTUARIES.

HOOLE, E. [Election, xxiii. 257; Resignation, xxvii. 131.]

HOOPER, E. [Decease, xxix. 217]

HOOPER, H.

Piers and landing stages. " Description

HUISH.

of the New Ferry and the New Brighton piers and landing stages on the River Mersey, near Liverpool," xxviii. 217.

HOPKINS, E.

Tunnelling operations. Rate of progress, and expense of, xxiii. 307.

HOPKINS, J. I. [Election, xxix. 322.]

HOPKINS, W. R. I. [Election, xxvii. 443.]

Permanent way. Wearing powers of fibrous as compared with crystalline iron rails, xxvii. 346.—Form of rails, 346.

HORN, G. W. [Election, xxv. 65.]

HORN, T. [Election, xxix. 322.]

HOSEASON, J. C., Captain, R.N.

Steam navigation, ocean, xxix. 173.—Performance of man-of-war steam transports between England and Bombay, 173.—Navigation of the Indian and China seas, 174.

HOUGHTON, G. [Election, xxvi. 310.]

HOVENDEN, J. St. J., Major, R E. [Election, xxv. 65.]

HOWARD, J. [Election, xxvii. 55.]

HOWARD, J. [Election, xxviii. 518.]

HOWARD, W. S. [Election, xxvii. 443.]

HOWARTH, O. H. [Admission, xxvii. 180.]

HOWDEN, A. C. [Election, xxiii. 320; Manby premium, xxviii. 161, 179.]

Rivers, flood discharge of. " Floods in the Nerbudda valley : with remarks on monsoon floods in India generally,'' xxvii. 218.

HOWKINS, J., jun. [Election, xxii. 242.]

Hownes Gill viaduct, on the Stockton and Darlington railway (Cudworth, W.), xxii. 44. *Vide* also VIADUCTS.

HOWSON, B.

Barometer, long tube, xxi. 32.

HUGHES, E. W. [Election, xxiii. 151.]

HUISH, Captain M. [Memoir, xxvii. 600.]

India-rubber and gutta-percha, relative insulating qualities of, xxv. 27.

Railway telegraphs, xxii. 213.—Continuous repetition of telegraphic signals producing weariness and liability to error, 213.—London and North Western telegraphic train-signalling system, 214.—Danger of working

HULBERT.

single lines of railway by the telegraph alone, 214.—'Train staff,' 214.

Telegraphic communication with India, xxv. 27.—Inefficient working of the Indo-European telegraph through the Turkish dominions, 28.

HULBERT, H. G. [Election, xxii. 398.]

HULSE, W. W. [Election, xxvi. 544.]

HUMBER, W. [Telford premium, xxvi. 121, 138.]

Railway stations, &c. "On the design and arrangement of railway stations, repairing-shops, engine-sheds," &c., xxv. 263.

HUMBLE, E. B. [Election, xxv. 262.]

HUMPHREYS, H. T. [Election, xxiv. 184.]
Surveying. Setting out railway or other curves, cycloscope for, xxv. 508.

HUMPHRYS, E. [Memoir, xxvii. 592.]
Steam-vessels running between Kingstown and Holyhead, disadvantage of the relatively great length of the, xxii. 598.—Duration of superheaters, 599.—Slip of the feathering wheels, 599.

HUNT, H. A., jun. [Election, xxi. 173.]

HUNT, W. [Election, xxii. 320.]

HUNTER, J. L. [Election, xxiv. 144.]

HUNTER, W. [Election, xxiv. 458.]

HUNTINGTON, J. B.
Mauritius railways, gradients, traffic, and cost of the, xxviii. 259.—Destruction of a viaduct by a hurricane, 260.

HURST, T. G. [Election, xxvi. 544.]

HURST, W., jun. [Election, xxvii. 580.]

HURWOOD, G. [Council premium, xxi. 135, 152; Memoir, xxiv. 531.]

HUSBAND, W. [Election, xxv. 479.]
Steam-engines. Cornish pumping engines, xxiii. 75.—Increase of diagonal shafts in mines, and their effect on the rods of ditto, 75.—Economical returns of ditto, 76.—Adoption of the

HYDRAULIC.

Cornish engine by the East London Waterworks Company, 76.—Wagon boiler, Cornish boiler, Woolf's engine, Gribel's engine, and Sim's engine, 77.—Combined engine, used for the drainage of the Haarlem lake, 77.—Abandonment of double-cylinder engines for pumping in Cornwall, 78.—Economy and non-liability to accident of Cornish engines, 78.—Indicator diagrams, 79.—Ditto from the Wheal Towan engine, the Wheal Tremayne engine, and from an engine at the Kent Waterworks, 79.—Excessive expansion not requisite for Cornish engines, 80.—High duty obtainable by wire-drawing steam and low rate of expansion, 80.—Cause of failure of Hornblower's engines, 81.—Safety of working of Cornish pumping engines, 81.—Question of the superiority of the Wagon boiler for evaporating water, 82.—Velocity of the piston the secret of the high duty of the Cornish engine, 82.—Expediency of introducing direct-acting engines, 82.

HUTCHINS, G. A. [Election, xxvi. 242.]

HUTTON, D. [Election, xxi. 258.]

HYDE, H., Captain, B.E. [Election, xxi. 48.]

Hydraulic apparatus and machinery, as applied to lock-gates and docks. *Vide* DOCKS; and PORTS.

Hydraulic lift graving dock, the (Clark, E.), xxv. 292. *Vide* also DOCKS, GRAVING.

Hydraulic limes and cements. *Vide* CEMENTS; DOCKS, Marseilles; and STRUCTURES IN THE SEA.

Hydraulic system of propulsion, xxvi. 22, 206.—For towing purposes, xxix. 176, 186.

I.

IKIN.

IKIN, J. D. [Election, xxv. 508.]

Illuminating power of coal-gas, experiments on the standards of comparison employed for testing the (Kirkham, T. N.), xxviii. 440. *Vide* also GAS.

INJECTOR.

"Giffard's Injector." By J. England, xxiv. 198.—Brief record of what has been done by others, for raising or forcing water by means of a jet of steam and apparatus without moving parts, 198.—Solomon de Caus, 198.—David Ramseye, 198.—The Marquis of Worcester, 198.—Savery, 198.—The Marquis de Manoury d'Ectot, 199.—The mechanism of the injector, 199.—The 'lance,' 201.—The 'divergent tube,' 202.—The 'sheaf,' 202.—Quantity of heat spent in the work done by the injector, 204.—Loss of heat found in M. Deloy's experiment, 205.—Description of a table showing the results of calculations of the resistance, power required, and heat for working a No. 9 injector, 205, *et seq.*—Whether expansion of the steam takes place on quitting the tuyère, 207.—Excess of heat in steam at 212° over an equal weight of water at 212°, 208.—Determination of the increase of temperature in the 'sheaf,' 208.—Results of experiments as to the maximum heat of the feed-water at which the 'sheaf' will act, 208.—Means of regulating the quantity of water injected, 209.—Tabular statement of quantity of water injected per square millimètre of area of throat per minute, by instruments of four companies, 210. —Overflow or running to waste, 211. —Depth from which water may be raised, 212.—Injector compared with pumps, 212.—Mr. Beattie's feed-water heating apparatus, 212.—Points of

IRON.

comparison between it and the injector, 214.—Superiority of the injector, 215.—Disadvantages of pumps, 215.—Injectors most advantageously compared with pumps in the case of marine engines, 215.—Mode of working with the injector on the Western railway system of France, 215.—Application of the injector as an elevator, 216.—List of publications on the injector, 217.

Discussion.—Armstrong, Sir W. G., 222, 240.—Beattie, W. G., 251.—Bidder, G. P., jun., 241, 244.—Bramwell, F. J., 219, 228.—Colburn, Z., 243.—Craven, J. C., 238.—England, J., 234.—Hawkshaw, J., 238.—Hawksley, T., 244.—Maudslay, H., 226.—Phipps, G. H., 219, 222, 225.—Robinson, J., 218, 225, 250.—Russell, J. S., 247.—Siemens, C. W., 222, 236.—Thorman, E. H., 219.

INMAN, T. [Admission, xxviii. 325.]

Institution of C.E. Papers, xxii. 383.—Value of plain and accurate descriptions of important works, 383.—Early history of the Institution, its progress and present position, xxv. 223.—Facilities it affords to members and students, 226.—Completion of the new building, xxviii. 1.—Original members of the Institution, xxix. 273.—Connection between the Royal Engineers and the members, 319. *Vide* also ADDRESSES OF PRESIDENTS; and ANNUAL REPORTS OF COUNCIL.

INNES, W., Lieutenant, R.E. [Election, xxi. 98.]

Iron, deterioration of, in hot and moist climates, xxii. 415.—In fresh, brackish, and salt water, 442; xxviii. 228, *et seq.* —Preservation of iron piles and cylinders in contact with water, 228. —Ironwork preserved by being boiled

IRON.

in a preparation of tar and asphalte, xxiv. 21; xxvii. 575; xxviii. 230.

Iron, uses of, and improvements in the manufacture of, xxi. 181.—Strength of American, xxii. 543, 558; xxviii. 395.—Annual production of iron in the United Kingdom, xxiii. 158.— Value exported in 1862, 158.—Inconvenience of being guided by set rules in reference to the strain upon iron, xxv. 259, 260.—Permanent set of iron structures, xxvii. 114. — Cohesion of fibres, xxix. 74.—Comparative value of hot and cold blast, xxx. 321.

——, cast, strength of, under compression, xxii. 567.—Tensile strength, xxviii. 409, 418, 419.

——, chilled, xxviii. 407.

Vide also BRIDGES, IRON; IRON AND STEEL; MATERIALS; PERMANENT WAY; SHIPS OF WAR; and STOVES.

Iron-plated ships, xxi. 180.

——, on the form and materials for, and the points requiring attention in their construction (Samuda, J. D'A.), xxi. 187. Vide also SHIPS OF WAR.

IRON AND STEEL.

Strength and resistance, xxi. 240, 242; xxix. 33.—Specific gravity, 34, 75.— Testing iron or steel, 73.—Methods of distinguishing ditto, 76.

" On the strength of iron and steel, and on the design of parts of structures which consist of those materials." By G. Berkley, xxx. 215.—Explanation of the absence of uniformity in the strength of wrought iron, 215.— Best method of representing the strength of ditto, 215.—Average strength of iron plates, and of L and T irons, 216.—Limit of strain to which 1 square inch in section of wrought iron may safely be subjected, 216.—Permanent set, 216.—Progressive increase of stretch in proportion to the unit of strain, 217.— Influence of repeated strains on the durability of iron, 217.—Influence of repeated strains on Bessemer metal, 218.—Result of Sir W. Fairbairn's

IRON AND STEEL.

experiments with respect to repeated strains of wrought iron, 218.—Practical strength of wrought iron in structures of a permanent character, 218.—Limit of strains generally adopted for railway bridges, 218.— Precautions to be observed for the possible weakness of parts of structures, 219.—Ditto, with respect to ordinary riveted connections of plates or bars, 219.—Results of experiments to determine the proper proportions of pins and heads of links for Warren girder bridges for the Great Indian Peninsula railway, 219, et seq.— Question of the strength of wrought iron in compression, 223.—Discrepancies of formulæ proposed for facilitating calculations to determine the strain which columns will bear under compression, 224.—Results of experiments on various forms of wrought iron subjected to compression, 224.— Advantages of cast iron for sustaining a statical compressive force, where the supports are not liable to flexure, 225.—Extract from specification of cast-iron sleepers provided for the Great Indian Peninsula railway, 225.—Results of proving test-bars and sleepers, 226.— Strength of iron test-bars, 227.— Results of experiments on ditto, 227. —Conditions requisite for the manufacture of iron test-bars, 228.—Considerations in respect of the strength of castings, 228.—Strength of Bessemer steel, 229.—Experiments on the strength of steel, and conclusions arrived at, 229.—Appendix, Tables Nos. 1-5. Experiments on the fracture of iron links, with different proportions of bar and head, 231.—Table No. 6. Ditto on bars and rectangular tubes, 236.—Ditto on cylindrical tubes, 244.—Ditto on angle iron, 248 —Ditto on T iron, 248.—Ditto on channel iron, 250.—Ditto on cruciform iron, 250.—Table No. 7. Experiments on cast-iron girders, 252.— Table No. 8. Statement of tests

IRRIGATION.

taken weekly from October, 1869, to April, 1870, 255.

Discussion.—Berkley, G., 256, 274.— Bramwell, F. J., 267.—Brereton, R. P., 270, 272.—Bruce, G. B., 266.— Cochrane, J., 265, 267.—Fox, Sir C., 272.—Morrison, G. J., 266.—Parsey, W., 263.—Phipps, G. H., 256, 272.— Redman, J. B., 269.—Reilly, C., 258. —Rich, W. E., 270.—Siemens, C. W., 268.—Vignoles, C. B., 274.

Vide also BRIDGES, IRON; IRON; MATERIALS; PERMANENT WAY; SHIPS OF WAR; and STOVES.

IRRIGATION.

" On irrigation in India." By A. Wilson, xxvii. 454.—Necessity of irrigation to meet seasons of drought, 454.—Irrigation works prior to the establishment of the British rule, 454.—Decay of the works, 455.—Recent completion of irrigation works, 455.—Diminution of the ravages of famine since the opening of the Delhi and Doab canals, 455.—Importance of even limited supplies of water for irrigation, 455. —Sites for reservoirs, 456.—Tanks and reservoir embankments, 456.— Retaining walls in front of the Hindoo works, 456.—Waste weirs constructed by natives often not of sufficient capacity, 457.—Different forms and dimensions of 'calingulahs' or waste weirs. 457.—Sluices, 458.— Cistern at end of sluice tunnel, 458.— Instance of favourable contour of the land for forming reservoirs of large capacity, 458.—Anicut or dam across the river Toombuddra, 459.—Anicuts of stone, 459.—Ditto of sand, 460.— Modern anicut on the Toombuddra, 460.—Masonry anicuts, 460.—Precautions to be observed in constructing anicuts, 460.—Sluices, 461.— Difficulty experienced for want of a system for regulating the supply of water to each cultivator, 461.—Cost of storing and distributing water over the land requiring to be irrigated, 462.—Quantity of water required for irrigating an acre of land, 462.—Abstract of observations on evaporation at the Red Hills, near Madras, from April to August, 1844, 463.—Mode of preparing land for wet cultivation, 464.—Irrigation canals and distributing channels, 464.—Methods of raising water for irrigation purposes, 464.—The môt, 464.—The picottah pump, 465.—Three systems of baling out water for the foundations of a bridge, 465.—Basket scoops, 465.— Statement of the quantities and cost of water raised by native methods in different parts of India, 466.—Relative value to Government of irrigated and dry cultivation illustrated by the revenue returns of the Madras Presidency, 467.—Gain to the cultivator from irrigated land, 467.—Losses from unirrigated land, 467.—Superiority of river and tank water for irrigation purposes, as compared with well and spring water, 468.—Improvements to be effected in the system of irrigation in Southern India, 468.—Diminished rainfall from destruction of trees, 468.—Augmentation of revenue due to the returns from irrigation works, 469.—Extent of land at present irrigated, 469.— Irrigation works should be carried on by private companies, 460.—Construction of works with a view to the combination of navigation and irrigation, 470.

" On the benefits of irrigation in India, and on the proper construction of irrigating canals." By T. Login, xxvii. 471.—Irregularities of the seasons, 471.—Climate improved by irrigation, 471.—Political advantages of irrigation, 471.—Canals in Northern India remunerative, 472.—Prevention of famine the principal argument in favour of canals, 472.—Development of irrigation would enlarge the commerce between England and India, 472.—Value of the Ganges canal in mitigating the famine of 1865–66, 472.—Traffic in grain of the East Indian railway in 1866, 472.—Power

94

IRRIGATION.

of water in motion to hold matters in suspension, 473.—How to regulate the slope of canals illustrated in the case of the Ganges canal, 473.— Natural courses of rivers through countries with a steep slope, 474.— Method of reducing the slope of the bed of canals by giving them a tortuous course, as in the case of the Western Jumna canal and the canal of Ali Murdan Khan, 474.—Introduction of falls on canals in India, 475.—Ogee form of fall on the Ganges canal, 475, 481, 482.—Perpendicular falls and rapids on the Barree Doab canal, 476.—Perpendicular falls in Madras, 476.—System of undersluices suggested by Colonel Fyfe, 476.—Considerations in favour of adopting weirs for overcoming excessive slopes, 476.—Natural weirs across rivers in Southern India, 477. —Action on the bed of rivers on the up-stream side of weirs, 477.—Slope of the surface of rivers varies according to the volume discharged, 477.— Effect of velocity of water on the bed of rivers dependent on the matters held in suspension, 478.—Best slope for canals in Upper India, 478.— Table showing approximately the sections and slopes probably best adapted for irrigation canals and watercourses for Northern India, 479. — Proposed zigzag falls, 480.—Expedients carried out for protecting the falls on the Ganges canal, 482.

" Irrigation in Spain: chiefly in reference to the construction of the Henares and the Esla canals in that country." By G. Higgin, xxvii. 483. —Importance of irrigation by canals in India and Spain, 483.—Construction of irrigation works in Spain by the Moors, 483, 486.—Vegetable productions, 483.—Table of mean monthly rainfall in various parts of Spain for an average of four years, 484.—Table of mean monthly temperature in various parts of Spain, taken from an average of four years,

IRRIGATION.

484.—Comparative table of mean temperature during the seven irrigating months in Italy and Spain, 485.— Table of mean annual rainfall in Italy, Algiers, and Spain, 485.—Table of comparative mean and maximum temperature and mean rainfall of Italy and Spain, during the seven irrigating months from March to September, 486.—Principal rivers in Spain not applied to purposes of irrigation, 486.—Date of execution of various irrigation works, 486.—Principal large irrigated areas in Spain, 487.—Proportion of irrigated to unirrigated land, 488.—Population in the irrigated and unirrigated districts, 488.—Price of irrigated and unirrigated land, 488.—Value of a cubic foot of water per second per annum in Piedmont, Lombardy, and Spain, 488, 489.—Establishment of a Company in London for constructing irrigation canals in Spain, 489.—Date of projects for irrigating the Henares and the Esla valleys, 489.—Physical features of the Henares valley and river, 489.—The Henares canal, 490. —Tunnel through limestone cliff, 491, et seq.—Weir across the river Henares, 491, et seq.—Sluices and overflow weir, 492.—Progress of the works, 492.—Prices paid for weir, 493.— Spanish bricks, 494.—Prices paid for the tunnel, 495.—Bridge under the Madrid and Saragossa railway, 495. —Tube over the Arroyo Majanar, 494.—Aqueduct over the Arroyo Dueñas, 496.—Methods of crossing the canal severally adopted for roads, bridges, and torrents, 496.—Mill falls, 497.—Average prices paid for the smaller works, 497.—Method of executing the excavations, 497.—The labourers, 497.—Sections of the canal and velocity of water, 498.—Quantity of water supplied to an acre of land from various canals, 498.—Quantity of water, when abundant, employed by cultivators, 499.—Frequency with which the whole of the Esla and

IRRIGATION.

Henares valleys can be irrigated, 500.
—Canon fixed by Government for the
Henares canal, 500.—Ditto, for the
Esla canal, 500.—Price of water in
Spain, 500.—Method of dividing the
water in the old Moorish works, as
adopted at Elche, 500.—Method of
dividing the water in Lorca, 501.—
Principal objects to be sought in a
module, 501.—The Milanese module,
502.—Method of measuring water on
the Marseilles canal, 502.—Ribera's
module, 503.—Lieutenant Carrol's
method of measuring water, 503.—
Module adopted on the Henares and
the Esla canals, 503.—Probable losses
of water by filtration and evaporation,
504.—Evaporation in Madrid in 1867,
505.—System of distribution of water
on the irrigated portion of the
Henares valley, 505.—Cost of the
Esla canal, 506.—Comparative cost of

IRRIGATION.

irrigation by the Esla and Henares
canals, 506.—Features of the Esla
valley, 506.
Discussion.—Atkinson, W., 552.—Bal-
four, General, 525.—Barry, J. D.,
517.—Bateman, J. F., 512.—Beardmore, N., 537.—Brereton, R. P., 537.
—Cotton, Sir A., 511, 533.—Delano,
W. H., 548.—Denison, Col. Sir W.,
515.—Dickinson, J., 526.—Harrison,
J. T., 539.—Hawkshaw, J., 539.—
Johnson, Captain W. R., 523 —Jones,
J., 524.—Kilgour, G., 522.—Login,
T., 508, 545.—Longridge, J. A., 537.
—Moncrieff, Lieut. C. C. S., 532.—
Phipps, G. H., 548.—Vignoles, C. B.,
525.—Webb, E. B., 551.—Wilson, A.,
546.
Irrigation in Egypt, xxvii. 548.—Cost of
the barrage of the Nile, 548.—Produce
from irrigated land, 548.

J.

JACKSON.

JACKSON, M. B. [Resignation, xxi. 148.]
JACKSON, R. W.
Rivers and estuaries. River Tees, xxiv. 78.—Shoaling consequent on the construction of cross jetties, 78.— Evil effects of contracting the entrance of tidal rivers by piers, 79.—Advantage of diagonal jetties for fixing the channel of a river in a given direction, 79.
JACKSON, T., Jun. [Election, xxvi. 398.]
JACOB, A. [Election, xxiv. 62.]
JACOMB, W. [Election, xxv. 203.]
JAMES, A. [Memoir, xxvi. 580.]
JAMES, E. R., Captain, R.E.
Rainfall on, and drainage from, the rivers Eden and Wey, xxvii. 233.— Basins of ditto, 233.
JAMES, Frederick. [Election, xxv. 262.]
JAMES, Frank. [Election, xxx. 106.]
JAMES, Sir H., Colonel, R.E. [Resignation, xxix. 217.]
JAMES, J. W. [Election, xxviii. 59.]
JEFFCOCK, P. [Memoir, xxvii. 594.]
JEFFREY, R. [Election, xxi. 48.]
JEFFREYS, E. A. [Election, xxiii. 110.]
JENKIN, F.
Girders, iron, principles of construction of, xxiv. 446.—Effect of loading a column out of the centre of gravity of its section, 446.
Iron, cast, under compression, xxii. 567.
Lighthouses in the Red Sea, temperature in, xxiii. 29.
Railway telegraphs, xxii. 215.—Tyer's telegraph for train-signalling, 215.— —E. Clark's instrument, 215.— Means of protecting ditto from demagnetization by lightning, 216.— Liability of the semaphore to get out of order in Preece's telegraphic system, 217.—Propriety of permanent visible signals, 218.
Steam-engines. Cornish pumping engines, xxiii. 65.—Comparison be-

JENOURE.

tween the actual duty recorded by Cornish engines, and the duty calculated from the dynamic theory of heat, 65, 66.—Analogy between the heat-engine and the water-engine in an ordinary mill, 65.—Calculation of the maximum power to be obtained from a given steam-engine, instanced in the case of the Fowey Consols engine, 65.
Telegraphic communication with India, xxv. 31.—Telegraph route to India by the Red Sea and the Arabian Sea, 31. —Stability of submarine cables compared with that of land lines, especially the land lines in India, 31.
Water supply of Paris, xxv. 505.— Methods of supplying private consumers with water in French towns, 505.—Prices charged for water at Rouen, Havre, and Bordeaux, 506.
JENKINSON, C. H. G. [Admission, xxvii. 54 ; Miller prize, xxix. 213.]
JENNINGS, J.
Cements. Behaviour of Portland cement and Roman cement under water, xxv. 130.—Portland cement concrete blocks for building purposes, 130.— Effect of fire upon Portland cement, 130.
Concrete. Iron bond in concrete work, xxii. 445.—Manufacture of concrete, 445.—Use of concrete blocks, xxiv. 183.
Docks and warehouses at Marseilles, xxiv. 183.
JENOUR, A. C. [Election, xxviii. 517.]
JENOURE, A.
Railway telegraphs, xxii. 230.—Expediency of teaching the manipulation of telegraphs in schools, 230.— 'Block' system on the Stockton and Darlington railway, 230. — Traffic worked without electrical signals on the Glasgow and Paisley railway, 231.

JERMYN.

Timber, durability of, xxii. 259.

JERMYN, G. A. [Decease, xxviii. 168.]

JERVOIS, W. F. D., Colonel, R.E. [Associate of Council, xxiii. 112.]

JOEL, H. F. [Admission, xxix. 98.]

JOHNS, J. W. [Resignation, xxvi. 129.]

JOHNSON, H.
Coal-mining, xxviii. 131.—Mr. S. P. Bidder's apparatus for breaking down coal, 131.

JOHNSON, J. [Election, xxviii. 325.]

JOHNSON, J. H. [Election, xxiv. 458.]

JOHNSON, James Trubshaw. [Election, xxvii. 320.]

JOHNSON, John Thewlis. [Election, xxvi. 79.]

JOHNSON, R. [Election, xxi. 493.]
Permanent way, xxv. 405.—Economy that would be effected by the substitution of steel for iron rails on the Great Northern railway, 405.—Flat-bottomed and double-headed rails, 407.

JOHNSON, S. W. [Election, xxvii. 55.]
Railway rolling stock, xxx. 213.

JOHNSON, T. M. [Auditor, xxiii. 111; xxiv. 105.]
Bridges, suspension, xxvi. 294.—Comparative deflection of a suspension bridge with stiffened chain and with stiffened roadway, 294.—Effect of changes of temperature on suspension bridges, 294.—Inverted arch bridge, 294.—Economy of material in suspension bridges, 295.—Economy of the stiffened suspension bridge when compared with a bridge on the principle of that at Saltash, 295.
Materials, durability of, xxvii. 573.—Durability of bridges, and rapid decay of sleepers in America, 574.
Railway telegraphs, xxii. 228.—Spagnoletti's system of train-signalling in use on the Metropolitan railway, 228.
Rivers and estuaries, xxiv. 98.—Improvement of tidal rivers, 98.—Tidal range diminished by the serpentine course of a river, 98.—Cause of the diminution of the tidal receptacle in the Tees, 98.—Necessity of dredging the clay beds of tidal rivers, 99.—

JONES.

Jetties and training walls, 99.—Proposed junction of the outfalls of the Witham and the Ouze, xxviii. 101.—Lincolnshire Estuary Company, 102. —Slopes of the banks of cuts in the Fens, 102.—Prejudicial effects of the Grand Sluice at Boston, 103.—Drainage by the Witham, 103.

JOHNSON, W. [Memoir, xxv. 528.]

JOHNSON, W. R., Captain, M.S.C.
Irrigation in India, xxvii. 523.—Distribution of water for irrigation, 523.— Irrigation works in Mysore, 524.

JOHNSTON, E. [Election, xxi. 258; Telford premium, xxv. 164, 180.]
Bridge. "The Chey-Air bridge, Madras railway," xxiv. 184.

JOHNSTON, R. E. [Election, xxvi. 310.]

JOHNSTONE, W. [Election, xxvi. 79.]

JOLL, H. [Election, xxx. 1.]

JONES, C. E. [Admission, xxvii. 218.]

JONES, E. J. [Election, xxvii. 553.]

JONES, G.
Coal-mining, xxviii. 128.—Machines for breaking down coal to avoid the use of gunpowder, 128, 129.

JONES, H.
Gas, illuminating power of coal, xxviii. 456.—Burners for testing the quality of gas, 456, 461.—Difference in the rate of consumption of oil or sperm burnt through different wicks, 462.

JONES, Sir H. D., Lieut.-General, R.E. [Memoir, xxx. 438.]

JONES, H. E. [Election, xxviii. 518.]
Gas, illuminating power of coal, xxviii. 463.—Chemical analysis of quality, 463.—Means for ascertaining the illuminating power by electricity, 464.

JONES, James. [Memoir, xxiv. 532.]

JONES, John.
Iron and steel, xxix. 76.—Methods of distinguishing, 76.
Irrigation, importance of, xxvii. 524.— Benefit of, in Wales, 524.—Indian irrigation companies as an investment, 525.—Value of water for irrigation when pure, and when charged with mud, 525.

JONES, M. [Decease, xxiii. 497.]

JONES, O. [Admission, xxvii. 54.]

H

JONES.

JONES, R. [Election, xxx. 215.]
JONES, R. W. [Memoir, xxviii. 608.]
JONES, T. M. R. [Election, xxvii. 55.]
JOPLING, C. M. [Memoir, xxiii. 508.]
JORDAN, T. B.

JOY.

Copper ores, sizing, xxx. 131.
JOULE, Dr.
  Injector, Giffard's, xxiv. 240.
JOWETT, J. [Election, xxiii. 459.]
JOY, A. [Election, xxii. 604.]

K.

KEEFER.

Keefer, S. [Election, xxx. 1.]
Keeling, H. H. [Election, xxi. 173.]
Kelk, J. [Associate of Council, xxv. 161.]
Kendrew, J. A. [Election, xxx. 215.]
Kennard, H. J.
Foundations, cylinder, xxviii. 345.—Superiority of Milroy's excavator to the sand-pump for sinking, 345.—Working of the sand-pump, 345.—Various methods of sinking cylinders, 346.
Kennedy, J. P., Lieut.-Colonel. [Election, xxvii. 320.]
Bridges. Sectional areas of bridges to void the waters of drainage basins, xxvii. 257.—Bridges on the Bombay, Baroda, and Central India railway, 258.—Danger to bridges in India from scour in monsoon floods and from drift timber, 258.
Rivers, freshwater floods of, xxvii. 257.—Periodical floods of India, 257.
Kershaw, J. [Election, xxi. 258.]
Locomotives, single-cylinder, xxii. 99.
Kessner, A. H. [Election, xxviii. 216.]
Ketchum, H. G. C. [Election, xxv. 479.]
Kilgour, G. [Election, xxiii. 110.]
Irrigation in India, xxvii. 522.—Type of fall used on the Baree Doab canal, 522.—Whether irrigation canals in India should be worked by Government or by private companies, 522.—Fitness of the Punjab for canal irrigation, 523.—Occurrence of salt-petre in wells of a few years' standing in the Punjab, 523.
Kincaid, J. [Election, xxx. 106.]
Kinch, W. H. [Admission, xxvii. 54.]
King, A. [Memoir, xxx. 440.]
King, C. U. [Admission, xxix. 98.]
King, Francis. [Election, xxv. 65.]
King, Frederick.
River Thames. Gradual decline of the navigation of the Upper Thames, and want of a proper outfall, xxii. 366.—

KIRKHAM.

Injurious effect on the meadow-land from damming up the river for the purpose of 'flashes,' and the remedy to be obtained by canalizing the river, 367.—Neighbourhood of Oxford flooded from raising the cills at Wolvercot mill, King's Weir, and Wytham mill-streams, 368.
Rivers. Treatment of navigable valleys a national question, xxii. 368.
King, J. H. R. [Admission, xxviii. 439.]
King, W. H. [Admission, xxvii. 180.]
Kinipple, W. R. [Election, xxiv. 184.]
Bridges, suspension, improved form of, xxvi. 293.
Cements and concrete, xxv. 125.—Use of Portland cement concrete in water, 125, et seq.—Advantages of mixing and allowing cement concrete partially to set before using it, 126.—Brickwork with cement under water, 127.—Neat cement for grouting between sheet piles under water, 127.—Preparation of concrete, 127.
Docks, graving, xxv. 323.—Pontoons, 323.—Pontoon sunk at the London docks, 323.—Cost of the Limekiln dock, 324.—Buckling of the copper of a vessel on the pontoon of the hydraulic lift graving dock, 341.
Kirby, C. [Election, xxv. 65.]
Kirk, A. C. [Election, xxiv. 184.]
Kirkham, T N. [Election, xxiv. 511 ; Telford medal and premium, xxix. 211.]
Gas, illuminating power of coal. "Experiments on the standards of comparison employed for testing the illuminating power of coal-gas," xxviii. 440.—Remarks, 453. — Standard of illumination recognised by Parliament, 453. — Gas-burners, 453.—Candles for testing the illuminating power of gas, 470. — Differences of vision of experimenters, 470.—Superiority of lamp to candle tests of illu-

KITSON.

mination, 470, 471.—Chemical analysis of coal-gas, 471.

KITSON, F. W. [Election, xxviii. 216.]

KITSON, J.

Locomotive engines, disturbing forces of, xxii. 83.—Oscillatory movement in double-cylinder engines, 83.

KNIGHT, J. G. [Election, xxiii. 375.]

KNIGHT, J. P.

Railway trains, communication in, xxvi.

KOE.

105.—Electrical system of signalling on the South Eastern railway, 105, 106.

KNIGHT, R. V. J. [Election, xxvi. 544.]

KNORPP, C. B. [Election, xxviii. 439.]

KNOWLES, G. [Election, xxv. 352.]

KNOWLES, J. [Election, xxix. 98.]

Coal-mining, xxx. 406.—Temperature of mines, 406.

KOE, S. L. [Election, xxii. 241.]

L.

LAGERHEIM.

LAGERHEIM, Captain G.[Decease, xxv. 531.]

LAGOONS AND MARSHES.

"On the lagoons and marshes of certain parts of the shores of the Mediterranean." By D. T. Ansted, xxviii. 287.—Mode in which the lagoons have been formed suggestive of a method of sanitary improvement, or of reclaiming the marshy lands, 287.—Eastward advance of the embouchure of the Rhone, 288.—Form of the present delta, 288.—Tributaries of the Rhone, 288. — Formation of the delta, 288, 290.—Changes in, and present limits of ditto, 289.—Silt and sand carried by the Rhone, 289.—Physical features of the delta, 290.—Origin of the sandhills, 290. — The étang of Valcares, 291.—Obstacles to the reclamation of the inner lagoons, 291.—Small amount of change in the surface of the Camargue, 291.—Works for draining the lagoons of the Rhone delta, 292. — Distance along the coast to which deposits brought down by the Rhone are conveyed, 292.—The Vidourle mud used to warp up the étang de Repousset, 292.—Physical geography and geology of the country drained by the Rhone, of its delta, and of the gulf of Lyons, 292.—Drainage area of the Rhone, 293. — Sandbanks, lagoons, and marshes, between the lighthouse of Aigues Mortes and the hills inland, 293.—The lagoon of Mauguio, 294.—The lagoons of Pérols and Grec, 294.—Proposed drainage of ditto, 295.—Features of the system of lagoons and marshes between the Vidourle and the Lez, 295.—Heavy showers of rain, 295.—The étangs of Villeneuve, Vic, and Frontignan, 296.—The lagoon of Thau, 296.—Effect of heavy rain on the lagoons, 297.—

LANDING STAGES.

Works carried on in the district, 297. —Lagoons and streams south of the cape of Agde, 299.—Lagoons on the eastern side of Corsica, 299.—Physical features of the island, 299.—The river Golo and the lagoon of Biguglia, 299. — Sandbank between the lagoon and the sea, 300.—Drainage area supplying water to the lagoon, 300.—Effect of the river Bevinco on the lagoon, 301.—Insalubrity of the surrounding country, 301, 302.—Proposal to canalize the Bevinco, 302. —Lagoons of Diana, Urbino, and Palo, 303.—Measures required for the improvement of the eastern coast of Corsica, 303.—Rainfall on the Corsican coast, 303.—Ditto at Montpellier and over the delta of the Rhone, 304.—Ditto at Bastia, 305.—Other lagoons in the Mediterranean and Black Sea, 305.—Practical bearings of the facts and inferences submitted, 305.

Discussion.—Ansted, Professor D. T., 307, 322.—Bateman, J. F., 307.—Giles, A., 322.—Gregory, C. H., 323.—Harrison, J. T., 315.—Hawkshaw, J., 317.—Mallet, R., 311.—Pole, W., 317.—Redman, J. B., 321.

Vide also COASTS; and RECLAIMING LAND FROM THE SEA.

LAIRD, W.

Steam navigation, xxix. 203. — Performance of the steamship 'Belgian' on a voyage from Liverpool to London, 203.

LAMBERT, S. [Admission, xxix. 98.]

LAMBERT, T.

Coal, distillation of, xxiii. 455.—Coke manufactured at the Vauxhall gasworks, 455.

"Land Drainage Act, 1861," xxxi. 63.
Vide also DRAINAGE OF LAND.

Landing Stages. *Vide* PIERS AND LANDING STAGES.

LANDON.

LANDON, F. H. [Admission, xxvii. 180.]

LANE, C. B.

Bridge, suspension, at Caxanga, xxiv. 29.

Bridges, lattice girder, xxiv. 449.

Cements, **xxv.** 135. — Expediency of establishing an equality between the strength of cement and that of bricks, 135.—Relative merits of blue lias lime and of Portland cement, 136.

Locomotive engines, disturbing forces of, xxii. 106.—Sinuous motion of broad-gauge locomotives, 106.

Materials, decay of, in tropical climates, xxiv. 28.—Depredations of the white ant, 28.—Deterioration of bricks in Brazil, 28.

Permanent way, xxi. 414. — Double-headed reversible rail, suited for new countries where the traffic is small, 415.—Advantages of placing wooden keys inside instead of outside the road, 415. — Sleepers used on Brazilian railways, xxiv. 27.—Preparing native timber for sleepers in Brazil, 28.—Introduction of fish-joints on Brazilian railways, 28. — Deteriorating effects produced by passing loads on permanent way, xxv. 427.

Public works and railways in Brazil, xxii. 409.—Perishable nature of native timber, 410.—Propriety of using creosoted North of Europe timber for railway purposes, 410.—Efficiency of European labour less in a tropical climate, 411.—Efficiency of Portuguese masons, 412.—Carriages used on the Pernambuco railway, xxiv. 28.—Introduction of railways in Brazil due to the Baron de Mauá, xxx. 62.—Original surveys for the São Paulo railway, 62.—Final plans for ditto as decided on by Mr. Brunlees, 63. — Commercial success of ditto, 63.

Railway accidents, xxi. 415.—Adoption of two whistles on an engine, 415.—Trial by jury in cases of railway accidents, 415.

River Liffey, xxvi. 440.—Removal of the bar at the mouth due to scour, 440.

LEAD ORES.

Surveying and levelling, xxi. 46.—Measuring distances by the telescope, 46.

Tunnels, xxii. 381.—Stapleton tunnel on the Bristol and Gloucester railway, 381.—Difficulties of construction, from the unstable condition of the ground, owing to an old tunnel having been carried through the same place, 381.—Centres for tunnels, 382.—Stapleton tunnel as completed, 382.—Invert put in where there was much lateral pressure, 383.—Cost of materials used in the construction, 383.

Water supply. Calculous diseases more rife in the districts of England where chalk-water is drunk than in others, xxv. 505.

Weights and areas of a crowd of men, xxvi. 289.

LANE, E. [Election, xxviii. 59.]

LANE, M. [Memoir, xxx. 441.]

LANG, W. [Election, xxv. 65.]

LANGE, D. A.

Canal, Suez, xxvi. 455. — Dredging operations, 455.— Extensive preparations required, 456.—Present rate of progress, 457.—Probable date of completion, 458.

LANGLEY, A. A. [Election, xxix. 272.]

LANGRISHE, R. [Election, xxiii. 442.]

LATHAM, B. [Election, xxiv. 458.]

LATHAM, G. [Election, xxiv. 62.]

LATHBURY, R. [Admission, xxix. 98.]

LA TOUCHE, H. C. D. [Election, xxviii. 59.]

LAW, H. [Election, xxvi. 242.]

Bridges, suspension, xxvi. 268.

River Amazon, xxvii. 257.

LAWFORD, A. C. [Election, xxx. 323.]

LAWFORD, W. [Election, xxvi. 242.]

LAWRENCE, E. [Election, xxix. 98.]

LAWRENCE, F. [Memoir, xxiv. 541.]

Bridge, Saltash, centre pier of, xxi. 275.—Difficulty of keeping the cylinder free from water, 275.

LAWRENCE, W. F. [Election, xxviii. 439.]

LAWS, W. G. [Election, xxx. 1.]

LAYBOURNE, R. [Election, xxvii. 320.]

LEAD ORES.

"The dressing of lead ores." By

LEAD ORES.

T. Sopwith, Jun., xxx. 106.—Paucity of printed information on ore-dressing machinery, 106. — Recent progress of this branch of mechanical engineering, 106.—Definition of the term 'dressing,' 107. — Argentiferous lead ores, 107.—Principle of separation in dressing ores by machinery, 107.—Treatment of the ore on the dressing-floors, 108.—Delivery of the mine-stuff on the higher floors, 108.—System of payment in mineral mines, 109.—Standard of ordinary mine-stuff, 109.—Separation at the first grate, 109.—Ditto at the second grate, 109. —Wages, 109.—Comparison of cost of production of clean ore in England and in Spain, 109.—Stirring, 110.—Hotching, 110.—Treatment of chatts and smiddum, 110.—Ditto of sludge, 111, 118.—Modified form of buddle, 111.—Treatment of the slime with Brunton's cloth, 112.—Enrichment of slimes in the dolly tub, 112.—Crushing mill in general use in England, 113.—Treatment of mine-stuff on the crushing mill-floors, 114.—General arrangement of crushing mill dressing-floors, 115. — Crushing mill, 115.—Rollers, 115.—Effect of gravitation in separating the materials in the hotching machine, 116.—Classification of the material crushed, 116. — Self-acting hotching machines, 117.—Method of moving the piston, 117.—Most suitable number of strokes per minute for different sizes of work, and length of stroke, 118.—Removal of waste, 118.—Amount of stuff treated per day, 119.—Weight of ore per 100 cubic feet treated, 119.—Comparison of the cost of labour in dressing ore by machinery in England and in Spain, 120.—Cost of producing a ton of clean ore, 120.—Cost of mills and machinery, 120.—Machinery manufactured in Germany, 120.—Subsequent treatment of chatts, 121.—Stamping apparatus not necessary for lead ores, 121.—Enumeration of other comparatively modern machines, 121. —Manufacture of dressing machinery,

LETHEBY.

121. — Argument against replacing manual labour by machinery controverted, 122. — Imperfect appliances used in Spanish mines, 122.—Difficulties attendant on the establishment of the floors and machinery, 122.—Comparative value of ores in England and in Spain, 123.

Discussion. — Jordan, T. B., 131.—Smyth, W. W., 124.—Sopwith, T., Jun., 133.—Taylor, J., 126.—Thomas, J. L., 128.—Williams, Capt. R. H., 131.

LEAN, J. [Election, xxv. 352.]

LEATHER, J. T. [Associate of Council, xxii. 112.]

LE BRETON, A. H. [Admission, xxvii. 180.]

LECKY, R. J.

Rivers and estuaries. Result of dredging in, and embankment of, Cork river, xxiv. 83.

LEDGER, J. C. [Election, xxv. 352.]

LEE, H., JUN. [Election, xxiv. 184.]

LEECHMAN, W. C. [Election, xxv. 479.]

LEEMAN, G. [Election, xxv. 352.]

LE FEUVRE, W. H.

Bridges, suspension, with multiple spans, xxvi. 273.

LEGG, G. [Resignation, xxix. 217.]

LE LIEVRE, C. [Admission, xxvii. 54.]

LE MESURIER, H. P. [Election, xxi. 257.]

LEMON, J. [Election, xxiv. 511.]

Drainage of towns, xxiv. 350.—Drainage of Paris, 350.

LEONARD, H. [Election, xxv. 65.]

LESLIE, A. [Election, xxix. 98.]

LESLIE, F. [Election, xxiii. 442.]

LESLIE, J.

Reclaiming lands from the sea, xxiii. 184. — Stopping of the Dagenham breach, by Captain Perry, 184.—Reclamations in the river Tay, 184.

Rivers and estuaries, xxi. 341.—Comparative effect of freshwater and tidal scour, 341.

LETHEBY, Dr. H.

Water supply and filtration, xxvii. 6.—Hardness of water supplied by public companies, 6.—Determination of the quantity of organic matter in water by incineration, 6.—Action of animal charcoal on organic matter, 6, et seq.

LEVEL.

—Rate of filtration of water, 7.—Impracticability of filtering all the water supplied to the metropolis, 7.—Examination of charcoal which had been in use as a filtering agent, 35.—Purifying power of charcoal principally dependent on its power of oxidation, 36. — Effects of organic matter on health, 37.

Level supported upon a gimbal joint (Doering, F. B.), xxiv. 104.

Levelling. *Vide* SURVEYING AND LEVELLING.

LEWIN, W. [Decease, xxiii. 121.]

LEWIS, J. [Election, xxii. 451; Memoir, xxv. 514.]

LEWIS, W. B. [Election, xxv. 262.]
Railway rolling stock, xxviii. 396.—Cast-iron wheels used on the Grand Trunk railway of Canada, 396.

LEWIS, W. T. [Election, xxiv. 257.]
Coal-getting apparatus (Chubb, C. J.), xxviii. 149.

LEY, J. V. [Admission, xxvii. 218.]

LIDDELL, A. J. [Admission, xxix. 272.]

LIGHT, A. L. [Election, xxi. 173.]

LIGHT, C. J. [Election, xxiii. 257.]

LIGHTHOUSES.
Apparatus, &c. " Optical apparatus used in lighthouses." By J. T. Chance, xxvi. 477.—Authorities on lighthouse apparatus, 477.—Object of lighthouse optical apparatus, 477.—Ordinary source of illumination, 477.—Application of the magneto-electric spark, 478.—The dioptric system, 478.—The glass zones, 478.—Definition of fixed lights and revolving lights, 478.—Relation of the flame to the emergent beams of light, 479.—Respective merits of revolving and fixed lights, 479.—Various orders of lights, 479.—Adjustment of the flame, 480.—Space occupied by, and relative illuminating values of, the refracting belt and reflectors, 480. — Separate foci for ditto, 481.—Proper direction to be given to the emergent beams, 481. — Causes of the diminution of light, 482.—Objections to coloured lights, 482.—Annular lens of Augustin

LIGHTHOUSES.

Fresnel, 483. — Buffon's and Condorcet's previous suggestions, 484.—Count Rumford's multiple burner, 485.—Illuminating effect of the improved lamps, 485.—Collective effect of the lens, 486.—The refracting belt, 486.—Original form of ditto, 486.—Introduction of the cylindrical refractor, 487.—Fresnel's invention adopted by the Commissioners of Northern Lighthouses, 487.—Sir D. Brewster's advocacy of the dioptric system, 487.—The catadioptric, or totally-reflecting, zones, 487.—Ditto first introduced, on a large scale, in the Skerryvore lighthouse, 487. — Labours of the Messrs. Stevenson on the subject, 487.—Superiority of reflecting prisms generated round a horizontal axis to Fresnel's and Sir D. Brewster's systems, 488.—Solution of the problem, 488.—Objections to the proposal of the Royal Commission on lights, &c., 490.—Precaution to prevent the loss of light in the smaller sizes of fixed lights, 490.—The method of testing and adjusting, 490.—System of internal observation, 491.—Method of adjusting by the image of the horizon, 491.—Superior method discovered in adjusting the Whitby lights, 492.—Precautions necessary in the construction and adjustment of the glass zones, 493.—The parabolic metallic reflector, 493.—Numbers of dioptric and catoptric sea-lights on the coasts of the United Kingdom, 493. — Argand's cylindrical burner, 494.—Teulère's reflector, 494. — Parabolic reflectors at Kinnairdhead, 495. — Inferiority of the parabolic reflector to the dioptric instrument, 494, *et seq.*—Description of the parabolic reflectors used in Great Britain, 494.—Modification by Mr. Thomas Stevenson, 495.—Experiments by the French lighthouse engineers on the relative intensity of catoptric and dioptric lights, 496.—Arrangement of reflectors necessary to produce the effect of a first order dioptric revolving appara-

LIGHTHOUSES.

tus, 496. — Catadioptric, or totally-reflecting, spherical mirror, 497. — Objections to the metallic spherical reflector, 498. — Catadioptric mirror first constructed by Mr. Chance, 499. —Mr. Thomas Stevenson's azimuthal condensing system, 499.—Adopted at Isle Oronsay and at Great Orme's Head, 499. — Design for Gibraltar, 500.—Subsidiary parabolic reflectors not required, 500. — Suit-ability of the dioptric azimuthal system for leading lights, 501.—Lead-ing lights for Hoylake and Buddon-ness, 501. — Appendix: generating section of a refracting zone, or straight prism, 502.—To determine the path of any ray, 503. — Totally-reflecting prism, 504.—To determine the path of any ray, 505.—The apparent diameter of the flame in the focal plane of a fixed apparatus is not changed by the interposition of the refracting zone, 506.

Discussion.—Airy, G. B., 507.—Arrow, Capt. F., 516, 525.—Babbage, C., 525.—Brereton, R. P., 521. — Campbell, J. F., 532.—Chance, J. T., 507, 535.—Douglass, J. N., 527.—Gregory, C. H., 507.—Hamilton, Admiral W. A. B., 524.—Ryder, Admiral A. P., 533.—Redman, J. B., 540.—Siemens, C. W., 529.—Smith, Col. J. T., 511.—Steven-son, T., 510.

——" On lighthouse apparatus and lan-terns." By D. M. Henderson, xxviii. 2. —Firms engaged in the manufacture of catadioptric apparatus for lighthouses, 2.—Authorities on lighthouse work, 3. —Glass used in lighthouse apparatus, 3.—Furnace, pots, and other appli-ances necessary for the production of cast-glass, 5.—Glass grinding and polishing, 7.—Various sizes of cata-dioptric lights, 9. — Distinction of catadioptric lights, 11.—Method of mounting the lenses and prisms, 14.—Arrangement of the panels and lantern framing, 19.—Lanterns, 22.—Catadioptric mirrors, 26.—Lamps, 27. —Clockwork, 30. — Odessa harbour

LIGHTHOUSES.

and apparent light, 31.—Appendix: description of Mr. Alan Brebner's refraction protractor, 34.

Discussion.—Airy, W., 35.—Beazeley, A., 44.—Collinson, Admiral R., 36.—Cutler, W. H., 42.—Douglass, J. N., 37.—Gladstone, Dr. J. H., 43.—Hen-derson, D. M., 2, 45.—Owen, Capt. J. F., 43.—Parkes, W., 41.—Redman, J. B., 35.—Rochussen, T. A., 45.

Red Sea. " Description of lighthouses lately erected in the Red Sea." By W. Parkes, xxiii. 1.—Agreement as to the parts to be undertaken by the Egyp-tian government and English govern-ment respectively, 1.—Survey and choice of sites, 1.—Physical features of coral reefs, 2.—Zafarana point, 2. —Straits of Jubal and the Ushruffee reef, 2.—Dædalus reef, 2. —Light-house at Zafarana point, 3.—Depth of soundings near the Dædalus reef, 4. —Details of the structure of a coral reef, 4.—Dædalus and Ushruffee coral reefs, 5.—Peculiar conditions to be considered in erecting a structure on coral reefs, 5.—Structure of wrought iron supported on piles resting on con-crete adopted, 5.—General features of the design for the Dædalus light-house, 6.—Conditions involved in the construction of the Ushruffee light, 6. —Details of the structures, parti-cularly of the Ushruffee, 6.—The piles, 6.—Framework of the super-structure, 8.—Separate pieces of no great weight, 8.—Floors and water-tank, 8.—Galleries and rooms, 8.—Force of wind in the Red Sea, 9.—Diagonal crosses to prevent the possible effect of the action of the wind, 9.—Small vibration in gales of wind, 10.—General principles of the construction of the Dædalus light-house, 10.—Construction of the lanterns, 11. — Ventilators, 11. — Sliding door leading from the light room, 12.—Lanterns and light appa-ratus of different orders, 12.—Ra-pidity of progress made in the under-taking, 12.—Vessel provided for the

LIGHTHOUSES.

service, 12.—General arrangements, 13.—Concrete, 13.—Arrival of materials from England, 14.—Delays and abandonment of the work for the season, 14.—Groundless fears for the security of the foundation, 15.—Determination to renew the attempt in the following season, 15.—Mr. C. W. Scott appointed superintendent at Ushruffee, 15.—Arrangements for the concrete changed, 16.—The 'Union' vessel manned by Europeans alone, 16.—Portland cement sent out, 16.—Delay in the commencement of operations, 16.—Gravel for the concrete procured from the desert of Suez, 17.—Resumption of operations at Ushruffee, 17.—Deposition of the concrete base, 17.—Site for the lighthouse selected at the Dædalus, 18.—Surface of the reef, 19.—Raising the piles, 19.—Cargo discharged from the vessel, 19.—Deposition of the concrete, 20.—Whole conduct of the undertaking committed to Mr. Scott, 20.—Sickness among the workmen, 20.—Completion of the framework of the Dædalus lighthouse, 20.—Completion of the nautical part of the undertaking, 21.—Sequel of the Dædalus works, 21.—Progress and completion of the works at Ushruffee under difficulties, 22.—Freedom from accidents, 22.—Cost of the undertaking, 23.

Discussion.—Arrow, Capt., 27.—Belcher, Admiral Sir E., 29.—Bower, J., 28.—Collyer, Colonel G. C., 34.—Cowper, E. A., 28.—Curtis, J. G. C., 31.—Douglass, J. N., 29.—Gordon, A., 24, 28, 36.—Grissell, H., 35.—Hemans, G. W., 30.—Jenkin, F., 29.—Maury, Capt. F. M., 34.—Parkes, W., 24, 26, 30, 36.—Porter, J. H., 29.—Smith, Colonel J. T., 34.—Vignoles, C. B., 26, 27, 36.

Roman rock. "The Roman rock lighthouse, Simon's bay, Cape of Good Hope." By J. F. Bourne, xxviii. 49 —Simon's bay, 49.—The Roman rocks, 49, 50.—Original design of the lighthouse, 49.—Cause of failure 50,

LIGHTHOUSES.

51.—Works for strengthening, 51.—Difficulties encountered, 53, 54.—Progress and completion, 55, *et seq.*—Workmen's sick fund, 57.

Discussion.—Bourne, J. F., 58.

Wolf Rock. "The Wolf Rock lighthouse." By J. N. Douglass, xxx. 1. —Lights and beacons previously in existence in the vicinity of the Land's End, 1.—Longships lighthouse, 2.—Rundlestone beacons, 2.—Buoy now in existence at the Rundlestone, 3.—Bearings and description of the Wolf rock, 4.—Original design for a lighthouse, 5.—Iron beacons on Wolf rock, 5.—Arrangements for commencing a lighthouse, 6.—Form and dimensions of the tower, 6.—Dovetailing and other methods of securing the courses of masonry, 7.—Damage during construction caused by wreck, 8.—Internal arrangements and fittings, 8.—Lantern, 8.—Light, 8, 9.—Experiments with red and white lights, 9.—Fog-bell, 9.—Landing platform, 9.—Season of 1861, 10.—Ditto, 1862, 10.—Ditto, 1863, 11.—Ditto, 1864, 11.—Iron derrick landing-crane, 11.—Stone barges, 11.—Positions of barges, buoys, landing boat, and barrack schooner when engaged at the rock, 12.—Landing boat, 12.—Moorings, 12.—Wear of the chains, 13.—Season of 1865, 13.—Ditto, 1866, 14.—Wrought-iron setting crane, 14.—Season of 1867, 14.—Ditto, 1868, 14.—Steam-winch for raising stones, 15.—Season of 1869: Exhibition of the light, 15.—Successful termination of the work without accident, 15.—System under which the workmen were employed, 15.—Cost, 16.—Average number of persons employed, 16.

Discussion.—Arrow, Sir F., 17.—Beardmore, N., 25.—Beazeley, M., 25.—Coode, J., 24.—Douglass, J. N., 26.—Gregory, C. H., 19.—Hawksley, T., 28.—Owen, Capt. J. F., 21.—Parkes, W., 17, 26.—Pole, W., 19.—Redman, J. B., 22.—Stephenson, G. R., 21.—Vignoles, C. B., 17.

LIGHT RAILWAYS.

Light railways. On the Festiniog railway for passengers; as a 2-feet gauge with sharp curves, and worked by locomotive engines (Tyler, Capt. W. H.), xxiv. 359.

——, on, in Norway, India, and Queensland (Fox, C. D.), xvi. 49.

Vide also RAILWAYS.

LIVESAY, J. G. [Election, xxv. 508.]

LIVESEY, F. [Admission, xxvii. 54; Election, xxix. 98.]

LIVESEY, J. [Election, xxvii. 55.]

LIZARS, W. H. [Election, xxiv. 62.]

LLEWELLIN, D. [Election, xxiv. 62.]

LLEWELLIN, W. [Decease, xxiv. 117.]

LLOYD, J. H. [Associate of Council, xxvii. 122.]

Bridges, Victoria, Pimlico, xxvii. 112.

Drainage of land, xxi. 110.—Generally admitted benefits accruing to land from under-drainage, 110.—Irregularities produced in the even flow of rivers, 111.—Examples of the rivers Trent and Derwent 112.—The Land Drainage Act not sufficiently comprehensive or prospective, 113.

Ports of Calcutta and of the Mutla, xxi. 31.

Railway income and expenditure, xxix. 358.—Importance of statistical results, 359.—Finance of railway companies, 361. — Railway administration and management, 362.—Question of low fares and distribution of the classes, 363.—Compensation for railway accidents, 363.

LLOYD, W. [Telford medal and premium, xxiv. 109, 124.]

Locomotive engines proposed for a railway with steep gradients in Mexico, xxvi. 351. — English and American locomotives, xxviii. 421.

Railway. "Description of the Santiago and Valparaiso railway, Chilé, South America; with remarks upon resistances from curves of railways, and upon coal-burning locomotives," xxiii. 376.

Railway inclines, xxvi. 349.—Gradients on the Valparaiso and Santiago railway, 350.—Result of working the gradients of the Copiapo extension railway from Pabellon to Chanarcillo, 350.—Working the Serra do Mar incline as a locomotive line, xxx. 66.—Ditto of the Pomaron mineral railway, Portugal, 67.

Railway rolling stock. Weight of railway carriages, xxviii. 422.—American ditto, 422.—Bogie trucks, 423.

Railways, maintenance and working expenses of, xxviii. 420.

Loch Ken viaduct, Portpatrick railway, description of the (Blyth, E. L. I.), xxi. 258. *Vide* also VIADUCTS.

LOCOMOTIVE ENGINES.

American. *Vide* LOCOMOTIVE ENGINES AND ROLLING STOCK.

Coal-burning. "Description of the Santiago and Valparaiso railway, Chilé, South America; with remarks upon resistances from curves on railways, and upon coal-burning locomotives." By W. Lloyd, xxiii. 376. *Vide* also RAILWAYS.

Disturbing forces of. " On some of the internal disturbing forces of locomotive engines." By A. W. Makinson, xxii. 65.—Improvements in the permanent way of railways, 65.— General considerations of the effect of internal forces causing transverse erratic movements of locomotives, 65. —Forces essentially required in locomotives, 66.—Description of the indicator diagrams illustrative of the working of the ' Great Britain ' locomotive, 66, *et seq.*—Definition and enumeration of the disturbing forces of locomotives, 67.—Detailed account of the nature and origin of the forces accumulated in the piston, piston-rod, and crank-pin, 68.—Variation in the tractive force developed through one stroke of either piston, 70.—Variation in the amount of the entire tractive force of the engine throughout an entire revolution of the driving-wheel, 70.—Comparative merits of the double-cylinder and single-cylinder locomotive, as far as regards uni-

LOCOMOTIVE ENGINES.

formity of motion, 72. — Sinuous motion produced in modern locomotives, 72.—Disturbing action of the steam in the double-cylinder engine, 73.—Tendency to sinuous motion produced by all the disturbing forces, and the effect on the permanent way, 73.—Cause of the jarring and vibration of the carriages and of engines leaving the rails, 74. — Practical remedy to be obtained by the adoption of balanced single-cylinder engines, 75.—Resistance to be overcome in starting the double-cylinder and single-cylinder engine, 76.—The single-cylinder engine recommended for adoption, 78.—Appendix: formula showing the relation between the pressure on the piston, as observed by the indicator, and the equivalent pressure at the crank-pin of locomotives, 79.—Disturbing forces generated by the unbalanced revolving masses, 80.—Method of finding the pressures, referred to the crank-pin, generated by the vis-inertiæ and varying velocity of the reciprocating parts of a locomotive in motion, 81.

Discussion.—Bidder, G. P., 102.—Bramwell, F. J., 85.—Cowper, E. A., 94.—Gravatt, W., 99.—Harrison, T. E., 84.—Hemans, G. W., 101.—Kershaw, J., 99.—Kitson, J., 83.—Lane, C. B., 106.—M'Clean, J. R., 83.—Makinson, A. W., 83, 84, 106.—Molesworth, G. L., 100.—Naylor, W., 106.—Phipps, G. H., 97.—Sinclair, R., 98.—Reynolds, E., 104.—Russell, J. S., 92.—Vignoles, C. B., 100.

Structure of, for ascending steep inclines, with sharp curves on railways (Cross, J.), xxiii. 406. *Vide* also RAILWAY LOCOMOTION.

Vide also LOCOMOTIVE ENGINES AND ROLLING STOCK; MACHINES AND ENGINES; PERMANENT WAY; RAILWAY ACCIDENTS; RAILWAY CURVES AND INCLINES; RAILWAY INCOME AND EXPENDITURE; RAILWAY LOCOMOTION; RAILWAY ROLLING STOCK; and RAILWAYS.

LOCOMOTIVE ENGINES, &c.

LOCOMOTIVE ENGINES AND ROLLING STOCK. " American locomotives and rolling stock." By Z. Colburn, xxviii. 360. —Differences in the systems of the railway machinery of America and England external rather than fundamental, 360, 362, 383.—First locomotives worked in America, 360.—Bogies, 361, 362, 363, 379, 380.—Spark arresters and cabs, 361.—Method of obtaining great steam tractive power, 362.—Compensating levers for distributing and equalizing the weight of the engine on the wheels, 362.—Pressure on the wheels of the engines of the Baltimore and Ohio and Reading railroads, 363.—Dimensions of wheels and wheel-base, 363. — Coupled wheels for goods engines, 364. — General form of passenger engines, 365. — Rate of speed and stoppages, 365.—Consumption of fuel, 365.—Goods engines, 367.—Goods traffic, 368.—Adhesion, 369, 383.—Experimental train on the Erie railroad, 369.—Engine, 369.—Train, 370. — Tractive force, 370. — Superiority of oil to yellow grease for lubricating axles, 371.—Chilled cast-iron wheels, 372, 383.—Cost of ditto enhanced by taxation, 372.—Engine driving-wheels, with chilled faces and without tires, 373.—Wood and coal fuel, 373.—Steel fire-boxes and iron tubes for locomotives burning coal, 373, 383. — Boiler explosions and 'furrowing,' 373. — Decoration of locomotives, 374.—Steep inclines, 375. —Locomotives for working ditto, 375. —Difficulty of arriving at the comparative cost of maintenance of locomotives in Great Britain and America, 376.—Causes conducive to economy in repairs of American locomotives, 377.—Comparative mileage of engines in America and on the London and North Western railway, 377.—Carriage and wagon stock, 378, 382, 384. —Oil-tight axle-box, 381. — Breaks, 381. — Bogie tenders, 383. — Peculiarities of American practice fitted

LOEFFLER.

for colonial and foreign lines in new districts, 384.

Discussion.—Adams, W. A., 397.—Adams, W. B., 386, 402.—Atkinson, W., 404.—Berkley, G., 393.—Birckell, J. J., 430.—Brereton, R. P., 396.—Colburn, Z., 385, 423.—Cowper, E. A., 406, 409.—Fox, Sir C., 415.—Gregory, C. H., 430.—Harrison, T. E., 397.—Hemans, G. W., 385, 411.—Hodge, P. R., 402. — Lewis, W. B., 396.—Lloyd, W., 420.—Palliser, Major W., 407.—Pole, W., 408.—Radford, G. K., 423.—Tyler, Capt. H. W., 411.—Younghusband, O., 433.

Vide also LOCOMOTIVE ENGINES; MACHINES AND ENGINES; PERMANENT WAY; RAILWAY ACCIDENTS; RAILWAY CURVES AND INCLINES; RAILWAY INCOME AND EXPENDITURE; RAILWAY LOCOMOTION; RAILWAY ROLLING STOCK; and RAILWAYS.

LOEFFLER, J. C. L. [Election, xxiv. 184.]

LOGAN, D. [Election, xxvii. 55.]

LOGIN, T. [Election, xxvii. 580; Telford premium, xxviii. 161, 178.]

Drainage of land, xxviii. 85.—Effect of changes of spring level on the vegetation of the Puttree valley, 85.—Drainage and navigation of the Fens, 85.

Irrigation. "On the benefits of irrigation in India, and on the proper construction of irrigating canals," xxvii. 471.—Remarks, 508.—Fall of rain in. and revenue of, the Rechna Doab, 508.—Revenue of the western and eastern Jumna canals, 508.—Financial state of the Ganges canal, 508.—Flow of water over the Solani aqueduct, 509.—Effect of change of slope on the bed of the Ganges canal, 545.

Rivers and estuaries. Transporting power of water, illustrated in the case of Indian and Burmese rivers, xxviii. 84.—Liability of Indian rivers to change their course, 85.—Navigation and drainage of the Fens, 85.—Annual silting-up of the Pyn Kyoung creek through the tidal 'bore' in the Sittang river, 86.

LONDON AND DUBLIN.

LONDON AND DUBLIN COMMUNICATION. "On the communication between London and Dublin." By W. Watson, xxii. 574.—Holyhead a convenient port of departure for Dublin, 574.—Communication between London and Dublin very irregular, and journey very protracted in the last century, 574.—Note as to the Skerries rock lighthouse, 574.—Improvements effected in the land part of the journey from London to Holyhead in the first quarter of the present century, 575.—Inferiority of the vessels employed, 576.—Construction of the packet harbour at Howth, 576.—Successful introduction of steam-vessels, 576.—Direct postal service established between Liverpool and Dublin, 577. — Regular steam communication between Liverpool and Dublin, originated by C. Wye Williams, 577.—Iron seagoing vessels first built by A. Manby, 578.—Completion of the railway from London to Liverpool, and between London and Holyhead, 578. — Approximate cost of maintaining the service between Great Britain and Ireland, prior to its concentration at Holyhead, 578.—Completion of the Asylum harbour of Kingstown, 579.—Holyhead harbour of refuge, 579.—Introduction of a superior class of vessels, 579.—Vessels provided by the Chester and Holyhead Railway Company, 579.—Admiralty contract for the packet-service, 579.—Gradual improvements in acceleration of time occupied in the journey at various periods, 580.—Plan for further improvements in the train and steam-packet service, 581.—Recommendation of a Committee of the House of Commons rejected, 581.—Ultimate agreement between the Government and the London and North Western Railway Company and the City of Dublin Steam Packet Company for an accelerated service, 582.—Extract from Treasury Minute, dated October 19, 1855, 582.—Main provisions of

LONG.

the new postal contract, 583 — Vessels constructed for the service, 584.—Details of the 'Connaught,' 584.—Engines of the 'Connaught' and the 'Leinster,' 586.—The 'Ulster' and the 'Munster,' 587. — Internal arrangements of the vessels, 587.—Opportunity for attaining good results, 588.—Cost of the vessels, 588. —Post-office for sorting letters during the passage, 589.—Commencement of the service and gain in speed realised by the new vessels, 589.—Stone jetty for landing in Kingstown harbour, 590.—Piers and quays not yet finished at Holyhead, 590.—Timber jetty for temporary use, 591. — Manner in which the new service has been performed, 591.—Consumption of coal, 593. — No breakdown experienced, 593.—Difficulty in obtaining sufficiently sound forgings for the large intermediate air-pump crank-shafts, 593.—No repairs to the ships hitherto needed, 594.—Bottoms of the vessels cleaned by divers, 594.—Appendix: particulars of trial-trips, 595.

Discussion. — Brereton, R. P., 597. — Cowper, E. A., 597.—Hawksley, T., 600.—Humphreys, E., 598.—Phipps, G. H., 598.—Robertson, A. J., 600.—Russell, J. S., 596, 601.—Samuda, J. D'A., 596.—Watson, W., 597, 602.

LONG, W. H. [Election, xxix. 98.]

Long tube barometer (Howson, B.), xxi. 32.

LONGLANDS, R. [Election, xxx. 1.]

LONGRIDGE, J. A. [Council premium, xxii. 121, 131.]

Artillery, xxvi. 198.

Bridges and viaducts, xxv. 248.—Grand river viaduct, Mauritius railways, 248.—Launching the girders, 249, 260. —Method of pushing a girder over the Tolly's canal on the Calcutta and South Eastern railway, 261.—Proper material for arched bridges, xxvii. 108.—Girder-bridge built on a quicksand near Calcutta, 296.

Bridges, suspension, xxvi. 270, 272.

Cements, lime and concrete, xxv. 133.

LONGRIDGE.

—Use of salt-water in slaking cement and lime, 133.—Concrete used in connection with the Suez canal at Port Saïd, 133.—Concrete used in Grand river viaduct, 248.

Foundations, xxvii. 296.

Locomotive engines, xxvi. 371; xxvii. 391; xxviii. 257, 259.

Low-water basin at Birkenhead, xxix. 9.

Permanent way, xxvi. 372.—Steel rails, 372.—Malleable-iron rails first used at the Bedlington ironworks, xxvii. 390 —Testing rails by a falling weight, 390.—Form of rails, 391.

Pile-driving in loose sand, xxvii. 296.

Railway inclines, xxvi. 371.—Results of working a railway with steep gradients in the Mauritius, 371.—Locomotive engines for ascending steep inclines, 371.—Question of working railway inclines by locomotives or rope-traction, xxx. 73.

Railway locomotion, xxvii. 391.—Means of diminishing the grinding action of the driving-wheels of locomotives, 391.

Railways. Cost of the Charing Cross railway, xxvii. 434. — Gradients of the Mauritius railways, xxviii. 256, 258. — Cost of working the Mont Cenis railway compared with the Mauritius railways, 257.—Weight of the engines on the Mont Cenis railway, 258.—Gauge of ditto, 259.—Springs applied to the wheels of the engines, 259.—Cost of working the traffic on the Mont Cenis railway, xxx. 73.

River Tyne, xxvi. 429.—Improvements effected by Mr. Brooks, 429.—Dredging operations subsequently carried out, 430.—Littoral current, 431.

Rivers and estuaries. "The Hooghly and the Mutla," xxi. 2.—Remarks, 25.—Quantity of mud brought down by the Ganges, 25.

Telegraph cables. Malta and Alexandria submarine cable, xxv. 54. — Necessity of constructing deep-sea cables of low specific gravity, 54.—Atlantic telegraph, 54.—Raising submarine cables, 62.

LONGSDON.

Telegraphic communication with India, xxv. 53.—Inadvisability of attempting to establish and maintain telegraphic communication through the Turkish dominions, 53.—Telegraph route to India from Suez to Aden, and from Aden to Bombay, 56.

Water, filtration of, xxvii. 41.—Mechanical operation of removing matters in suspension, 41.—Removal of matter in solution, 42.

LONGSDON, A. [Election, xxvii. 443.]
LOUTTIT, S. H. [Election, xxv. 352.]
LOVATT, H. [Election, xxiv. 257.]
LOVEGROVE, J.

Drainage of towns, xxii. 301.—Cleansing the sewers at Dundee, 301.—Needless expense incurred in constructing ditto, 301.—Escape of noxious gases through untrapped and imperfect gullies, 302.—Course of the draft in sewers, 302.—Vertical inspection-shaft to facilitate the cleansing and ventilation of small sewers, 303.—Form of gully-trap, 303.

LOVELL, T. [Election, xxii. 65.]
LOW, W. [Election, xxvii. 55.]
LOWE, C. H. [Election, xxvi. 310.]
LOWE, G. [Memoir, xxx. 442.]
LÖWINGER, C. [Election, xxii. 451.]
LOW-WATER BASIN at BIRKENHEAD.

"Description of the low-water basin at Birkenhead." By J. Ellacott, xxviii. 518.—Plans sanctioned by Parliament in 1844, 518.—Advantages of the situation chosen for the works, 519.—Site fixed on for the low-water basin, 519.—Alterations in the dock plans, 519.—Projected communication between the basin and the Mersey, 519.—Intended depth of the basin, 519.—Range of the tides, 519.—The great dam, 520.—Plan for clearing the basin by the discharge of water from the great float by sluices, 520.—Transfer of the estate to the Mersey Docks and Harbour Board, 521.—Substitution of Mr. J. B. Hartley's plans for those of Mr. Rendel, 521.—The low-water basin as carried out, 522.—The dam, 522.—Arrange-

LUBBOCK.

ments for sluicing, 522.—Sluicing chambers, 523.—Division walls, 523.—Sluicing paddles, 524.—Masonry, 524.—Hydraulic power, 524—Culverts for scouring away deposit from near the wings, 524.—Bursting-in of the dam, 525.—Results of, 525.—Accident from running the water through the culvert in the south wall of the basin, 525.—Sluicing operations, 525.—Events which occurred during the different trials, 526.—Removal of deposit from the bottom of the basin, 527.—Table of the results of the operations, 528.—Rate of accumulation of deposit, 528, 529.—Details of sluicing operations, 528.—Effect of the scour over the main portion of the basin, 530.—Velocities of the currents of water when the sluices were open, 530. —Record of sluicing operations in August, 1864, 531.—Dangerous nature of the operations, 531.—Sluicing capable of maintaining the low-water basin at its proper depth, 532. —Determination to convert the low-water basin into a wet-dock, 532.—Extract from the preamble of the Act of 1866, 532.—Gradual silting-up of the basin since the close of the sluicing operations, 533.—Capital expenditure on the basin, and estimate for forming it into a wet-dock, 533.—Summary of the records of the direction of the wind at Liverpool observatory, 533.—Tables of the results of soundings across the river Mersey between Liverpool and Birkenhead, in 1822 and 1827, 535. —Changes in the bed of the river Mersey, 535.

Discussion.—Abernethy, J., 5.—Beardmore, N., 21.—Blair, J. F., 19.—Giles, A., 18.—Hawksley, T., 19.—Longridge, J. A., 9.—Murray, J., 3.—Parkes, W., 17.—Rawlinson, R., 16.—Webster, J., 7, 17.

LOYSEL, E. [Memoir, xxx. 475.]
LUARD, W. C. [Election, xxix. 322.]
LUBBOCK, Sir J. W., Bart. [Memoir, xxv. 510.]

112

LUCAS.

LUCAS, C. T. [Election, xxiv. 62; Associate of Council, xxvi. 119.]

LUCAS, T. [Election, xxiv. 62.]

LUCAS, W. H. [Election, xxv. 262.]

LÜDERS, F. W. W. [Election, xxviii. 517.]

LUKE, W. [Election, xxvii. 55.]

LUNGLEY, A. R. [Admission, xxvii. 54.]

LUPTON, A.

Coal-mining, xxviii. 131.—Loss of life

LYSTER.

in connection with coal-mining operations, 131.—Getting coal by undercutting and wedging, 131.—Coalbreaking apparatus invented by Mr. S. P. Bidder, Mr. C. J. Chubb, and Mr. Grafton Jones, 133.—Waste from holing coal, 134.

LYNDHURST, Lord. [Memoir, xxiii. 478.]

LYSTER, G. F.

River Mersey, xxvi. 425.

M.

MABERLY.

MABERLY, A. W. [Election, xxiii. 459.]

M'ALPINE, W. J. [Election, xxvi. 310; Telford medal, xxviii. 161, 178.]

Piles. "The supporting power of piles; and on the pneumatic process for sinking iron columns, as practised in America," xxvii. 275.

M'CLEAN, F. [Election, xxiii. 375.]

M'CLEAN, J. R. [Vice-President, xxi. 133; xxii. 112; President, xxiii. 112; xxiv. 106; Past-President, xxv. 202; xxvi. 164; xxvii. 179; xxviii. 215; xxix. 271.]

Address on taking the chair for the first time after his election as President, xxiii. 151.—Effects of the railway system in promoting the material and intellectual progress of Great Britain, 151.—Erroneous opinion that the increased prosperity of the country has resulted from improvements in the cultivation of the land, 152.—Comparison of the property and income of the country in the years 1815 and 1856, 152.—Tables of the net amount of the property and income of Great Britain, from all sources, liable to assessment for taxation in the years 1815 and 1856, 153.—Causes of the increase of income, 154.—Railway securities a safe medium for investment, 154.—Construction of railways has established a wealthy and educated middle-class in Europe, 155.—The railway system in Great Britain occupies one half per cent. of the area of the land, yet pays nearly an equal amount of tax to the land under culture, 155. —Coal raised annually in Great Britain equivalent to the annual production of timber on an area equal to that of France, 156.—Development of coal the main cause of increase of wealth, 156.—Question as to the permanence of coal supply, 156.—Theory

M'CLEAN.

of central heat, 157.—Equivalent in horse-power of daily consumption of coal, 157.—Coal may be drawn profitably from almost any depth, 158.— Annual production of iron in the United Kingdom, 158.—Value of coal and iron exported in 1862, 158.— Quantities of other minerals produced in 1862, 158.—Failure of cotton supply obviated to a great extent by the profits from minerals, 158.—Iron shipbuilding, 158.—Iron screw-steamships practically an extension of the railway system, 159.—General reflections on the increase and distribution of wealth since 1815, 159.—Extension of the railway system in the metropolis, 159.—Railways should be constructed by means of private funds, 160.— Unproductive works of national importance may be executed at the public expense, 160.—The Isthmus of Suez canal, 160.—Statement respecting the labours of the English members of the International Commission appointed for examining the question of the practicability of forming a ship-canal through the Isthmus of Suez, 160.—English plan for a high-level canal with locks rejected, 161.— Mr. Hawkshaw's report on the ship-canal in 1863, 162.—Extension of the railway system necessary for the prospects and wellbeing of the world, 162.—Disastrous effects that would result from making the railway system a protected interest, 162.—Desirability of free-trade, and of the abolition of all restrictions on commerce, 163.— Comparative advantages of the two systems proposed for constructing a direct canal between the Mediterranean and Red seas, 164.—List of members of the International Commission on the Isthmus of Suez canal, 167.

M'CLELLAND.

Drainage of towns. Main-drainage of London, xxiv. 358.

Locomotive engines, single-cylinder, xxii. 83.

Rivers and estuaries, xxi. 28.—Tidal scour in the Barrow estuary, 28.— Works at the Sulina mouth of the Danube, 294.

M'CLELLAND, W. [Election, xxvii. 55.]

M'CONNELL, J. E.

Steam-engines, xxiii. 98. — Results of experiments to ascertain the duty of a pair of double-acting Cornish engines, 98.

M'CONNOCHIE, J. [Election, xxiii. 375.]

M'CONNOCHIE, J. A, [Election, xxiv. 144.]

MACDONALD, J. O. [Election, xxvii. 218.]

MACEDO, M. B. de. [Election, xxvi. 544.]

MACHINES AND ENGINES.

"On the manufacture of duplicate machines and engines." By J. Fernie, xxii. 604.—Introduction of the system of special machines, each adapted to perform a particular operation, 604.— Saving effected by the introduction of the block machinery at Portsmouth dockyards, 604.—Ditto by the dupli- cate system at Enfield, 605.—Impor- tance of fine measurements demon- strated by Mr. Whitworth, 605.— Description of a machine introduced in the workshops of the Midland railway, 606.—Manner of obtaining duplicates, 607.—Table of experiments on differences in diameter in boring and turning wheels, 607.—Results of the experiments, 607.—Results found in shrinking on outside cranks, 608.— Gauges used, 608.—Method by which the lengths of the eccentric rods are preserved uniform, 608.—Improve- ments in plate-moulding, 609.—Plan for securing the fitting together of the various pieces of a locomotive, so as to insure uniformity in erection as well as in construction, 610.—Advantages of the system, 611.

Discussion.—Beyer, C. F., 612.—Bram- well, F. J., 612.—Fernie, J., 612, 613. —Vignoles, C. B., 613.

MAKINSON.

MACINTOSH, J.

Ships of war, xxvi. 224.—Monitors, 224. — Ventilation of ditto, 224.—Small buoyancy of ditto, 225.

Telegraph cables, xxi. 536.—Relative absorption of water by indiarubber and by gutta-percha, 536.—Impervious coverings, 536.—Iron-wire and hemp spiral coverings a source of weakness, xxv. 51.—Strong form of cable with the insulator consisting of numerous films of indiarubber or gutta-percha, 51.—Construction of ditto, 51.—India- rubber coverings, 52.—Insulating pro- perties of paraffin compound, 53.

MACINTYRE, J. S. [Election, xxvii. 55.]

MACKENZIE, H. A. O. [Election, xxvii. 553.]

M'KERROW, A. [Election, xxv. 203.] ·

MACKESY, Captain W. H. [Election, xxi. 492.]

MACKIE, S. J. [Election, xxvii. 580.]

MACKINLAY, J. [Election, xxvii. 55.]

MACKINNON, A. K. [Election, xxx. 106.]

MACKINNON, M. C. [Election, xxx. 323.]

MACKINTOSH, C. E. [Election, xxvi. 242.]

MACKISON, F. [Election, xxiv. 458.]

MACKWORTH, Sir A. W., Bart., Lieut. R.E. [Election, xxvii. 443.]

McMASTER, B.

Railway sleepers. "On the woods used for sleepers on the Madras railway," xxi. 241.

M'MURDO, Colonel W. M. S. [Election, xxv. 65.]

MACNAY, T. F. [Election, xxx. 106.]

MACTIER, —.

Ports of Calcutta and of the Hooghly. Extracts from his report of the 15th February, 1853 (Longridge, J. A.), xxi. 3.

M'VEAGH, J. [Memoir, xxi. 563.]

MAGNUS, W. A. [Admission, xxix. 272.]

MAKINSON, A. W. [Telford premium, xxiii. 114, 126.]

Locomotive engines. "On some of the internal disturbing forces of locomotive engines," xxii. 65.—Remarks, 83.— Plan for starting a single-cylinder engine, 83.—Sinuous motion produced by the pressure of the steam only,

MALINS.

84, 106.—Question of the moving force increasing more rapidly than the velocity, 107.—Theoretical demonstration of the lateral movement of the front of a locomotive, 107.—Movement exemplified in the case of the 'Great Britain' locomotive, 108.—Possibility of the engine leaving the rails from this cause, 108.—Effect of the varying tractive power, 109.—Violent oscillations at high speeds on a seemingly perfect road, 110.

MALINS, W. [Resignation, xxiv. 117.]

MALLET, R.

Artillery, xxvi. 199.—Penetration of shells, 199.—Effect of heavy shot on armour-plates, 199.

Bridges and viaducts. Iron lattice bridges in Germany, xxii. 38.—Rapid deterioration of timber bridges in America, 325.—Durability of European wooden bridges, 325.—River Nore viaduct, 325.—Principles of construction of iron girder bridges, xxiv. 435.

Canals, steam-power on, xxvi. 28.—Introduction of flyboats towed by horses on the Grand and Royal Irish canals, 29.—Experiments with a steam paddle-boat on ditto, 29.—Ditto at the port of Dublin, 30.—Modifications of the wave from the use of different paddle-floats, 30.—Expediency of vertical walls for the sides of canals, 31, 33.—Slope assumed by the Irish canals, 32.

Coal-mining, xxviii. 129. — Hydraulic machine for breaking down coal, invented by Mr. Grafton Jones, 129.—Hydraulic press for breaking down coal, devised by Mr. Joseph Bramah, 136.—Conical splitting screw, 137.—Donisthorpe's coal-hewing machinery, 140.—Mr. S. P. Bidder's apparatus, 140.

Drainage, arterial, in Ireland, xxi. 114.—Effect in accelerating the passage of flood-water, 114.—Results of drainage-works on the climate of Ireland, 115.—Declivity of the surface of catchment basins an important element of the rapidity of discharge, 115.

MALLET.

Engineers, advantages of a sound technical education for, xxii. 38, *et seq.*

German industry, rapid extension of, xxvii. 39.

Iron, decay of, in water, and the means of preserving it, xxviii. 229, 231.

Lagoons, formation of, on the shores of the Mediterranean, xxviii. 311.—Lagoons in the delta of the Rhone, 313.—Plans by M. Duponchel for reclaiming ditto, 315.

Materials, resistance of, xxix. 54.—Experiments for determining strength, 55.—Sir W. Fairbairn's experimental researches as to the resistance to collapse of the tubes of boilers, 56.—Experiments on 'repeated vibrations of girders,' 58.—Vibration in elastic solids, 59.—Elastic limit of structural materials, 59.—Ascertaining the specific gravity of metals, 60.

Piers and landing stages, xxviii. 229.—Movement of the large landing stages on the Mersey, 229.

Railway system of Germany, xxii. 37.—Freedom from accidents on German railways, 39.—Narrow-gauge railway between Antwerp and Ghent, xxiv. 375.—Advantages of narrow-gauge lines generally, 376.—Rolling stock to be used on ditto, 376.—Choice of gauge primarily dependent upon the traffic to be accommodated, 388.

Surveying and levelling, xxi. 45.—Measuring distances by the telescope, 45.

Tunnels, xxiii. 297.—Machinery for perforation, 297.—Hand 'jumping,' 298.—Use of deep holes and great charges of powder, 298. — Project of M. de Fontenay, as to the Mont Cenis tunnel, 299.

Weight per square foot of a crowd of men, xxii. 532.

MALLET, R. T. [Election, xxii. 540.]

Locomotive engines, xxvi. 381.

Railway inclines. Tramway on a steep incline on the Ottoman railway as worked by ordinary locomotives, xxvi. 381.

MALTA.

Malta and Alexandria submarine telegraph cable, the (Forde, H. C.), xxi. 493. *Vide* also TELEGRAPH CABLES.

MANBY, C. [Honorary Secretary, xxi. 133; xxii. 112; xxiii. 112; xxiv. 106; xxv. 161; xxvi. 119; xxvii. 122; xxviii. 158; xxix. 208.]

MANBY, E. O. [Memoir, xxiv. 531.]

MANBY, J. L. [Memoir, xxii. 629.]

MANBY, J. R. [Memoir, xxx. 446.]

Manby premiums. *Vide* PREMIUMS AND PRIZES.

MANISTY, E. [Election, xxx. 323.]

MANN, F. G. [Admission, xxvii. 54.]

MANN, G. O. [Election, xxiv. 62; Telford premium, xxv. 165, 180.]

Materials, durability of. "On the decay of materials in tropical climates, and the methods employed for arresting and preventing it," xxiv. 1.

MANNERS, C. R. [Election, xxx. 323.]

MANNING, J. R. [Election, xxiv. 62.]

MANNING, R. [Telford medal and Manby premium, xxvi. 121, 138.]

Rivers, circumstances which influence the maximum discharge of, xxvii. 261. —Maximum discharge from various drainage areas in Ireland, 261.

Water, flow of. "On the results of a series of observations on the flow of water off the ground in the Woodburn district, near Carrickfergus, Ireland; with rain-gauge registries in the same locality for a period of twelve months, ending 30th June, 1865," xxv. 458.— Remarks, 470.—Record of the rain-gauge observations at Belfast and in the Woodburn district, 470, 476.— Observations of the flow off the ground, 470.—Additional observations of the flow off the Woodburn district by Mr. Lanyon, 471.—General results of the Woodburn observations, 471.— Mill-power at Woodlawn, 472.—Published statements of the rainfall available for the supply of water to Belfast, 477. — Storage for ditto, 478.— Mill-power in the Woodburn district, 478. —Lowell formula for calculating the discharge of water, 478.

MAPPIN, F. T. [Election, xxiv. 184.]

MARTLEY.

MARGARY, P. J.

Railway inclines, results of working steep, xxvi. 365.

Railways. Atmospheric system on the South Devon railway, xxvi. 365.— Sledge-breaks, 366. — Fell's central rail system for branch lines, 366.

Steel, manufacture of, xxvi. 365.

MARILLIER, R. A. [Election, xxv. 262.]

Marine boilers and engines, decay of, xxvii. 575.—*Vide* also MATERIALS; SHIPS OF WAR; SHIPS AND STEAM-VESSELS; and STEAM NAVIGATION.

MARKHAM, C. [Election, xxiii. 375.]

Railway stations, xxx. 98.—Advantages of a railway station with a roof of a single span, 98. — Defacing railway stations with pasteboard advertisements, 99.—St. Pancras station of the Midland railway, 99.

MARLEY, J. [Election, xxvi. 398.]

MARRABLE, F. [Associate of Council, xxii. 112.]

Marseilles, account of the docks and warehouses at (Hawthorne, T.), xxiv. 144. *Vide* also DOCKS.

MARSH, T. E. M. [Election, xxi. 258.]

Permanent way. Iron rails made from 1846 to 1850 for the South Wales railway, xxvii. 375, *et seq.*—Samples of various rails in use on the Great Western system of railways, 376.—Letter by Mr. Brunel to twelve of the principal ironmasters respecting rails, 377. —South Western Railway company's specifications for rails, 379.

MARSHALL, E. [Decease, xxv. 532.]

MARSHALL, F. C. [Election, xxv. 203]

MARSHALL, P. P. [Election, xxiii. 110.]

MARSHALL, W. J. [Admission, xxvii. 54.]

Marshes. *Vide* COASTS; LAGOONS and MARSHES; and RECLAIMING LAND FROM THE SEA.

MARSHMAN, J. [Election, xxx. 1.]

MARTIN, C. [Election, xxx. 1.]

MARTIN, E. [Election, xxv. 352.]

MARTIN, S. G. [Election, xxiii. 375.]

MARTIN, T. [Election, xxvi. 79.]

MARTLEY, W. [Election, xxvi. 398.]

Railway rolling stock, xxx. 201.—Cost of repairs on long and short lines of

MASON.

railway, 201.—Disparity between train mileage and engine mileage in published mileage accounts, 201.

MASON, W. [Election, xxv. 262.]

Masonry, relative durability of ashlar and rubble, xxv. 115.

MATERIALS.

Choice of, xxv. 209.

Decay of. " On the decay of materials in tropical climates, and the methods employed for arresting and preventing it." By G. O. Mann, xxiv. 1.—Climate of Brazil, 1.—Rainfall, 1.—Durability of half-round creosoted sleepers from the North of Europe, 2.—Ballast best adapted for the preservation of sleepers in the tropics, 2.— Trial of native sleepers, 3.—Brazilian timber fit for railway purposes, 3.— Why the supply of wood has not been made available, 3.—Excellent quality of some woods in Brazil, 4.—Rules for preparing timber for sleepers, 4.— Cost of sleepers delivered on the Pernambuco railway, 4. — Character of timber suited to withstand the climate and ravages of the white ant, 4.— Application of coal-tar to the ends of timbers, 5.—Age of the old Recife wooden bridge, 5. — Precautions for insuring satisfactory results in preparing timber, 5.—Suspension of the transverse girders of iron bridges by bolts injudicious, 5.—Durability of iron bridges in the tropics, 5, *et seq.*— Bridge over the Pirapama river, 6.— Over the Saboatão, 6.—Over the mouth of the river Ibura, 6.—Cast-iron pipe piles, 7.—Preservation of iron bridges sent to the tropics by paint, tar, and oil, 7.—Protection by galvanising, 8.—Stone, 8.—Bricks, 9.—Tiles, 9.—Rafters, 9.—Laths, 10. —Permanent-way keys of native timber used on the Pernambuco railway, 10.—Rapid wear of permanent-way rails and wheel-tires in the tropics, 10.—Chairs and spikes, 10.— Use of Greaves's 'pot' sleepers on the Pernambuco railway, 11.—Carriages, 11. —Railway wagons, 11.—Subject of

MATERIALS.

the decay of materials in tropical climates but little known, 11.— List of Brazilian timbers used as sleepers on the Pernambuco railway, and suitable for general purposes in permanent structures, 13.— Table of specific gravities of Brazilian timber suitable for shipbuilding, 13.

—— " On the decay of materials in tropical climates, and the methods employed for arresting and preventing it." By W. J. W. Heath, 14.—Materials most used in the construction of permanent buildings in Ceylon, 14.— Huts built of 'wattle and dab,' 14.— 'Cabook,' 14.—Rubble masonry, 15.— Perishable character of brickwork, 15. —Lime, 15.—Best means of preserving timber, 16. —Iron and other metals, 16.—Paper, leather, and gutta-percha, 17.

Discussion.—Aitken, R., 20.—Berkley, G., 18.—Bethell, J., 30.—Bruce, G. B., 20.—Brunlees, J., 20.—Burt, H. P., 22. —Calvert, J., 34.—Curtis, J. G. C., 36.—De Mornay, A., 29.—Gregory, C. H., 25.—Hawkshaw, J., 18, 19, 22. —Heppel, J. M., 36.—Lane, C. B., 27. —Mann, G. O., 19.—Rendel, A. M., 22.—Sale, Col. T. H., 25.—Sheilds, F. W., 32.—Turnbull, G., 22.—Waugh, Gen. Sir A., 24.—Webster, T., 36.

Durability of. "On engineering philosophy: the durability of materials." By E. Clark, xxvii. 554.—Papers contributed to the Institution, principally practical, 554.—Questions which can be discussed more effectually in their abstract capacity than in connection with the practical applications out of which they arise, 554.—Materials used by the engineer, 555.—Durability of materials dependent on the agencies to which they are exposed, 555.—Tufa, marble, and telegraph wires, 555.—Varying durability of galvanized zinc roofs, timber, iron plates, and animal remains in various situations, 555.— Humidity under peculiar conditions the principal cause of decay, 556.— Vegetation in the form of fungus

MATERIALS.

always present in the decay of organic substances, 557.—Moisture an indispensable element of decay, 558.—Durability of metals dependent on the resistance they offer to combination with oxygen, 558.—Conditions that affect the durability of wrought iron, 559. — Preservative power of paint shown in the case of the Britannia bridge, 559. Slow deterioration of cast iron, 560.—Oxidation of zinc, and its destruction by galvanic action, 560. — Danger from the contact of metals of different conductive powers, 560.—Galvanized iron, 561.—Action of sea-water on copper, 561.—Cause of the comparative durability of paint, 562.—Gutta-percha, 562. — Value of silicious sand as a coating for paint, 562.—Constant destruction and reconstruction of matter on the earth, 563.—Unchangeable aspect of the moon, 563.

Discussion. — Barlow, W. H., 570. — Bazalgette, J. W., 572.—Beardmore, N., 569, 570.—Boulton, S. B., 564.—Brunlees, J., 575. — Clark, E., 564, 577.—Conybeare, H., 506.—Cowper, E. A., 576.—De Rusett, E. W., 575.—Farren, G., 567. — Giles, A., 573.—Gregory, C. H., 578.—Heppel, J. M., 569.—Johnson, T. M., 573.—Pole, W., 571.—Shoolbred, J. N., 568.—Symons, G. J., 570.—Vignoles, C. B., 572.—Webb, E. B., 574.

Preservation of, by chloride of zinc, xxii. 495.

Strength and resistance of. "On the present state of knowledge as to the strength and resistance of materials." By J. Gaudard (translated from the French by W. Pole), xxviii. 536. — Introductory remarks, 536. —Extension, 537.—Compression, 539.—Sliding, 541.—Texture of bodies, 542.—Limits of safety, 543.—Torsion, 544.—Flexure, 549.—Sliding due to flexure, 553.—Continuous beams, 555.—Lattice girders, 557.—Rupture imminent by flexure, 557.—Compound deformations, 559.—Formulæ for the

MAY.

general deformation of curved structures, 559.—Formulæ of M. Barré de St. Venant, 562.—Combination of different materials, 565.—Dynamical, or living resistance, 565. — Transverse vibrations for a homogeneous beam, 567.—List of works which the author has quoted, 571.

Discussion.—Barlow, W. H., 48.—Bow, R. H., 76. — Bramwell, F. J., 76.—Brereton, R. P., 63.— Brooke, C., 53, 75.—Cowper, E. A., 71.—Gaudard, J., 95.—Gregory, C. H., 95.—Hemans, G. W., 74.—Heppel, J. M., 41.—Jones, J., 76.—Mallet, R., 54.—Murray, A., 73.—Pole, W., 25.—Phipps, G. H., 70.—Reilly, C., 27, 77.—Siemens, C. W., 32. — Stoney, B. B., 75. — Thomson, Sir W., 74.—Unwin, W. C., 38.—Young, E. W., 34.

Vide also BRIDGES, IRON; BRIDGES, TIMBER; CEMENT; GIRDERS, IRON; IRON AND STEEL; PERMANENT WAY; RAILWAY SLEEPERS; TIMBER.

MATHER, W.
Well-boring machine, xxiii. 475.
MATHEW, F. [Election, xxix. 98.]
MATHEWS, E. D. [Election, xxvi. 398.]
MATHIAS, J. [Election, xxvii. 443.]
MATTHEW, J. [Memoir, xxx. 446.]
MATTHEWS, H. G. [Election, xxiv. 144.]
MATTHEWS, H. M. [Election, xxiv. 257.]
MAUDSLAY, H.
Cement, Portland, in actual contact with iron, xxv. 129.
Injector, Giffard's, xxv. 226.
MAUDSLAY, J. [Memoir, xxi. 560.]
Mauritius railways, the Grand River Viaduct (Ridley, W.), xxv. 237. *Vide* also VIADUCTS.
—— Midland line (Mosse, J. R.), xxviii. 232. *Vide* also RAILWAYS.
MAURY, Captain F. M.
Lighthouses, efficiency of, dependent on meteorological conditions, xxiii. 34.
Waves. Deadening effect of coral reefs on a rough sea, xxiii. 35.
MAXWELL, J. P. [Admission, xxviii. 59.]
MAY, G. [Memoir, xxvii. 595.]
MAY, J. [Election, xxiii. 442.]

MAY.

MAY, R. C.
  Drainage, xxviii. 83.—Outfall of the
  Welland and Denge marshes at Jury's
  Gut, 83.
MAYER, E. A. F. [Election, xxv. 352.]
MAYNARD, H. N. [Election, xxviii. 325.]
Measuring distances by the telescope,
  on (Bray, W. B.), xxi. 34. *Vide* also
  SURVEYING and LEVELLING.
MEDEIROS, Captain V. de. [Election, xxii.
  540.]
MEIK, P. W. [Admission, xxix. 98.]
MEIK, T. [Election, xxv. 479.]
Memoirs of deceased members, xxi. 542;
  xxii. 615; xxiii. 478; xxiv. 526; xxv.
  510; xxvi. 556; xxvii. 582; xxviii.
  573; xxx. 418.
MENELAUS, W. [Election, xxvii. 55.]
  Permanent way. Wrought-iron rails,
  xxvii. 353.—Manufacture of Bessemer
  steel rails, 353.—Steel-headed rails,
  354.
MERCER, W. [Election, xxvi. 79.]
MEREDITH, G. [Memoir, xxv. 515.]
MERRY, W.
  Drainage of towns, xxii. 297.—General
  principles to be discussed before
  entering into the details of sewers,
  297.—Difference between sewage in
  densely-populated and provincial
  towns, 298.
MESSENT, P. J.
  Rivers and estuaries. Depth of water
  on the bars of the Tees and of the
  Tyne, xxiv. 100.
MESSER, R. [Election, xxv. 65.]
METFORD, W. E.
  Surveying and levelling. Measuring
  distances by the telescope, xxi. 42.
MEULEN, J. P. van der. [Admission,
  xxviii. 232.]
MICHELE, B. M. de. [Election, xxviii. 232.]
Middle Level drainage, account of the
  cofferdam, the syphons, and other
  works, constructed in consequence of
  the failure of the St. Germains sluice
  of the (Hawkshaw, J.), xxii. 497.
  Vide also COFFERDAM AND SYPHONS.
—— destruction of sluice, xxi. 486, 491;
  xxii 498; xxvii. 538, 539.
MIDDLETON, R. E. [Election, xxix. 322.]

MITCHELL.

MIERS, F. C. [Election, xxii. 336.]
MIERS, J. W. [Election, xxix. 98.]
MILLER, D. [Telford premium, xxiii.
  114, 126; Election, 375.]
  Structures in the sea. "Structures in
  the sea, without cofferdams; with a
  description of the works of the new
  Albert harbour at Greenock," xxii. 417.
  —Remarks, 439.—Cost of the pier at
  Greenock, 439.—Concrete used, 448.—
  System of casing adopted, 449.—
  Stability of ditto, 449.
MILLER, G. M. [Memoir, xxiv. 532.]
MILLER, T. [Election, xxviii. 518.]
Miller prizes. *Vide* PREMIUMS.
MILLIGAN, R. [Election, xxi. 258.]
MILLS, W. [Election, xxx. 1.]
  Permanent way. Durability of steel and
  iron rails on the London, Chatham,
  and Dover railway, xxvii. 379.
MILLS, W. H. [Election, xxi. 345; Tel-
  ford premium, xxvi. 121, 138.]
  Viaduct. "The Craigellachie viaduct,"
  xxv. 229.
MILNE, J.
  Canals, steam-power on, xxvi. 10.—
  Introduction of steam-power on the
  Forth and Clyde and Monkland
  canals, 10,—Steamers and engines,
  10, *et seq.*—Locks, 13.—Introduction of carrying-steamers with high-
  pressure engines and screw-propellers,
  13.—Increase in the number of
  steamers, 14.
MILNER, H. E. [Election, xxx. 106.]
MILROY, J. [Election, xxvii. 553; Telford premium, xxix. 211.]
  Foundations. "Description of apparatus
  for excavating under water, and for
  sinking cylinders," xxviii. 339.—
  Remarks, 357.—Use of, at the Glasgow (City) Union railway bridge, 357.
  —Superiority of, to other machines for
  excavating, 358.
MILROY, J., Jun.
  Foundations, use of the excavator and
  the sand-pump in, xxviii. 349.
MITCHELL, J.
  Concrete, disintegration of, xxii. 439.
  Permanent way, xxvii. 402.—Best form
  of rail for different bearings, 402.—

MITCHELL.

Importance of good ballast in securing a sound and cheap permanent way, 403.—Necessity of procuring an accurate estimate of the cost of the maintenance of permanent way under every variety of circumstances, 403.

Railway, Mont Cenis, xxviii. 259.

Railway traffic, elasticity of, xxix. 355. —Unremunerative character of railway property, 355.—Expediency of low fares for promoting traffic, 357.—Through communication in trains in America, 358.

MITCHELL, T. T. [Memoir, xxiv. 542.]

MOLESWORTH, G. L.

Locomotive engines, disturbing forces of, xxii. 100.—Difficulties in starting a single-cylinder locomotive, 100.

MOLLETT, F. H. [Admission, xxvii. 180.]

MONCRIEFF, C. C. S., Lieutenant R.E. [Election, xxvii. 553.]

Irrigation in India, xxvii. 532.

MONSON, E. [Election, xxv. 262.]

Mont Cenis railway. *Vide* RAILWAY CURVES AND INCLINES.

Mont Cenis tunnel, the actual state of the works on the, and description of the machinery employed (Sopwith, T.), xxiii. 258. *Vide* also TUNNELS.

MONTGOMERIE, P., Lieutenant R.E. [Election, xxvii. 553.]

MOORE, A. [Election, xxv. 508.]

MOORE, W. [Election, xxx. 215.]

MOORE, W. G. [Admission, xxvii. 54.]

MOORSOM, L. H. [Election, xxvi. 165.]

MOORSOM, Captain W. S. [Memoir, xxiii. 498.]

Bridges and viaducts. Timber bridges on railways in Devonshire and Cornwall, xxii. 324.—Durability of timber lattice bridges on the Birmingham and Gloucester railway, 324.—Lattice bridges readily repaired, 325.

Railway curves and inclines, xxii. 33.—Cost of working the Lickey incline at different speeds, 34.

Railways, economy in the construction of, xxii. 33.

Surveying and levelling, xxi. 39.—Measuring distances by the telescope, 39.—Determining the speed of the

MOULTON.

'Great Eastern' from telescopic observation, 39.—Advantages of the pocket sextant for measuring distances, 43.

MORE, C. J. [Election, xxvi. 79.]

MOREL, E. [Election, xxiv. 511.]

MORELAND, R., Jun. [Election, xxviii. 517.]

MORGAN, J. [Election, xxiv. 458; Resignation, xxviii. 167.]

MORGAN, J. L. [Election, xxiv. 184.]

Copper ores. "On the smelting of refractory copper ores with wood as fuel, in Australia," xxvi. 44.—Remarks, 48.—Failure of the cupola form of furnace for smelting purposes in Australia, 48.

MORGAN, R. [Election, xxv. 352.]

MORIARTY, E. O. [Election, xxv. 65.]

MORRIS, F. [Election, xxix. 322.]

MORRIS, W. [Election, xxx. 1.]

MORRIS, W. R. [Election, xxv. 479.]

Steam-engines, increase of duty of Cornish, pumping water in London, xxiii. 69.

MORRISON, G. J. [Election, xxix. 322.]

Iron bars, strength of, xxx. 267.

Piles, formulæ for determining the resisting power of, xxvii. 313.

MORRISON, Colonel W. L., R.E. [Election, xxvii. 320.]

Railways, Mauritius, construction and cost of the, xxviii. 275.—Traffic, 276.—Working expenses, 277.—Accommodation, 278.—Propriety of making, 278.

MORSHEAD, W., Jun.

Steam-engines. "On the duty of the Cornish pumping-engines," xxiii. 45.

MORT, F. H. [Admission, xxvii. 55; Miller prize, xxix. 213.]

MORTON, F. [Decease, xxiii. 121.]

MOSELEY, R. [Election, xxv. 65; Resignation, xxix. 217.]

MOSELEY, T. B. [Election, xxiv. 257.]

MOSSE, J. R. [Election, xxi. 173.—Telford medal and premium, xxiii. 114, 126; Telford premium, xxix. 211.]

Bridges, timber. "American timber bridges," xxii. 305.

Railways. "The Mauritius railways—Midland Line," xxviii. 232.

MOULTON, S. [Resignation, xxix. 217.]

MOYLE.

MOYLE, S. [Admission, xxviii. 325.]

MUIR, J. [Election, xxv. 479.]

MUIR, M. A. [Election, xxiv. 184.]

MULLER, J. H. [Telford medal and Miller prize, xxi. 120, 130.]
Reclaiming land from the sea. "On reclaiming land from seas and estuaries," xxi. 466.—Remarks, 488.—Antiquity of cradles for closing gaps in reclamation banks in Holland, 488.—Enclosure of large areas as easy as the enclosure of small areas, 488.—Expensiveness of stone for reclamation banks, 488.—Causes that led to the formation of the Zuyder Zee and the Bies Bosch, and the extent of the Bies Bosch, 489.—Circumstances attending the irruption of the sea which formed the Bies Bosch, 490.—Slips of foreshore salt-marsh, 490.—System of closing gaps and breaches, 491.—Application of cradles for constructing quays and breakwaters, 491.

MUMFORD, C. [Election, xxvi. 79.]

MUNDAY, H. T. [Admission, xxvii. 54.]

MURDOCH, G. B. [Election, xxvi. 477.]

MURPHY, H. de la P. [Election, xxviii. 517.]

MURRAY, A.
Materials, strength of, Sir W. Fairbairn's researches on the, xxix. 78.
Steam-vessels, economies recently introduced in, mainly attributable to expansion, surface condensation, and superheating, xxix. 178.—Compound engines, 178.—Surface condensation, 179, 193.—Consumption of fuel for marine engines dependent on the boilers, 180.—Form of vessels, 180.—Necessity of maintaining the bottoms of vessels clean, 180.—Materials of which ships are built, 180.—'Co-efficient' of steam-vessels, 181.—Vessels with auxiliary steam-power, 181.—Hydraulic propellers, 182.

MURRAY, J. [Member of Council, xxi. 133; xxii. 112; xxiii. 112; xxiv. 106; xxv. 161; xxvi. 119; xxvii. 122; xxviii. 158; xxix. 208.]
Breakwaters and piers, xxiv. 173.—New mole at Leghorn, 173.—Breakwaters

MURRAY.

at Marseilles, Algiers, Holyhead, and Dover, 174.—Brick blocks, xxiv. 175.
Canal, Suez, xxvi. 454.—Cost of dredging, 454.—Formation of the Delta of the Nile, 465.—Bitter Lakes, 465.—Relative levels of the Mediterranean and the Red Sea, 466.—Supply of water to the Bitter Lakes, 466.—Probable formation of a bar at Port Said, 467.—Necessity for locks at each end of the Suez canal, 468.
Cofferdams. Cofferdam of the Great Grimsby docks, xxiv. 57.—Leakage through the puddle in cofferdams, 57.
Dock at Silloth, xxi. 337.
Docks, graving, xxv. 332.—Cost of the hydraulic lift graving dock, and of graving docks in various ports of the country, 333.
Harbours. Harbour of refuge contemplated at Redcar, xxiv. 76.—Harbours in the Gulf of Lyons, 171.—History of Marseilles, 171.—Present port of ditto, 171, et seq.—Harbour at Frioul, 172.
Low-water basin at Birkenhead, xxix. 3.
Rivers and estuaries, xxi. 26.—The Hooghly and the Mutla, 26.—Amount of solid matter contained in the waters of the Hooghly, 27.—Cost of maintaining the navigation of the Nuddea rivers, 28.—Improvement of the Sunderbund district, 28.—Improvements that might be effected in the St. George branch of the Danube, 294.—Direction of the piers executed at the Sulina mouth, 295.—Changes in the harbour of Aberdeen, 335.—Mr. Smeaton's plan for the improvement of ditto, 335.—Absence of a bar due to freshes, 336.—Velocity of the water in Aberdeen harbour, and of streams in the Pentland Frith, 341.—Junction of the rivers Orwell and Stour, xxiii. 245.—Harwich harbour, 245.—Expediency of breakwaters for preserving ditto, 246.—Yarmouth roads, 247.—Travel of the sands into the Wash, 247.—Maintenance of the estuaries of Blakeney and Wells, 248.—Mr. Price's plan for deepening the river Tees at the coal-staithes of the

MURRAY.

Stockton and Darlington railway company and the Clarence railway staithes, xxiv. 75.—Jetties carried out in accordance with ditto, 75.—Improvement of a river generally, and the comparative advantages of jetties and longitudinal training-walls, 75.—Improvements contemplated at various times in the estuary of the Tees, 75.—Comparative state of the river Tees between the bar and Stockton in 1824 and 1839, 80.—Cargo Fleet reach in 1836 and 1839, 81.—Improvement in the river Tees effected by the works carried on between 1824 and 1839, 81. —Cost of the cuts and jetties for contracting the channel of ditto, 82.—Transverse stone dykes and longitudinal walls in the Clyde, 82.—Depth of water in the Clyde, 82.—Expenditure on the works up to the year 1846, 82.—Relative expenditure on dredging in the Clyde and Tees, 83.—River Witham, xxviii. 86.—Effect of the Grand Sluice, 87.—Outfalls of the

MYRES.

Witham and Welland, 88.—Action and course of the tides in the Wash, 88.—Improvements executed on the Ouze, 88, 90.—Course and range of the tides in the Humber, and their effect on the bed of the estuary, 504.—Increased tidal flow in the Mersey, consequent on the formation of the docks at Liverpool, 505.—Protection of the seaward frontage of Spurn point, 506.

Sluicing operations at Birkenhead, xxix. 4.

Water supply. Fall and length of the New River, xxv. 498.

MURTON, F. [Election, xxiii. 320.]

Lime. Use of Theil lime in the works at Marseilles, Algiers, and Cherbourg, xxiv. 169.

MUSGRAVE, J. [Election, xxviii. 232.]

Mutla, the Hooghly, and the (Longridge, J. A.), xxi. 2. *Vide* also RIVERS AND ESTUARIES.

MYLNE, W. C. [Memoir, xxx. 448.]

MYRES, J. J., Jun. [Election, xxvi. 242.]

N.

NAPIER.

NAPIER, F. [Election, xxv. 203.]

NAPIER, J. [Election, xxiv. 458.]

NAPIER, W. H. E. [Election, xxvii. 320.]

NAPOLEON III., Emperor of the French. [Election, xxviii. 438, 518.]

Rivers, freshwater floods of. Letter to M. Rouher, the Minister of Public Works, respecting the ravages caused by inundations in France in 1856, and the means for preventing similar disasters (Redman, J. B.), xxvii. 270.

Naval architecture. *Vide* LONDON AND DUBLIN COMMUNICATION; SHIPS AND STEAM-VESSELS; SHIPS OF WAR; and STEAM NAVIGATION.

NAYLOR, W. [Election, xxiv. 358.]

Railway crossings and sidings for a railway on the central rail system, xxvi. 347.

Railway curves and inclines, xxvi. 347. —Effect of snow, 347.—Instances of working steep railway inclines, 347.— Amount of friction on curves, 348.

Railway locomotion, xxii. 106.—Sinuous and oscillatory motions, 106.

NEALE, H. W. O'N. [Admission, xxx. 106.]

NEAME, A. [Admission, xxvii. 54.]

NEATE, C.

Railways, São Paulo and Dom Pedro Segundo, xxx. 69.

NEILL, W. [Election, xxii. 604.]

NEILSON, J. B. [Memoir, xxx. 451.]

NEILSON, W. [Election, xxvii. 553.]

NEILSON, W. M.

Permanent way, testing rails, xxvii. 404.

NELSON, T. B. [Election, xxvii. 218.]

NEPVEU, C. M. A. [Decease, xxvi. 129.]

NESHAM, W. J. [Decease, xxvii. 131.]

NETHERSOLE, W. [Election, xxiv. 184.]

NEUMANN, G.

Tunnel, Mont Cenis, choice of the route of, xxiii. 287.—Drilling machinery used, 287.—Advantage that

NOYES.

would have resulted from a system of shafts, 287.—Present rate of progress of tunnel, 288.—Estimated cost, 288.

NEVILLE, H. J. W. [Election, xxiii. 459.]

NEVILLE, P. [Election, xxv. 65.]

NEWBIGGING, T. [Election, xxx. 106.]

New Ferry and the New Brighton piers and landing stages on the river Mersey, near Liverpool, description of the (Hooper, H.), xxviii. 217. *Vide* also PIERS AND LANDING STAGES.

NEWMAN, F. [Election, xxv. 262.]

NEWMAN, G. W.

Railway telegraphs, xxii. 230.—Clark's railway telegraph signals on the London and North Western railway, 230.

NEWMAN, J. [Admission, xxvii. 54.]

NEWMARCH, W. [Election, xxv. 65.]

NEWTON, J.

Drainage of towns, xxii. 295.—Relative gradients proper for main and tributary sewers, 295.—Street gullies, 295. —Size of sewer required to carry off a given depth of rain falling in a limited time at Preston, 295.—Necessary velocity of flow of sewage to prevent silting, 296.—Some of the sewers at Newport larger than necessary, 297.— Mortuary returns of Newport, 297.

NEWTON, S. B. [Election, xxvii. 553.]

NEWTON, W. [Memoir, xxi. 592.]

NICHOLLS, N. [Decease, xxix. 217.]

NICOLSON, A. [Election, xxx. 323.]

NIMMO, A. L. [Election, xxx. 215.]

NOAD, Dr. H. M.

Iron, report upon the West Cumberland Bessemer pig (Boyd, J.), xxvii. 393.

NOAD, W. I. [Admission, xxix. 98.]

NOBLE, J. [Election, xxviii. 517.]

NOYES, P. A. H. [Admission, xxvii. 54; Election, xxix. 322.]

O.

OAKLEY.

OAKLEY, H. [Election, xxv. 352.]

O'BRIEN, Captain D. [Resignation, xxiii. 120.]

O'BRIEN, T. E. [Election, xxvii. 55; Decease, xxix. 217.]

O'CALLAGHAN, F. L. [Election, xxviii. 216.]

Ocean steam-navigation with a view to its further development (Grantham, J.), xxix. 126. *Vide* also STEAM NAVIGATION.

O'CONNELL, P. P. L., Lieutenant-Colonel, R.E. [Election, xxv. 262; Telford medal and premium, xxviii. 161, 178.]

Rivers, flood discharge of. "On the relation of the freshwater floods of rivers to the areas and physical features of their basins; and on a method of classifying rivers and streams, with reference to the magnitude of their floods, proposed as a means of facilitating the investigation of the laws of drainage," xxvii. 204.

ODLING, F. J. [Admission, xxx. 323.]

OGILVIE, A. [Associate of Council, xxiv. 106.]

OGILVIE, C. E. W. [Election, xxi. 492.]

OGILVIE, P. [Election, xxvii. 320.]

O'HAGAN, H. [Memoir, xxx. 453.]

OKES, J. C. R. [Election, xxiv. 358.]

OLDHAM, J. [Council premium, xxii. 121, 131.]

Reclaiming land from seas and estuaries. "On reclaiming land from seas and estuaries," xxi. 454.—Remarks, 488.—

OWEN.

Peat lands silted over by tidal deposit in the neighbourhood of Hatfield, in Yorkshire, 488.—Land that might be added to Reed's island, 488.

OLIVEIRA, B. [Election, xxiv. 144.]

OLIVER, J. [Election, xxi. 258.]

OLIVER, T. [Election, xxiv. 358.]

OLRICK, L.

Water supply. Fatal effects of drinking water impregnated with decaying organic matter, xxvii. 43.—Absorption of mephitic gases by water in ordinary cisterns, 44.—Speed of filtration of water, 44.—Water-testing apparatus, 44.—Danchell's filter, 45.

O'NEILL, C. [Election, xxvi. 242.]

ONSLOW, D. A. [Election, xxiii. 320.]

Optical apparatus used in lighthouses, on (Chance, J. T.), xxvi. 477. *Vide* also LIGHTHOUSES.

Ores, the dressing of lead (Sopwith, T.), xxx. 106. *Vide* also LEAD ORES.

ORMSBY, A. S. [Election, xxii. 241.]

Bridges, timber, expense of the insurance of, on the Richmond and Petersburgh railway, xxii. 323.

OSBURN, H. [Election, xxiv. 358.]

OWEN, G. [Election, xxvi. 242.]

OWEN, J. A. [Admission, xxvii. 553.]

OWEN, Captain J. F.

Engineers, technical qualifications of, xxx. 21.

Fog-horns, xxviii. 43.

OWEN, T. E. [Election, xxvii. 180.]

P.

PADDISON.

PADDISON, G. [Election, xxii. 336.]
Railway, Santiago and Valparaiso, xxiii.
399.—Route originally proposed, 399.
—Reasons for abandoning it, 399.—
Reverse curves, 399.—Price of earth-
work, 399.
Railway curves, xxiii. 399. — Super-
elevation given to the outer rails on
reverse curves, 401.
PADDON, J. B. [Election, xxi. 48.]
PAGE, G. E. [Admission, xxvii. 443.]
PAGE, G. G. [Election, xxiv. 184.]
PAIN, A. C. [Election, xxix. 322.]
PALEZIEUX FALCONNET, G. P. de, Captain,
R.E. [Election, xxx. 215.]
PALLISER, Major W. [Election, xxvi. 310.]
Artillery and projectiles, xxviii. 407.
Iron chilled, xxviii. 407.—Chilled shot
and shells, 407.
PALMER, G. H. [Decease, xxviii. 168.]
PALMERSTON, Lord.
Drainage of land. Letter on the theory
of under-drainage in connection with
the amelioration of climate, and the
supply of water to rivers (Denton,
J. B.), xxi. 125.
Palmyra palm, on the use of the timber
of the, in the construction of bridges,
xxii. 58. *Vide* also BRIDGES, TIMBER.
PARKER, Captain F. G. S. [Election, xxvi.
79.]
PARKER, J. L. [Election, xxvi. 165.]
PARKES, T. F. [Admission, xxvii. 54.]
PARKES, W. [Telford premium, xxiv. 109,
124.]
Cements and hydraulic limes, xxii.
446.
Concrete, deposition of, in the sea near
Marseilles, for the erection of a beacon,
xxiv. 169.
Harbour, Kurrachee, xxii. 488.
Lighthouses. "Description of light-
houses lately erected in the Red Sea,"
xxiii. 1.—Remarks, 24.—Use of timber
piles, 26.—Force of the waves, 30.—

PARKES.

Portland cement concrete used for the
foundations, 36.—Choice of wooden
piles instead of iron piles for the
supports, 38.— Durability of teak,
39.—Use of the diagonals in the
Ushruffee lighthouse, as shown in
raising the structure in the contractors' yard, 40.—Line of the support not continuous from the ironwork
to the piles in ditto, 41.—Satisfactory
arrangements for mitigating the heat
in ditto, 41.—Cost of the Red Sea
lighthouses, 42.—Comparison of the
Lobos Cay with the Red Sea lighthouses, 42.—Labour employed on the
Red Sea lighthouses, 44.
Lighthouses. Obstruction of light caused
by lighthouse lantern framing, xxviii.
41.—Construction of stone lighthouses,
xxx. 17.—Failure of cast-iron lighthouses in exposed situations, 18.—
Use of cement in the construction of
lighthouses, 25, 26.
Low-water basin at Birkenhead, xxix. 17.
Pier at Greenock, construction of, xxii.
447.
Rivers, Colonel O'Connell's formula for
classifying, as flood-producers, xxvii.
243.—Flood moderators, 243.—Natural
drainage of lake Fucino, 244.—Lakes
as flood moderators, 245.
Rivers and estuaries. Treatment of the
river Dee, xxiv. 91.—Points of difference between the rivers Clyde and
Dee, 91.—Decadence of the port of
Chester, 92.—Reclamation of land in
the estuary of the Dee by Kinderley,
94.—Depth of water maintained at
Chester by the River Dee Company,
94.—Effect produced upon the propagation of the tide up rivers by changes
in the condition of the channel, particularly in the case of the Thames,
xxviii. 509.—No change in the level
of highwater caused by the construc-

PARSEY.

tion of a groyne at the harbour of Kurrachee, 510. —Difference between the level of spring and neap tides bears an analogy to the difference between an improved and an unimproved channel, as illustrated in the case of the tides of the Humber, 510, *et seq.*

Tides. Errors in the published Ordnance mean-tide levels, xxviii. 511.

PARSEY, W. [Election, xxii. 336.]

Iron and steel. Strength of iron plates, xxx. 263.—Extension of iron and steel bars under strain, 263.—Size of the pin in proportion to the bar in tension-bars, 264.

Viaducts. Apparatus used for the erection of the girders of the Mhow-ke-Mullee viaduct, xxix. 398.

PARSON, J. [Election, xxvi. 544.]

PARTRIDGE, W. [Admission, xxvii. 54.]

PASLEY, Major C., R.E. [Election, xxv. 429.]

PASLEY, General Sir C. W. [Memoir, xxi. 545.]

PASSMORE, F. B. [Election, xxviii. 517.]

PASSOS, F. P. [Election, xxvi. 544.]

PATERSON, T. [Election, xxv. 429.]

PATON, J. [Telford medal and Miller prize, xxii. 120, 130; Election, xxvii. 443.]

Reclaiming land from the sea. "On the sea-dykes of Schleswig and Holstein, and on reclaiming land from the sea," xxi. 426.—Remarks, 487.—Amount of water-pressure exerted against reclamation banks, as illustrated in the case of the Schelenkulen bank, 487.—Banks most liable to injury from the waves overtopping and then undermining the footing on the inner side, 488.

PATTEN, W. [Admission, xxx. 106.]

PATTERSON, E. C. [Election, xxvii. 55.]

PATTERSON, M. [Election, xxvi. 79.]

PAXTON, Sir J.

Railways. Proportion of railway accidents attributed to faults of management excessive, xxi. 387.—Fishjoints, 387.—Increased weight of engines and the capacity of trucks now used, 388.

PERMANENT WAY.

—Continuous breaks, 388.— Inexpediency of employing better-educated men as pointsmen and engine-drivers, 388.

Rivers and estuaries. Inapplicability of comparison between the works executed at the mouths of the Adour, Liffey, and Danube, xxi. 296.—Efficient manner in which the works at the Sulina entrance of the Danube were carried out, 296.

PEACOCK, R.

Locomotive engines. Dimensions of two tank-engines built for the Norwegian railway on the 3 feet 6 inches gauge, xxvi. 77.—Double locomotives, 77.

PEARSALL, H. D. [Admission, xxvii. 54.]

PEARSE, G. [Decease, xxiii. 121.]

PEASE, J. W. [Election, xxix. 98.]

PECK, F. [Election, xxviii. 518.]

PEELE, A. J. [Election, xxv. 203.]

PELLATT, A. [Memoir, xxiii. 511.]

PEMELL, E. [Decease, xxvi. 129.]

PENISTON, W. M. [Telford premium, xxiii. 114, 126; Decease, xxix. 217.]

Public works in Brazil. "Public works in Pernambuco, in the empire of Brazil," xxii. 385.—Remarks, 409.

PENN, T. [Election, xxv. 262.]

PENNELL, G. B. [Election, xxiii. 375.]

PENNY, A.

Coke, xxiii. 456.

Gas obtained in coke-making, xxiii. 456. —Incorrectness of the present methods of ascertaining the illuminating power of coal-gas, xxviii. 459.

PERDONNET, A. [Memoir, xxvii. 596.]

PERKINS, J. [Memoir, xxv. 516.]

PERMANENT WAY.

Maintenance and renewal of. "On the maintenance and renewal of permanent way." By R. P. Williams, xxv. 353. — Durability of the permanent way has not improved with the demands made upon it, 353, 362.— Increased percentage on the gross traffic receipts of maintenance of way on the Great Northern railway in fourteen years, 353.—Permanent way of the Liverpool and Manchester

PERMANENT WAY.

railway not strong enough for the 'Rocket,' 353.—Improvements of permanent way to be effected by the use of a better and more durable class of materials, 354.—Elasticity in the substructure necessary for a good form of permanent way, 354.—Tables and diagrams showing that the durability of the permanent way has been over-estimated, 354. — Precautions taken to render the accounts of the cost of maintenance of ditto on different railways strictly comparable, 355.—Classification of the different charges usually comprehended under the head of 'maintenance and renewal of way and works,' 356. — Explanation of diagrams, 356.—London and North Western railway, 356.—Expenditure for renewals of permanent way, 357.—Average annual expenditure for ditto, 357.—Average life of a rail on the London and North Western railway, 358.—Ditto on other railways, 358.—Particulars relative to the permanent way of the Great Northern railway, 359. — Detailed account of cost of renewing a mile of single line, 360.—Effect of heavy coal traffic on the condition of the road, 360, et seq.—Average annual cost of renewals on the Great Northern railway, 361.—Relative proportion of renewals greater on the up than on the down line, 361. — Weight and amount of traffic on the up line of the Great Northern railway near Barnet required to destroy the rails in periods of three years, 362.—Tonnage required to wear out the rails on the Lancashire and Yorkshire railway in seven years and a quarter, 362.—Rapid deterioration of the permanent way attributable to the increased weight and speed of the traffic, 362.—Reference to the mode of manufacturing iron rails at the principal ironworks in South Wales, 363.—Objections to the different forms of piling, 364.—Introduction of Bessemer steel rails, 364.—Wear of steel rails at the

PERMANENT WAY.

Camden Town and Crewe stations of the London and North Western railway, 364.—Advantages to be derived from the adoption of steel rails on main lines where the traffic is heavy, 365.—First cost of steel rails compared with that of iron, 365.—What is the best form of section for the double-headed, bridge, and foot rails? 366.—Appendix. List of diagrams and tables accompanying the paper, 367.—List of the tables in the Appendix, 368.—Table 1. Summary of mileage maintained, increase of mileage, and amount expended in renewals, with the estimated number of miles renewed on seven lines, from June, 1847, to June, 1865, 369.—Table 2. Ditto on nine lines, from June, 1847, to June, 1864, 370.—Table 3. Abstract showing amounts expended in renewals of way, miles maintained, and increase of mileage, half-yearly, during a period of years on various railways, 370.—Table 4. Abstract showing comparative cost per mile per annum of maintenance of way, maintenance of way and works, and renewals of way, together with the cost per mile per annum of the total charge under the head of 'maintenance and renewals of way, works, stations,' &c., on various railways, 370.—Table 5. Statement showing the duration of certain iron rails on the descending gradients of the Great Northern railway, between Hatfield and London; and on a similar ascending gradient between the 63rd and the 66th miles, 371.—Table 6. Statement showing the number and gross weight of trains passing over the Great Northern railway, from Hatfield to London, 1856 to 1865, 372.—Table 7. Statement showing the number and gross weight of trains passing over certain portions of the Lancashire and Yorkshire railway, from 1858 to 1865; with the average life of experimental rails at various stations, 372. — Table 8. Statement showing a comparison between guaran-

PERMANENT WAY.

teed iron rails at £7 15s. per ton, estimated to last three years, with steel
rails at £15 per ton, supposed to last
twenty years, 372.—Table 9. Statement showing comparative percentage
on gross traffic receipts, of locomotive
charges, and maintenance of way and
works, for a period of years, on the
Great Northern railway, 373.—Table
10. Experiments on Bessemer steel
rails, section 34, showing the relation
between the carbon contained and the
resistance to pressure, 374.—Tables 11
and 12. Results of experiments to ascertain the resistance to deflection and
set under a gradually increased bending
strain, of rails of various materials,
form, and size, made at Mr. Kirkaldy's
testing works, 374.—Table 13. Statement showing the separate and collective expenditure in renewals during
a period of eighteen years on various
railways, 374.—Statement showing the
cost at the end of each year from one
year to twenty years (including compound interest at 5 per cent. per
annum), of steel and iron rails, for
1 mile of single line, 374.
Discussion.— Barlow, W. H., 408.—
Berkley, G., 382.—Bessemer, H., 401,
414.—Bramwell, F. J., 407, 426.—
Brotherhood, R., 416.—Crossley, J. S.,
414, 417.—Cubitt, J., 410.—Fowler, J.,
379, 427.—Fox, Sir C., 381.—Fox, F.,
392.—Harrison, T. E., 411.—Hawkshaw, J., 404.—Hemans, G. W., 397,
414.—Johnson, R., 405.—Lane, C. B.,
427.—Phipps, G. H., 309, 408.—
Rochussen, T. A., 396.—Schneider,
H. W., 418, 426.—Siemens, C. W.,
379.—Stileman, F., 417.—Struvé, W.
P., 377.—Vignoles, C. B., 379, 380,
395.—Webb, F. W., 409, 410, 426.—
Williams, R. P., 375, 380, 426.
—— "The manufacture and wear of
rails." By C. P. Sandberg, xxvii. 320.
—Mode of manufacturing rails for the
Swedish railways, as carried out in
Wales between the years 1856 and
1860, 320.—Experiments on the wear
of rails at Camden Town by the London

PERMANENT WAY.

and North Western Railway Company,
322.—Tables showing the results deduced from the experiments, 322.—
Superiority of rails from rolled slabs
as compared with hammered slabs, 323.
—Importance of perfectly welding iron
rails, 323.—Comparative endurance of
iron rails on the Great Northern railway and at Camden Town station,
323.—Endurance of rails calculated
from the renewals on the Swedish
state railways, 324.—Best method of
manufacturing rails of Welsh iron,
324.—Method of ascertaining the life
of iron rails in years, 325.—Disposal
of rails when worn-out, 325.—Steel-
headed rails, 325.—How far the process of re-rolling old rails may be
profitably carried on in various
countries, 326.—Under what conditions it becomes most economical to
employ iron or steel, or a combination
of the two, in the construction of rails,
327.—Manner in which the safety of
the permanent way constructed of
different kinds of rails is affected by
high speeds, severe climate, &c., 330.
—Comparative strength of a rail in
winter and in summer, 332.—Importance of good raw material for the
Bessemer process, 333.—Appendix.
Result of the wear of the experimental
rails at Camden Town station, according to Mr. Woodhouse's report,
334.—Life of the experimental rails in
time, 335.—Cost of building a rolling
mill for the manufacture of 10,000
tons of rails per annum, 336.—Estimate
of the cost of manufacturing rails in
Sweden, rolled from worn rails, with
Bessemer steel for the head, 336.—
Calculation of annuities, 337.—Note
by the author, 408.
Discussion.—Adams, W., 380.—Adams,
W. B., 396.— Ashcroft, P., 379.—
Baker, B., 386.—Banister, F. D., 394.
—Bell, I. L., 349.—Bidder, G. P., 384.
—Boyd, J., 392.—Bragge, W., 381.—
Brereton, R. P., 375.—Bruce, G. B.,
374.—Bruulees, J., 402.—Colburn, Z.,
380.—Conybeare, H., 357.—Cowper,

PERNOLET.

E. A., 398.—Deas, J., 352.—Forbes, D., 356.—Fox, Sir C., 342.—Gregory, C. H., 408.—Harrison, T. E., 343.—Heppel, J. M., 403.—Hopkins, W. R. I., 346.—Fowler, J., 346.—Longridge, J. A., 390.—Marsh, T. E. M., 375, 379.—Menelaus, W., 353.—Mills, W., 379.—Mitchell, J., 402.—Neilson, W. M., 404.—Rochussen, T. A., 385.—Sandberg, C. P., 310, 405, 408.—Shaw, J., 354.—Stileman, F., 401.—Strapp, J., 378.—Taylor, J., 379.—Tyler, Capt. H. W., 387, 392.—Vignoles, C. B., 355.—Williams, E., 341.—Williams, R. P., 381.

Vide also MATERIALS; RAILWAY ACCIDENTS; RAILWAY INCOME AND EXPENDITURE; RAILWAY LOCOMOTION; RAILWAY SLEEPERS; RAILWAYS; and TIMBER.

PERNOLET, C. M. A. [Telford medal, xxiv. 109, 124.]

Coal. " On the distillation of coal, the utilization of the resulting products, and the manufacture of coke," xxiii. 443.—Remarks, 457.

PERRAM, G. J. [Admission, xxvii. 54.]

PERRING, J. S. [Memoir, xxx. 455.]

PETO, M. K. [Admission, xxvii. 218.]

PETO, W. H. [Admission, xxvii. 218.]

PHILLIPS, D. [Election, xxvii. 180.]

PHILLIPS, J.

Foundations. Cost of sinking cylinders, xxxviii. 347.—Sand-pump, and Milroy's excavator, 347.—Pneumatic apparatus for sinking cylinders, 348.

PHILLPOTTS, W. C., Captain R.E. [Election, xxiv. 358.]

PHIPPS, G. H. [Telford medal and Manby premium, xxiv. 109, 124.]

Arches. Strain upon an iron arch under pressure, xxii. 571.

Bridges, launching girders of, xxv. 251.—Bridge over the Sarine, 252.—Board of Trade requirements, 259.—Stability of the Victoria bridge, xxvii. 88.—Superstructure, 89.—Widening, 91.—Computation of the strains, 108.—Pressure per square foot on the foundations of the Cannon Street and the Charing Cross railway bridges, 439.

PHIPPS.

Bridges, suspension, xxvi. 301.—Clifton, 301, *et seq.* Means of rendering suspension bridges sufficiently rigid for railway purposes, 301.—Back chains, 304.—Design for a suspended tubular bridge on the site of the Victoria bridge, xxvii. 88.

Canals, steam-power on, xxvi. 22.—Experiments upon the Stoke canal with Ruthven's system of propulsion, 22.—Necessary elements of success for screw propulsion in narrow canals, 22.

Coal-mining, xxviii. 147.

Docks, graving, xxv. 340.—Hydraulic lift graving dock, 340, 341.—Elast city in pontoons, 340.

Drainage of towns, xxiv. 339.—Of large towns by steam-pumping, 339.—Drainage of London, 339.—Mr. Wicksteed's plan, 340.

Girders. Strains on the main girders of the Charing Cross bridge. xxii. 528, 535—Uniform stress in girder-work, xxiv. 427.—Importance of confining the line of force exerted upon any member of a truss to its true axial line, 428.—Bad effects of straining matter transversely, 431.—Injurious action on the booms of girders, 447.

Injector, Giffard's, xxiv. 219, 222, 225.

Iron, degree to which the limit of elasticity in, may be approached with safety, xxx. 256.—Proper form for the heads and eyes of suspension links, 257.—Iron used as struts under compression, 257.—Transverse strength of cast iron, 257.—Effect of equal strains applied in compression and in tension on cast-iron bars, 258.

Irrigation canals, xxvii. 549.

Locomotive engines. Comparative rotatory power of single-cylinder and double-cylinder engines, xxii. 97.

Materials, strength of, xxix. 70.

Permanent way. Invention of the fish-joint, xxv. 399.—Amount of adhesion of locomotive wheels with steel tires upon steel rails, 400.—Destructive effects of high speed, 400, 408.—Coal traffic upon the Great Northern

PHIPPS.

railway, 401.—Rails without chairs, 401.

Piers and landing stages, New Ferry and New Brighton, xxviii. 228.

Piles, M'Alpine's, Weisbach's, and Molesworth's formulæ for determining the resisting power of, xxvii. 297.

Railway curves, xxiii. 401.

Railway locomotion, xxiii. 431, 435.— Radial axles, 431. Spring tires, 435. —Proportion between the weight of the engines and the weight of the trains on the Metropolitan railway, xxvi. 357.—Resistances to trains upon curves, 357.—Formula expressing the resistance due to curves generally, 380.

Railways, economy of narrow-gauge, xxiv. 375.—Size of carriages, xxvi. 73. —Railways over mountainous regions, xxvi. 356.

Rivers and estuaries, formation of bars at the mouths of, xxvi. 431.—Bar of the river Tyne, 432.

Rivers, freshwater floods of, xxvii. 239.

Roofs of the St. Pancras, Cannon Street, Charing Cross, and Victoria railway stations, xxx. 97, 98.

Ships and steam-vessels, xxii. 598.— Skin resistance, 598.

—— "On the resistance to bodies passing through water," xxiii. 321.— Remarks, 340.—Resistance of the ship 'Atrato,' 340.— Mr. Colthurst's experiments, 340.—Resistance to vessels as the square of the velocity, 369.— Effect of the slip of the screw in H.M.S. 'Rattler,' 369.—Difficulties attending the steering of large and long ships, and of turning them round rapidly on a short radius, 370.—Beaufoy's experiments, 370.—Effect of roughness in diminishng the flow of water through pipes, 371.—Deductions from the results of ne trial-trip of the 'Atrato,' 371.— Frictional resistance on the internal surfaces of pipes and open watercourses, as compared with that on the exterior of floating bodies, 372.—Resistances of prows of various shapes, 373.— Surface friction in vessels, xxix. 186.

PILES.

—Hydraulic system of propulsion for towing purposes, 186.

Ships of war, xxi. 200.

Steam-engines. Employment of high-pressure steam, with large expansion, in the Cornish engine, xxiii. 74.—Surface condemnation in marine engines, xxix. 186.—Mode of analysing the various parts of an engine subject to the greatest amount of wear, xxx. 205.

Viaducts. Strength of the Craigellachie viaduct, xxv. 250.—Trellis-work, 251. —Grand River viaduct, Mauritius railways, 251.

PHIPSON, W. W. [Election, xxviii. 216.]

PICKERING, J. [Election, xxi. 258.]

PIERS AND LANDING STAGES.

"Description of the New Ferry and the New Brighton piers and landing stages on the River Mersey, near Liverpool." By H. Hooper, xxviii. 217.—Success of the Southport pier, 217.—Ferry accommodation of the river Mersey, 217.— Proposed pier and stage at Waterloo, 218—Requirements of the Mersey River Steamboat Company led to the construction of the New Ferry pier and landing, 218.— Original slipway, 218.—The pier, 218.—Connecting joint between the pier and bridge, 220.—The bridge, 220.—The floating stage, 222.—Mooring of ditto, 222.—Dioptric light over bridge, 223. —Gas and water supply, 223.—Cost of works, 223.—Design for the New Brighton pier and landing stage, 223. —The pier, 223.—The bridge, 224. —The floating stage, 224.—Cost of works, 225.

Discussion.—Bazalgette, J. W., 227.— Bramwell, F. J., 226.—Brunlees, J., 226, 228, 230.—Grover, J. W., 228.— Haughton, B., 226.—Hemans, G. W., 222.—Mallet, R., 229, 231.—Phipps, G. H., 228.—Redman, J. B., 230.

Vide also PILES.

PILES.

"The supporting power of piles; and on the pneumatic process for sinking iron columns as practised in America." By W. J. M'Alpine, xxvii. 275.—

PILES.

Molesworth's formula, 275.—Weisbach's formula, 275.—Conditions under which piles are used, 275.—Government graving-dock at Brooklyn, N. Y., 276.—Material removed from the excavations, 276.—Number and size of piles used in the foundations, 276.—Record of the effect of driving the piles, 276.—The piling machines, 277.—Result of driving a trial pile by a Nasmyth hammer, 278.—Result of driving a trial pile by a ram weighing one ton, falling from ½ to 35 feet, 278.—Cause of the better results from the use of the Nasmyth machine, 278.—Effect of driving on the material penetrated, 279.—Supporting power, 279.—General laws, ascertained from an analysis of the experiments, 280.—Formula based thereon, 280.—Comparison with those of Weisbach and Molesworth, 280.—Bearing support due to the sectional area of the pile, 281.—Supporting power of large cast-iron piles due to friction of the surface, 281,291.—Croton aqueduct bridge over the Harlem river, 281.—Third avenue bridge over ditto, 281.—Adoption of Dr. Potts' method of sinking piles for various works in America, 282.—Account of sinking piles for the Harlem bridge, 283.—Experiments to determine the resistance of the material in sinking ditto, 283.—Bearing support of wooden piles driven into fine sand at Brooklyn navy-yard, 286.—Relative supporting power of iron and wooden piles, 286. — Expansion of the base of the column at Harlem bridge by concrete, 287.—Behaviour of concrete under pressure, 288, 292.—Conical cylinder for the base of iron columns recommended, 289.—Operation and cost of labour and plant in sinking columns at Harlem bridge, 289.—Effect of condensed air on the workmen, 289.—Advantages of cylinder piles, 290.—Method to be adopted when the material below and around the column is impervious to air and water, 291.—

POLE.

Support from the area of the bottom of piles, 292.—Iron shell not injuriously affected by cold, 292.—Corrosion of the metal, 292.—Iron columns as inverted caissons, 292.

Discussions.—Beazeley, A., 306.—Bethell, H. S., 294.—Brereton, R. P., 303.—Bruce, G. B., 314.—Brunlees, J., 309.—Eckersley, W., 317.—Fox, Sir C., 298, 300.—Gregory, C. H., 294.—Hawkshaw, J., 295.—Hemans, G. W., 295.—Heppel, J. M., 314.—Longridge, J. A, 296.—Morrison, G. J., 313.—Phipps, G. H., 297.—Redman, J. B., 304.—Rennie, Sir J., 300. —Ridley, T. D., 311.—Wright, J., 308.

PILKINGTON, W. [Election, xxiv. 511.]
PIM, B. C. T., Captain, R.N.
Ships of war, xxi. 225.—Mode of fastening armour-plates by double dovetailed rivets, 225.

PITT, R. [Election, xxx. 323.]
PLEWS, J. [Memoir, xxi. 564.]
PLOWDEN, Lieut -Colonel J. C. [Resignation, xxi. 148.]
PLUCKNETT, G. [Resignation, xxvi. 129.]
POCOCK, G. P. [Admission, xxvii. 180.]
POINGDESTRE, W. W. [Resignation, xxviii. 167.]

POLE, W.
Bridges. Principles of construction of iron-girder bridges, xxiv. 449.—Durability of bridges of cast iron and wrought iron, xxvii. 571.
Canals, steam-power on, xxvi. 17.—Experiments with the steam-tug 'Pioneer' on the Ashby-de-la-Zouch canal, 17.—Wave caused by the passage of the steamer, 18.—Injurious effect of the wave at high speed, 19.
Fog-horn, xxx. 19.
Iron and steel. Strength of iron, xxi. 242.—Strength of cast iron, xxviii. 409.
Lagoon of Venice. xxviii. 317.
Locomotive engines, use of steel in, xxvi. 345.
Materials, strength of. Translation from the French of M. J. Gaudard's

POLE.

paper, "On the present state of knowledge as to the strength and resistance of materials," xxviii. 536. Remarks, xxix. 25.—History of the theory, 25.—Practical investigation of the numerical data, 27.

Railway inclines, atmospheric system for working steep, xxx. 67.

Railways. Use of iron in works of construction on Indian railways a saving of time, xxii. 55.—Apparent greater transverse strength of palm-wood when compared with teak, 63.—Railway across the Brenner pass between Munich and Verona, xxvi. 342, 344.—Atmospheric system of propulsion as a means of crossing Alpine passes, 344.

Ships of war. Comparative values of iron and steel for armour-plates, xxi. 241.—Proceedings of the Iron Armour-plate Committee, 242.

Steam-engines. Cornish pumping, xxiii. 85.—Cause of high duty, 85.—Slow combustion generally used in the Cornish boiler, 86.—Precautions taken for economising the heat, 86.—Expansion of the steam in the Cornish engine after it has been cut off from the boiler, 86. —Weight of pump-rods in deep mines favourable to the economical working of Cornish engines, 86.—Necessity of a certain mass of matter, to moderate the velocity produced by initial excess of steam-pressure, 87.—Cornish principle of high-pressure steam, with considerable expansion, applied in double-acting engines for rotary motion, 87.—Irregularity of pressure upon the piston at different parts of the stroke, 87.—Difficulty of carrying the degree of expansion to the same extent with the rotary as with the Cornish single-acting pumping engine, 88.—Merits of the double cylinder engine invented by Hornblower, 89.—His patents relative to the steam-engine, 89.—Invention of the double-cylinder engine attributed by Watt to Hornblower, 90. —Cause of Hornblower's engine fall-

PORTER.

ing into disuse, 90.—Application of high-pressure steam to the single-cylinder and double-cylinder engines by Trevithick and Woolf respectively, 90.—Woolf's invention simply the application of high-pressure steam to Hornblower's engine, 91.—Introduction of ditto into use, 91.—Woolf's engine ultimately superseded by Trevithick's, 91.—Introduction by the Lambeth Waterworks Company of the compound-cylinder Cornish engine for pumping water along a main from Ditton to Brixton Hill, 92.—Small cylinder in a double-cylinder engine merely useful for equalizing the action of the steam during the stroke, 93. —Action of the steam in Hornblower's and Woolf's compound-cylinder engine, 93.—Mr. Pole's discovery that there is a certain part of the stroke at which it is most advantageous to cut off the steam from the smaller cylinder, 94.—Illustrations of ditto, 94.—Table showing the results for various degrees of expansion, 95.—Importance of reducing the initial blow, 96.—Arrangement of the valves and steam-passages in the double-cylinder Cornish engine, 96. — General considerations which tend to prove the superiority of compound-cylinder engines for pumping purposes, 97.—Note on the theory of the action of the compound-cylinder engine, 97.

Steel, strength and toughness of well-worked, xxi. 241.

POLLARD, C., Major, R.E. [Election, xxix. 98.]

PONTIFEX, E. A. [Election, xxiv. 511.]

PORTER, J. F. [Memoir, xxvi. 582.]

PORTER, J. H.

Bridges and viaducts, xxv. 254.—Erection of continuous girder-bridges, 254. —Foundations of the Craigellachie and Grand River viaducts, 254.

Bridges, suspension, xxvi. 285. — Stiffening effect of the vertical and diagonal trussing in the Lambeth bridge, 285.—Bars or beams of varying section, 285.

PORTLAND CEMENT.

Lighthouses, utility of diagonal bracing in, xxiii. 29.

Roofs of the stations at New Street, Birmingham, St. Pancras, and Cannon Street, xxvii. 435.—Large roof in St. Petersburg, 435.

Weight of a crowd of men per square foot of surface, xvvi. 285.

Portland Cement. *Vide* CEMENTS; CONCRETE; and STRUCTURES IN THE SEA.

PORTS.

East Indies. Port of Calcutta, and of the Mutla, xxi. 2, *et seq.*—Kurrachee, xxii. 451, 453, 481.—Its capabilities, 482.—Position, especially as compared with the port of Bombay, 483.—Improvement of the harbour, 484, 487, *et seq.*—Necessity for perfecting the ports of India, 489. *Vide* also RAILWAYS—Scinde; and RIVERS and ESTUARIES—Hooghly and Mutla.

Hull, Liverpool, London, and Newcastle, annual tonnage of, xxvi. 435; xxviii. 496.

Saïd, renseignements sur les jetées de, xxv. 133. *Vide* also CANALS, Suez.

Swansea, Blyth, and Silloth. "Description of works at the ports of Swansea, Blyth, and Silloth." By J. Abernethy, xxi. 309.—Situation and exposure of the port of Swansea, 309.—Rise and set of the tides, 309.—History, 310.—Piers constructed, 310.—Plans for improvement by Telford, Hartley, and others, 310.—New cut executed, 311.—Construction of docks in the Town Reach, 311.—Progress and cost of the works, 312.—New cut improved, 312.—Hydraulic power for opening and shutting the dock-gates, 312. — Swansea South dock recommended by Mr. Brunel, 313.—Description and cost of the several works, 313.—Geological section of the site, 314.—Method of executing the works, 314.—Materials used, 314.—Details of the lock and entrance, 315.—Description of the system of hydraulic machinery, 316.—Ballast-cranes for the shipment of coal, 317.—Machinery for delivering coal, 317.—Method of discharging

PORTS.

the wagons, 318. — Table of performance of the hydraulic machinery for the year ending October, 1860, 319.—Cost of working, 320.—Statement of the work that can be performed by the 80 H.P. steam-engine for working the hydraulic machinery, and the estimated cost of the same, 320.—Increasing trade of the port of Swansea, 321.—Present state of the entrance of the port of Blyth, as compared with its original condition, 322.—Works executed, and their cost, 322.—Results similar to those obtained at the entrance of Aberdeen harbour, 323.—Account of the works executed at Aberdeen harbour, 323.—Bar opposite Blyth harbour entirely removed by the works carried out, 324.—Topography of the harbour of Silloth, 324.—Enumeration of works designed by Mr. J. Hartley, and carried out by Mr. Abernethy, 324.—Objections urged against the scheme in Parliament, 325.—Sandbanks in the Solway Frith; velocity, rise and course of the tide, 325.—The tidal current must always be deflected to the English side, and there form the navigable channel, 326.—The changes that take place in the upper portion of the estuary, 326.—Plan for improving the Solway navigation below Annan Point, 326.—Effect of the jetty on the foreshore at Silloth, 326.—Entrance channel successful, 327.—Method of constructing the foundations of the dock, and of keeping the foundations dry during the course of construction, 327.—Machinery employed, 327.—Advantages of the low-level system for loading coal, 327.—Details of coal hoists, 328.—Method of shipping coal, 328.—Cost of the works at Silloth, 328.—The port of Silloth affords an entrance to shipping at an early period of the tide, 328.—Appendix: Table of details of hydraulic machinery, steam-engines, pumps, and boilers at Swansea harbour, 330.—Ditto; Statement showing

POST.

the expense of working the steam-engines in connection with the hydraulic machinery at Swansea for the year ending October, 1860, 334.

Discussion.—Abernethy, J., 342.—Armstrong, Sir W. G., 338.—Belcher, Admiral Sir E., 339.—Curtis, J. G. C., 340.—Giles, A., 337.—Harrison, T. E., 338.—Hawkshaw, J., 344.—Leslie, J., 341.—Murray, J., 335, 341.—Rawlinson, R., 342.—Rennie, Sir J., 341.—Stevenson, D., 337, 340.

Vide also Docks—Harbours; Low-water Basin at Birkenhead; and Structures in the Sea.

Post. —

Bridges, timber, classification of, on the most important lines of railway in the United States (Colburn, Z), xxii. 318.

Potter, E. [Resignation, xxix. 217.]

Potter, W. A. [Election, xxvi. 477.]

Potts, J. [Election, xxvi. 544.]

Potts, J. T. [Election, xxix. 322.]

Powell, W. [Election, xxx. 1.]

Power, S.

Rivers, flood discharge of. Report on the effects of a flood in Beerbhoom on the East Indian railway, and on the subject of the floods of the southern tributaries of the Ganges (Vaux, A. H.), xxvii. 266.

Pownall, C. A. W. [Admission, xxvii. 320.]

Pownall, G. [Election, xxi. 345; Resignation, xxviii. 167.]

Pratt, H. J. [Admission, xxx. 323.]

Prebble, C. T. [Election, xxiii. 320.]

Preece, W. H. [Telford medal and Council premium, xxi. 135, 152; Telford premium, xxiii. 114, 126; Telford premium, xxvii. 124, 142.]

Electric telegraph, working of the, in India, xxv. 19.—Persian Gulf cable, 19.—Route for a line of telegraph between Bagdad and Beyrout, 19.

Railway telegraphs. "On railway telegraphs, and the application of electricity to the signalling and working of trains," xxii. 167.—Remarks, 193.—Variety of systems in use, 193, *et seq.*—Mr. Tyer's system, 194.—'Space' system and 'block' system, 194.—

PRESTON.

Superiority of the semaphore arrangement, 195.—The telegraph chiefly valuable as an auxiliary agent, 232.—Impracticability of the train-staff system, 232.—Superiority of visual signals to bell-signals, 233.—Advantage of permanent railway telegraph signals, 233.—Danger arising from the inductive effect of atmospheric electricity on telegraph signalling instruments worked by momentary currents, 234.—Ditto exemplified in the case of the Great North of Scotland railway, 234.—Effect of earth-currents, 235.—Temporary signals interrupted by accidental and artificial causes, exemplified in the case of an accident near the Victoria station, 235.—Wrong signals by Tyer's instrument from pressing the wrong button, 236.—Superiority of the semaphore system to the needle system of railway telegraphing, 236.—Question of priority in the invention of the semaphore system, 237.

Railway trains, communication in. "On the best means of communicating between the passengers, guards, and drivers of trains in motion," xxvi. 80.—Remarks, 92.—Perfect system of communication in trains by means of electricity, 92.—Rope-and-bell system between passengers and guard, 95.—Cost of ditto on the Great Northern railway, 113.—Simplicity of the electrical system of intercommunication in trains, and the results of its adoption hitherto, 114.

Premiums awarded, xxi. 132, 135, 152; xxii. 111, 120, 130; xxiii. 111, 114, 126; xxiv. 106, 109, 124; xxv. 161, 164, 180; xxvi. 118, 121, 138; xxvii. 121, 123, 142; xxviii. 157, 160, 178; xxix. 207, 210.

Presents received, xxi. 144, 161; xxii. 124, 141; xxiii. 137; xxiv. 134; xxv. 171, 189; xxvi. 126, 146; xxvii. 150; xxviii. 187; xxix. 245.

Preston, E. W. [Election, xxviii. 232.]

Preston, J. [Election, xxvii. 55.]

Preston, S. [Admission, xxix. 322.]

PRESTWICH.

PRESTWICH, J. [Election, xxix. 98.]
PRICE, A. P. [Election, xxiv. 511.]
PRICE, J. [Election, xxx. 1.]
PRICE, W. H. [Election, xxv. 65.]
PRIME, C. [Election, xxix. 98.]
PRINCE, H. [Election, xxii. 336.]
PRITCHARD, D. B. [Election, xxiv. 184.]
PRITCHARD, E. [Election, xxvi. 310.]
PRITCHARD, L. W. [Election, xxviii. 216.]
PROCTOR-SIMS, R. [Election, xxvii. 553.]
PROSSER, T. [Election, xxvi. 544.]
PUBLIC WORKS.

Brazil. "Public works in Pernambuco, in the empire of Brazil." By W. M. Peniston, xxii. 385.—Position and size of the province, 385.—Appearance of the town of Recife or Pernambuco, 385. — Harbour, 386. — Absence of quays and charge for lighterage, 386. —Tonnage of foreign vessels entering, 386.—The Pernambucana Steamboat Company, 386.—The São Francisco river, 386. — Vegetable productions and exports, 387.—Principal imports, and duty charged on imports and exports, 387. — The currency, 387. —Measures of weight, capacity, and length, 387.—Healthiness of the climate, 388.—Meteorology, 388.— Rainfall, 389.—Winds, 389.—Geology, 389.—Water supply, 389.—Gasworks, 390.—Contemplated drainage of Recife, 390.—Street-paving and roads, 390.—Bridges, 391.—Road-metalling, 391.—Cost of roads, 391.—Bullock tracks, 391.—Traffic carried on by pack-horses, 392.—Bullock carts, 392. —Parallel drawn between the condition of Pernambuco and England. 392.—Excellency of the roads at Rio Janeiro, 393.—Railway scheme projected by, and concession granted to, the Messrs. de Mornay, 393.—Original estimate and actual cost of the line, 393.—Government inspection, 393.— Character of the country traversed by the first portion of the Recife and São Francisco railway, 394.—Construction of a tunnel, 394.—Earthworks, 395.— Iron bridges, 395.—Culverts, 395.— Fencing, 395.—Permanent way, 395.

PUBLIC WORKS.

—Stations and line arrangements, 396. —Rolling-stock, 396.—Engine-shed and repairing-shops, with list of tools, 397. —Dates of concessions and completion of the work, 398.—Working arrangements carried out successfully under great difficulties, 398.—Maintenance of the permanent way carried on by natives, 398.—The labour question, 398.—Labourers and method of working, 399.—Artisans, 400.—Foreigners must be imported for the higher orders of work, 401.—Native carpenters, 402.—Divers, 402.—Timber 402.—Mode of preparing timber for the market, 403.—Woods for dyeing purposes and furniture, 403.—Stone, 404.—Bricks, 404.—Brazilian tile, 404.—Sand available for ballast, 405. —Materials required to be imported for public works, 405.—Authorities for statistics, 405.—Standard dimensions of the Recife and São Francisco railway, and of the principal structures upon it, 406.—Table of the wages of the different classes of labourers and artisans, 407.—Prices of materials, and of various kinds of work and of transport, 407.—Actual cost per mile per annum of the maintenance of the way and works of the Recife and São Francisco railway, 408.

Discussion.—De Mornay, E., 409.— Lane, C. B., 409.—Sheilds, F. W., 414.—Webb, E. B., 413.—Whitfield, J., 415.—Wood, J. T., 412.

Ceylon, xxii. 63.
England, xxvii. 184; xxix. 285, et seq.
English colonies, xxvii. 183.
France, xxix. 276, et seq.
India, xxix. 286, 287.
New Zealand. "Memoir on the public works in the province of Canterbury, New Zealand." By E. Dobson, xxix. 99.—Colonization by the Canterbury Association, 99.—Establishment of a department of public works, 99.— Progress of the province, 99.—Expenditure, 99.—Price of waste land, 100.—Topographical survey, 100.—

PUBLIC WORKS.

Extension of roads, 100.—Social and political difficulties incurred in the settlement of the province, 101.—Principal works executed by the government, 102.—System pursued by the provincial engineer in the management of his department, 103.—Want of timber, 103.—Introduction and spread of the watercress plant, 104.—Appendix a : reports from the provincial engineers on the progress of the public works, 104.—Appendix b : returns showing the cost of the public works, and the working of the road boards, 104.—Appendix c : papers relating to the Sumner road, and to the Heathcote navigation, 105.—Appendix d : railway reports, and the Moorhouse tunnel, 106.—Appendix e : reports on the passes through the New Zealand alps, 108.—Appendix f : reports on the encroachments of the Waimakariri river, 110.—Appendix g : papers relating to the Lyttelton harbour works, 111.—Appendix h : reports on the telegraph department of New Zealand, 113.—Appendix i : statistical maps ; principal coach roads, 113.—Drainage districts, 115.—River navigations, 115.—Railways surveyed, 116.—Railways completed, 117.—Wooden tramways, 118.—Telegraph lines, 119.—Appendix k : topographical maps, 119.—Appendix l : maps and sections illustrating the several plans proposed for connecting Port Lyttelton with the Canterbury plains, 119.—Appendix m : sections of the Little River and the Great Southern railways, 119.—Appendix n : Northern and Western railways, 119.—Appendix o : timber bridges, 120.—Appendix p : Lyttelton tunnel ; engineering details, 120.—Appendix q : Lyttelton tunnel ; geological section, 121.—Appendix r : views illustrating the physical geography of Canterbury, 121.

Discussion.—Abernethy, J., 124.—Baynes, C., 123, 124.—Cowper, E. A., 125.—Gregory, C. H., 122, 125.—Hemans, G. W., 122.—Heppel, J. M., 124.—Vignoles, C. B., 123, 125.

Table showing the facilities of internal communication in the United Kingdom, France, Prussia, Spain, and the United States of North America, for the year 1868–69, xxix. 286.

Vide also MATERIALS, decay of ; and RAILWAYS, São Paulo.

Pumping engines, on the duty of the Cornish (Morshead, W., Jun.), xxiii. 45. *Vide* also STEAM-ENGINES.

PURCHAS.

PURCHAS, S. G. [Election, xxix. 322.]

Q.

QUINETTE.

QUINETTE DE ROCHEMONT, E. T. [Election, xxix. 322.]

R.

RADFORD.

RADFORD, G. K. [Election, xxii. 336.]
Bridge, suspension, erected over the river Ohio, at Cincinnati, by Mr. Roebling, xxvi. 267.

Locomotive engines. Table of locomotive expenses on the eastern division of the Pittsburg, Fort Wayne, and Chicago railway, xxviii. 423, 424.

Radial axle locomotive engine. *Vide* RAILWAY LOCOMOTION.

Rails, the manufacture and wear of (Sandberg, C. B.), xxvii. 320. *Vide also* PERMANENT WAY; RAILWAY LOCOMOTION; and RAILWAY INCOME AND EXPENDITURE.

RAILWAY ACCIDENTS.
" Railway accidents—their causes and means of prevention." By J. Brunlees, xxi. 345.—Number of accidents and their causes in the seven years from 1854 to 1860, 345.—Tabular statement of ditto, 346.—Accidents arising from a defective state of the permanent way, 347.—Accidents most frequent in winter from the effect of the weather on the road, 347.—Placing the fish-joint between two sleepers objectionable, 348.—Turning the rails should be avoided, 348.—Chairs should be fixed to the sleepers by iron spikes, 348.—Superior economy of steeled rails, points, and crossings, 349.—Accidents caused by the defective condition of the permanent way, 349. —Causes leading to the explosion of the boilers of locomotive engines, 351. —Roads made at an early period not strong enough for the ponderous locomotives and high speeds of the present day, 351.—Accidents arising from the breakage of axles and wheel-tires, 352.—Steeled tires recommended, 353. —On the best mode of fixing tires, 353.—Injuries to which tires are subjected at high speed, 354.—Im-

RAILWAY ACCIDENTS.

provements by Mr. Beattie, 354.—Want of uniformity in the carriage portion of the rolling stock a cause of frequent accidents, 354.—Plan for carriages and buffers recommended, 354. —Great percentage of accidents from bad management, 355.—Excessive speed to make up for unpunctuality dangerous, 355.—Accidents arising from unpunctuality, 356.—An interval of space between trains far superior to an interval of time, 356.—Irregularity of excursion-trains a fruitful source of accidents, 356.—Accidents from defective signals, and precautionary measures recommended, 357.—Beneficial effects to be derived from working the traffic by the use of the electric telegraph, 358.—Need of communication between the engine-driver and guard, 359.—Efficient break-power required, 359.—Continuous breaks recommended, 360.—Accidents caused by negligence principally due to ignorance or inefficiency, 360.—Recommendations on this point, by a French commission, in 1857, 361.—Over-working of railway servants an element of danger, 361.—Great expense often entailed from defective management, 362.— Government interference not likely to render railways safer or more available, 362.

" Railway accidents—showing the bearing which existing legislation has upon them." By Captain D. Galton, 363.—Length of railway communication open in the British Isles at the end of 1860, the number of passengers and accidents to passengers from causes beyond their own control, in the seven years ending 1860, 363.— Average sum paid annually by railway companies as compensation for railway accidents, 363.—Instances of

RAILWAY ACCIDENTS.

large sums paid as compensation, 364 —Conveyance by railway safer than by any other mode, 364.—Coach accidents compared with accidents on British, Belgian, Prussian, and French railways, 364.—Lines of small traffic comparatively safe, 365.—Table showing the ratio of traffic to the degree of safety upon certain railways on an average of seven years, 365.— Accidents classified, 366.—Table of the general results of accidents which could not be guarded against, and of those which were within the control of the working staff, 366. —Table showing accidents from trains leaving the rails and from collisions, 367.—Large proportion of acidents due to preventible causes, 367.—Fractured tires, axles, and rails, where no flaw had been previously visible, the chief cause of accidents which could not be guarded against, 367.—Association of railway companies in Germany for the purpose of collecting, investigating, and diffusing information on suggested improvements in railway construction, 368.— Accidents through negligence generally caused by faulty arrangements, 368.—Instances of accidents from simple negligence, 368.—Instances in which negligence has been attributable to the defective arrangements of the company, 369.—Railway companies can prosecute their servants for acts endangering life or limb, 369.—Small number of accidents caused by negligence on the part of the inferior servants alone, attributed to the efficacy of this direct responsibility, 370.—Companies must be held responsible for the acts of their agents, 370.—Causes of accidents within the control of the management, 370.— Accidents of this class principally occur for the want of a continued enforcement of good rules and manner of working the traffic, 371.— Fewer accidents in France and in Germany from the rigidly method-

RAILWAY ACCIDENTS.

ical manner in which every detail of working is treated, 372.—Directors often insufficiently remunerated, and able to devote only a portion of their time to their charge, 372.—Recommendations of Mr. Cardwell's Parliamentary Committee in 1853, 372.— Ditto of Mr. Bentinck's Committee in 1857, that a law should be passed to compel all railways to be worked by the electric telegraph, and that punctuality should be enforced, by enabling passengers to obtain cheap and prompt legal redress for delays, 372.—Recommendations not acted upon, 373.— Extent of Government control over railway companies, 373.—Objections urged against Parliamentary control, 373.—The selection of the appliances for safety should rest with the manager, 374.—Freedom from railway accidents not to be obtained by Government interference, but by an effective and responsible internal management, 375.—An organization among railway companies recommended, analogous to the Association for the Prevention of Boiler Explosions, 375.—Faults of the system of compensation, 375.— Instances of hardship entailed upon railway companies from simple act of negligence of one of the inferior servants, 376.—Exaggerated and unfounded claims to which railway companies are exposed, 376.—The present state of the law gives great facilities for fraudulent claims, 377.— Extract from the summing-up on a case in point by Mr. Justice Williams, 377.—Offer of compensation by the company frequently used as a means of extortion, 377.—Quotation from Mr. Baron Wilde's summing-up on a case in point, 377.—How the law of compensation has arisen, 378.—Compensation partly a penalty on a railway company for carelessness, and partly compensation to the sufferer for the injury he has received, 378.—Amount of compensation depends upon the condition in life of the travellers, 379.

RAILWAY ARCHES.

—How the present law of compensation gives rise to litigation, 379.—Extent of liability of shipowners by the Merchant Shipping Act, 380.—If the same limitation were applied to compensation for railway accidents, the sufferer would sometimes not receive adequate remuneration, 380.—Inducements to carefulness on the part of directors and employés, 380.—Suggestion for diminishing litigation, 380.—The true remedy against railway accidents lies in improved management and machinery, and in the formation of an association among railway companies for mutual insurance in case of accidents, 381.

Discussion.—Airy, G. B., 383, 411.—Babbage, C., 385.—Bidder, G. P., 389.—Bruce, G. B., 407.—Brunlees, J , 418.—Clarke, S., 389.—Galton, Capt. D., 416, 422.—Gregory, C. H., 406.—Hawkshaw, J., 406, 420, 422.—Lane, C. B., 415.—Paxton, Sir J., 387.—Ransome, J. A., 413.—Shaw, H., 408.—Shelburne, The Earl of, 411.—Siemens, C. W., 383.—Tyler, Captain H. W., 383, 409.—Webster, T., 408.—Yolland, Colonel W., 396, 413.

Vide also RAILWAY TELEGRAPHS.

Railway arches, rental to be derived from, in London, xxvii. 438, 441.

Railway breaks, xxi. 408; xxii. 240; xxviii. 260, *et seq.*; xxx. 69, 74. *Vide* also RAILWAY ACCIDENTS; and RAILWAY CURVES AND INCLINES.

RAILWAY BRIDGES AND VIADUCTS.

" On the new Mhow-ke-Mullee viaduct, Great Indian Peninsula railway." By A. R. Terry, xxix. 373.—Situation on the Bhore Ghaut, 373.—Old viaduct, 373.—Collapse of viaduct, 373.—Temporary arrangements for carrying on the traffic, 373.—Alterations in the new structure from the former design, 375.—Masonry contract, 375.—Foundation and pier, 375.—Abutments, 375.—Staging for the erection of the girders, 376.—Girders, 376, 380.—Fixing roadways on ditto, 377.—Hoisting ditto, 378.—Hindrances in

RAILWAY CURVES.

the operation, 379.—Superstructure, 379.—Testing the girders, 379.—Workmen employed, 380.— Expenditure, 380.—Supervision of the work, 381.

" Description of the Pennair bridge, Madras railway, N. W. line." By E. W. Stoney, xxix. 382.—Dimensions, 382.—Superstructure, 382, 385.—Pennair river, 382.—Geological features of site of bridge, 382.—Foundations, 383.—Fair work, 385.—Girders, 385.—Mode of erecting ditto, 387.—Rolling girders, 388.—Cost of erecting and fixing girders, 390.—Cost of bridge complete, 391.—Testing the bridge, 391.—Appendix : calculation of strains in the girders of the Pennair bridge, 392.

Discussion.—Berkley, G., 399.—Heppel, J. M., 400.—Parsey, W., 398.—Vignoles, C. B., 402.

Railway communication, xxiv. 388.—Desirability of a uniform gauge on railways in each country, 388.—Trade between Great Britain and the East, xxvi. 331.—Effect the passage of the Alps by a railway would have on ditto, 332.—Table of Alpine roadway passes, 333.

RAILWAY CURVES AND INCLINES.

" Description of the Santiago and Valparaiso railway, Chile, South America ; with remarks upon resistances from curves of railways, and upon coal-burning locomotives." By W. Lloyd, xxiii. 376. *Vide* also RAILWAYS.

" On the working of steep gradients and sharp curves on railways." By Captain H. W. Tyler, xxvi. 310.—Coefficient of adhesion underestimated in the first instance, 310.—Defects of the rack rail system and of grooved wheels, 310.—Objections to the screw of Signor Grassi, 311.—Instances of the earlier steep inclines, 311.—M. Flachat's proposal to utilise the adhesion of all the vehicles composing a train in ascending steep gradients, 311.—M. Thouvenot's and Mr. Fairlie's systems, 312.—Method of calculating

RAILWAY CURVES.

the limit of the gradient up which an engine can take a load, 312.—Reason for adopting the central rail system on the Mont Cenis, 313.—Introduction of the central rail system, 313.—Experimental lines on the Cromford and High Peak railway, and on the road over the Mont Cenis, 313.— First engine for ditto, 313.—Second engine for ditto, 314.—Programme submitted to the French and Italian Governments as a basis for locomotive trials on the Mont Cenis, 315.—Results of locomotive trials on the Mont Cenis railway, 316, *et seq*—Probable horsepower per ton to be ultimately attained by the engines, 319.—Cause of increased velocity round curves during the trials, 319.—Advantage of the middle rail system for mountain passes and steep gradients, 319, 324. —Signor Agudio's system for working steep inclines, 319.—Results of experiments on the Dusino incline, 320. —Useful effect of the system, 321.— Proposed alterations of the machinery, 321.—Advantages of a modified Agudio system for passenger traffic on very steep gradients, 321.—Superiority of the central rail system, 322. —Economy of the Mont Cenis railway compared with the Grand Alpine tunnel, 322.—Gradients on which the central rail may properly be applied, 323.—Table of results of M. Desbrière's calculations as to ditto, 323.

Discussion.—Abernethy, J., 270.—Alexander, A., 329.—Bramwell, F. J., 358, 380.—Brereton, R. P., 378.—Brunlees, J., 341, 394.—Beyer, C. F., 352.— Clark, J., 385.—Cohen, M., 330.— Conybeare, H., 334.—Cowper, E. A., 376.—Crampton, T. R., 382, 384.— Doull, A., 367.—Drew, E. A., 382.— Edwards, G., 395.—Ellis, W. I., 372.— Fairlie, R. F., 367.—Fell, J. B., 326.— Fox, Sir C., 386.—Gregory, C. H., 340.—Grover, J. W., 387.—Hawkshaw, J., 382.—Hemans, G. W., 346, 387.— Holt, W. L., 379.—Lloyd, W., 349.—

RAILWAY INCOME.

Longridge, J. A., 371.—Mallet, R. T., 381.—Margary, P. J., 365, 366.— Naylor, W., 347.—Phipps, G. H., 356, 380.—Pole, W., 342.—Reilly, C., 354. —Roney, Sir C. P., 331.—Stephenson, G. R., 384.—Tyler, Captain H. W., 325, 366, 388.—Vignoles, C. B., 354.— Woods, E., 352.

Gradients on the Mauritius and the Mont Cenis railways, xxviii. 256, *et seq.*—Working steep inclines by locomotive engines, or by stationary engines, xxx. 39, *et seq.*

Vide also Locomotive Engines; Railway Locomotion; Railway System of Germany; and Railways.

Railway embankments on the seashore, xxi. 483. *Vide* also Reclaiming Land from the Sea.

Railway facing - points, apparatus for wedging (Harrison, T. E.), xxix. 22.

Vide also Railway Switches.

Railway inclines. *Vide* Railway Curves and Inclines.

RAILWAY INCOME AND EXPENDITURE.

" On the statistics of railway income and expenditure, and their bearing on future railway policy and management." By J. T. Harrison, xxix. 322. —Privileges and responsibilities, 322. —Questions affecting the railway interest, 323.—Board of Trade returns, 323.—Characteristics of railway traffic, 323.—Passenger traffic, 324.—Goods traffic, 326.—Further extension of railways, 327.—Comparison of annual receipts and expenditure, 328.—Expenditure on revenue account, 328.— Maintenance of works, 328.—Repairs of passenger carriages, 328.—Repairs of goods trucks, 328.—Locomotive charges, 329.—Repairs, 329.—Running expenses, 329.—Wages, 329.—Fuel, 329.—Net revenue, 330.—Amount available for dividend, 330.—General review, 331.—Funded property, 331. —Railway property, 331.—Comparison of funded and railway property, 331. —Railway expenditure in last twenty years, 331.—Explanation of large

RAILWAY LOCOMOTION.

outlay, 332.—Closing capital accounts, 332.—Points affecting value of railway property, 332.—First cost, 332.— Leased lines and guaranteed stock, 333.—Loans and debentures, 333.— Proposals for relieving burdens, 333. Government loans, 333.—Associated companies, 333.—Means of increasing income, 334.—Reduction of expenditure, 334.—Concluding remarks, 334. Discussion.—Barlow, W. H., 336.—Chadwick, E., 349.—Currie, G. W., 345, 355.—Dutton, F. S., 353.—Fowler, J., 347.—Harrison, J. T., 367.—Harrison, T. E., 364.—Hawkshaw, J., 352.— Hemans, G. W., 343.—Hill, F. H., 345.—Lloyd, J. H., 358.—Mitchell, J., 355.—Taylor, J., 366.—Vignoles, C. B., 371.—Williams, R. P., 338.

Vide also LOCOMOTIVE ENGINES AND ROLLING STOCK; PERMANENT WAY; RAILWAY ROLLING STOCK; and RAILWAY SYSTEM OF GERMANY.

RAILWAY LOCOMOTION.

" On the structure of locomotive engines for ascending steep inclines with sharp curves on railways." By James Cross, xxiii. 406. — General requirements, 406.—Injurious effects of an ordinary locomotive passing round curves, 406. —Rapid destruction of tires and rails from the tension on the axles, 407—Long locomotives sometimes railbound on ascending curves, 407.—Locomotive fitted with Adams's radial axle-boxes and spring-tires, 407. — Principal details, 407.—Effect of the radial axle-boxes in reducing the real wheel base, 408.—Action of the axle-boxes, 408.—Capabilities of the engine, 409.

" On the impedimental friction between wheel-tire and rails, with plans for improvement." By W. B. Adams, xxiii. 411.—Difference in the movement of a rolling cone and a rolling cylinder, 411.—Movement of a pair of railway wheels on a fixed shaft resembles that of a rolling cylinder, 411.—Conditions that arise when a single pair of wheels are placed on rails, 411.— Ditto when two pairs of wheels are

RAILWAY LOCOMOTION.

connected together to a frame to form a carriage of the usual plan, 411.— Actual conditions found in practice, 412.—Theory of conic compensation not reduced to practice, 412.—Practical compensation in a sliding movement resulting in impedimental friction, 412.—Proofs of the above, 412.— Method of coupling a cause of increased friction in goods trains, 413.—Causes of the strains upon rails, 413.—Parts worn on the inner and on the outer rails on a curve, 413.—Cost of different kinds of iron and steel for tires and rails, 414.—Mechanical difference between iron and steel, 414.—Instance of a steel tire wearing more quickly than an iron tire, 414.—Objections to the loose wheel and spring wheel, 415.—Advantages of an elastic tire, 415.—Spring-tire wheels tried with success on the North London railway, 415.—Remarkable facts developed on another line in the wheels of an engine fitted with similar tires, 416.— Further good results of the application of spring tires to the wheels of engines on the same line, 416.—New system of wheels with double-spring hoops applied by the engineer of the St. Helens railway, Lancashire, 416.— Report by Mr. Cross as to ditto, 416. —Results of performance of four classes of tires on the St. Helens railway, 417.—Tabular statement of ditto, 417. —Spring-tires do not need turning up so frequently, 417.—Reason why the tires with the smallest load wear most, 417.—Advantages of radiating axles, 418.—Invention of the ' bow-spring,' 418.—Bow-springs used without axle-guards, 418.—Bow-spring carriages not suited for going round curves, 418. —Adaptations to the axle-boxes for causing them to radiate on curves, 419.—Engine in which the above principle was introduced, 419.—Question of giving elasticity to the rails, 419.—Firm foundation for the permanent way might be secured by paving, 420.—Rigid way destructive

RAILWAY LOCOMOTION.'

to the substructure, 420.—Effect of the passage of trains over an ordinary way, 421.—Elastic way, made by fastening longitudinal timbers upon the transverse sleepers, tried on the North London main line, 421.—Plan similar in appearance tried on the Great Western railway, but abandoned, 421.—Advantage of the system on the North London line, 421.—Objections to the use of timber for sleepers, 422. —Cost of a first-class cross-sleeper road tabulated in quantities per mile, 422.—Ditto upon elastic system, 422.— Economy of the elastic system both as to wheels and rails, 423.—Plan for constructing an elastic railway wholly of metal, 423.—Calculation of the cost of ditto, 423.—Suitability of a metal spring way for India, 423.—Desirability and economy of applying the system of longitudinal timbers to permanent metal sleepers, 424.—Cost of such a line, 424.—Durability of the elastic way on the North London line, 424.—Chief sources of destruction in rolling stock and permanent way result from blows and friction between tires and rails, 425.—Best mode of preventing the blow by providing for elastic resilience, 425.—Rail joints, 425.—How to prevent the sliding movement of the tires on the rails, 426.—Firm foundations for the permanent way, 426.—Best arrangement for spring tires, 426.—Rigid way with a continuous bearing for the rail where speeds are not excessive, 427.

Discussion.—Adams, W., 438.—Adams, W. B., 438.—Barlow, W. H., 434.— Berkley, G., 434.— Bidder, G. P., 441.—Cross, J., 438.—Gregory, C. H., 428, 434.—Harrison, T. E., 436.— Hawkshaw, J., 437.—Hemans, G. W., 432, 435.— Heppel, J. M., 436.— Phipps, G. H., 431, 435.—Russell, J. S., 432.—Woods, E., 435.—Vignoles, C. B., 430, 431.

Vide also LOCOMOTIVE ENGINES; LOCOMOTIVE ENGINES AND ROLLING STOCK; PERMANENT WAY; RAILWAY ACCIDENTS;

RAILWAY ROLLING STOCK.

RAILWAY ROLLING STOCK ; RAILWAY SYSTEM OF GERMANY; RAILWAYS, &c. RAILWAY ROLLING STOCK.

" On the maintenance of railway rolling stock." By E. Fletcher, xxiv. 459.— Statistics of the rolling stock belonging to the North Eastern Railway Company, 459.—General results, 460. —Statement showing the total number of the different descriptions of stock, the average age of each, the cost of repairing per vehicle per annum, and the percentage of repairs, and of rebuilding on the first cost, 461.—Appendix, tables giving the ages of the stock for the years 1852-64 inclusive, 462.—First-class carriages, 462.—Composite carriages, 463.—Second-class carriages, 464.—Third-class carriages, 465.—Luggage and parcels vans, 466. —Horse-boxes, 467.—Carriage-trucks, 468.—Goods break-vans, 469.—Stores vans, 470.—Goods wagons, 471.— Covered goods wagons, 472.—Sheep and box wagons, 473.—Cattle wagons, 474.—Timber wagons, 475.—Six-ton coal wagons, 476.—Eight-ton coal wagons, 477.—Coke and lime wagons, 478.—Hopper iron wagons, 479.— Ironstone wagons, 479.—Ballast wagons, 480.—Water and creosote tanks, 481.—Stone wagons, 482.— Locomotive engines, 483.—Table showing the number, average age, cost, &c., of the locomotive engine stock at the different periods, 484. —Ditto of the carriage stock, 485. —Ditto of the total cost of carriage stock, cost of repairs, cost per vehicle per annum, for repairing and upholding, 486.—Ditto showing the number, description, and average age of the wagon stock, 487.—Ditto of the total cost of wagon stock, cost of repairs, and cost per vehicle per annum, for repairing and upholding, 489.—Ditto of the number, original cost, &c., of the chaldron wagon stock, with the cost per wagon per annum for upholding, 490.

Discussion.—Adams, W. A., 496, 497.—

RAILWAY ROLLING STOCK.

Bidder, G. P., 501.—Gibson, J., 499.
—Harrison, T. E., 491, 497, 509.—
Hawkshaw, J., 495.

"On the maintenance of the rolling
stock on the Cologne-Minden and
other Prussian railways." By T.
A. Rochussen, xxv. 430.—Districts
through which the Cologne-Minden
railway passes, 430.—Ditto the
Bergish-Maerkish railway, 430.—
Ditto the Rhenish railway, 431.—
Rails in use on the above railways,
431.—Sleepers, 431.—Slag used for
ballast on the Bergish-Maerkish railway, 431.—Explanation of the tables
in the Appendix, 431.—Improvements
in the construction of the carriage-
wheels introduced by the Prussian
Railway Company, 432.—Wooden
disc-wheels of Mr. Daelen, 432.—Iron
disc-wheels, 432.—The Bochum corrugated cast-steel wheels of combined
disc and tire, 433.—Corrugated
wrought-iron disc wheels with steel
tires, 433.—Method of grinding the
steel tires on the Cologne-Minden
railway, 434.—Appendix: Table A,
general circumstances, 435.—Table B,
description of engines, 436.—Table C,
work done by engines in 1864, 437.—
Table D, cost of motive power, 438.—
Table E, repairs and renewal of
engine tires, 438.—Table F, summary
of repair and renewal of engines, 438.
—Table G, description of carriages
and wagons, 439.—Table H, repairs
and renewals of carriages and wagons,
inclusive of cleaning, 440.—Table K,
commercial results, 441.—Table L,
statutory reserve, for renewal fund,
442.—Table M, experience of the
wear of tires on the Cologne-Minden
railway from 1845 to 1863, reduced to
a diameter of 5 feet and a weight of
10 tons on each axle, the wear calculated in the inverse ratio of the
diameter and the direct ratio of the
load, 443.—Table N, experience of
the wear of tires on the Cologne-
Minden railway from 1845 to 1863,
taken from the effective mileage,

RAILWAY ROLLING STOCK.

irrespective of quality of material and
diameter, 443.—Table O, performance
and wear of carriage and wagon tires
on the Cologne-Minden railway,
taken from the average of 3,046 cast-
steel, 18,458 puddled-steel, and 4,086
iron tires, 444, et seq.

Discussion.—Bidder, G. P., 449.—Bram-
well, F. J., 451.—Gregory, C. H., 456.
—Phipps, G. H., 456.—Rochussen,
T. A., 447, 457.

"The maintenance and renewal of railway rolling stock." By R. P.
Williams, xxx. 136.—Average life,
136.—Engine valuation: Table A a.
Locomotive valuation, 137.—Table
B b. Tender valuation, 139.—Valuation of engine and tender combined,
139.—Table C. Summary of tables
A a and B b, 140.—Table F. Summary
of tables D d and E e, 141.—Scrap
valuation, 141.—Stages of depreciation of an engine, 142.—Irregularity
of the depreciation of different parts
of ditto, 143.—Definition of the stages
of the life of an engine, 143.—Value
of an engine at each of these stages,
144.—Normal dilapidation, 144.—
Successive renewals required by an
engine and tender during thirty years,
145.—North Eastern railway locomotive stock, 147.—Practical application of tables, 148.—Method of
arriving at an accurate knowledge of
the condition of rolling stock, 150.—
Capital expenditure, and cost of repairs and renewals, for locomotives on
the Great Northern railway, 150.—
Tables 4 and 5. Average cost of
repairs and renewals on twelve
English railways, 151.—Locomotive
expenses, 152.—Train mileage, 152.—
Number of engines per mile worked
on the London and South Western
and London and North Western railways, 152.—Comparative working expenses on different railways, 153.—
Table 6. Details of locomotive expenses per train mile, and per engine,
153.—Repairs and renewals of carriages and wagons, 154.—Table 7.

RAILWAY SLEEPERS.

Carriage repairs and renewals, 155.— Table 8. Wagon repairs and renewals, 155.—Cost of wagons on the North Eastern railway, 155.—Fallacy of estimating the cost of repairs and renewals of carriages and wagons per train mile, 155.—Importance of having few types of engines, 156.—Appendix: enumeration of tables and diagrams, 157.—Table A. Engine valuation, 158.—Table B. Tender valuation, 180. —Summary of table A. Engine valuation, 186.—Summary of table B. Tender valuation, 187.—Table D d. Locomotive valuation, 188.—Table E e. Tender valuation, 189.—Table 1 a. Valuation of engine, based on the assumption of uniform wear, 190.— Table 2 a. Valuation of tender, 190. —Table 3 a. Summary of results of valuation in tables 1 a and 2 a, 191.

Discussion.—Adams, W., 200.—Bramwell, F. J., 202.—Clark, D. K., 197. —Gregory, C. H., 206.—Harrison, J. T., 194.—Harrison, T. E., 203.— Johnson, S. W., 213—Martley, W., 201.—Phipps, G. H., 205.—Rapier, R. C., 205.—Vignoles, C. B., 194, 204, 213.—Williams, R. P., 192, 206.— Woodhouse, J. T., 206.

Vide also LOCOMOTIVE ENGINES; LOCOMOTIVE ENGINES AND ROLLING STOCK; and RAILWAY INCOME AND EXPENDITURE.

RAILWAY SLEEPERS.

" On the woods used for sleepers on the Madras railway." By B. McMaster, xxii. 241.—Question whether the resources of India can supply the demand for the substructure of the permanent way, 241.—Rapid decay of sleepers when cut from young trees or from woods unfit for the purpose, 241. —Arrangement of the sleepers on the Madras railway, 242.—Tabular statement of the Tamil and botanical names of the woods, and the state of the sleepers at the end of the second year, 243.—Small proportion sound at the end of that period, 243. —Advantages resulting from the

system of leaving the sleepers as much as possible uncovered, 243.— Proportion of sleepers split and decayed in uncovered and covered ballast, 244.—Keys and trenails rapidly decay when in contact with ballast, 244.—Road does not twist and buckle when not buried in ballast, 244.—Trenails and keys of excellent quality obtainable, 244.— Tamil and botanical names of twelve woods that would make good sleepers, to be used plain, 245.—Sleepers generally begin to rot under the chairs, and probable cause thereof, 245.— Seats of the chairs in the sleepers should be tarred, 246.—Sleepers of sapwood always decay before the expiration of a year, 246.—Account of the means used to obtain a supply of sleepers from the jungles, 246.—Contract system found to fail, 247.—Experience gained of the woods suitable for sleepers, 247.—Railway companies in India can procure good sleepers by sending their own agents into the jungle to cut them, 248.—English creosoted sleepers successfully resist the influences of the Indian climate, 249.—Sleepers of common light native woods if creosoted would probably be as durable as any others, 249.—Resources of the country likely to prove sufficient to meet the demand, 250.— Calculation of the supply that could be obtained from the Madras forests, 251.—Analysis of 246,000 sleepers cut in the Salem jungles in the year 1858 –59, 251.—Argument in favour of preparing the sleepers by creosoting or otherwise, 251.—Estimate of the cost of one mile of single line of four different kinds of permanent way in the Madras presidency, 252.—Comparison in favour of native creosoted sleepers, 252.—Pot sleepers liable to breakage, 253.—All native woods which will not last plain should be creosoted or otherwise prepared, 253. —Difficulty in obtaining the results of the experience of engineers in

RAILWAY STATIONS.

India, 253.—Extract from 'The Times' confirmatory of the statements in the foregoing paper, 254.

Discussion.—Berkley, G., 256.—Bryce, A., 258.—Burt, H P., 255.—Coode, J., 258.—Curtis, J. G. O., 257.—Greaves, C., 259.—Gregory, C. H., 260.—Jenoure, A., 259.—Sale, Col. T. H., 259. — Sheilds, F. W., 258.—Walker, J., 257.

Vide also MATERIALS ; PERMANENT WAY ; and TIMBER.

RAILWAY STATIONS.

Cannon Street, Charing Cross railway. xxvii. 419, *et seq. Vide* also RAILWAYS, Charing Cross.

Design and arrangement of. " On the design and arrangement of railway stations, repairing-shops, engine-sheds, &c." By W. Humber, xxv. 263.— ' Terminal-intermediate' stations, 263. —Classification, 263.—Leading principles to be observed in general, 264. —Requirements for terminal stations, 264. — Terminal passenger stations, 264.—Arrangement of booking-offices, 264.—Facilities to passengers, 265. —Urinals, closets, and lavatories, 266.—Height of platforms, 266.—Station roofs, 266. — Gas, 267.—Platform arrangements, 267.—Most suitable arrangements for roadside stations, 267.— Goods stations, 268. —Proper situations for manufacturing, maintaining, and storing the rolling stock, 268. — Disadvantages of placing repairing shops at a distance, 269.—Respective merits of rectangular, circular, and radial engine-sheds, 269. —Reference to different stations embodying the points touched upon, 270. —Victoria station of the London, Chatham, and Dover and Great Western railways, 271. — West End terminus of the London, Brighton, and South Coast railway, 271. — Euston station, 271.—New Street station, Birmingham, 272.—Stafford station, 272. —Newton Junction station, 272. —Goods station of the Great Northern railway at King's Cross, 273.—Loco-

RAILWAY STATIONS.

motive workshops of the London, Chatham, and Dover railway at Stewart's Lane, 274. — Britannia carriage works of Messrs. Brown, Marshall, & Co., of Birmingham, 274.—Impossibility of laying down rules applicable to all railway stations, 275.—Appendix : reference index to the plates, 276.

Discussion.—Allport, J. J., 284, 286.—Brereton, R. P., 286.—Berkley, G., 287.—Cawkwell, W., 289.—Clarke, S., 280, 288.—Eborall, C. W., 277.—Findlay, G., 283.—Forbes, J. S., 278. —Gregory, C. H., 291.—Harrison, T. E., 280.—Hawkshaw, J., 290.—Hood, R. J., 277.—Valentine, J. S., 286.—Vignoles, C. B., 280.

St. Pancras, Midland railway. " Description of the St. Pancras station and roof, Midland railway." By W. H. Barlow, xxx. 78.—System of lines forming the Midland railway, 78.—Line from Bedford to London, 78.—Site secured for station, 79.—Junction with the Metropolitan railway, 79.—Arrangement of the station floors, and original design for the station roof, 79. —Considerations which led to the adoption of a one-span roof, 80.—Estimated additional cost, as compared with a roof of two spans, 81. —Substructure of the station, 82.—Competitive designs, 82. — General arrangement of the station, 82.—Arrangements for the delivery of coal outside the station, 82. — Relative roofed area of some of the principal terminal stations in London, 83.—Description of the lower floor, 83.—Ditto of the roof, 83.—Strength of the roof, 85.—Principal dimensions and structural values of the five largest roof-trusses erected, 86.—Cost of the roof, 88.—Cost compared with that of some other large roofs, 89.—Cost no criterion of structural value, as exemplified in the case of the ironwork of the Cannon Street and the Charing Cross roofs, 89.—Advantages of one span instead of two spans, 89.

RAILWAY SWITCHES.

—General question of the cost of roofing considered from a structural point of view, 90.—The covering, 90. —The principals, 90.—Limiting spans, 91.—Limiting spans of several girders, and the more commonly used weight-bearing structures, 91.—Method of obtaining approximately the weight of an intended structure from its limiting span, 92.

Discussion.—Allport, J. J., 94, 99.—Barlow, W. H., 104.—Barry, J. W., 95. —Cowper, E. A., 102.—Grover, J. W., 100.—Heppel, J. M., 99.—Markham, C., 98.—Phipps, G. H., 97.—Rich, Col. F. H., 95 —Vignoles, C. B., 105.

Railway switches (Williams, R. P.), xxix. 23.

—— Improvement in the mode of actuating and locking (Brunton, J.), xxix. 24.

RAILWAY SYSTEM OF GERMANY.

"The railway system of Germany." By R. Crawford, xxii. 2.—Horse tramway first used, 3.—Development of the system, 4.—Mileage and local distribution, 5.—Proprietary, 5.—Association of German railway directions for management, 6.—Gauge, gradients, and curves, 7.—Instances of heavy gradients, 8.—Semmering railway, 9.—Description of engines used for working the Semmering line, 11.—Embankments and cuttings, 12.—Tunnels, 13. —Bridges of timber or cast-iron inadmissible, 13. — Goeltzsch valley viaduct, 13.—Elser valley viaduct, 14. —Neisse viaduct, 14.—Examples of bridges, 14.—Bridge over the Neckar, 14.—Gauthey's and Desjardin's formula for bridge-building compared with Perronet's, 15.—Bridge at Offenburg injudiciously constructed, 16.—Dirschau bridge, 17. — Marienburg bridge, 19.—Cologne bridge, 20.—Kehl bridge, 21.—Lattice bridges on the Eastern railway of Bavaria, 22.—Permanent way, 23.—Table of dimensions and weight of rails, 23.—Method of impregnating sleepers with sulphate of copper, 24.—Stone blocks formerly used for rail supports on the Taunus

RAILWAY TELEGRAPHS.

railway, 24.—Space outside the ballast filled with earth, 25.—Fencing seldom used, 25.—Rolling stock, 25.—Tests applied to locomotive engines, 25.—Table of break-power for different gradients, 26.—Rate of speed, 26.

Discussion.—Crawford, R., 43.—Curtis, J. G. C., 41.—Gregory, C. H., 42.—Harrison, T. E., 30.—Mallet, R., 37, 43.—Moorsom, Capt. W. S., 33.—Russell, J. S., 35.—Sheilds, F. W., 40.—Vignoles, C. B., 27.

Vide also RAILWAY ROLLING STOCK.

RAILWAY TELEGRAPHS.

"On railway telegraphs, and the application of electricity to the signalling and working of trains." By W. H. Preece, xxii. 167.—Many railway accidents due to the absence of the electric telegraph, 167.—Accident in the Clayton tunnel due to inefficient telegraphic regulations, 167.—Collision in the Tottenham tunnel prevented by the use of the telegraph, 168.—Accidents at the Stoke tunnel preventible by telegraphic means, 169.—Localities where the adoption of the telegraph for signalling trains is essential, 169.—Chief advantage of the electric telegraph in its auxiliary character, 169.—Cost trifling in respect of the advantages secured, 170.—Question of maintaining trains at certain intervals of time or space, 170.—Description of Cooke's system, now called the ' block' system, 171.—Ditto, first established on the Eastern Counties line between Norwich and Yarmouth, 172.—Inefficiency of the single-needle speaking instrument for working trains through long tunnels, 172.—Cooke's system, improved by Clark, in use on the London and North Western line, 173.—Faults of this system, 174.—Accident at Wolverton, 174.—Superiority of the time system to the block system, 175.—Inferior system used on the Great Northern railway, 175.—The needle telegraph used as a medium of conversation, and an accident thereby

RAILWAY TELEGRAPHS.

avoided at Roade, 176.—Description of Bartholomew's and of Tyer's systems, 177.—C. V. Walker's system of signalling by bells alone, 179.—Regnault's system used in France inferior to those adopted in England, 179.—German system of bell-ringing impracticable in England, 180.—Want of distinctions in the opposite indications in the above systems, and improvements introduced by Highton and by Spagnoletti on the Metropolitan railway, 180.—An electric signalling instrument for all practical purposes a distant signal worked by electricity, 181.—Preece's system an exact counterpart, on a small scale, of the signals used on the line, 181.—Description of semaphore worked by electricity, 183.—Resemblance to the 'block' system, 184.—Method of working, 184.—Used on the London and South Western railway, 184.—Comparison of the London and North Western, Mr. Tyer's, and the London and South Western systems, 184.—Mr. E. Clark's remarks as to improvements in the London and North Western Railway Company's system, 185.—Needle system liable to derangement by lightning, 185.—Faults of Tyer's system, 185.—Its inferiority to the needle and semaphore systems, 186.—Self-acting mechanical arrangements impracticable, 186.—Application of the telegraph to the working of single lines, 187.—Collision on the Shrewsbury and Hereford railway from an inaccurate message, 188.—System employed on the London and South Western railway, 188.—Accident near Rainham from delay in sending a message, 189.—'Block' system in use in the West of England, 189.—Advantages of record books, 189.—American system similar to the London and South Western, 190.—Single line of railway may be worked with perfect security by telegraph, 190.—Telegraph held in low estimation on most railways,

RAILWAY TRAINS.

191.—Captain Tyler's remarks, 191.—The telegraph a source of danger when indiscriminately used, 191. Discussion.—Adley, C. C., 227.—Bartholomew, E. G., 218.—Bramwell, F. J., 229.—Cowper, E. A., 226.—Culley, R. S., 221.—Eborall, C. W., 210, 212.—Hawkins, G., 212.—Hawkshaw, J., 238.—Hemans, G. W., 224.—Huish, Capt. M., 213.—Jenkin, F., 215.—Jenoure, A., 230.—Johnson, T. M., 228.—Newman, G. W., 230.—Preece, W. H., 193, 232.—Scott, A., 211.—Tyer, E., 196.—Tyler, Capt. H. W., 225.—Walker, C. V., 203.

Vide also RAILWAY ACCIDENTS.

Railway traction, respective merits of rope, and of locomotive. *Vide* RAILWAYS, São Paulo.

Railway traffic. *Vide* RAILWAY INCOME AND EXPENDITURE.

RAILWAY TRAINS.

Autographic record of the times of starting and stopping, the velocity at every instant, the tractive force employed, and the curve of progression, xxi. 385.

Bell used on American railways for communicating between the guards and the drivers, xxi. 408.

Communication in. "On the best means of communicating between the passengers, guards, and drivers of trains in motion." By W. H. Preece, xxvi. 80.—No necessity for mechanical contrivances in early days of railway travelling, 80.—Difficulties resulting from the growth of the railway system, 80.—Various inquiries into the subject, 80.—Reports of parliamentary committees, 80.—Ditto of general managers, 81.—Ditto of Captain Tyler, 81.—French commission of inquiry, 81.—Continued investigation of the sub-committee of the Railway Clearing House, 82.—Necessity of attracting the attention of those who have the control of the train in case of accidents, 82.—Objections on the part of railway authorities to place the control of the train in the hands of passengers, 82.

RAILWAYS.

—Success of the system of passenger signals on the London and South Western railway, 82.—Proposed establishment of a footboard and handrail on every carriage, 83.—Dangers of external circulation, 83.—Objections raised by the sub-committee of general managers to the American system of internal circulation, 83.—System of glass partitions between the compartments of carriages, 84.—Ineffective plans for calling the attention of guards and drivers, 84.—Objections to the cord-and-bell system, 85.—Signals dependent on sound and sight not to be relied on, 85.—Advantages of electricity for signalling purposes, 86.—Systems of electrical communication between guards and drivers hitherto tried, 86.—General arrangement of Mr. Preece's system of communication in trains, 86, et seq.—Appendix No. 1. Instructions issued to the guards and drivers of the London and South Western railway, 90.—No. 2. Instructions inserted in carriages, 91.

Discussion.—Allport, J. J., 94, 95, 96.—Barlow, W. H., 117.—Bazalgette, J. W., 105, 112.—Beardmore, N., 97, 106.—Bramwell, F. J., 96.—Gregory, C. H., 115.—Harrison, T. E., 112.—Knight, J. P., 105, 106.—Preece, W. H., 92, 95, 113.—Spagnoletti, H., 98.—Tattersall, E., 95.—Tyler, Capt. H. W., 106.—Varley, S. A., 97.—Walker, C. V., 101.

Vide also RAILWAY ACCIDENTS.

RAILWAYS.
Alpine, xxvi. 333, 344, 395.—Atmospheric propulsion a means of crossing Alpine passes, 344.—Vide also RAILWAY CURVES AND INCLINES.

Atlantic, xxvi. 300.

Atmospheric, xxvi. 344, 365.—Atmospheric system on the South Devon railway, 365.

Australian, xxix. 353.—Indirect advantages of ditto, 353.—Particulars respecting the South Australian railways, 354.

RAILWAYS.

Battersea, new railways at, in connection with the Victoria bridges, Pimlico, xxvii. 78. Vide also BRIDGES.

Brazilian, xxx. 69. Vide also PUBLIC WORKS.

Brenner, across the Brenner pass, between Munich and Verona, xxvi. 342.

Canterbury, New Zealand, xxix. 116.

Cape of Good Hope, xxviii. 270.

Charing cross. "The City terminus extension of the Charing Cross railway." By J. W. Barry, xxvii. 410.—Accommodation afforded to the public, 410.—Works authorized by Act of Parliament, 410.—Engineers and contractors, 410.—Bridge over the river Thames, 411.—Abutments, 412.—Staging for the bridge, 413.—Piers, 413.—Sinking the cylinders, 414.—Weighting and testing ditto, 415.—Bedplate girders, 415.—Outside main girders, 416.—Intermediate main girders, 416.—Flooring, 416.—Cross strutting, 417.—Footway, 417.—Signal bridge, 418.—Cost, &c. of the bridge, 418.—Cannon Street station, 419.—Substructure, 419.—Walls, 421.—Roof, 421.—Gable screen, 423.—Staging for the roof, 423.—Cost of the roof, 423.—Arrangement of the station, 424.—Platforms, &c., 425.—Station-yard and signals, 426.—Cost of the station, 427.—The viaducts, &c. south of the Thames, 428.—Engine depôt, 428.—Permanent way, 428.—The total cost, 429.—Conclusion, 429.

Discussion.—Barlow, W. H., 431.—Barry, J. W., 431, 440.—Bazalgette, J. W., 438.—Brereton, R. P., 434.—Gregory, C. H., 441.—Grover, J. W., 437.—Harrison, J. T., 432.—Harrison, T. E., 439.—Hawkshaw, J., 432, 439.—Hemans, G. W., 435.—Hood, R. J., 433, 437.—Longridge, J. A., 434.—Phipps, G. H., 439.—Porter, J. H., 435.—Ryde, E., 438.

Dom Pedro Segundo, xxx. 69.

East Indian, comparative statement of waterway on the several districts of the main line, Bengal division, xxvii. 269.

RAILWAYS.

Festiniog. "On the Festiniog railway for passengers; as a 2-feet gauge with sharp curves, and worked by locomotive engines." By H. W. Tyler, Captain, R.E., xxiv. 359.— Objects of the construction of this railway, or tramroad, 359.—Powers under Act of Parliament, 359. — Description of the line and mode of working the traffic, 360.—Employment of locomotive engines, first for minerals, and subsequently for passengers, 361.—Details of the engines, and their performances, 361.—Carriages, 362.—Permanent way, 363.— Difficulties with which the company had to contend, in transferring a horse tramway into a passenger line to be worked by locomotives, 363.—Situations in which railways on a narrower gauge than 4 feet 8½ inches may possibly be adopted, 364.—Railways in Norway on a gauge of 3 feet 6 inches, 365.—Illegal at present to construct passenger lines in Great Britain on a narrower gauge than 4 feet 8½ inches, 365.—Desirable that this Act should be amended, and that a narrower gauge should be recognised, 365.—Locomotive engine at the Crewe workshops on a gauge of 18 inches, 366.

Discussion.—Adams, W. B., 380.—Allport, J. J., 385.—Barlow, P. W., 388.—Bidder, G. P., 377.—Bruff, P., 371, 375. —Brunlees, J., 386.—Colburn, Z., 386. —England, G., 389.—Fox, Sir C., 369. —Galbraith, W. R., 387.—Giles, A., 384.—Gregory, C. H., 375, 382.— Harrison, T. E., 388.—Hemans, G. W., 368.—Mallet, R., 375, 388.—Phipps, G. H., 375.—Roney, Sir C., 388.— Savin, T., 377.—Tyler, Capt. H. W., 367.—Woods, E., 379.

Germany. *Vide* RAILWAY ROLLING STOCK; and RAILWAY SYSTEM OF GERMANY.

History of, xxi. 174; xxix. 307.—The Stockton and Darlington and the Liverpool and Manchester railways, 307.—The 'Rainhill experiments,' 310. — Introduction of the railway system

RAILWAYS.

into France hindered by M. Thiers, 313.—The 'Irish Railway Commissioners,' 315.

Madras, xxiv. 184, 190, *et seq. Vide* also BRIDGES.

Mauritius. "The Mauritius railways—Midland line." By J. R. Mosse, xxviii. 232.—Physical features of the island, 232.—Soil, 232.—Dimensions, 233.—Population, 233.—Products and trade, 233.—Revenue and expenditure, 233.—Causes which led to the introduction of railways, 234.—Conveyance of sugar, 234.—Survey for the railway, and its construction, 234.—Routes of the North and Midland lines, 234.—Rails, 235.—Chairs, 235.—Sleepers, 235.—Cost of railways, 235.—Causes for large expenditure, 236.—Gradients and curves on the Midland line, 236, 250.—Locomotives, 238. —Carriages and wagons, 239.—Train service, 239. —Trains, 239.—Speed of ditto, 240.— Locomotive power employed, 240.— Results of a trial trip, 241.—Breakpower, 242.—Heaviest passenger train from Mahebourg to Port Louis, 243.— Freedom from accidents, 243.—Limitation of speed in descending the inclines, 243.—Goods trains, 243.—Break-power for ditto, 244.—Instance of a goods train getting beyond control, 244.— Safety sidings, 244.—Electric telegraph, 245.—Rules respecting runaway vehicles, 245.—Mauritian woods used for break-blocks, 245.—Rules for working the sidings, 246. — Traffic returns, 246.—Passenger and goods rates, 247.—Locomotive cost per engine mile, 248.—Salaries and wages, 248 —. Maintenance of the permanent way, 249.—Coal, oil, and tallow, 249.—Percentage of working expenses, 250.— Appendix No. 1. Midland line. Summary of gradients rising from Port Louis to Mahebourg, 252.—No. 2. Summary of curves, 253. —No. 3. Principal dimensions of tank-engines, 254.—No. 4. Schedule of rolling stock, 255.

Discussion. — Adams, W. B., 260. —

RAILWAYS.

Atkinson, W., 267.—Barlow, W. H., 271.—Barry, J. W., 269.—Berkley, G., 271.—Bidder, G. P., 280.—Bramwell, F. J., 258—Brereton, R. P., 274.—Fell, J. B., 279.—Gregory, C. H., 257, 260, 286.—Harrison, T. E., 264.—Hawkshaw, J., 266, 283.—Hemans, G. W., 256.—Huntington, J. B., 259.—Mitchell, J., 259.—Morrison, Col. W. L., 275.—Longridge, J. A., 256, 257, 258.

Mont Cenis, xxiii. 258, 315; xxvi. 312, et seq.; xxviii. 256, et seq.; xxix. 301. Vide also TUNNELS; and RAILWAY CURVES AND INCLINES.

Norway, narrow-gauge, between Throndhjein and Storen, and between Hamar and Eleverum, the character of the lines, the details of the works upon them, especially the bridges and viaducts, and their economy of construction, with particulars of the rolling stock, xxiv. 365, 371, 375.

Norway, India, and Queensland. "On light railways in Norway, India, and Queensland." By C. D. Fox, xxvi. 49.—Railways of Europe and America contrasted, 49.—Class of railways required for thinly populated countries, 49.—Definition of the term 'light railways,' 49.—Light railways in Norway, 50.—Permanent way, 50.—Locomotives and rolling stock, 51.—Financial results, 51.—Railway from Arconum junction of the Madras railway to Conjeveram described, 51.—Cost per mile of ditto and traffic, 52.—Queensland government railways, 53.—Features of the country, 53.—Direction of the Southern and Western railway of Queensland, 53.—Inclines and tunnels on ditto, 53.—Bridge over the river Bremer, 53.—Stations, 54.—Rolling stock, 54.—Locomotives, 55.—Permanent way, 57.—Results of testing rails, 58.—Cost of Queensland railways per mile, 59.—Great Northern railway of Queensland, 59.—Relative cost of different railways in Australia, 60.—Concluding remarks, 60.

Discussion.—Abernethy, J., 72.—Adams,

RAILWAYS.

W. B., 74.—Blair. J. F., 66.—Bramwell, F. J., 72.—Bruce, G. B., 65.—Fox, C. D., 61, 79.—Harrison, T. E., 73.—Hemans, G. W., 63, 72.—Hodge, P. R., 69.—Peacock, R, 76.—Phipps, G. H., 73.—Sheilds, F. W., 70.—Tyler, Capt. H. W., 72.—Woods, E., 67.

Prussian. Vide RAILWAY ROLLING STOCK.

Santiago and Valparaiso. "Description of the Santiago and Valparaiso railway, Chilé, South America; with remarks upon resistances from curves on railways, and upon coal-burning locomotives." By W. Lloyd, xxiii. 376.—Original plans and estimates, 376.—Adoption of a new route, 376.—Construction of railway works imperfectly understood, 377.—Establishment of the contract system, 377.—Opening of the line for traffic, 377, 378.—Difficulty experienced in raising the requisite capital, 377.—Difficulty of the execution of the work, 378.—Physical features of the country, 378.—The first cost of construction more important than the future cost of working, 378.—Valparaiso and Santiago, 379.—Coach road between ditto, 379.—Economy of railway conveyance, 380.—Route selected by Mr. Campbell, 380.—Deviation from ditto finally carried out, 381.—Comparison of the Tabon with other steep inclines, 381.—General description of the line, 382.—Sea-walls, 382.—Viaducts, 382.—Bridges over the Limache river, 383.—San Pedro tunnel, 383.—Provisional line at San Pedro during the construction of the tunnel, 383.—Successful stoppage of a slip in the tunnel, 384.—Quillota, 384.—Valley of the Aconcagua, 385.—Bridge over the Vichiculen river, 385.—The Tabon incline, 385.—Railway carried along the face of the mountains, 386.—Works on this portion of the line, 386.—The Maquis viaduct, 386.—Bridges over the Tabon river, 387.—Summit of the incline, 387.—Guard rails for the curves, 387.—Permanent way,

RAILWAYS.

387.—Bridges over the river Lampa, in the San Ramon ravine, 388.—Declivity of the valley at Tiltil and Polpaico, 388.—Embankment across the Batuco lake, 388.—Bridge over the Mapocho river, 388.—Station at Valparaiso, 389.—Stress laid upon the combination of steep gradients with abrupt curves, 389.—Resistances due to such combinations as shown by experiments made upon the Paso Hondo incline, and the level line near Valparaiso, 389, et seq.—Method of conducting the experiments, 390.—Rules for determining the resistance due to curvature, 391.—Dimensions of the engines now in use, 391.—Native coal employed for fuel, 392.—Alterations made in engines intended to burn coke, for adapting them to consume coal, 392.—Application of a jet of water from the boiler upon the flanges of the leading wheels of the engines, 393, 397.—Mileage of the engines in October, 1863, 393.—Duty that the engines can perform, as shown by trains conveyed up the inclines, 393.—Application of water to prevent the burning of the break-blocks, and to ease the train round the curves in working the Tabon incline, 395.—Traffic returns, 395.—Table of the length, cost, plant, and consumption of fuel of the railways of Chilé, 396.—Exceptional features of the Chañarcello line, 396.—General characteristics of the country through which the railway passes, 396.—Social contrasts presented by this railway, 396.—Means for resisting the effects of earthquakes, 397.—Superiority of Chilian coal, 397.—Unsatisfactory results of an attempt to adapt screw piles as foundations for a bridge upon a quicksand, 397.

Discussion.—Bidder, G. P., 404.—Colburn, Z., 403, 404.—Fowler, J., 399.—Giles, A., 402.—Paddison, G., 399, 401.—Phipps, G. H., 401.—Vignoles, C. B., 401, 402.—Woods, E., 399, 401, 402.

RAILWAYS.

São Paulo, Brazil. "Description of the line and works of the São Paulo railway, in the empire of Brazil." By D. M. Fox, xxx. 29.—Mr. R. Stephenson's remarks on the enterprise, 29.—Commencement of ditto, 29. — Concession, 30. — Preliminary surveys, 30.—Contract for, and cost of the works, 31.—Results of working the line, 32.—Physical features of the province of São Paulo, 32.—Santos, 33.—Productions of the province, 33.—Engineering features of the line from Santos to the foot of the Serra, 34.—Ditto from the summit of the Serra to Jundiahy, 34.—Stations, 35.—Summit tunnel, 35.—Land-slide north of tunnel, 36.—Earthworks, 36.—Serra inclines, 36. — Measures adopted for preventing slips, 37.—Slip cleared by the agency of water, 37.—Iron viaduct at foot of fourth incline, 37.—Mode of working inclines, 39.—Winding machinery, 39.—Break-wagons, 40.—Traffic on the inclines, 40.—Permanent way, 41.—Iron pot sleepers preferred to timber sleepers, 41.—Fencing, 42.—Telegraph, 43.—Geological formation of the district, 43.—Climate, 44.—Table of rainfall and temperature, 44.—Locomotives, 44.—Carriages and goods wagons, 45.—Railway materials obtainable in the province, 45.—Timber, 46.—Brickwork, 46.—Gravel, 46.—Ironwork, 46.—Methods of preserving ditto, 46.—Cost of haulage of materials, 47.—Labourers and wages, 47.—Total cost of line and revenue, 48.—Appendices : A. Table of curves and straight lines, 50.—B. Table of gradients on locomotive line, 50.—C. List of principal bridges, 51.—D. Table of culverts and smaller bridges, 51.—E. Sections of steel tire, 52.—F. Schedule of locomotives and rolling stock, 53.—G. Table of wages during construction, 53.—H. Comparative statement of receipts and expenditure for the half-year ending June 30, 1869, showing the loss per

RAILWAYS.

mile in working the inclined planes at locomotive rates, 54.—I. Comparative statement *showing cost of working a given traffic up and down the Serra do Mar by, first, steep inclines worked by fixed engines and ropes, and, secondly, locomotives on a gradient of 1 in 40, 54.

Discussion.—Aubertin, J. J., 58.—Bayliss, J., 71.—Bell, V. G., 69.—Broadrick, G., 69.—Bramwell, F. J., 67.—Brunlees, J., 57, 76.—Coode, J., 74.—Douglass, J. N., 76.—Hawkshaw, J., 68.—Hemans, G. W., 64.—Heppel, J. M., 66.—Lane, C. B., 62.—Lloyd, W., 66.—Longridge, J. A., 73.—Neate, C., 69.—Pole, W., 67.

Scinde. "Description of the line and works of the Scinde railway." By J. Brunton, xxii. 451.—Importance of the Indus Valley route pointed out by Sir C. Napier and others, 451.—Inauguration of railways in India, 452.—Schemes undertaken by the Scinde Railway Company, 452.—First section of the line between Kurrachee and Kotree, 452.—Description of the town and port of Kurrachee, 453.—Table of the number of vessels entering and clearing outwards, 453.—Articles of export and import, 453.—Table showing the increase of the import and export trade, 454.—Increased accommodation, 454.—Obstructions to commercial communication hitherto, 454.—Administrative difficulties encountered in the commencement of the railway works, 455.—Introduction of the piece-work system, 457.—Average prices paid for earth and rock work, 458.—Table of total quantities of different classes of work, and average cost of each kind, 458.—Table of the rainfall, 459.—Rainfall at the end of July, 459.—Well-water more or less saline, 459.—Tables of the results of the analyses of the water, 459, 460.—Geological and physical features of the neighbourhood of Kurrachee, 461.—Earthquakes, 462.—Table of gradients of the railway

RAILWAYS.

between Kurrachee and Kotree, 462.—Table of curves, 463.—Earthworks executed for a single line of railway; bridges, culverts, &c., adapted for two lines, 463.—Permanent way, 463.—Timber used for sleepers, 463.—Deodar timber floated down the Indus, 463.—Respective cost of sleepers of creosoted pine, Australian blue gum, Eyne, and Deodar, 464.—Value of Deodar timber, 464.—Creosoted pine sleepers liable to split, 464.—Cost of creosoting and of Burnettising sleepers in India, 465.—Quality, cost, and weight per cubic foot of different kinds of timber used in Scinde, 465.—Fencing used on the railway, 466.—Locomotive erecting and repairing shops at Kurrachee, 466.—Native carpenters and smiths, 466.—European workmen and plan for keeping up the supply, 467.—Electric telegraph, 467.—Train-signalling stations, 468.—Provision in the construction of the line over plains against damage by floods, 468—Difficulty in obtaining pure water for the use of the locomotive engines, 469.—Cost of the haulage of materials, 469.—List of the different-sized culverts erected on the line, 470.—Details of culverts, 470.—Bridges, 470.—Viaduct across the Bahrun river, 470.—Other viaducts with iron girders on Warren's principle, 471.—The Mulleer viaduct, 471.—Defects of Warren's girders, 471.—Objections to the departmental system of executing works, 472.—General considerations of the extension of railways in uncivilized countries, and the position occupied by the European employé in regard to the natives, 473.—Appendix: details of quantities and cost of the Bahrun viaduct, 475.

Discussion.—Andrew, W. P., 480.—Berkley, G., 486.—Bidder, G. P., 489.—Brooks, W. A., 487, 489.—Bruce, G. B., 484.—Brunton, J., 494.—Parkes, W., 488.

——Devastating flood on the Scinde

RAINFALL.

railway in 1866 (Bidder, G. P.), xxvii. 249.—Report to the Directors of the Scinde Railway Company with regard to ditto, 250, 256.—*Vide* also RIVERS, FRESHWATER FLOODS OF.

Talyllyn, narrow-gauge, xxvi. 72.

Victoria station and Pimlico, xxvii. 56. *Vide* also BRIDGES.

Rainfall, in England, xxi. 100.—Results produced by rain falling on different geological formations, xxii. 360.

—— in India, xxii. 459.

Vide also RIVERS, FRESHWATER FLOODS OF; and WATER, FLOW OF.

RAKE, A. S. [Election, xxii. 241.]

RAMSBOTTOM, J. [Election, xxv. 429.]

RANDALL, —.

River Thames, xxii. 355.—Sudden floods about Oxford, caused by increased agricultural drainage, 355.—Floods caused from the changing deposit of gravel and soil in the bed of the river, and suggestions for relief, 355.

RANDOLPH, G. W. [Admission, xxix. 98.]

RANKIN, W. H. [Election, xxiv. 184.]

RANKINE, Professor W. J. M.

Ships and steam-vessels, xxiii. 368.—Method of estimating the probable speed of steam-vessels with a given indicated H.P., and the converse, 368.—Frictional resistance of vessels depends on the nature and condition of the surface, 368.—Sensible resistance to a ship of truly proportioned lines caused only by frictional eddies, 368.—Computation of the "augmented surface of a vessel," 368.—Method of ascertaining the cube of the probable speed of a steam-vessel in knots, 368—Probable speed of the 'Warrior,' 369.

RANSOME, A., Jun. [Election, xxiii. 320.]

RANSOME, F. [Associate of Council, xxviii. 158.]

RANSOME, J. A.

Permanent way, xxi. 413.—Compressed oak trenails, 413.

RANSOME, R. [Memoir, xxv. 529.]

RAPIER, R. C. [Election, xxii. 451.]

Railway locomotion, xxx. 205.—Speed

RAWLINSON.

of trains on entering and leaving stations, 205.

RAVENHILL, J. R. [Election, xxiv. 184.]

Steam navigation, xxix. 168.—Surface and jet condensation for marine engines, 168.—Effect of surface condensing on the boilers of the 'Ripon,' 168.—Superheating steam, 169.—Consumption of fuel per indicated H.P., by the Peninsular and Oriental company's vessels, 169.—Recent improvements in steam-vessels, 170.

RAWLINSON, R.

Canal, Suez, xxvi. 454.—Cost of maintenance, 455.—Facing the sides with concrete, 455.

Cements, xxv. 114.—Portland cement, 114.—Cost of ditto, 115.—Halkin mountain limestone, 116.

Drainage of land, xxi. 98.—Evaporation from plants, 98.—Utilisation of drainage-water from upland districts, 99.

Drainage of towns, xxii. 285.—Relative amount of sewage discharged from the outlet sewers at Dundee in dry weather, and during storms, 285.—Necessity of the ventilation of sewers, 286.—Flow of gases to the upper and higher levels, 286.—Method of cleansing sewers proposed by Mr. Fulton, 286.—Impolicy of constructing sewers of a larger size than absolutely necessary, 286.—Construction of a sewer in which the invert and sides consist of a double ring of bricks and the crown of a single ring, 287.—System of ventilation, 287.—Use of steps, flap-valves, and ventilating grates where the gradients are steep, and the sewers long, 287.—Proper outlet of a sewer to a river having a low summer level and a high or flood level, 288.—Cast-iron invert of the main outlet sewer at West Ham, 290.—Sewer junctions, 290.—Sizes and cost of brick sewers executed at various places, 292.—Leading principles for the construction of sewers, 292.—Ill-effect of ventilating openings leading direct into the sewer, 292.—

RAWLINSON.

Impossibility of scamping work in a straight sewer with a true gradient, 293.—Pipe drains choked up when brought into a sewer with level inverts, 293.—Débris discharged at the outlets of the Birmingham sewers, 293.—Main sewer at Carlisle, 293.—Flushing apparatus to ditto at the manholes, 293.—Injurious effects of allowing sewage to foul rivers, 294.—The land the proper receptacle of soil refuse, 294.—Results of the analysis of sewer-water from different places generally the same, 298.—Sewerage of Alnwick and Worksop, 298.—Sewers of London and Paris, xxiv. 317, et seq.—Ventilation of sewers, 318.—Sewage outfalls at Barking and Deptford, 320.—Sewerage of Lyons and Marseilles, 320.

Low-water basin at Birkenhead, xxix. 16.

Masonry of Liverpool docks and Cherbourg harbour, xxv. 115.

Rivers and estuaries, xxi. 342.—Inexpediency of canalising rivers subject to flood, 342.—Estuary of the Dee, 342.—Velocity of the stream in the Mersey at half-tide, 342.

Water, flow of, off the ground from the Woodburn district, xxv. 476.

Water supply of Paris and London, xxv. 494.—Prejudicial effects of drinking hard water, 494.—Waste of water in London and Paris, 495.—Plugs for fire-service, 496.—Service reservoirs, 496.—Conduits, 496.

RAWLINSON, W. [Election, xxix. 272.]

RAYNE, M. [Election, xxvii. 180.]

RAYNER, T. C. [Election, xxviii. 517.]

READ, W. H. [Admission, xxviii. 59.]

RECLAIMING LAND FROM THE SEA.

" On the sea-dykes of Schleswig and Holstein, and on reclaiming land from the sea." By J. Paton, xxi. 426.—Extent of marsh-lands reclaimed in Jutland, Schleswig, and Holstein, 426.—Engineering works of the ancient Scandinavians, 426.—Evidence of a gradual upheaving of the land in the North of Denmark, 427.—Diminution

RECLAIMING LAND.

of land on the west coast, 428.—Form of the coast of Schleswig at three different periods, 428.—Evidences of land being overwhelmed by the sea, 429.—Peat-mosses, 429.—Cause of present slow subsidence of land, 429.—Great part of the marsh-lands rest on peat-mosses, 430.—The Wilster and Cremper marshes rest on water, and are gradually subsiding, 430.—Bursting out of salt-water springs in a storm-flood in 1825, 430.—Stone thrown into the Elbe to divert the current of the river, 430.—Rise of water in the wells in Eiderstedt during the great flood, 430.—Zuyder Zee probably formed by the bursting of the marsh and eruption of water from below, 431.—The Bies Bosch and the Dollart probably formed in the same manner, 431.—Breaches in the main dyke of Schleswig and Holstein probably caused by the sea breaking over the top and undermining the foot of the bank, 431.—Other local peculiarities influencing the features of the country, 432.—The Cimbrian flood, 432.—Changes in the island of Amrom, 432.—No great changes on these coasts for over 600 years, 433.—The Lyster Deep the only available inlet for ordinary-sized vessels on the western coast, 433.—The Agger channel to the Liim fiord formed by the storm in 1825, 433.—Results of the above storm, 434.—The flood probably connected with volcanic movements of the bottom of the sea, 434.—Sea violently agitated off the coast of Holland and Friesland during the great earthquake of Lisbon, 434.—Extent of the dams, 435.—The sand singularly productive in grasses, 435.—Constituents of the Flyve sand, 435.—Antiquity of the construction of dykes, 435. — Description of the 'Halligs,' and importance of their preservation, 436.—The area of the 'Halligs' decreased one-half between the years 1713 and 1778, 436.—Importance of maintaining the island of Pelworm, 436.—Surface of the island

RECLAIMING LAND.

gradually subsiding, 437.—Whether the existing stone dykes will absolutely free Pelworm from danger, 437.—Description of the summer, inside, and sea dykes of Ditmarsh and Eiderstedt, 437. —Dykes of the Eider and Elbe, 438.— Range of the tides in Schleswig, 438.— Height of the dykes, 438.—Slope of the dykes, 438.—Variations of the rise of the water in great storm-floods, 439.— Construction and form of the dykes in exposed situations, 439. — Materials used in the formation of dykes, 440.— Precautions in procuring the materials, 440.—Composition of the dykes where every ordinary tide reaches the foot of the dyke, and there is a low exposed 'watt' or outer ground, 441.—System of groynes, 441.—Pitching the sea slope with stone, 441.—Pitching only the foot of the dyke and increasing the slope, 442.—Covering the sea-face with straw matting, 422.—Protecting the dyke with fascine and hurdle-work, 443.—Dykes of seaweed and stones, and temporary dyke of hay, 443.— Means used for suddenly raising dykes in exposed situations, 443.—Scale of contribution towards the maintenance of the main dyke, 444.—Reclamation of 'Friedrichen Koog,' 444.—Advantages of reclamations from the sea exemplified in the result of the exports from Denmark, 445.—Results of reclamations in the Fen districts, 446.—Reclamations in Holland, 446.— Extent and value of the reclamations in the three cases above mentioned, 446.—Estimate, by Mr. Hyde Clarke, of the further extent of land that might be reclaimed in Great Britain, 447.— Appendix I. King Waldemar's rent-roll, etc., 448.—II. The great Danneverke, 448.—III. Account of the greatest storm-floods on the coast of Denmark, etc., 449.—IV. Authorities consulted, 452.

"On reclaiming land from seas and estuaries." By J. Oldham, xxi. 454.— Description of the lower part of the Humber, 454.—Geological section of

RECLAIMING LAND.

the banks of the Humber, 455.— Yielding nature of the foreshores, 455. —Mode of 'warping,' or raising the surface of low lands by tidal deposits, 455.—Waste of land on the banks of the Humber, 456.—Protection of the banks against the tide by piles and chalk-stone facings, 456.—Waste of land on the seaboard of Holderness, 456.—Extract from Dr. Bell's "Observations on the character and measurements of degradation of the Yorkshire coast," 457.—Rate of the waste of land on the Holderness coast, 457.—Situation and extent of Sunk island, 457.— Formed from materials transported by the tide from the Holderness coast, 458.—Particulars of the substrata of Sunk island, 459.—Constituents of the Humber mud, 459.—Progress of vegetable growth on the mud flats, 460.— Vegetable growth and diatomaceæ render the Humber mud fit for cultivation, 460.—Preparation of the land before embanking, 460.—Permanent drainage of the land, 461.—Formation of the sea-bank, 461.—Description of the works of the last embankment at Sunk island, 462.—Restrictions imposed on the contractor as to procuring the materials of the embankment, 463. — Progress and completion of the works, 463.—Cost of the works, 463.— Soil of Sunk island impervious to the pressure of water, 463. — Self-acting draining sluice, 464. — Freshwater door, 464.—Spontaneous appearance of white clover within three or four years of the date of the exclusion of salt-water, 464.—Remarkable fertility of Sunk island, 464.—Patrington channel, 465.—Probable future reclamation of land from Sunk island to the Spurn, 465.

"On reclaiming land from seas and estuaries." By J. H. Muller (of the Hague), xxi. 466.—Considerations as to the expediency of reclaiming land in any particular district, 466.—Sea-bank should be constructed at right angles to the current and the full force

RECLAIMING LAND.

of the sea, 467.—Large areas of enclosure preferred, 467.—Embankments on salt marsh of clay, on samphire ground slake or mud, and on hard sea-sand, 468.—Banks on samphire ground and mud most difficult to construct, 468. — No necessity for cradge banks to diminish scour from the exit of tidal water from the enclosure, 468. — Banks on a lower level than that of the half-tide mark unadvisable, 469.—Cross-section of the bank, 469.—Force of violently agitated sea-water, 470.—Materials employed for the defence of slopes in Holland, 470.—A cess or bench recommended, 471.—Wood or fascine-work protection, 471.—Four different sections of banks proposed to be constructed at various levels, 472.—Flatter slopes recommended with stone defences, 473. — Relative advantages of stone and wooden slopes, 473.—Detailed account of the construction and sinking of cradles for closing reclamation banks which cross creeks, 474.

Discussion.—Bidder, G. P., 483.—Brunlees, J., 481.—Forchammer, Professor, 483.—Gibbs, J., 479.—Giles, A., 481. —Hawkshaw, J., 478, 491.—Hemans, G. W., 482.—Muller, J. H., 488.—Oldham, J., 488.—Paton, J., 487.—Vignoles, C. B., 478.

" On the closing of reclamation banks." By J. M. Heppel, xxiii. 168.—Various opinions as to the extent to which the difficulty of closing the banks would be influenced by the area to be reclaimed, 168.—Site of operations proposed on the Essex coast, 168.—Closing places should be constructed of solid materials to resist scour, 168.—General effect of the size of the openings on the relative level of the water inside and outside at different heights of the tide, 169. — Difficulty of expressing the various conditions of flowing water by convenient formulæ, 169. — Table showing the areas of the several interior water surfaces at various

REDMAN.

heights of the tide, 170.—Explanation of method of calculating the discharge through the opening, 170. — Table showing influx or efflux discharge in cubic feet per minute, corresponding to any heights H and h, of which H is the greater, for each foot of width of opening, the bottom being supposed to be at low-water level, 171.—Description of curves showing Admiralty form of rise and fall of tide, 172.—Ditto of the 'graphic integration' of the rise and fall of the interior water, 172.—Return of water to the same level after a full period of a tide indicative of the curves having reached a permanent condition, 175.—Indications afforded by the curves when established, openings of 1,000 feet, 800 feet, and 500 feet, 176, 177.—The junction of the banks with the closing places is to be effected by bringing up the banks evenly and simultaneously in horizontal layers, 177.—Consideration of the effect of a space of 1200 feet being left open at different heights, 178.—Final closing of the 800-feet opening should be done at a single tide, 178. — General result of the inquiry, 178.—Approximate rule for the aggregate width of the final closing places, 179.—Variation in the level of the interior water diminishes in proportion with the smallness of the openings, 179.—Method of ascertaining the height of the fixed level, 179.

Discussion. — Bidder, G. P., 182. — Brooks, W. A., 184.—Giles, A., 182.— Hemans, G. W., 180.—Heppel, J. M., 185.—Leslie, J., 184.—Russell, J. S., 184.—Vignoles, C. B., 181, 183.

Vide also LAGOONS AND MARSHES; and RIVER WITHAM.

REDMAN, J. B. [Telford premium, xxiv. 109, 124.]

Breakwaters and sea-walls, xxiv. 179.— Comparative cost of the Marseilles, Portland, Alderney, and Dover breakwaters, 179.—Comparisons of foreign and British works for defending tid- ˙

REDMAN.

slopes, 180.—Instances of the deterioration of concrete river and sea walls, 180.

Canal, Suez, xxvi. 469.—Levels of the Mediterranean and the Red Sea, 469. —Slope of the banks, 470.—Effect of the western pier at Port Saïd in arresting the drift of sand, 470.—Cost of dredging, 470.

Cements. Relative strength of Portland cement and natural stones, xxv. 141.— Employment of Roman cement in tidal works, 142.

Coasts, &c. "The East Coast between the Thames and the Wash estuaries," xxiii. 186. — Remarks, 225. — Recent changes in the Thames estuary, 225. —Upper reaches, 225.—Annual shifting of the 'Beach End' buoy at Harwich, 226.—Registered tonnage of the thirteen ports from Maldon to Boston, 226.—Effect of the groynes at Cromer, 226.—Sea-bed off Cromer and Mundesley, 251.—Impossibility of the shingle of the Chesil Bank and of Landguard Point being ploughed up from the bottom of the sea, 253.—Landslip at the Isle of Sheppey, 255.—Changes on the south side of the estuary of the Thames, 255. —Occurrence of shingle between the Naze and St. Osyth, 255.—Changes in the channels at the mouth of the Thames, 255.—Motion of the beaches on the east coast, 255.—Elongation of Dungeness Point, 256.—'Suffolk Crag' affords a large supply of flints, 256.— Deteriorating action at Harwich, 256. —'Suffolk Crag' supplies the material of the beaches south of Hunstanton, 256.

Docks and warehouses at Marseilles, xxiv. 178.—Commerce of the port of Marseilles, 178.—Cost of the docks and warehouses, 179. — Cost of docks in London, 179.

Docks, graving, xxv. 330.—Metropolitan dry docks, 330. — Trafalgar graving dock, 330. — Early timber docks of London, 331.—Cost of docks per yard cube of capacity, 331.—Decline of the

REDMAN.

shipbuilding trade of the port of London, 332.

Foundations, xxvii. 304.—Weight sustained by the pile foundations of a swingbridge at Kingston-upon-Hull, 304.—Sinking cylinders on the open-well system to ascertain the level of the chalk substratum beneath the Goodwin sands, 305.—Plenum process adopted by French engineers to penetrate a quicksand in the Loire, 305.—Case of a cylinder sunk on the plenum process flooded by the rise of the tide, 305.—Vacuum process, 306.— Sinking cylinders through sand and gravel to the chalk at Milton-on-Thames, xxviii. 355.—Use of the air lock, 356.

Iron and steel. Decay of iron structures exposed to the action of salt or brackish water, xxviii. 230.—Kirkaldy's experiments on the strength of iron and steel, xxx. 269.

Lagoons on the western coast of France below Bordeaux, xxviii. 321.—Ditto on the shores of the Mediterranean, 321. — Ancient lagoons on the east coast of England, 322.

Lighthouses, optical apparatus of, xxvi. 540.—English origin of the use of lenses for lighthouse purposes, xxviii. 35.—Tuskar rock and beacon. xxx. 22. —Construction of stone lighthouses, 22.—Dovetailing the masonry courses, 22.—Saving of life by the establishment of lights, 23.

Ports of Hull. Liverpool, London, and Newcastle, annual tonnage of, xxvi. 435; xxviii. 496.

River Tyne, xxvi. 435.—Influence of Jarrow Slake, 436.—Bar, 437.

Rivers and estuaries. Effect of the operations carried out in Dublin bay, xxvi. 437.—Ditto at the Sulina mouth of the Danube, 437.—Deterioration of the port of Boston from the construction of the Grand sluice, xxviii. 95.— Effect of Denver sluice on the Ouze and on Lynn harbour, 96.—Relative drainage area of the Humber, Severn, and Thames, 493.—Degrada-

REED.

tion of the coast between Flamborough Head and Saint Edmund's point, 493. —Spurn point, 495.—Natural facilities for navigation of the river Humber, 496, 497.—Sand Haile, 497.

REED, E. J. [Election, xxx. 1.]

Ships of war, xxvi. 180.—Monitor system of vessels, 180.—Armour of the 'Bellerophon' and the 'Warrior,' 187.—Armour-plates of the 'Dictator,' 187, 189.—Difficulty of fitting the 'Dictator' with masts, 188.—Capability of the 'Bellerophon' to ram the 'Dictator,' 188.—Depth of armour-plating of the 'Dictator,' 189.—Armour of the 'Hercules' frigate, 190.—Vessels with a low freeboard, 191.—Inexpediency of heavily-armoured vessels carrying masts and sails, 192.—'Hercules' target, 197.

REID, G. L. [Election, xxvii. 443.]

REID, W. [Resignation, xxix. 217.]

REILLY, C. [Election, xxiv. 62 ; Telford medal and premium, xxv. 164, 180.]

Bridges, iron, xxvii. 84.—Different systems of construction in the iron arches of the Victoria bridges, 85.

——— "Studies of iron girder bridges, recently executed, illustrating some applications of the modern theory of the elastic resistance of materials," xxix. 403.

Bridges, suspension, xxvi. 272.—Forces tending to overturn the piers of suspension bridges, 272.—Economical design for a suspension bridge of several spans adapted to carry a railway load, 274.—'Hanging girders,' 275.—Effects of change of temperature on suspension bridges, 275.—Stiffening suspension railway bridges by means of suspended girders, 275.—Holding down the ends of stiffening girders, 276.—Proper proportion of the pins and eyes connecting the links of the chains of suspension bridges, 277.

Concrete, use of, in a sea-wall at Callao, xxiv. 170.

Girders. "On uniform stress in girderwork, illustrated by reference to two

REILLY.

bridges recently built," xxiv. 391.—Remarks, 426.—Cost of the ironwork of the two bridges, 426.—Trough form of section, 426.—Inequality of the stress in the top boom diminished, towards the centre of the span, by the accumulated effect of flexure, 450.—Whether the unequal stress upon a trough-shaped lower boom, subject only to tension, is similarly diminished, 452.—Quantity of material required to give a certain constant degree of stiffness to a long strut, 453.—Objections to the form of No. 2 truss, 454.—T and trough-shaped sections of boom, 455.—Tests applied to a pair of diagonal trusses for a single-line railway bridge in Italy, 456.—Stress in loaded beams, xxix. 79.—Continuous girders, 83, et seq.

Iron and steel, strength of, xxx. 258.—Stresses to which a piece of elastic metal is liable, 258.—Definitions of the limit of elasticity, 259.—Hodgkinson's experiments on the elongations of a long bar of 'best' wrought-iron, 259. —Morin's experiments on the elongations and permanent sets of a long wire of hardened charcoal iron, 261.—Morin's experiments on annealed iron wire and copper wires, 263.—Limit of elasticity of bar iron, 263.

Materials, strength of, xxix. 27.—Mathematical definitions as adopted by French and by English writers on the subject, 27.—Progress of discovery in the resistance of materials, 77.—Ultimate strength, 78.—Divisions of theoretical mechanics, 80.—Ratio of linear lateral contraction to elongation, 81.—'Theorem of the three moments,' 83. —Resistance of lateral adhesion, 86.—Hypothesis of the theory of the resistance of materials, 87.—Simple extension or compression, 88.—Simple sliding, 89.—Simple flexure, 90.—Simple torsion, 92.—Experimental branch of the science, 93.

Mathematics, study of, in England and in France, xxix. 94.

Railway locomotion, xxvi. 354. —Pressure

REMINGTON.

of the wheels of a locomotive upon the rails on an incline, 354.—Co-efficients of friction of wrought-iron upon wrought-iron increase with the increase of pressure, 355.

REMINGTON, G., Jun. [Admission, xxix. 98.]

RENDEL, A. M. [Election, xxi. 492.]
Cofferdams, exclusion of water from, by puddle, xxiv. 58.
Docks, Great Grimsby, xxiv. 57.—Fill-ing-in of the land on each side of ditto, 58.—Grimsby dock basin, 58.
Docks, graving, xxv. 324.—Pontoon sunk at the London docks, 324.—Dry dock at Leith, 324.
Materials, deterioration of, in tropical climates, xxiv. 22.

RENDEL, G. W. [Election, xxii. 451.]
RENDEL, S. [Election, xxii. 336.]
RENNIE, G. [Memoir, xxviii. 610.]
River Danube, xxi. 297.—Dredging operations at the Sulina mouth, 298.

RENNIE, G. B.
Docks, graving, xxv. 333.—Floating docks at Carthagena and Pola, 333.—Hydraulic lift graving dock, 334.

RENNIE, Sir J. [Past-President, xxi. 172; xxii. 166; xxiii. 150; xxiv. 143; xxv. 202; xxvi. 164; xxvii. 179; xxviii. 215; xxix. 271.]
Breakwaters, use of concrete in the construction of, xxiv. 177.—Harbour works at Algiers, 177.—Comparative cost of breakwaters in tidal and tideless seas, 178.
Bridge, Chey-Air, xxiv. 196.
Coasts, &c. Origin of the great banks of shingle on the southern and eastern coasts of England, xxiii. 231.—In-stances of the consequence of neg-lecting the study of the changes of the coast, and the causes which pro-duced them, in the cases of Rye harbour and Harwich harbour, 232.—Harbour of Lowestoft, 233.
Concrete blocks, xxiv. 178.
Docks at Marseilles, entrance to the, xxiv. 176.
Drainage of land, xxi. 97.—Lowering the water-level in the Fen districts, 97.

RICHARDSON.

—Utilising surplus drainage-water in dry seasons, 98.
Foundations of London Bridge, xxvii.300.
Rivers and estuaries, xxi. 341.—Pre-ponderance of tidal water in a harbour gives it the character of a lagoon, 341.—Improvement of the outlets of rivers on the east coast of England, xxiii. 233.—Fluvial estuary harbours, xxiv. 83.—Best mode of treating ditto, 84.—Reduction of the bar at the mouth of the Tees, 84.—Jetties and guide piers at the entrances of rivers, 85.

Reports, annual, of Council. Vide ANNUAL REPORTS OF COUNCIL.
Resistance of materials. Vide MATERIALS, resistance of.
Resistance to bodies passing through water, on the (Phipps, G. H.), xxiii. 321. Vide also SHIPS AND STEAM-VESSELS.

REYNOLDS, E.
Locomotive engines, disturbing forces of, xxii. 104.—Sinuous motion, 104.—Satisfactory results of balance weights, 105.

REYNOLDS, F. C. [Election, xxv. 203; Memoir, xxx. 475.]
REYNOLDS, R. [Election, xxvii. 443.]
REYNOLDS, T. [Admission, xxvii. 55.]
RHODES, T. [Memoir, xxviii. 615.]
RHODES, W. [Election, xxv. 203.]
RICH, F. H., Colonel, R.E.
Railway stations, xxx. 95.—Strains in the roof of the St. Pancras station of the Midland railway, 95.—Under-pinning the principals of ditto, 95.

RICH, W. E. [Election, xxix. 98.]
Bridges, suspension, xxx. 270.—Failure of links and pins in suspension chains, 270.

RICHARDSON, H. Y. [Election, xxvii. 180.]
RICHARDSON, J. [Election, xxiv. 184.]
RICHARDSON, R.
Bridges, suspension, xxvi. 268.—Testing weight, 268.—Suspension bridges of iron and steel combined, 268.—Angles of the chains with the summits of the piers, 273.

RICHARDSON, T. [Election, xxiii. 442; Memoir, xxx. 476.]

RICHMOND.

RICHMOND, D. [Election, xxvii. 443.]
RICKARD, Major F. J. [Election, xxx. 1.]
RICKETTS, E. B. [Election, xxx. 106.]
RICKMAN, W. C.
Sailing yacht ' America,' xxviii. 364.
RIDINGS, H. S. [Election, xxiv. 511.]
RIDLEY, T. D.
Cements, testing, xxv. 153.
Piles, resisting power of, xxvii. 310.—
M'Alpine's formula, 310.—Superiority
of a heavy hammer with a low fall
over a light ram with a long stroke,
312.
RIDLEY, W. [Election, xxvi. 79 ; Telford
premium, xxvi. 121, 138.]
Viaduct. "The Grand River viaduct,
Mauritius railways," xxv. 237.
RIGBY, W. [Decease, xxiii. 121.]
RIVER DANUBE.
" Description of the Delta of the Danube,
and of the works recently executed at
the Sulina mouth." By C. A. Hartley,
xxi. 277.—Objects of the Commission
appointed in 1856 to carry out works
at the mouths of the Danube, 277.—
Mr. Hartley appointed engineer to
the undertaking, 277.—The Upper
Danube, 278.—Head of the Delta and
relative volumes of water passing by
the Kilia and Toulcha branches, 278.
—Description of the course of the
Kilia, 278.—Ditto of the St. George,
279.—Ditto of the Sulina, 280.—
Description of the Delta proper of the
Danube, 280.—Delta almost sub-
merged in floods, 281.—Volume of
water discharged, 281.—Amount of
silt held in suspension, 281.—Position
and size of the bars across the several
mouths of the river subject to changes,
282.—Level of the water in the Black
Sea solely influenced by the winds,
282.—Sea depths opposite the Delta
decrease to the north, 283.—Kilia
unsuitable for successful treatment,
283.—Merits of the St. George superior to those of the Sulina branch,
283.—Conflicting opinions as to the
best branch to improve permanently,
284.—Sea entry and gates, indepen-
dent of the mouth, proposed for the

RIVER HUMBER.

St. George branch, 284.—Raking the
bar at the Sulina mouth of no avail in
removing the mud, 284.—Resolution
to carry out guiding-piers across the
bar of the Sulina, 285.—Original
design for the permanent works at the
Sulina mouth, 285.—Two piers on
which the expenditure was not to
exceed 80,000l., and capable of lasting
uninjured six or eight years, determined on, 286.—Various plans for
carrying out the work, 286.—Choice
made of a structure of piling and
' pierre perdue,' 287.—System of execution, 287.—Instance of the scouring
action of the sea, 288.—Plans adopted
for remedying the evil, 288.—Length
of time occupied in the constructi.
of the piers, their dimensions and cos .
289.—Comparison of surveys of the
coast-line and depth of water at the
Sulina mouth, in 1829, 1857, and 1862,
290.—Increased depth of water obtained from carrying out the works,
290.—Immense gain to the shipping
interest, 291.—Reflections as to the
profitable expenditure on the works,
291.

Discussion.—Belcher, Admiral Sir E.,
298 —Bidder, G. P., 299.—Brooks,
W. A.. 296.—Giles, A., 297.—Harrison,
T. E., 293.—Hartley, C. A., 293, 300.—
Hawkshaw, J., 307.—Hemans, G. W.,
296.—M'Clean, J. R., 294.—Murray,
J., 294.—Paxton, Sir J., 296.—Rennie,
G., 297.—Sheilds, F. W., 298.—Vig-
noles, C. B., 295.

RIVER HUMBER.
General description and foreshores, xxi.
454.—Tides, xxiv 53.
" On the outfall of the River Humber."
By W. Shelford, xxviii. 472.—Spurn
point, 472.—Drainage area of the
Humber, 472.—Geological structure
of the district, 473.—Marshes and fen
lands draining into the Humber, 473.
—Valley of Ancholme, 473.—The
Great Level, 474.—Sunk Island and
Cherry Cobb sands, 474.—Degrada-
tion of the east coast of Holderness,
474.—Spurn point at the landing of

RIVER HUMBER.

the Danes, 474.—Ravensburg, 475.—
Gradual destruction of ditto by the
sea, 476.—Establishment of lights at
Spurn point by Angell, 476.—Green-
ville Collins' chart of the Humber,
476, 477.—Formation of Sunk Island,
477.—Frismersh, 477.—Clee Ness,
477.—The Old Den, 477.—Mitchell's
chart, 478.—Smeaton's lighthouses,
478.—Hewett's chart, 479.—Breach
in Spurn neck, 479.—Groynes for
strengthening Spurn point, 479.—
Calver's chart, 479.—Tidal flood and
ebb streams in the Humber, 479.—
Movement of Spurn point, 480.—
History of Spurn lights, 480.—Present
condition of Spurn point, 481.—Increase of tidal range in the Humber
in the fourteenth century, 481.—Tidal
range in the Ouze and the Humber at
subsequent dates, 482.—Highest recorded tide, 482.—Effect of Naburn
lock on the tide in the Ouze, 483.—
Explanation of discrepancies in the
charts of Hewett and Calver, 483.—
Increase of tidal capacity of the
Humber below low-water between
1828 and 1852, 484.—Relative value
of tidal and fresh water at the outfall,
484.—Condition of the estuary under
droughts and freshes, 484.—Relation
of the operations of nature and of
engineering works to the facts recorded, 484.—Tendency to encroachment on the tidal area, 485.—Probable
increase in the depth of the estuary,
485.—Changes brought about by the
increased tidal range and scour, 485.
—Ditto by the sea, 486.—Authorities,
487.—Appendix: Copy of tidal observations taken at Grimsby (Royal
dock) in May and June, 1864, 488-
490.—Tidal observations taken at
Spurn lights (Humber side) and Hull
docks, 21st April, 1866, 491-492.
Discussion.—Abernethy, J., 497.—Airy,
G. B., 512.—Bateman, J. F., 498.—
Bartholomew, W. H., 508.—Calver,
Capt. E. K., 499.—Coode, J., 501.—
Harrison, J. T., 506.—Harrison, T.
E, 514.—Murray, J., 504.—Parkes,

RIVER TEES.

W., 509.—Redman, J. B., 493.—
Shelford, W., 493, 515.—Webster, T.,
513.
Vide also DOCKS, Great Grimsby; and
RECLAIMING LAND FROM THE SEA.

RIVER TEES.

" Description of the River Tees, and the
works upon it connected with the
navigation." By J. Taylor, xxiv. 62.
—Physical and geological features of
the district through which the river
flows, 62.—Waterworks above Darlington, 63.—Total course, 63.—Cut made
between Stockton and Portrack, 63,
65.—Increase of trade effected by the
Stockton and Darlington railway, 64.
—Second cut made by the Tees
Navigation company from Blue House
point to near Newport, 64, 65.—
Groynes erected between Stockton
and Cargo Fleet, 64.—Railway suspension bridge carried over the river
above Stockton, 64.—Coal staithes at
Stockton and Middlesbro', 64.—Dock
for the shipment of coal constructed a
little below Middlesbro', 65.—Tonnage
of the port of Middlesbro' affected by
the opening of the West Hartlepool
railway and dock, 65.—Combined
effect of the groynes and artificial
channels on the channel of the river,
65.—Accumulation of mud within the
enclosure of the jetties, and at
Middlesbro', 66.—Bad state of the
river under the operation of the
groynes, 67.—Expenditure of the Tees
Navigation Company, 67.—Advance
of the foreshore to the extremities of
the groynes, and consequent exclusion of tidal water, 67.—Comparison
of the state of the river with what it
was prior to the construction of any
works in the channel, 67.—Reduction
in depth below Middlesbro', 68.—
Estimate of the cost of removing the
shoal in the south channel, 68.—
Works carried out by the Tees Con-
servancy Commissioners, 69.—Construction of piers and groynes of iron
slag, 69.—Depth of water on the
bar, 70.—Importance of obtaining a

RIVER THAMES.

deep-water channel from the sea to Middlesbro', 70.—Appendix, relative to the South Gare breakwater, 71.

Discussion.—Abernethy, J., 77.—Beardmore, N., 35.—Brooks, W. A., 72, 76, 96.—Hawkshaw, J., 100.—Hemans, G. W., 95.—Jackson, R. W., 78.—Johnson, T. M., 98.—Lecky, R. J., 83. —Messent, P. J., 100.—Murray, J., 74, 79.—Parkes, W., 91.—Taylor, J., 101.—Rennie, Sir J., 83.—Russell, J. S., 86, 100 —Williams, E. L., Jun., 77.

RIVER THAMES.

Floods of the Upper Thames, xxi. 84.—Effect of the tide in maintaining the depth of the Lower Thames, 299, 307. Strata of fresh and salt water at Woolwich, 339.

" The perennial and flood waters of the Upper Thames." By the Rev. J. C. Clutterbuck, xxii. 336.—Geological character of the watershed, 336.—The Thames from its source to its junction with the Thames stream, 336.—Flows over a clay bed, while its tributaries flow from oolitic sources in the north, and from chalk hills in the south, 337.—The Swill brook, 337.—The Churn, 337.—The Ray, 338.—The Coln, 338.—The Cole, 338.—The Leach, 338.—The Windrush, 338.—The Evenlode, 338.—The Glyme, 339. —The Cherwell, 339.—The Ray, 339. —The Ock, 339.—The Thames, 340. —Geological condition of the source, 340.—Effect of pumping operations to supply the Thames and Severn Canal shown in the diminution of the water at the source, 341.—Cause of the deviations to which the bed is liable, 341.—Mills on the river and its tributaries, 342.—Deficiency of gaugings of the tributaries, and difficulties that beset the guaging of the main stream, 342.—Result of gaugings of the flow of the Thames at Wolvercot, 343.—Ditto at Wolvercot and Clifden Hampden after heavy rain in January, 1863, 344.—Tabular comparison of floods, 345.—Deplorable state of the navigation between Lechlade and

RIVER TYNE.

Oxford, 345.—Injurious effects of flashes, 346.—Improved state of the river below Oxford, 346.—Geological conditions that account for the large body of flood-water thrown into the Thames, 347.—Principal floods of the Thames, 347.—Detailed account of the floods of March to May, 1862, with statement of the rainfall and the date of maximum flood at various points, 347, et seq.—Action of land drainage on flood-water, 350.—Ditto on perennial waters, 350.—Improvements recently carried out to effect the better drainage of the meadows bordering the river, 351.

Discussion.—Bateman, J. F., 362.—Braithwaite, F., 364.—Clutterbuck, Rev. J. C., 353, 357, 368.—Grantham, R. B., 365.—Gravatt. W., 366.—Hawkshaw, J., 369.—Homersham, S. C., 360.—King, F., 366.—Randall, Aldn., 355.—Taunton, J. H., 357.—Taylor, J., 359.—Towle, J., 354.

Changes resulting from sea-currents at the mouth, xxiii. 231.—Influence of the chalk formation on the floods, xxvii. 229.—Drainage area, xxviii. 493. —Effect of the removal of Old London Bridge, 509.—Vide also COASTS.

RIVER TYNE.

Depth of water on the bar, xxiv. 100.

" Memoir on the River Tyne." By W. A. Brooks, xxvi. 398.—Elevation of watershed, 398.—Fall per mile, 398.—Effect of inefficient drainage in checking the ingress of flood-tide, as demonstrated by tidal observations, 399.—Former depression of the level of highwater at Newcastle, 400.—Progress of the tidal wave, and proper mode of estimating it, 401.—Early charts of the Tyne, 402.—Messrs. Giles' survey for Mr. Rennie in 1813, 402.—Progressive improvement in the state of the navigation between 1813 and 1854, 403.—Groynes executed by Mr. Rennie, 403.—Channels of the Dee and Clyde at first too much contracted by groynes, 403.—Connecting river-walls and dredging

RIVER TYNE.

operations subsequently carried out in the Clyde, 404.—Timber groynes and river-walls executed by Mr. Brooks for deepening the river Tyne from below Newcastle bridge, and their cost, 404.—Improvement of the Hay Hole channel, and execution of the Northumberland dock, 405. — Improvement effected at Bill point, 406. —Admiral Washington's report on ditto, 406.—Quay at Dent's Hole, 407.—Removal of Hebburn shoal, 407.—Conditions under which dredging operations prove permanently useful, 408.—Scouring effect of the current on the bed of the Tyne, 408.— Utility of the drainage of a country in the preservation of harbours, 408. —Depression of the low-water surface produced by the river-works, 409.— The North Pool, 409.—Tynemouth Dock planned, 410.—Reference to unexecuted works, 410.—Investigation into the condition of bar harbours, 410.—Views of Mr. Rennie and Mr. Walker as to the supposed influence of Jarrow Slake in accelerating the current of the flood-tide over the bar of the Tyne, 410.—Extract from Mr. Rennie's report on the Tyne, 411. —Mr. John MacGregor's views relative to the transit of the tidal wave, 411.—Extract from Smeaton's reports in reference to the influence of Jarrow Slake on the transit of the tidal wave, 412.—Probable effects that would follow the inclosure of Jarrow Slake, 412.—River-works executed by Mr. Brooks between Newcastle and Shields, 414.—Ditto in the tidal navigation above Newcastle bridge, 415.—Shields Harbour, 415.—Sea reach and bar, 416.—Tyne piers, 417, et seq.

Discussion.—Abernethy, J., 438.—Bateman, J. F., 424, 425.—Beardmore, N., 432, 434.—Brooks, W. A., 421, 424, 434, 439.—Brunlees, J., 438.—Cubitt, J., 431.—Graham, J., 434.—Gregory, C. H., 423.—Harrison, T. E., 428.— Hemans, G. W., 425.—Lane, C. B., 440.—Longridge, J. A., 429, 431.—

RIVER WITHAM.

Lyster, G. F., 425.—Phipps, G. H., 431.—Redman, J. B., 435.—Stephenson, G. R., 425.—Vignoles, C. B., 423, 424.

Results of works executed, xxviii. 497.

RIVER WITHAM.

" Description of the River Witham and its estuary, and of the various works carried out in connection therewith, for the drainage of the Fens, and the improvement of the navigation." By W. H. Wheeler, xxviii. 59.—Course of the Witham, 60.—Tidal flow, 60. —Drainage area, 60, 69.—Evidences of changes of level of the Fens, 60, et seq. —Embankments constructed by the Romans for keeping out the tidal water, 61, 62.—Importance of ditto in the case of an extraordinarily high tide, 62.—Former condition of the low land, 63.—Extent of the Lincolnshire fens, 63.—Condition of the East Fen and Holland Fen in the reign of Elizabeth, 63.—Drainage and enclosure of Holland Fen, 64.—Drainage of the districts between Holland Fen and the Witham, 65.—Deterioration of the navigation of the Witham and subsequent works for its improvement, 65. — Drainage and navigation interests hostile to each other, 66.— Drainage and enclosure of the East, West, and Wildmore Fens, 67.— Sinking of the land caused by the cultivation of the soil, 68.—Present condition of Boston haven, 69.— Causes of the silting-up of the estuary, 70, et seq.—Present state of the Wash, 74.—Works proposed and carried out for the improvement of the estuary, 75.—Plans recommended by Kindersley, Huddart, Rennie, and Hawkshaw, 76.—Reclamations effected by Sir John Rennie, 77.—The Lincolnshire Estuary Company, 77.— Method of guiding the rivers in the Fens by training-walls of faggots, clay, and chalk, 78, 79.—General results of the enclosure of the Fens, 79, 80.

Discussion. — Abernethy, J., 101.—

RIVERS.

Brereton, R. P., 82.—Brunlees, J., 98.
—Cubitt, J., 82.—Frow, C., 90.—
Giles, A., 82.—Hawkshaw, J., 96.—
Hawksley, T., 83, 99.—Hemans, G.
W., 82.—Johnson, T. M., 101.—Login,
T., 84.—May, R. C., 83.—Murray, J.,
86.—Redman, J. B., 95.—Shelford,
W., 97.—Taylor, J., 94.—Vignoles,
C. B., 81.—Wheeler, W. H., 81, 83,
104.

RIVERS, FRESHWATER FLOODS OF.
" On the relation of the freshwater
floods of rivers to the areas and
physical features of their basins; and
on a method of classifying rivers and
streams, with reference to the magnitude of their floods; proposed as a
means of facilitating the investigation
of the laws of drainage." By Lieut.-
Col. P. P. L. O'Connell, R.E., xxvii.
204.—Water forms its own drainage
vehicle, 204.—First stage of natural
surface drainage, 204.—Dimensions of
the drainage area as affecting the
discharge, 204. — Lakes as flood
moderators, 205, 212.—River-channels
as flood moderators, 205.—Rate of
discharge from a surface receiving
rain varies inversely with its area,
205.—Obstacles to the graphical re-
presentation by a regular curve of the
rate of discharge in floods, 206.—
Method of classifying rivers as flood-
producers, 206.—Ditto as shown in
the case of the river Mississippi and
its tributaries, 206, et seq.—Exceptional floods not regulated by the
ordinary laws of drainage, 207.—
Indian rivers, 208.—Variation of the
annual fall of rain in Hindostan, 208.
—Modulus of rivers as flood-producers
in North America, 209.—Ditto in
Great Britain, 209.—Ditto on the
Continent of Europe, 209.—The Nile,
209.—Causes which affect the modulus
of rivers as flood-producers, 209, et seq.
—Rate of fall of heavy rain, 210.—
Formulæ for computing the discharge
from districts of various sizes in proportion to the rate of rainfall, 210.—
Table of results, 211.—Influence of

the great lakes on the river St.
Lawrence, 211.—Floods of the river
Seine, 212.—Computation of the height
of the greatest probable flood, 212.
—Effect of the chalk districts in
moderating the floods of the Thames,
213.—Floods of the Pennair moderated
by sand-beds, 213.—Moderating influence of the channel on the Mississippi floods, 213.—Flood in the
river Loire relieved by the channel of
the Maine, 214.—Appendix: Table
exhibiting a few of the physical
features of certain rivers, 215.
" Floods in the Nerbudda valley, with
remarks on monsoon floods in India
generally." By A. C. Howden, xxvii.
218.—Scantiness of information re-
garding the periodical monsoon floods,
218.—Limited extent of the district,
218.—Physical features of the Nerbudda valley and river, 219.—Tributaries of the Nerbudda, 219.—Floods
affecting plains, 219.—Average rainfall in the valley, 219.—Railway
embankment intercepts the surface
flow and causes floods, 220.—Floods
inflicted great injury on Indian railways in 1864 and 1866, 220, 221.—
Precautions to be taken in the construction of embankments, 221.—
Bridges in an open plain, 221.—
Floods affecting the rivers, 221.—
Principal rivers crossed by the Great
Indian Peninsula railway, 221.—
River Towah, 222.—Injury to the
Towah viaduct by floods in 1864,
1865, and 1866, 222, et seq.—Alterations in the design of the bridge, 223,
224.—River Gunjai or Moorum, 224.
—Table showing the velocity and
discharge of the Gunjal and Towah
rivers during the floods of 1864 and
1866, 224.—Viaduct over the river
Gunjal, 225.—Effect of the force of
the current of the river at the Mul-
kapoor viaduct, 225.—Wide spans for
the viaducts indispensable, 225.—Necessity of giving the piers great
strength, 225.—Instance of the non-
setting properties of Indian lime, 226.

RIVERS AND ESTUARIES.

—Face of the cutwaters of piers should be tool-dressed, 226.—Precautions to be taken where rubble backing is used in the piers, 226.—Hindrances to engineering operations in India, 226.—Appendix containing extracts from various sources relating to floods and rainfall, 227.

Discussion.—Ansted, Prof. T. D., 230.—Bateman, J. F., 253.—Beardmore, N., 235.—Bidder, G. P., 248.—Brereton, R. P., 241, 242.—Brunton, J., 256.—Clutterbuck, Rev. J. C., 229.—Curtis, J. G. C., 248.—Denison, Sir W., 254.—Fowler, F., 262.—Graham, R. W., 246.—Gregory, C. H., 229.—Hassard, B., 238.—Heppel, J. M., 259.—James, Capt. E. R., 233.—Kennedy, Lieut.-Col. J. P., 257.—Law, H., 257.—Phipps, G. H., 239.—Manning, R., 261.—Parkes, W., 243.—Redman, J. B., 270.—Smith, Col. J. T., 240.—Symons, G. J., 258.—Vaux, A. H., 265.—Vignoles, C. B., 242.—West, A. A., 264.

Vide also DRAINAGE OF LAND; RIVER THAMES; and WATER, FLOW OF.

RIVERS AND ESTUARIES.

Adour, xxi. 303.

Amazon, xxvii. 257.

Barrow estuary, xxi. 28.

Catchment areas of the principal rivers in England, xxii. 365.

Churn, xxii. 359.

Clyde, xxii. 363; xxiv. 77, *et seq.*; xxvi. 433. — Low-water of spring-tides at Glasgow, xxix. 19.

Cork river, xxiv. 83.

Cromarty Frith, xxi. 340.

Danube. *Vide* RIVER DANUBE.

Dee (Aberdeen), xxi. 323, 335, *et seq.*

Dee (Chester), xxiv. 77, *et seq.*

Düna, xxi. 338.

Ganges, xxi. 3; xxiii. 231. *Vide* also Hooghly and Mutla.

Hooghly and Mutla. "The Hooghly and the Mutla." By J. A. Longridge, xxi. 2.—Commercial importance and trade of the port of Calcutta, 3.—Water routes available to Calcutta in the different seasons, 3.—Obstructions from the press of traffic, 4.—Relative cost of the transport of merchandise from various places in the interior, by railway and by water, in 1857, 5.—Depth of water in the rivers derivative from the Ganges, 6.—Changes in the bed of the Damoodah, 7.—Description of the tributaries of the Hooghly, 7.—Report on the state of the Hooghly in 1853, 8.—Changes in the channels leading towards Calcutta, 8.—Effects of the monsoon in modifying the channel of the James-and-Mary reach, 10.—Description of the Hooghly above Fulta point, 11.—Tides of the Hooghly, 12.—Volume of water derived by the Hooghly from the Ganges, 13.—Silt held in suspension, and amount from all sources deposited in the estuary of the Hooghly, 15.—The delta of the Ganges, 16.—The Mutla and its tributaries, 17.—Its tides, 18.—Easy of access, 18.—Superiority of the navigation of the Mutla to the Hooghly, 19.—Instance of detention from shoals in the Hooghly, 20.—Causes of the difference in the conditions of the Hooghly and Mutla, 20.—The James and Mary shoal produced by the Damoodah river, 22.—Improvement of the lower part of the Hooghly hopeless, 23.—Calcutta not likely to be ruined by opening a port at the head of the Mutla, 23.

Discussion.—Ayrton, A. S., 31.—Bidder, G. P., 32.—Borradaile, J., 31.—Brooks, W. A., 30.—Giles, A., 29.—Hawkshaw, J., 29.—Henderson, A., 25.—Lloyd, J. H., 31.—Longridge, J. A., 25.—M'Clean, J. R., 28.—Murray, J., 26.— Sale, Col. T. H., 25.—Ward, Lieut. C. V., 30.

Humber. *Vide* RIVER HUMBER.

India. Character of rivers crossed by the Madras railway, xxiv. 190.—Depth of sand-beds in some of the rivers in Madras, 194.

Irrawadi, xxviii. 84.

Liffey and Dublin Bay, xxi. 295; xxvi. 424, 437, 440.

ROACH.

Medlock at Manchester, xxii. 362.

Mersey, xxi. 342; xxvi. 425, 434, 440; xxviii. 499, 505, 514.—Tables of the results of soundings between Liverpool and Birkenhead, in 1822 and 1827, 535.—Silt, xxix. 19. *Vide* also LOW-WATER BASIN AT BIRKENHEAD.

Nene, xxviii. 91, 93, 514.

Ouze, xxviii. 83, 93, 95, 514.

Pentland Frith, xxi. 341.

Punjab rivers, xxvii. 263.

Rhone, xxviii. 288, *et seq. Vide* also LAGOONS AND MARSHES.

Severn, xxviii. 493.

Shannon, xxi. 99; xxvii. 253.

Sittang, xxviii. 84.

Spey, xxv. 229.

Tay, xxi. 341.

Tees. *Vide* RIVER TEES.

Thames. *Vide* RIVER THAMES.

Tyne. *Vide* RIVER TYNE.

Weaver, xxvi. 23.

Welland, xxviii. 76. *Vide* also RIVER WITHAM.

Witham. *Vide* RIVER WITHAM.

Vide also COASTS; LAGOONS AND MARSHES; and RIVERS, FRESHWATER FLOODS OF.

ROACH, W. I. [Election, xxix. 98.]

ROBERTS, A. [Election, xxviii. 59.]

ROBERTS, G. H. [Admission, xxvii. 180; Miller prize, xxix. 213.]

ROBERTS, L. R. [Election, xxii. 241.]

ROBERTS, Richard. [Memoir, xxiv. 536.]

Ships of war, armour-plating, xxi. 194.—Framework of iron vessels, 194.

ROBERTS, Robert. [Election, xxviii. 59.]

ROBERTS, T. D. [Election, xxvii. 55.]

ROBERTS, W. [Election, xxx. 215.]

ROBERTSON, A. J.

Ships and steam-vessels, xxii. 600.—Resistance per square foot of midship section of the 'Connaught' steam-vessel, 600.

ROBERTSON, E. L. [Admission, xxvii. 180.]

ROBERTSON, R., Captain, R.N. [Election, xxvi. 242.]

ROBERTSON, R. A. [Election, xxviii. 325.]

ROBINS, C. [Election, xxvi. 242.]

ROBINSON, A. [Resignation, xxviii. 167.]

ROBINSON, C. E. [Admission, xxvii. 218.]

ROBINSON, F. W. [Election, xxvii. 443.]

ROCHUSSEN.

ROBINSON, H. [Election, xxiii. 257.]

ROBINSON, John. [Election, xxv. 352.]

Injector, Giffard's, xxiv. 218, 225, 250.—Application of, on the London and North Western railway, 218.

ROBINSON, Joseph. [Election, xxv. 262.]

ROBSON, A. [Election, xxiv. 358.]

ROBSON, N. [Memoir, xxx. 456.]

ROBSON, O. C. [Admission, xxviii. 216.]

ROCHUSSEN, T. A. [Election, xxiv. 184; Telford premium, xxvi. 121, 138.]

Lighthouses, xxviii. 45.—Steel sashes for lighthouse lanterns, 45.—Dispersion of light from lighthouses, 45.

Permanent way, xxv. 396.—Life of iron and of compound steel rails at the Hamm station of the Cologne-Minden railway, 396.—Conversion of old Bessemer rails into telegraph wire, 397.—Steel and iron welded rails manufactured at Hörde, in Prussia, xxvii. 385.—Cause of fracture of American rails, 386.

Railway rolling stock. "On the maintenance of the rolling stock on the Cologne-Minden and other Prussian railways," xxv. 430.—Remarks, 447.—Break-power on the Prussian railways, 447.—Iron permanent way on ditto, 447.—Tables of statistics relating to the rolling stock on ditto, 447.—Grinding the tires of wheels, 449.—Defects of American cast-iron wheels, 457.—Wrought-iron disc and spoke wheels, 457.—Iron axle-bars with steel heads made at Hörde, xxvii. 386.

Ships of war, xxvi. 200.—Monitors used as floating gun-carriages, 200.—Want of buoyancy in monitors, 200.—Special uses of ditto, 201.

Steam navigation, xxix. 182.—Economy of steam navigation dependent on the relation between the engine, ship, and freight, 183.—Navigation of the Indian seas, 185.—Means of cleansing the skin of iron steamships from marine growths by hot water from the boilers, 184.—Vessels successful in trade, 184.—Substitutes for coal for raising steam-power, 185.

Steel, Bessemer cast, xxv. 397.

RODWELL.

RODWELL, J. K. [Admission, xxvii. 54.]

ROGET, Dr. P. M. [Memoir, xxx. 419.]

ROLFE, C. [Election, xxiv. 458.]

Rolling stock. *Vide* RAILWAY ROLLING STOCK.

RONEY, Sir C. P. [Resignation, xxi. 148.]
Railway communication, xxiv. 388.— Desirability of a uniform gauge on railways in each country, 388.—Trade between Great Britain and the East, xxvi. 331.—Effect the passage of the Alps by a railway would have on ditto, 332.— Table of Alpine roadway passes, 333.

Roofs. *Vide* RAILWAY STATIONS.

——, American timber, xxii. 317.

ROOKE, C. S. [Election, xiii. 375.]

ROSE, H. [Election, xxiv. 184.]

ROSE, R. B. [Admission, xxvii. 54.]

ROSSE, Earl of. [Memoir, xxvii. 584.]

Rotary Fans. *Vide* FANS.

ROTHEROE, J. [Election, xxx. 323.]

ROTTON, H. B. [Election, xxvi. 398.]

ROUSE, H. J.
Telegraphic communication between England and India, xxv. 42.

ROWLAND, O.
Telegraph cables, xxv. 56.—Commercial prospects of submarine telegraphs, 56. —Insulating properties of gutta-percha, 57.

RUMBALL, A. [Election, xxii. 451.]

RUNDLE, C. S. [Election, xxv. 65.]

RUSHTON, J. R. [Election, xxvi. 79.]

RUSSELL, J. Scott. [Member of Council, xxi. 133 ; Vice-President, xxii. 112 ; xxiii. 112 ; xxiv. 106 ; xxv. 161 ; xxvi. 119.]
Blasting rock, advantages of gun-cotton for, xxiii. 318.
Bridge, Charing Cross, xxii. 530.— Strains on the top and bottom members of the main girders, 534.
Cements, xxv. 129.—Use of Portland cement in the insides of ships to preserve the iron from corrosion, 129, 130. —Quality of sand used with cement for making concrete, 134.
Coasts, &c., xxiii. 236.—Origin of the stones of the Chesil Bank, 236.—Motive power of a wave, 237.—Dungeness beach, 237.—Influence of the pre-

RUSSELL.

valent sea in the formation of beaches, 237.
Dock-gates of the Grimsby docks, xxiv. 59.
Docks, graving, xxv. 311.—Comparative merits of stone and floating docks, 311. —Ditto of the hydraulic lift and ordinary graving docks, 345.—Patent slip for lifting vessels, 345.—Circumstances under which the ordinary floating dock is superior to the hydraulic lift graving dock, 346.
Engineering, German, xxii. 35.—Readiness of German engineers in adopting improvements, 35.—Value of recording mistakes, xxiv. 86.—Usefulness of general principles, 90.
Girders, advantages of continuous, xxii. 531.
Injector, Giffard's, xxiv. 247.
Locomotive engines, disturbing forces of, xxii. 92.
Railway curves, xxiii. 432.— Reversed curves, 432.—Propriety of taking the extreme speed for the measure of the cant of the outer rail, 432.
Railways, German, xxii. 36.— Earthworks, permanent way, and rolling stock, 36.—Want of accommodation, great cost and slow speed of travelling, 36.
Reclaiming land from the sea, xxiii. 184. —Process of tentatively ascertaining the laws which regulate the rise and fall of water within the area of reclamation embankments, 184.— Closing reclamation banks, 184.
Rivers and estuaries, xxiv. 86.—Treatment of the river Clyde, 86, 89.— Ditto of the river Dee, 86.—Danger of interfering with the natural course of a river, 87.—Injury resulting to the river Dee from straightening its channel, 88.—Parallel groynes, 90.— Superficial area for receiving tidal waters for purposes of scour, 90 —Superiority of straight courses, 100.
Ships and steam-vessels, xxii. 596.—Performance of the vessels on the postal service between Holyhead and Kings-

RUSSELL.

town, 596.—Displacement of ditto, 596.—Skin resistance, 601.—Condition of the ribbon of water surrounding a vessel when moving fast, 602.—H.P. per foot of midship section of a vessel for the purposes of comparison, 602.— Value of 'graphic integration,' in calculating the qualities of ships, xxiii. 184.—Character of the majority of experiments made upon the resistance of water to bodies passing through it, 345.—Amount of resistance of any body dragged through water at any speed, 345.—Difference of head resistance depends upon the density of the water, 345.—Theory of the resistance of inclined planes, 345.—General disagreement of ditto with the results of experiments, 346.—Summary of experiments on angular wedge-bows by the Academy of Sciences, 346.— Amount of resistance of square-ended vessels, 346.—Diminution of resistance due to sharp inclinations of bow, 346.—' Angle of escape,' 347.—Resistance of the screw-propeller, 347.— Power of the rudder in turning a vessel, 347.—Advantages of wave-lines, 347.—Measure of value of the hollow bow or approximate wave-line entrance in diminished head resistance, 348.—Minus resistance at the stern of a vessel, 348. — Frictional surface resistance, 348. — Value of shape in diminishing resistance, 349. —Use of Portland cement in the insides of ships to preserve the iron from corrosion, xxv. 129, 130.

RYDON.

Ships of war, xxi. 195.—Construction of iron vessels, 195.—Serviceable thickness for armour-plates, 196.—Whether speed should be ` sacrificed to entire protection in iron ships of war, 197.— Requisite conditions for ironclad vessels, xxvi. 181.—Monitors, 181.— Seagoing qualities of ditto, 182.— Relative merits of the monitor form of turret and that of Captain Coles, 183. — Combination of the turret system of vessel with the broadside system, 185.

Surveying and levelling, xxi. 43. — Measuring distances by the telescope, 43.—Determining the speed of vessels, 43.—Surveying a large lake, 44.— Personal equation, 46.

Timber. Difference between endogenous and exogenous trees, xxii. 62.

Viaducts. Spread of the buttresses in the bridge aqueduct of Roquefavour and the Hownes Gill viaduct, xxii. 56.

RYAN, J. [Election, xxv. 65.]

RYDE, E.

Railways. Charing Cross railway, xxvii. 438.—Comparative advantage and cost of underground and overground railways in London, 438.

RYDER, Admiral A. P.

Lighthouses, xxvi. 533. — Mismanagement of the revolving dioptric light at Bermuda, 533.—Ditto of a catoptric light at Halifax, 534.—Advisability of the periodical visitation of the Colonial lighthouses, 535.

RYDON, H. J. [Election, xxvii. 553.]

S.

SABINE.

SABINE, R. [Election, xxvii. 320.]

SACRÉ, A. L. [Election, xxviii. 232.]

SACRÉ, C. [Election, xxvi. 165.]

SACRÉ, E. A. [Election, xxviii. 59.]

SADASEWJEE, J. [Election, xxvii. 180.]

SAÏD-BEY, Colonel. [Election, xxiv. 144.]

SALE, T. H., Colonel, B.E.

Ports of Calcutta and of the Mutla, xxi. 25.

Timber. Durability of Indian woods, xxii. 259.—Preservation of timber in tropical climates, xxiv. 25.—Teak and Saul woods, 25.

SALKELD, J. [Resignation, xxiv. 117.]

SALOMONS, D. [Election, xxi. 257.]

Saltash bridge, description of the centre pier of the, on the Cornwall railway, and of the means employed for its construction (Brereton, R. P.), xxi. 268. *Vide* also BRIDGES.

SAMSON, H. J. [Admission, xxviii. 2.]

SAMUDA, J. D'A. [Election, xxi. 492; Watt medal, xxii. 120, 130.]

Ships and steam-vessels. Trial-trip of the steamship 'Leinster,' xxii. 596.—Use of steam for ocean navigation, xxix. 161.—Improved results obtained from steam-vessels, 162.—Dimensions of vessels suitable for the Australian trade, 162.—Government subsidies for ditto, 163.

Ships of war. "On the form and materials for iron-plated ships, and the points requiring attention in their construction," xxi. 187.—Remarks, 194.—Insertion of canvas and india-rubber between the armour and skin of mail-clad vessels, xxi. 194.—Armour-plated vessels entirely constructed of iron, 199.—Speed and invulnerability essential conditions for a good war-vessel, 249.—Advantages of readily replacing injured armour-plates, 249.—Armour-plates entering into the composition and structure of

SANDBERG.

vessels, 250.—Defects of wood backing, 250.—Superiority in resisting shot of a single thickness of iron-plate, 251.—Fastenings of armour-plates, 251.—Possibility of constructing a completely ironclad vessel, of smaller dimensions than the 'Warrior,' yet of equal speed, 252.—Experiments on the passage of projectiles through a series of plates placed at given distances apart, 252.—Expediency of plating with iron the wooden ships of the Navy, 253.—Superiority of turret to porthole ships, xxvi. 193.—Vessels of war constructed of steel, 193.—Armour of monitors, 194.—Penetrating powers of guns, 194.—Solid armour compared with laminated armour-plates, 195.—Penetration of armour by solid shot and shell, 195.—Proportions of an armour-plated vessel, 196.—Disadvantages of a form of bow suitable for ramming purposes, 196.

SAMUEL, L. W. [Resignation, xxix. 217.]

SAMUELSON, A. [Election, xxi. 345.]

SAMUELSON, B. [Election, xxviii. 517.]

SMAUELSON, M. [Election, xxii. 65.]

SANDBERG, C. P. [Election, xxvi. 79; Telford medal and premium, xxviii. 161, 178.]

Iron and steel. Testing the toughness of steel, xxvii. 340.—Steel less subject to the influence of cold than iron, 406.

Permanent way. "The manufacture and wear of rails," xxvii. 320.—Remarks, 340.—Steel rails, 340.—Comparative wear of steel and iron rails on the London and North Western railway, 340.—Steel-headed rails, 404.—Life of steel rails, 405.—Supply of pig-iron for Bessemer rails, 406.—Tests of iron rails in Sweden and Russia, 406.—Fracture of steel rails through an excess of silicon, 407.

SARGEAUNT.

—Effect of the reduction of the price of iron and steel rails, 408.

SARGEAUNT, R. A., Lieutenant, R.E. [Election, xxviii. 439.]

SARTORIUS, Admiral Sir G.

Ships of war. Transition state of the navies of the world, xxi. 202.—Unwieldiness of the 'Warrior,' 203.—Defective armament of ditto, 204.—Vessels acting in the capacity of rams, 205.

SAUNDERS, A. [Election, xxiii. 442.]

SAUNDERS, Captain R.

Steam navigation, xxix. 177.—Navigation of the Red, Arabian, and China seas, 177.

SAVIN, T. [Election, xxiv. 257.]

Railways, gauge of, xxiv. 377.—Festiniog railway, 377.—Narrow-gauge lines in Wales, 377.

SCAMP, W.

Docks, graving, xxv. 334.—Hydraulic lift graving dock, 334.—Adoption of shoring-altars to ditto, 334, et seq.—Docking-duties in times of war, 335.—Docking 'hogged' vessels, 337.

SCANLAN, W. R. [Election, xxix. 98.]

Schleswig and Holstein, on the sea-dykes of, and on reclaiming land from the sea (Paton, J.), xxi. 426. Vide also RECLAIMING LAND FROM THE SEA.

SCHMIDT, B. [Election, xxv. 65.]

SCHNEIDER, H. [Election, xxv. 203.]

SCHNEIDER, H. W. [Election, xxiii. 320.]

Permanent way, xxv. 418.—Commercial value of steel rails compared with iron rails, 418.—Re-manufacture of steel rails, 420.—Compound iron and steel rails, 425.

Steel, cost of manufacture of, xxv. 421.—Experiments on the strength of, 422, et seq.—Welding Bessemer steel, 426.

SCOTT, A. [Election, xxv. 65.]

Railway telegraphs, xxii. 211.—'Block' system of train-signalling not universally suitable for working the traffic, 211.—Application of electric telegraph to railway purposes, 212.

SCOTT, C. W. [Memoir, xxiii. 512.]

SCOTT, D. J. [Election, xxiv. 358.]

SCOTT, E. B. [Election, xxviii. 325.]

SEWELL.

SCOTT, J. [Resignation, xxi. 148.]

SCOTT, M.

Canals, steam-power on, xxvi. 28.—Resistance to the passage of vessels dependent on the size of the channels, 28.

Rainfall in the Woodburn district, xxv. 477.

SCOTT, P. [Election, xxx. 215.]

SCOTT, R. A. E., Captain, R.N.

Ships of war, xxvi. 208.—Monitors at the siege of Charleston and at Mobile bay, 208.—Battle of Lissa, 208.—Rapidity of fire of monitors, turret vessels, and broadside ships, 209.—Liability of single-turret vessels to be shrouded in powder-smoke, 209.—Admiral Elliot's model war-vessel, 209.—'Monitor' turret system of working guns, 210.—Traversing guns, 210.—Gunnery practice, 210.—Mr. Reed's model war-vessel, 211.

SEACOME, T. H. [Election, xxv. 352.]

Sea Dykes. Vide RECLAIMING LAND FROM THE SEA.

SEARLE, J. C. [Admission, xxix. 98.]

SELBY, F. [Resignation, xxviii. 167.]

SELWYN, J. H., Captain, R.N.

Copper, duration of, under water, xxi. 534.

Ships of war, xxvi. 184.—Turret and broadside systems, 184.—Difference between ordinary vessels and monitors in a rough sea, 184.

Steam navigation, xxix. 194.—Economical production of steam, 194.—Rigging of steam-vessels, 196.

Telegraph cables, xxi. 534.—Duration of copper under water, 535.—Stowing and paying-out cables, 535.—Curve where there is any slack, xxv. 58.—Mechanical forces to which shallow-water cables are subject, 59.—Dangers of the proposed telegraphic route between Singapore and Australia, 59.—Laying deep-sea cables, 59.—Spiral wires outside deep-sea cables, 59.—Raising cables, 60.—Compound of indiarubber and paraffin as an insulating material, 60.

SEWELL, P. E. [Election, xxiii. 257.]

SEWERAGE.

Sewerage and drainage works of Newport, Monmouthshire, description of the (Williams, A.), xxii. 273. *Vide* also DRAINAGE OF TOWNS.

Sextant, for measuring large angles (Webb, F. C.), xxi. 540.

SHARLAND, R. [Admission, xxviii. 216.]

SHARP, J. F. [Election, xxi. 257.]

SHARPE, R. [Decease, xxviii. 168.]

SHAW, D. S. [Admission, xxvii. 180.]

SHAW, H.
Railway break block, xxi. 408.

SHAW, J. [Election, xxvii. 320.]
Permanent way. Specifications and tenders for rails, xxvii. 354.—Bessemer steel rails, 355.

SHEILDS, F. W. [Auditor, xxiv. 106; xxv. 160.]
Bridges, suspension, xxvi. 282.
Bridges and viaducts, xxii. 54.—Superior advantages of iron structures for large bridges, 54, *et seq.* — Framing of American timber bridges, 323. — Relative cost of timber and wrought-iron bridges, 323. — Charing Cross bridge, 532.—Weight that can be put on London clay, 533.—Object of bracing girder-bridges, 572.—Suspension cross-girders, xxiv. 33.—Construction of iron girder-bridges, 433.—Bow and string bridges, xxvi. 284. — Superstructure of the Victoria bridges, Pimlico, xxvii. 97.—Strains of ditto, 98.
Cements and concrete, xxii. 443.—Superiority of Portland to Roman cement, 443.
Docks, graving, xxv. 338.—Flexibility or rigidity of floating docks, 338.—Raising vessels by pontoons, 339.—Commercial returns of the Thames Graving Dock Company, 340.
Foundations. Weight that can be put on London clay, xxii. 533.
Girders, lattice, xxii. 41.—Strains on girders, xxiv. 433.
Ironwork in hot and moist climates, xxii. 415.
Materials, decay of, xxii. 414. — Expediency of sending out English materials to Brazil, 414.—Ravages of white ants, 415; xxiv. 32.—Timber

SHERVINTON.

seasoned in Bahia by burying it in sea-sand, 32.—'Iron-bark' wood of Australia, 33.—Effect of coal-tar in destroying white ants, 33. — Expediency of using wrought-iron sleepers in tropical climates, 33.

Railways in Prussia, xxii. 40.—Cost of light railways in comparison with those ordinarily in use, xxvi. 70.—Advantages of light railways in Australia, as compared with England, 71.

River Danube, xxi. 298.—Sulina branch, 298.—St. George branch, 298.

Ships of war, xxi. 206.—Construction of iron-plated ships, 206.

Timber, Australian, xxii. 258.

Tunnel, Mont Cenis, xxiii. 300.—Superiority of Mr. Bartlett's to M. Sommeiller's perforator, 301.

SHELBURNE, Earl of.
Railway accidents, xxi. 412.
Railway legislation, xxi. 412.—Evils of parliamentary contests, 412.

SHELFORD, W. [Election, xxv. 429; Telford medal and premium, xxix. 211.]
River Humber. "On the outfall of the River Humber," xxviii. 472.—Remarks, 493.—Hydraulic mean depth between Hull and Spurn point in 1828 and 1852, 493.—North channel, 515.—Exclusion of tidal water, 515.—Construction of groynes north of Spurn point, as a protection to the coast, 515.—Spurn point, 515.—Range of tide in the Humber, 515. — Beneficial and prejudicial actions affecting the outfall, 516.—Erosion of the Lincolnshire shore by the flood-tide, 516.
Rivers and estuaries. Effect of the Grand sluice on the river Witham, xxviii. 97.—Ditto of a sluice in the river Nene, above Wisbeach, 97.—Value of fresh water in keeping tidal rivers clear from the deposit of silt, 98.

SHEPHERD, C. E., Lieutenant, B.S.C. [Election, xxx. 323.]

SHERIFFS, J. [Memoir, xxiv. 543.]

SHERRIFF, A. C. [Election, xxvi. 242.]

SHERVINTON, T. R. [Election, xxvi. 398.]

SHERWOOD.

SHERWOOD, A. [Election, xxvii. 55.]

SHIELD, H. [Election, xxv. 203.]

Water supply, xxvii. 27.—Filtration of Thames water through sand and vegetable charcoal, 27, et seq.—Action of sand in purifying water, 31.—Magnetic carbide system of filtration, 31. —Purity of the water supplied by the London water companies, 31.

SHIELD, W. [Admission, xxvii. 54.]

SHIPS AND STEAM-VESSELS.

Improvements in, xxi. 175.—Application of the screw-propeller to steamships, 175.—Fouling of the bottoms of ditto, 254.—Strains to which iron vessels are subjected, 255.

"On the resistance to bodies passing through water." By G. H. Phipps, xxiii. 321.—Subject not confined to surface resistance only, 321.—Definition of the terms 'inertial resistance' and 'frictional resistance,' 321. —Experiment and theory differ widely on the subject, especially upon frictional resistance, 321.—Theory of inertial resistance, 321.—Resistance against the force of a column of water directed against a plane surface at rest dissimilar to the force against a plane moving in the water, 322.— Experiments of Dubuat and Beaufoy, 322, et seq.—Positive resistance, 322. —Minus resistance, 323.—Ditto less easily determined than positive resistance, 323.—Reason of the advantage of lengthening some ships, 323.— Beaufoy's experiments, 323.—Saving of power by increasing the length amidships, 324.—Illustration of ditto, 324.—Case of ship 'Candia,' 324.— Differs from experiments by Dubuat, 325.—Expression of the minus resistance, 325.—Ditto of the total resistance, 325.—Ditto of the positive resistance of an inclined plane in the direction of motion, 325.—Ditto of the minus resistance, 326.—Reason of positive resistance being denominated 'theoretical resistance,' 326.— Probable reason of the large positive resistance shown in Beaufoy's ex-

SHIPS AND STEAM-VESSELS.

periments, 326. — The ordinary screw-propeller, 326.— Proper proportion for the blades of ditto, 327.— Ricochet of a cannon-ball, 327.— Additional head resistance, 327.— Calculation of resistance of curved surfaces, 327.—Frictional resistance, 327.—No experiments since those of Beaufoy, 328.—Distinction between the friction of solids and fluids, 328. —Beaufoy's experiments, 328.— Influence of roughness in increasing friction, 328.—Ditto as shown in the diminished speed of the Holyhead and Kingstown steam-packets, 328.—Approximation to the frictional resistance of the surfaces of steam-vessels, 329. —Ditto of the steamship 'Leinster,' 329.—The steamship 'Leinster,' 330. —Roughness of pipes hitherto not considered as affecting the question of the friction of water passing through them, 330.—M. Henry Darcy's experiments, 330.—Cause for the excess of friction in pipes and watercourses over that on exterior surfaces, 331.— Consideration of the effect of the friction of the surface of a ship passing through a mass of water at rest, and the converse, 331.—Resistance to an iron ship moving at a speed of 30 feet per second, as applied to the steamship 'Leinster,' 332.—Determination of the power to propel a vessel at any required speed, 333. — Influence of form in reducing the resistance of vessels, 334.—Instances of the advantage derived from changes in a vessel's form, 334. — Appendix: description of the figures, 337.—Data upon which the calculation of the resistance of the Royal West India mail steamship 'Atrato,' on her trial-trip, was based, 338.—Experiment on the resistance to motion, due to the form of floating bodies, 339.

Discussion.— Armstrong, R., 342.— Atherton, C., 350.—Bidder, G. P., 358.—Bramwell, F. J., 364.—Cowper, E. A., 361.—Ditchburn, T., 359.— Gravatt, W., 363.—Hawksley, T., 353.

SHIPS OF WAR.

—Heppel, J. M., 341.—Phipps, G. H., 340, 369.—Rankine, Prof. W. J. M., 368.—Rickman, W. C., 364.—Russell, J. S., 344.

'Connector' steam-vessel, xxvi. 40.— Decay of iron plates in steam-vessels, xxvii. 575. *Vide* also LONDON AND DUBLIN COMMUNICATION; SHIPS OF WAR; and STEAM NAVIGATION.

SHIPS OF WAR.

Displacement, indicated horse-power, and speed of H.M.S. 'Warrior' and H.M.S. 'Howe,' xxi. 175.—Best mode of constructing iron ships of war, 176. Iron-plated ships, 180.

"On the forms and materials for iron-plated ships, and the points requiring attention in their construction." By J. D'A. Samuda, xxi. 187.—Indispensable conditions for the construction of iron-plated ships, 187.—Defects in the 'Warrior,' 'Defence,' and 'Valiant' class of vessels, 187.—The 'Warrior' constructed expensively and in a complicated manner, 188.—Armour hung on midship portion only, 188.—How the armour may be made to enter into the construction of the ship, 189. —Dimensions of armour-plates proposed, 190.—Best dimensions for vessel, 191.—Advantages of the proposed armour-skin vessels over the Admiralty model, 191.—Vessels for coast defences described, 192.—The Admiralty should avail themselves of the engineering skill of the country for the construction of vessels, 192.— The subject of the construction of mail-clad vessels should be freely discussed, 193.

Discussion.—Belcher, Admiral Sir E., 214.—Bidder, G. P., 245.—Brereton, R. P., 209.—Brooks, W. A., 232.— Brunlees, J., 240.—Clarke, G., 243.— Cowper, E. A., 207.—Ditchburn, T., 194.—Fairbairn, W., 223.—Fitzroy, Admiral R., 219.—Gibbs, J., 210.— Grantham, J., 198.—Halstead, Capt. E. P., 232.—Hawkshaw, J., 253.— Hay, Sir J. D., 212, 223.—Hemans, G. W., 240.—Phipps, G. H., 200.

SHIPS OF WAR.

—Pim, Captain B. C. T., 225.— Pole, W., 241.—Roberts, R., 194.— Russell, J. S., 195.—Samuda, J. D'A., 194, 199, 249. — Sartorius, Admiral Sir G., 202.—Sheilds, F. W., 206.— Thornton, P., 227.—Turner, G., 201.

"Ships of war." By J. Bourne, xxvi. 166.— The 'Warrior' and 'Bellerophon' types of ships of war, 166.— Their vulnerability, 166.—The 'Monitor' system of Ericsson, 167.—Ordinary ironclad ships and monitors contrasted, 167.— Kalamazoo class of monitors, 167.—Note as to heavy ordnance, 168.—Armament of broadside and of monitor vessels, 169.— Points of difference between Captain Coles' turret vessels and monitors, 171.—Details of the American war steamer 'Dictator,' 172.—Superiority of the 'Dictator' to the English ironclad 'Bellerophon,' 174.—Description of the 'revolving compressor' for expediting the firing of guns, 176.— Seaworthiness of monitors, 177.— Report by Commodore Rodgers on the performance of the 'Weehawken' in a gale, 177.—Causes of the loss of the 'Weehawken' and 'Monitor,' 178.— Comparative healthiness of the crews of monitors, 179.

Discussion.— Barnaby, N., 185.— Belcher, Admiral Sir E., 222.—Bramwell, F. J., 197.—Bourne, J., 180, 189, 228.—Colburn, Z., 201.—Cowper, E. A., 227.—Elliot, Admiral G., 201.— Gregory, C. H., 241.— Hamilton, Capt. J. R., 211.—Hemans, G. W., 226.—Henwood, C. F., 185.—Heppel, J. M., 226.—Longridge, J. A., 198.— Macintosh, J., 224.—Mallet, R., 199. —Reed, E. J., 180, 187, 189, 197.— Rochussen, T. A., 200.—Russell, J. S., 180.—Samuda, J. D'A., 192.—Scott, Capt. R. A. E., 208.—Selwyn, Capt. J. H., 184.—Symonds, Capt. T. E., 219.—Unwin, W. C., 218.—Vignoles, C. B., 201.

Improvements in the means of attack and defence consequent on the Crimean war, xxvii. 188.—Iron-cased floating

SHIRLEY.

batteries, 189. — Appointment and labours of the Iron Plate Committee, 189.—Progress in the manufacture of iron plates, 192.—The 'Warrior' and 'Hercules' contrasted, 196.—'Agincourt' class of vessels, 196.—Armament of the 'Invincible,' 197. — —Strength of the ironclad navy, 198. —Classification of ships of the various services of the Navy suggested, 202.

Vide also SHIPS AND STEAM-VESSELS.

SHIRLEY, L. H. [Election, xxvii. 218.]

SHOOLBRED, J. N. [Election, xxiii. 257.]
Iron, galvanised, xxvii. 569.
Materials, durability of, xxvii. 568.
Zinc, xxvii. 568.—Zinc roofs, 568.— Superiority of Belgian zinc to British zinc for sheathing vessels, 569.

SHORT, W. D. A. R., Lieutenant-Colonel, R.E. [Decease, xxvii. 131.]

SHORTREDE, G. [Admission, xxvii. 54.]

SICCAMA, H. T. H. [Election, xxviii. 232.]

SIDNEY, S.
Drainage of land in England and the Netherlands, xxi. 95.

SIEMENS, C. [Election, xxx. 323.]

SIEMENS, C. W. [Council premium, xxii. 121, 131.]
Coal, distillation of, xxiii. 452.—Primitive character of the coke-ovens in the North of England, 452.—Inferior quality of the coke produced in the ordinary ovens, 452.—Conversion of the ordinary coke-oven into a close oven, 452.—'Four Appold' coke-oven, 453.—Upright retort, somewhat resembling the 'Four Appold' coke-oven, 453.—Gas drawn from the bottom of the retort of a higher illuminating power than that obtained from the top, 453.—Wasteful process of coke-making as generally performed, and saving that might be effected, 453.
Coal-mining, xxviii. 141.—Apparatus for getting coal, invented by Mr. C. J. Chubb, Mr. Grafton Jones, and Mr. S. P. Bidder, 141.—Modification suggested by Mr. S. P. Bidder's machine, 142.
Copper ore, smelting, xxvi. 47.—Use of

SIEMENS.

wood fuel, 47.—Circumstances under which the cupola form of furnace is advantageous for copper-smelting, 48.
Injector, Giffard's, xxiv. 222, 236.
Iron and steel, xxv. 378.—Manufacture of cast steel from worn-out Bessemer iron, 378.—Resisting force of iron and steel, xxix. 33.—Specific gravity of ditto, 34.
Lighthouses, optical apparatus of, xxvi. 529.—South Foreland lights, 530.— Penetrating power of light of different intensities, 530.— Nickel parabolic reflectors, 531.— Electric flashing lights, 531.
Materials, resistance of, xxix. 32.—Limit of elasticity of materials, 32.—Definite limit of elasticity in metals, xxx. 268.
Permanent way, maintenance and renewal of, xxv. 378.—Manufacture of cast steel from worn-out Bessemer iron, 379.—Propriety of using homogeneous cast iron or steel for rails or tires, 379.—Conversion of Bessemer rails into cast-steel rails, 379.
Railway accidents, xxi. 383.—Cause of the comparative safety on German and other Continental railways, 383.— Cast-steel tires and axles on German railways introduced by Mr. Krupp, 384.— System of telegraphing the arrival or passage of trains from station to station in Germany, 384.— Apparatus used for the above purpose, 385.
Specific gravity, easy method of determining the, of metals, xxix. 34.
Stoves, regenerative hot-blast, xxx. 315. —Difference between ditto and the ordinary hot-blast stove, 315.—Expediency of using blast of very high temperature, 315.—Chemistry of the blast-furnace, 315.
Telegraph cables. "On the electrical tests employed during the construction of the Malta and Alexandria telegraph, and on insulating and protecting submarine cables," xxi. 515.— Remarks, 538.— Working speed of telegraphs, 538.— Progress in the manufacture of gutta-percha, 539.—

SILLOTH.

Solubility of indiarubber in sea-water, 539.—Durability of copper under sea-water, 540.—Persian Gulf cable, xxv. 18.— Outer coverings of submarine electric cables, 18.—Decay of ditto, 60.—Possibility of raising cables, 62.

Telegraphic communication, xxv. 18.— Difficulties in the transmission of messages through Turkey and India, 18.—Use of iron telegraph posts in India, 62.—Principal faults of land telegraph insulators, 62.—Mechanical transmission of telegraphic messages, 62.

Silloth, Swansea, and Blyth, description of works at the ports of (Abernethy, J.), xxi. 309. *Vide* also PORTS.

SIMMONS, J. A. L., Colonel, R.E. [Associate of Council, xxi. 133.]

SIMMS, F. W. [Memoir, xxv. 519.]

SIMONS, H. M. [Election, xxviii. 518.]

SIMPSON, A. T. [Election, xxvii. 218.]

SIMPSON, J. [Past-President, xxi. 172; xxii. 166; xxiii. 150; xxiv. 143; xxv. 202; xxvi. 164; xxvii. 179; xxviii. 215; Memoir, xxviii. 360, and xxx. 457.]

Drainage of land, xxi. 86.—Effect of under-drainage in producing a permanent spring on an estate on the borders of Kent and Sussex, 86.— Perennial spring drying up at Malvern from drainage operations, 87.— Flow of water in streams generally diminished by land drainage, 88.

Steam-engines, high-pressure condensing double-cylinder, at the water-works at Ditton and Chelsea, xxiii. 69.

SIMPSON, J., Jun. [Election, xxiv. 62.]

SIMPSON, J. B. [Election, xxix. 322.]

SIMPSON, J. C. [Election, xxiii. 151.]

SIMPSON, W. [Memoir, xxiv. 537.]

SINCLAIR, R.

Locomotive engines, disturbing forces of, xxii. 98. — Balance-weights for correcting irregularity of motion, 98. —Single-cylinder engines, 99.

SKETCHLEY, H. G. [Admission, xxix. 272.]

SKIPPER, H. de S. [Admission, xxviii. 2.]

SLAGG, C. [Election, xxi. 48.]

SMITH.

Sleepers, on the woods used for, on the Madras railway (McMaster, B.), xxii. 241. *Vide* also RAILWAY SLEEPERS.

SLESSOR, F. G. [Election, xxi. 48.]

Sluices. Disaster to the St. Germains Middle Level sluice, xxi. 486, 491; xxii. 497; xxvii. 538, 539.—Grand sluice on the river Witham, xxviii. 66, *et seq.*—Effect of sluices on tidal rivers, 81, *et seq.*—*Vide* also COFFER-DAM AND SYPHONS; and RIVER WITHAM.

Sluicing operations at Birkenhead. *Vide* LOW-WATER BASIN AT BIRKENHEAD.

Small-arms, xxvii. 186.—Improvement in rifle-shooting produced by good machinery and ammunition, 187.— Enumeration of rifles made and converted at Enfield, 187.

SMALLMAN, R. [Election, xxi. 258.]

SMALLPEICE, W. [Election, xxvii. 55.]

SMART, F. A. [Election, xxii. 65; Decease, xxviii. 168.]

SMART, W. G. [Election, xxi. 258.]

SMEE, A.

Water supply, xxvii. 22. — Organic matter in water, 22.—Subtle nature of organic poisons, 22.—Use of impure water causes cholera, 22.— Why impure water is sometimes preferred for drinking, 22.—Unwholesomeness of organic matter in a state of change, 23.—Pollution of the Wandle by the drainage of Croydon, 23.—Method of testing imperfectly-purified water, 23.—Purification of water by natural filtration, 24.

Smelting of refractory copper ores with wood as fuel, in Australia (Morgan, J. L.), xxvi. 44. *Vide* also COPPER ORES.

SMITH, A. [Decease, xxiv. 117.]

SMITH, A. T. [Admission, xxvii. 218.]

SMITH, C. F. S. [Election, xxi. 257; Memoir, xxviii. 621.]

SMITH, C. G. [Admission, xxx. 106.]

SMITH, C. H.

Blasting rock, xxiii. 299.

SMITH, E. P. [Election, xxiii. 257.]

SMITH, G., Jun. [Election, xxii. 604.]

SMITH, G. H. [Election, xxiv. 358.]

SMITH.

Smith, H. L. [Election, xxi. 48.]
Smith, H. O. [Admission, xxviii. 325.]
Smith, J. [Election, xxvi. 477.]
Smith, J. C. [Election, xxi. 173.]
Smith, J. N. [Election, xxviii. 59.]
Smith, J. P. [Memoir, xxi. 594.]
Smith, J. T. [Election, xxvii. 320.]
Smith, J. T., Colonel, M.E.
  Lighthouses. Lighting apparatus and lantern at Cape Rachadah, xxiii. 34.—Respective merits of the catoptric and dioptric systems of lights, xxvi. 511, *et seq.*—Irregularity of effect in fixed lights on the catoptric system, 512.— Possibility of producing absolute uniformity of distribution, and an equally good effect, by reflectors as by zones, 514.—Principle of separating the vertical from the horizontal divergence, 515. — Fresnel's system of crossed prisms, 515.—Means of increasing the horizontal divergence of a beam of light from ditto, 516.
  Rivers, freshwater floods of, xxvii. 240.—Heavy falls of rain at Madras, 240.—Formulæ for classifying rivers as flood-producers, 240.
Smith, M. [Election, xxv. 479.]
Smith, T. H. [Election, xxiii. 151; Decease, xxviii. 168.]
Smith, W. [Election, xxv. 508.]
Smyth, R. B. [Election, xxvii. 443.]
Smyth, William Scott. [Election, xxiv. 257.]
Smyth, William Stopford. [Election, xxiv. 62.]
Smyth, W. W.
  Coal-mines, causes of accidents in, xxviii. 129, 130.—Economy to be introduced by a ' falling' apparatus, 130.
  Lead ores. Peculiar nomenclature used in describing mining operations, xxx. 124.—Improvements in machines for crushing ores, 124.—Works at Clusthal, 124.—Hotching machines for separating metal from refuse, 124.—Petherick's patent separators, 125.—Dressing of argentiferous lead ores by jigging machines at the Hartz mines, 125.—Jigging pump, 125.— Sizing trommel, 125.—Round buddles in use

SPENCER.

  in Cornwall, 126.—Williams' buddle, 126.—Influence of the matrix in the separation of ores, 126.
Smythies, J. P. [Election, xxvii. 580.]
Sopwith, T., Jun. [Election, xxiii. 320; Watt medal and Telford premium, xxiv. 109, 124.]
  Lead ores. " The dressing of lead ores," xxx. 106. — Remarks, 106. — Performances of his round buddle, 133.—Lead ores of England and Spain, 133.—Ore-crushing mills, 133. — Self-acting hotchers, 134.—Sizing lead ore mixed with various gangues, 134.
  Tunnel, Mont Cenis. " The actual state of the works on the Mont Cenis tunnel, and the description of the machinery employed," xxiii. 258.—Remarks, 309.—Question of economy of M. Sommeiller's system of driving tunnels, 309.—Differences between M. Sommeiller's and Mr. Bartlett's boring machines, 310.—Length of the boring tools in M. Sommeiller's machine, 311.—Number of men employed at the Mont Cenis tunnel, 311.—Wages paid, 311.—Proportionate rates of progress made by the systems of hand labour and machine labour, 311.—Numerous holes made for the blasting operations, 312. — Power given out by the ' Compresseur à coup de. belier,' 312.—Clearance, 312.—Various rates of progress made with the ' Compresseur,' 313.—Cost per yard of the Mont Cenis tunnel, 313.—Probable time required for completion, 319.
Sörenson, B. [Resignation, xxviii. 167.]
Spagnoletti, H.
  Railway trains, communication in, xxvi. 98.—System of train-telegraphing introduced on the Great Western and Metropolitan railways, 98.
Sparks, J. B., Lieutenant, B.S.C. [Election, xxvi. 544.]
Specific gravity, easy method of determining the, of metals, xxix. 34.
Spencer, C. I. [Election, xxi. 345.]
Spencer, J. F. [Election, xxvii. 55.]
  Steam navigation and carrying trade

SPENCER.

by sea, xxix. 190.—Efficiency and performance of steamships running between Liverpool and the United States, 191.—Difficulties in estimating the efficiency of marine engines, 191.

SPENCER, T.

Water supply. Method of determining the amount of organic matter in water, xxvii. 10.—Permanganate of potash test for organic matter in water useless when iron is present, 11, et seq.—Small amount of organic matter contained in potable water, 11.— Question of depriving water of matter held in solution, 11.—Charcoal as a filtering medium, 11.—Silicated carbon and magnetic carbide, 12.—Alleged removal of inorganic matter from water by filtration, 12.—Derbyshire stone as a filter, 17.

Spurn Point. Vide Docks, Great Grimsby; and River Humber.

STANHOPE, Hon. P. J. [Admission, xxvii. 54.]

STANTON, F. S., Captain, R.E. [Election, xxx. 1.]

STATHAM, E. J. [Election, xxviii. 59.]

Stations. Vide Railway Stations.

STEAD, W. [Election, xxix. 322.]

STEAM-ENGINES.

Consumption of fuel, xxi. 185.—Steamjackets, xxii. 97; xxix. 170.

" On the duty of the Cornish pumping engines." By W. Morshead, Jun., xxiii. 45.—Declension of the duty of late years, 45. — Registration by counters, 45.—Table by Mr. Lean, showing the number of engines annually reported, and the average duty from 1840 to 1860, 46.—Consideration of ditto, 46.—Coal in use inferior to what it was, 47.—Unfair means formerly resorted to for indicating a high duty, 47.—Sinking the engine-shaft in a direction inclined to the course of the lode tends to diminish the reported duty of the engines, 47.—Increased depth of mines tends to diminish ditto, 48.—Practice of working expansively formerly carried to a greater extent

STEAM NAVIGATION.

than now, 48.—Primary cause of the decline of duty and proposed remedies, 48.—New form of duty-paper suggested, 50.—Advantages expected to be derived from ditto, 50.—Tables of form of duty-paper for first-class engines, and for engines from which a high duty cannot be expected, 52, 53.

Discussion.—Beardmore, N., 83.—Blake, H. W., 101, 102.—Bramwell, F. J., 54, 73.—Cowper, E. A., 61.—Fraser, A., 107.—Greaves, C., 67.—Hawkshaw, J., 102, 110.—Hawksley, T., 103.—Heppel, J. M., 84.—Homersham, S. C., 75, 82.—Husband, W., 75. — Jenkin, F., 65.—McConnell, J. E., 98.—Morris, W. R., 69.—Phipps, G. H., 74.—Pole, W., 85.—Simpson, J., 69.—Webster, T., 82.

Working non-condensing engines at low pressure, inexpediency and wastefulness of, xxvi. 33.—Formation of holes round the foot-valves of pumping engines, xxix. 22.—Pumping engines for raising the metropolitan sewage, 296, et seq. Vide also Drainage of Towns.

STEAM NAVIGATION.

" Ocean steam navigation, with a view to its further development." By J. Grantham, xxix. 126.—Importance of the saving of time, 126.—Examples for consideration, 127.—The ' Sarah Sands,' 127. — Decadence of the shipping interest in America, 127.—Superiority of iron ships to wooden ships, 128.—Loss of the ' Pacific' steamship, 128.—Excess of cost of building iron ships and machinery in America, 129. — Ameliorations in marine engines, 129.—Class of vessels unsuited for screw-propellers, 130.—' Silver's governor,' 131.—Machinery for driving screws, 131. — Marine boilers, 131.—Superheating steam, 132.—Ventilation of the boiler-room, 132.—Use of steam expansively, 132.—Altered condition of the cylinder, 133.—Slide-valve, 133.—Surface-condensers, 134.—Saving of fuel, 135.—

STEAM NAVIGATION.

Clothing of the boilers and engines, 135.—Form of engines as applied to the screw-propeller, 135.—Giffard's injector, 136.—Screw-propellers, 136. —Ruthven's hydraulic system, 136.— Characteristics found most serviceable in merchant steamships, 137.—Form, 187.—Length compared with the breadth of vessels, 137.—Employment of sails in steamships, 138.— 'Auxiliary steam-vessels,' 139.— Ocean routes, 139, *et seq.*—Great circle sailing, 139.—Mercator's sailing, 140.—Speed attained by vessels on long voyages, 142. — Table of distances between Liverpool and various ports, and average time spent on the voyage, 143.—Summary of ocean steamships trading from the various ports of Great Britain, 144.— The Cunard, Collins, and Inman steamship companies, 144.—German-American companies, 144.—Cunard Company's steam-vessels, 144.—Inman Company's steam-vessels, 145.—Peninsular and Oriental Company's steam-vessels, 146.—Royal West India Mail Company, 146.—Pacific Steam Navigation Company, 147.— Colonial Steam Navigation Company of New Zealand, 148.—Vessels used in the trade between England and the Mediterranean and Black Sea, 149. — Fully-rigged vessels having small steam-power and trading on long voyages, 150.—'Great Western,' 'Great Britain,' and 'Great Eastern' steamships, 151.—Austrian Lloyd's Company, 151. — 'Messagéries Impériales,' 151. — 'La Compagnie Générale Transatlantique,' 152. — Commercial success of the German-American steamship companies, 152. —Ocean steamships of America, 152. —Steamships supplanting sailing-vessels in the trade between England and America, 153.—Real value of total imports and exports to and from Great Britain and foreign countries and British possessions, with the total of sailing and steam-vessels em-

STEEL.

ployed in transporting them, 154.— Increase of steam-vessels in the Mediterranean trades, 155.—Carrying trade to India, China, Australia, and New Zealand, 155.—Suez Canal dependent on the development of ocean steam-navigation for its success as a commercial speculation, 155.—Problem of communication by steam between England and Australia *vid* the Cape of Good Hope, 156.—Steam communication outward by the Cape of Good Hope, and homeward by Cape Horn, 157.—Postal service, 157. —Engineering question of the Suez Canal, 157. – Progress made in adapting steam-vessels to the carriage of merchandise, 158.—Dimensions most suitable for passenger vessels and cargo vessels adapted for the longest sea-voyages, 159. — Authorities supplying information, 160.

Discussion.—Belcher, Admiral Sir E., 175.—Bramwell, F. J., 168, 187.— Brock, W., 197.—Cowper, E. A., 170. —Grantham, J., 161, 199.—Gregory, C. H., 161. — Hebson, D., 204.— Hoseason, Capt. J. C., 173.—Laird, W., 203.—Murray, A., 178, 193.— Phipps, G. H., 186.—Ravenhill, J. R., 168.—Rochussen, T. A., 182.— Samuda, J. D'A., 161.—Saunders, Capt. R., 177.—Selwyn, Capt. J. H., 194.—Spencer, J. F., 190.—Stephenson, G. R., 167, 192.—Thomson, D., 193.—Vignoles, C. B., 196.—Wigram, C., 163, 167.

Vide also LONDON AND DUBLIN COMMUNICATION; SHIPS AND STEAM-VESSELS; and SHIPS OF WAR.

Steam-power on canals. *Vide* CANALS.

Steam-vessels. *Vide* SHIPS AND STEAM-VESSELS.

Steel, strength of, xxv. 374, 385-391, 417, 422-425; xxvi. 295, 297, 365. *Vide* also PERMANENT WAY; and IRON AND STEEL.

STEEL, T. D. [Election, xxiii. 459.]
Coal-mines. Firing shots in fiery pits, xxviii. 148.—Getting coal by machinery, 148.

STENT.

STENT, F. W. [Election, xxx. 106.]

STEPHENSON, G. R. [Member of Council, xxi. 133; xxii. 112; xxiii. 112; xxiv. 106; xxv. 161; xxvi. 119; xxvii. 122; xxviii. 158; xxix. 208.]
Coal-mines, xxx. 406.—Danger of explosions from the collection of gas in the old workings of coal-mines, 405. —Safety lamps, 405.—Ventilation of coal-mines, 405.—Long-wall system of working mines, 406.
Lighthouse, Wolf rock. xxx. 21.
Railway inclines, xxvi. 385.—Oldham branch of the Lancashire and Yorkshire railway, as originally worked by a rope and stationary engine, 384.
River Tyne, xxvi. 425.—Effect of the enclosure of Jarrow Slake, 425.— Dredging the bar, 426.—Piers at the mouth, 427.
Steam navigation, xxix. 167.—Compound marine engines, 167.—Consumption of fuel per indicated H.P., 167, 192.—High-pressure boilers, 192. —Surface condensation, 192.—Performance of steam-vessels on trial-trips, 192.—Indicator diagram of the 'Great Eastern' on her trial-trip, 193.

STEPHENSON, H. P.
Coal, distillation of, xxiii. 457.—Superior quality of the coke produced in ovens partially opened, 457.—Improvement of the quality of coke effected at the expense of the illuminating power of the gas, 457.

STEPHENSON, R.
Portrait, xxvi. 126.

STEVENS, G. [Admission, xxviii. 216.]

STEVENS, W. [Election, xxviii. 216.]

STEVENSON, A. [Memoir, xxvi. 575.]

STEVENSON, D.
Rivers and estuaries, xxi. 337.—River Dee at Aberdeen, 337.—Exceptional nature of the phenomena of the currents at the entrance at flood-tide, 340. — Currents in the Cromarty Frith, 340.—Comparative inefficiency of river-water alone to maintain an effectual scour at the mouths of rivers, 340.

STEVENSON, F. [Election, xxvi. 242.]

STOVES.

STEVENSON, T. [Election, xxiii. 257.]
Lighthouses, optical apparatus of, xxvi. 511.—Dioptric spherical mirror, 510. —Most simple form of holophote, 510.

STEWART, J. [Election, xxvii. 180.]

STEWART, J. H. M. S., Major, R.E. [Election, xxviii. 325.]

STIFFE, A. W. [Election, xxii. 604.]

STILEMAN, F. C. [Auditor, xxi. 132.]
Permanent way, xxv. 417.—Relative strength of steel and iron rails, 417. —Mechanical appliances for fixing rails, 417.—Total annual cost for maintenance and renewal of the permanent way of railways, xxvii. 401.—Saving by the substitution of steel rails for iron rails on main lines, 401.

STILES, J. J. [Admission, xxviii. 216.]

STONE, C. [Election, xxiii. 257; Decease, xxvii. 131.]

STONE, E. H. [Admission, xxvii. 218.]

STONE, H. [Election, xxiii. 257.]

STONEY, B. B.
Viaduct, Boyne, points of inflection of, xxix. 75.

STONEY, E. W.
Railway bridges and viaducts. "Description of the Pennair bridge, Madras railway, N. W. line," xxix. 382.

Storm-floods, account of the greatest, on the coast of Denmark, xxi. 449.

STOTHERT, G. K. [Election, xxi. 48.]

STOVES.
"On recent improvements in regenerative hot-blast stoves for blast furnaces." By E. A. Cowper, xxx. 309.—Irregularity of the working of cold-blast furnaces, 309.—Introduction of hot blast by Mr. Neilson, 309.—Losses of heat by conduction. 309.—Objections to ordinary pipe stoves, 310.—Siemens' regenerative furnace, 310.—Detailed description of stoves, 310.—Hot-blast pipes, 311.—Condition of the regenerator when at work, 311.—Utilisation of waste gas from the top of the blast furnace for heating the stoves, 312. — Dust-catchers, 312. — Subsequent arrangements for blowing out dust, 312.—Effect of the form of

STRACHAN.

the passages in mixing the air passing through, 313.—Tests to ascertain the heat of the blast, 313.—Economical results obtained from the stoves, 313.—Results of several years' working with the old stoves and the regenerative stoves, 314.—Comparative economy of ordinary and of high temperature blast, 314.

Discussion.— Cowper, E. A., 319.—Crampton, T. R., 318.—Fairbairn, Sir W., 321.—Siemens, C. W., 315.—Vignoles, C. B., 321.—Williamson, Professor, 317.

STRACHAN, J. [Admission, xxix. 98.]

STRAPP, J.

Permanent way, xxvii. 378.—Wear of steel and iron rails on the South Western railway, 378.

STREET, J. C. [Election, xxiii. 375; Decease, xxvii. 131.]

Strength and resistance of materials, on the present state of knowledge as to the (Gaudard, J.), xxvii. 536. *Vide* also MATERIALS.

STRODE, W. [Decease, xxviii. 168.]

STRONG, J. F. [Election, xxii. 65.]

STRONGITHARM, A. H. [Election, xxviii. 232.]

STROUDLEY, W. [Election, xxx. 323.]

STRUCTURES IN THE SEA.

"Structures in the sea without cofferdams; with a description of the works of the new Albert Harbour at Greenock." By D. Miller, xxii. 417.—Novel method of construction introduced of late years, 417.—Objections to the several methods of founding works in deep water as at present practised, 417.—Quay-walls built on piling carried up to the level of low water have given way at Glasgow, from the decay of the piles, 418.—Great expense and frequent danger in the construction of cofferdams, 418.—System of building by diving-bells very costly, 418.—Vicat's system of founding piers of bridges without cofferdams, 418.—Modification in the construction of the Westminster and Chelsea bridges, 419.—Reintro-

STRUCTURES IN THE SEA.

duction of the use of concrete by the French engineers, 419.—Modes in which concrete may be applied for constructive purposes, as illustrated in the works at the Victoria (London) docks, Dover breakwater, Spithead forts, and the graving docks at Toulon, 419.—Facilities for making béton or hydraulic concrete, 420.—Hydraulic limes, and the proportions of some of the concretes made from them, 420.—Smeaton's and Vicat's discovery of the mode of composing artificial hydraulic limes, 421.—Portland cement, 421.—Hydraulic properties of pozzuolana due to the presence of silicate of alumina, 421.—Mole at Genoa, constructed, under water, of pozzuolana thrown into the sea, 421.—Mole at Algiers, 422.—Applications of béton by French engineers, for the construction of bridges and harbour works, 422.—Attention required in the manipulation of hydraulic concrete, 422.—Cofferdams or diving apparatus hitherto principally used for founding and constructing works in deep water, 423.—Destructive action of 'teredo navalis' on timber, and the corrosive action of sea-water on iron, prevent these materials being employed in sea-works where durability is essential, 423. — Existing docks at Greenock, 423. — Wet docks proposed by Rennie, Telford, and Walker and Burges, 423.—General description of the Albert harbour and proposed future works, 423.—Estimated cost of a cofferdam for proposed new pier, 424.—Design for a stone and concrete pier constructed without a cofferdam, 424.— Stone facing of granite, 425.—Cast-iron guide piles for placing the stone facing, 425.—Introduction of hydraulic concrete for the base of the wall, and detailed account of the construction of the pier, 425.—The hydraulic lime, 426.—Plan to preserve the cast-iron piling. 426.—Pier will serve as a cofferdam for the harbour, 426.—Cost of the sea pi-

STRUCTURES IN THE SEA.

427.—The concrete, 427.—Proposed increase in the area of the Albert harbour, 427.— Different modes of forming the stone casing in constructing quay walls on the foregoing principles, 427.—Purposes to which this system of founding marine structures is applicable, 428.—Applicability of the system to the construction of breakwaters, 428.—Various plans discussed by a Select Committee of the House of Lords for diminishing the cost of breakwaters, 428.—The 'pierre perdue' or 'long slope' system of forming breakwaters, 429.—The 'vertical system,' 429.—'Intermediate system,' 429.—Superiority of the 'vertical wall' to the 'long slope' breakwater, 429.—Disturbing action of the sea does not extend below 15 feet under low-water mark, as shown from sections of 'pierre perdue' breakwaters, 430.—Method of constructing 'pierre perdue' breakwaters as carried out at Holyhead and Portland, 431.— French method of constructing 'pierre perdue breakwaters, 431.—Costliness of the 'long slope' and 'vertical' systems of breakwaters as at present carried out, 431.—Proposed plan for constructing breakwaters, 432.— Principal features of ditto consist in a framework of iron piles for binding together a stone facing enclosing a hearting of concrete, 432.—Mode of executing the work, 432.—Occasional effect of the waves compressing the air in the joints of the masonry, and its after-expansion, 433.—Great solidity of the work, 433.—Cost of such a structure, 433.—Table of estimates, 434.—Blocks of béton may be used in the place of stone, 434.—Economy in this system of construction, 434.—Danger to timber staging from its buoyancy, 435.— Advantage in the great speed with which such a breakwater may be constructed, 435.—Estimate of the cost of such a breakwater at Dover, 435.—Objections to the method of making breakwaters and piers of tim-

SURVEYING AND LEVELLING.

ber framing and casing, confining a mass of rubble, 435.—Timber may be substituted for the cast-iron standards, 436.—Application to the foundations of marine fortifications, 436.—Consideration of the advantages that may be fairly claimed for the proposed system, 437.

Discussion.— Bateman, J. F., 440.— Beardmore, N., 440.—Bramwell, F. J., 440.—Brooks, W. A., 443.—Brunlees, J., 446.—Curtis, J. G. C., 443.— Gregory, C. H., 439.—Jennings, J., 445.—Miller, D., 439, 447.—Mitchell, J., 439.—Parkes, W., 446.—Sheilds, F. W., 443.—Wright, J., 445.

STRUVÉ, W. P.

Permanent way, maintenance and renewal of, xxv. 377.—Process of manufacture of iron rails at the Cwm Avon works in Glamorganshire, 377.— Comparative value of Bessemer steel and wrought-iron rails, 378.

STUBBS, W. [Decease, xxvi. 129.]

Students, Inst. C.E., Establishment of, xxvii. 126.—Miller prizes awarded to, xxix. 212.—Noticed in the address of the President, Mr. C. B. Vignoles, 316.

Submarine telegraph cable, the Malta and Alexandria (Forde, H. C., and Siemens, C. W.), xxi. 493, 515. Vide also TELEGRAPH CABLES.

Subway, Tower, xxix. 288.

Suez Canal. Vide CANALS.

SUGG, W. [Election, xxi. 492.]

Gas, illuminating power of coal, xxviii. 454.—Burners, 454.—Determination of illuminating power, 454.

SUMMERS, T. [Election, xxiii. 320.]

SURVEYING AND LEVELLING.

"On measuring distances by the telescope." By W. B. Bray, xxi. 34.— Method of measurement, 34.—Use of distance hairs on the diaphragm, 34. —Degree of accuracy attainable by theory, 35.—Method of measuring distances on sloping ground, 36.— Table for facilitating the above, 37.— Advantages of a second pair of distance hairs in levelling operations, 37.

SUTHERLAND.

Discussion.—Gordon, A., 34.—Gravatt, W., 38, 46.—Hemans, G. W., 42.— Lane, C. B., 46.—Mallet, R., 45, 46. —Metford, W. E., 42.—Moorsom, W. S., 43.—Russell, J. S., 43, 46.

Surveying and levelling instruments. Telemeter, xxi. 40.—Sextant, for measuring large angles, xxi. 540.— Level supported upon a gimbal joint, xxiv. 104.—Cycloscope for setting out railway or other curves, xxv. 508.

Suspension bridges. *Vide* BRIDGES, SUSPENSION.

SUTHERLAND, DUKE OF. [Election, xxiv. 458.]

SUTHERLAND, D. S. [Election, xxii. 336.] Tunnel, Mont Cenis, xxiii. 291.—Quality of the rock at the Modane end of the Mont Cenis tunnel, 291.—Method of boring and blasting adopted, 291, 293. —Rate of advancement, 292.—Injection of water into the bore-holes, 292.—Improvement in effecting the rotary motion of the drill, 293.— Description of the new drills, 294.

SWANN, W. [Decease, xxviii. 168.]

Swansea, Blyth, and Silloth, description of works at the ports of (Abernethy, J.), xxi. 309. *Vide* also PORTS.

SWARBRICK, S. [Election, xxvii. 320.]

SZLUMPER.

SWINBURNE, W. [Decease, xxviii. 168.]

SWYER, C. R. [Election, xxiv. 511.]

SYKES, W. [Election, xxvii. 443.]

SYMONDS, T. E., Captain, R.N. Ships of war, xxvi. 219.—Bad accommodation on board turret vessels, 219. —Ventilation and anchor-gear of monitors, 220.—Impossibility of rigging ditto, 220.—Proper sphere of action for ditto, 220.—'End on' and broadside firing, 221.—Ships' guns, 221.—Improvements effected in broadside ships, 222.

SYMONS, G. J. Materials, durability of, xxvii. 570.— Experiments on the wear of rails by the British Association, 570.—Destructive agency of damp distinguished from moisture, 570.— Oxidation of metals exposed to the atmosphere applicable to obtaining some of the softer tints in engraving, 570. Rivers, freshwater floods of, xxvii. 258. —Fall and distribution of rain, 258. —Influence of vegetation on rainfall, 259.

SYNNOT, R. H. I. [Election, xxiii. 257.]

SZERELMEY, N. C. [Admission, xxvii. 581.]

SZLUMPER, J. W. [Election, xxiv. 62.]

T.

TAIT.

TAIT, G. H. [Election, xxx. 1.]
TALMAN, J. J. [Admission, xxix. 98.]
TANCRED, T. S. [Election, xxviii. 59.]
TANNER, H. T. [Election, xxvi. 242.]
TANNER, J. E. [Election, xxi. 492.]
TARBOTTON, M. O. [Election, xxi. 345.]
TARBUTT, P. F. [Admission, xxvii. 320.]
TARRANT, C. [Election, xxv. 65.]
TATAM, E. J. [Election, xxx. 106.]
TATTERSALL, E.
  Railway trains, communication in, xxvi. 95.—Rope-and-bell system, 95.
TAUNTON, J. H.
  River Thames, xxii. 357.—Supply of water from the springs of Thames Head, 357.—Drainage area and volume of water yielded by the Thames Head springs, Swill Brook, Churn, Coln, and South Ampney springs, 357.—Average flow of the river Thames at Wolvercot, 358.—Rights of millowners, 358.
TAYLERSON, R.
  Ships and steam-vessels, iron, xxi. 229.—Superiority of the diagonal to the longitudinal system of construction of iron vessels, 229, 231.—Greater stability of a hollow girder keel and keelson combined, 230.—Reason of the inherent weakness of iron vessels, 231.
TAYLOR, H. A. [Election, xxix. 98.]
TAYLOR, John.
  Lead ores, xxx. 126.—Separating ore from gangue of light specific gravity in the South of Spain, 126.—Ore-crushing mills, 127.—Trommel and hotching machines, 127.
TAYLOR, John.
  River Churn, xxii. 359.—Loss of water by percolation through the bed, 359.—Fish and mill ponds, 359.—Geological character of the river, 359.
TAYLOR, John. [Election, xxii. 65.]
TAYLOR, Joseph. [Telford premium, xxv. 165, 181.]

TELEGRAPH CABLES.

Bridges, cast-iron and wrought-iron, xxvii. 111.
Permanent way, xxvii. 379.—Specifications and tests for iron rails, 379.
Railway income and expenditure, xxix. 366.—Beneficial effect of increasing the facilities for travelling by railway, 366.
River Tees. "Description of the River Tees, and of the works upon it connected with the navigation," xxiv. 62.—Remarks, 101.—Deep water at the coal staithes at Middlesbro', 101.—Shoaling of the Tees at Middlesbro', consequent on the works in Bamblet's Bight, 102.—Deterioration of the river below Cargo Fleet, 102.—Injurious effect of the groynes, 103.—Wattle jetties, 103.
River Witham, silting-up below the Grand Sluice, xxviii. 94.
TAYLOR, T. H. [Decease, xxix. 217.]
TAYLOR, W. B. [Election, xxvi. 79.]
TEASDEL, W. [Election, xxvii. 580.]
TELEGRAPH CABLES.
Progress of ocean telegraphy, xxi. 179.
"The Malta and Alexandria submarine telegraph cable." By H. C. Forde, xxi. 493.—Object of the paper, 493.—Contract for making and laying a cable between Falmouth and Gibraltar, 493. — Determination by Government to change the destination of the cable to join Rangoon and Singapore, and, finally, to join Malta and Alexandria, 493.—Table giving the specification of the Falmouth and Gibraltar telegraph, 494.—Mr. Robert Stephenson's design for a copper conductor covered with gutta-percha, 495.—Sir Charles Bright's design for a core protected by iron wire, 496.—Resemblance to Mr. L. Gisborne's and Mr. Forde's plan, 496.—Experi-

TELEGRAPH CABLES.

ments on a hemp and steel cable for the deep sea, 496.—Advantages and disadvantages of steel and hemp cables, 496.—Hemp and steel cable given up when the destination of the cable was changed, 496.—Large size of the wires of the cable as laid, 497. —Rate of working, 497.—Table showing the increase which has taken place in the size of the cores of telegraph cables, 497.—Contract for the manufacture of the cable, 498.— Rules observed in the manufacture of the cable, 498.—Cable tested and packed, 498.--Table showing the relative resistance per knot of the conductor and insulator of the Atlantic, Red Sea and India, and Malta and Alexandria telegraphs, 499.— Superiority of the Malta and Alexandria telegraph, 499.—Care requisite in making the joints of the core, 499. —Loss of insulation by the drying and oxidation of the wire, 500.— Report of Dr. W. A. Miller, supported by an experiment of Messrs. Glass, Elliot, and Co., 500.—The 'Malacca' and 'Rangoon' steam-vessels fitted with watertight tanks for receiving the cable, 501.—Weight carried by each vessel, 501.—Shipment of the cable, 501.—Fault detected and cut out in the coil on board the 'Rangoon,' 502.—Importance of the batteries being in thoroughly good order, 503.—Soundings taken on the line on which it was proposed the cable should be laid, 503.—Arrival of the 'Malacca' at Malta, 504.—Apparatus for paying out the cable, 504.—Selection of the routes upon which the cable was laid, 505.—Laying the line between Malta and Tripoli, 505.—Difficulties in splicing the main cable to the shore end at Tripoli, 506.—Cable remaining on board the 'Malacca' laid from Tripoli in the direction of Benghazi, 506.—Laying the cable from Alexandria towards Benghazi, 507.—Kink made in the cable on anchoring cut

TELEGRAPH CABLES.

out, 508.—Completion of the sections between Alexandria and Benghazi, and Benghazi and Tripoli, 508.— Laying the cable successful as a mechanical operation, 508.—Selection of landing-places for the cable, 509.— Tests during and after the laying of the cable, 509.—Improvements in the insulation of the different sections after being laid, owing to the cooler temperature and the pressure of the water, 510.—Table showing the final results of the official tests, 512.— Temperature of the cable unable to be calculated from the resistance of the copper, owing to the interference of earth currents, 512.—Results of experiments as to the rate of working through the different sections of the cable, 512.—Small amount of battery power employed, 512.—Table showing the above, 513.—Telegraphic communication between Belgrade and Constantinople, 514.
" On the electrical tests employed during the construction of the Malta and Alexandria telegraph, and on insulating and protecting submarine cables." By C. W. Siemens, 515.— Recent progress in the knowledge of submarine telegraphy, 515.—Failure of the Atlantic cable and of the Red Sea and India telegraph, 515.—Superiority of the insulation of the Malta and Alexandria telegraph to the Red Sea and India telegraph, 516.—Requirements under the electrical tests, 516.—Description of the standard measure of resistance by which to express the conductivity of the copper conductor, and of the insulating covering, 517.—Reference to diagrams representing the results of observations upon two different sections of the cable, between Malta and Tripoli, and between Alexandria and Benghazi, 518.—Effects of spontaneous heating on a portion of the Malta and Alexandria cable, 519.—Further reference to the above, 519.—Precautions used in order to discover

TELEGRAPHIC COMMUNICATION.
undue accumulation of heat at an early stage, 519.—Fault detected in the Alexandria and Benghazi section, 520.—Causes of the improvement in the insulation of the cable, 521.—Good condition of the Alexandria and Malta cable, 521.—Instruments for working the line and mode of transmitting messages, 521.—Reference to the "Report of the Joint Committee on the Construction of Submarine Telegraph Cables," 522.—Sources of deterioration to which submarine telegraphs are exposed, 522.—Comparative merits of indiarubber and gutta-percha as insulating materials, 522.—Reference to a diagram showing the results of experiments on the absorption of water by different insulating materials, 523.—Deductions from the experiments, 523.—Notice of the specific resistance of gutta-percha and of indiarubber, alone and combined, at different temperatures, 524.—Table showing the above, 525.—Table showing the specific induction of gutta-percha and indiarubber, alone and combined, 526.—Remarks on the above table, 526.—Advantages of indiarubber covered with gutta-percha as an insulating medium, 527.—Mechanical construction of a sound indiarubber and gutta-percha covered wire, 527. — Durability of wires covered in this manner, 528.—Iron sheathing not suitable for deep-sea cables, 528.—Permanent stretching of the copper core in paying out the wire, 528.—Description of cable recommended by Mr. Siemens, 529.—Probable duration of the cable, 530.

Discussion.—Bright, Sir C. T., 531.—Chatterton, J., 536.—Forde, H. C., 537.—Hawkshaw, J., 531, 540.—Macintosh, J., 536.—Selwyn, Capt. J. H., 534.—Siemens, C. W., 538.—Thomson, Prof. W., 535.

Vide also TELEGRAPHIC COMMUNICATION.

TELEGRAPHIC COMMUNICATION.
"The telegraph to India, and its extension to Australia and China." By

TELEGRAPHIC COMMUNICATION.
Sir C. T. Bright, xxv. 1.—Progress of the electric telegraph since the opening of the first line, 1.—Choice of telegraphic routes between Europe and India, 1.—Suez, Aden, and Kurrachee submarine cable, 1.—Extension of the telegraph in the Turkish dominions in Asia, 2.—Submarine telegraph from the head of the Persian Gulf to Gwadur and Kurrachee determined on, 2.—Line divided into sections, 3.—The cable, 3.—The conductor, 3.—Use of gutta-percha as an insulator in a warm climate, 4.—Electrical tests for defective joints made in the insulating material, 4.—Conductivity of the cable, 5.—Resistance tests of the coils, 5.—Condensers for determining the quantity of electricity, 6.—Effect of temperature on the conducting power of gutta-percha and india-rubber, 6.—Formula obtained from the mean results of experiments as to ditto, 6.—Tabular statement of numerical values, as found by experiment, and calculated from ditto, 7.—Formula for the Atlantic cable core, 7.—Testing of the core, 7.—Application of coverings to the core, 7, 8.—Completion of the manufacture of the cable, 8.—Lengths and weights of the several forms of ditto made, 8.—Shipment of cable, 8.—Appliances for laying ditto, 9.—Vessel for permanent service on the line, 9.—Protection from oxidation afforded by the outer bituminous covering of the cable, 9.—Records during the voyage of the currents produced by the earth's magnetism on the coils of the cable, at each roll of the vessel, 9.—Deposition of the cable between Gwadur and Mussendom, 10.—Laying cables from sailing-ships towed by steam-vessels, 10.—Electrical observations made during the paying-out of the cable, 11.—Completion of the other sections of the line, 11.—Character of the bottom along the line of telegraph, 12.—Temperature of the sea,

TELESCOPE.

12.—Insulation tests taken after immersion, 12.—Uniformity of the results, 13.—Working of the line, 13.—Completion of the Turkish land line, between Bagdad and the head of the Persian Gulf, 13, 14.—Room for improvement in the working of ditto, 14.—Indian telegraphs constructed to Rangoon, 14.—Feasibility of establishing a land line down the Malay peninsula, 14.—Expediency of the construction of submarine cables in uncivilized countries, 14.—Routes for telegraph communication between Singapore and China, 14.—Ditto between Singapore and Australia, by Banca, Java, and Timor, 15.—Death of Colonel Stewart, 15.

Discussion.—Allan, T., 57.—Ayrton, A. S., 20.—Bright, Sir C. T., 16, 62.—Champain, Major J. U., 22.—Clark, L., 45.—Crawford, R. W., 26.—Fowler, J., 53.—Galton, Capt. D., 19.—Gisborne, F., 43.—Glass, R. A., 29.—Huish, Capt. M., 27.—Jenkin, F., 31.—Longridge, J. A., 53, 62.—Macintosh, J., 51, 53.—Preece, W. H., 19.—Rouse, H. J., 42.—Rowland, O., 56.—Selwyn, Capt. J. H., 58.—Siemens, C. W., 18, 60.—Varley, C. F., 32, 50.

Vide also TELEGRAPH CABLES.

Telescope, on measuring distances by the (W. B. Bray), xxi. 34. *Vide* also SURVEYING AND LEVELLING.

Telford medals and premiums. *Vide* PREMIUMS AND PRIZES.

TENGBERGEN, A. G. [Admission, xxix. 98.]

TERRY, A. R. [Election, xxviii. 517.]
Railway bridges and viaducts. "On the new Mhow-ke-Mullee viaduct, Great Indian Peninsula railway," xxix. 373.

THACKERAY, E. T., Capt., R.E. [Election, xxviii. 325.]

Thames, the perennial and flood waters of the Upper (Clutterbuck, Rev. J. C.), xxii. 336. *Vide* also RIVER THAMES.

THOMAS, E. [Election, xxvi. 165.]
Canals, steam-power on, xxvi. 14.—Screw tug-boat 'Birmingham,' 14.—

THORNTON.

Steam-power on the Regent's Canal, 15.—Combination of the tug and cargo vessel, 15.

THOMAS, H.
Canals, steam-power on, xxvi. 24.—Engine-boat 'Dart,' 24.—Boilers and engines of ditto, 24.

THOMAS, J. L.
Lead ores, process of dressing, in England and in Spain, xxx. 128.—Revolving riddle or trommel, 128.—Machinery for crushing ore, 129.—Continuous hotching machine, 129.—Round buddles, 130.—Cost of dressing lead ores, 130.

THOMPSON, A. [Memoir, xxiv. 544.]
THOMPSON, H. S. [Election, xxv. 429.]
THOMPSON, T. J. [Election, xxvi. 242.]
THOMSON, C. [Admission, xxix. 98.]
THOMSON, D.
Steam navigation, xxix. 193.—Surface condensation in marine engines, 193.—Double-cylinder and single-cylinder engines, 193.

THOMSON, P. [Election, xxvi. 398.]
THOMSON, Sir W.
Materials, resistance of, xxix. 74.—Torsion of prisms, and elastic fatigue of metals, 74.
Telegraph cables. Working speed through the Malta and Alexandria telegraph cable, xxi. 535.—Speed from theoretical considerations, 535.—Desirability of effecting a permanent protection for the insulating medium, 535.

THORBURN, T. C.
Drainage of towns, xxii. 284.—Ventilation of sewers, 284.—Flushing of the sewers at Derby, 284.—Stoneware pipes for drainage purposes, 285.

THORMAN, E. H.
Injector, Giffard's, xxiv. 219.

THORNHILL, E. B. [Election, xxx. 215.]
THORNTON, G. [Election, xxv. 352.]
THORNTON, H. E. [Election, xxvii. 218; Resignation, xxix. 217.]
THORNTON, P.
Ships of war, xxi. 227.—Armour-plates, 227.—Effects of projectiles upon ditto, 227.—Speed of iron vessels, 228.—

THOROWGOOD.

Experience acquired by the Admiralty in building ditto, 229.

THOROWGOOD, F. N. [Admission, xxvii. 218.]

THWAITES, C. [Election, xxix. 98.]

THWAITES, D. [Election, xxi. 492; Resignation, xxiii. 120.]

Tides. Effect produced upon the propagation of the tidal wave by changes in the condition of a channel, xxviii. 499, 509. — Retardation and progressive increase of height of the tidal wave passing from the north down the east coast of Great Britain, 507.—Errors in the published Ordnance mean-tide levels, xxviii. 511. — Elevation of mean water in progressing up the Shannon estuary, 512.—Tides in the Humber, 513.—Effect of the Dogger and the Wells banks on the tides of the east coast of England, 513. *Vide* also COASTS; and RIVERS AND ESTUARIES.

TIJOU, W. [Election, xxvii. 55.]

Timber. Difference between endogenous and exogenous trees, xxii. 62.—Preservative effect against white ants, of the immersion of timber in chloride of zinc, 496.

——, Australian, xxii. 256, 258.

——, Brazilian, xxii. 402, 409, *et seq.*; xxiv. 3, 18, *et seq.; xxvii. 574.

——, creosoting, xxii. 62.—Similarity of Palmyra timber to creosoted wood, 62.—Creosoting operations not carried out with success in India, 255, 258.—Australian woods difficult of creosoting, 256.—Preparation of creosoted sleepers, xxiv. 22, *et seq.*—Arracan oil as a substitute for creosote, 24.—Advantage of creosoting piles, 54.—Creosoted timber not liable to attack by white ants, xxv. 416.—Experiments on the relative resistance to crushing weight, and the relative elasticity, of creosoted and uncreosoted timber, xxvii. 294. — Value of creosoting timber as a preservative against the attacks of marine insects in the case of piles in Holland and Belgium, 564.—Preparation of timber for creosoting by the French and Belgian govern-

TUNNELS.

ments, 565.—Necessity of thoroughly drying before creosoting, 566.

Timber, Madras Presidency, xxiv. 242, *et seq.*

——, Palmyra, xxii. 58.

——, Saul, xxiv. 25.

——, Singapore, and from Straits of Malacca, xxii. 258, 260.

——, Teak, xxiv. 25.

Vide also BRIDGES, TIMBER; PILES; PUBLIC WORKS; MATERIALS; and RAILWAY SLEEPERS.

TIMINS, H. C. A. [Election, xxix. 98.]

TODLEBEN, Lieutenant-General E. [Election, xxiv. 62.]

TOMKINS, S. L. [Election, xxi. 345.]

TOMKINS, W. G. [Memoir, xxx. 460.]

TOMLINS, R. H. [Admission, xxvii. 54.]

TOOKE, W. [Memoir, xxiii. 480.]

TOPLIS, F. [Admission, xxvii. 320.]

TOSH, Dr. E. G.

Iron, West Cumberland Bessemer (Boyd, J.), xxvii. 393.

TOWLE, J.

River Thames, floods round Oxford, xxii. 354.

TOWNSEND, F. E. [Admission, xxix. 98.]

TOWNSEND, T. C. [Election, xxii. 451.]

Trade, foreign, of Great Britain in 1865, exclusive of specie, xxvi. 332.

Trains in motion, on the best means of communicating between the passengers, guards, and drivers of (Preece, W. H.), xxvi. 80. *Vide* also RAILWAY TRAINS.

Tramways along suspended wire-ropes, xxix. 300.

TREGELLES, E. O. [Resignation, xxi. 148.]

TREHEARNE, W. J. [Election, xxvii. 553.]

TREHERNE, E. [Decease, xxi. 595.]

TREVERTON, W. H. [Election, xxviii. 216.]

TREWBY, G. C. [Election, xxv. 352.]

TROLLOPE, C. B. [Election, xxvi. 242.]

TROTTER, C. E. [Admission, xxvii. 54; Election, xxx. 106.]

TUCK, J. H. [Election, xxii. 604.]

TULLOCH, H., Captain, R.E. [Election, xxvii. 180.]

TUNNELS.

Lydgate and Buckhorn Weston. "Description of the Lydgate and of the Buckhorn Weston railway tunnels."

TUNNELS.

By J. G. Fraser, xxii. 371.—Paucity of information of a practical character on the subject of tunnels, 371.— Length of railway tunnels open, and their cost, 371.—Small number of tunnels hitherto described, 371.— Geological features of the Lydgate tunnel, on the Oldham branch of the London and North Western railway, 372.—Lengths of the different strata cut through, 372.—Shafts and measures for securing ventilation, 372. —Description of the shafts, 373.— Table of the depths and rate of sinking of the shafts, 373.—Table showing the lengths mined from the different shafts, 374.—Process of excavation and timbering from top heading, 374.—Advantages of the common mode of sinking shafts and multiplying the number of faces, 374. —Disadvantages of a bottom heading, 374.—Lengths mined before lining with masonry, and prices paid to the miners, 375.—Centering, 375.— Masonry used for building the side-walls and arch, with statement of prices, 375.—Mortar, 376.—Course pursued when much weight was shown, 376.—Importance of preventing any motion in the ground, 376.— Table showing the variation in the thickness of the masonry, 376.—Account of the tunnel as completed, 376.—Contract price, 377.—Geological features of the Buckhorn Weston tunnel, on the Salisbury and Yeovil railway, 377.—Vein of water remedied by driving a heading above the tunnel, and draining it away by a pipe, 377.—Failure of a bottom heading on the west side from the bulging of the clay, 377.—Description and cost of the shafts, 377.—Table showing the lengths mined from the different shafts, 378.—Method of mining pursued, lengths mined before lining with masonry, and cost of mining, 378.—Bars and centres, 378. —Extra thickness of masonry required on account of the pressure of

TUNNELS.

water, 378.—Substitute for sharp sand for making mortar, 378.—Precautions for preventing settlement, 379.—Water conveyed away in pipes, 379.—Table showing the variation in the thickness of the masonry, 379.— Account of the tunnel as completed, 379.—Tabular statement of the total cost of the tunnel, 380.

Discussion.—Fraser, J. G., 381.—Hawkshaw, J., 383.—Lane, C. B., 381.

Mont Cenis. "The actual state of the works on the Mont Cenis tunnel, and description of the machinery employed." By T. Sopwith, Jun., xxiii. 258.—Direct railway communication between France and Italy by the tunnel, 258.—Route to Alexandria from London, viâ Ancona, compared with that viâ Marseilles, 259.—Expected advantages of the former, 259. —Determination to use air compressed by water for driving machinery to bore the tunnel, 259.—Geological features of the district, 260.—Ventilation of the tunnel, 260, 273.— Dimensions of ditto, 260.—Establishment at each end of the tunnel, 261. —Captain Penrice's boring machine, 261.—M. Sommeiller's ditto, as used at the Mont Cenis tunnel, 262.—Time occupied in working a 'shift,' 263.— Boring and blasting the rock, 264.— Removal of the 'déblais,' 264.—Description of the machinery used for compressing the air, 265.—Pipe for conveying the air, 265.—Water raised by machinery at Modane for compressing the air, 265.—New system of compression introduced at Modane, 266.—Dates of the application of machinery, 266.—Rates of progress at Modane and Bardonnêche, 267.— Probable duration of the work, 268.— Large establishment and number of workmen required, 269.—Cost of tunnelling by machinery and hand labour compared, taking the operations at Mont Cenis as a basis for calculation, 269, et seq.—Supply of air in advanced gallery, 273.—Heads of agreement

TUNNER.

entered into between France and Italy, 273.—Sums to be paid to the Italian Government by France, 275.—Estimated cost of tunnel per mètre, 276.— Necessity of improving the present system of tunnelling, 276.—Description of the machinery in use, 276.— Available head of water, 276.—Pump compressors, 277.—Superior air-compressing machine at Modane, 280.— Description of a similar machine in use at Seraing, 280.—No injurious heat manifested during the working of M. Sommeiller's machines, 281.— Loss of power in conveying the air and amount of leakage inconsiderable, 281.—The supply pipes, 282.—The perforators, 282.—Requirements of a boring machine, 283.—Percussion and return of boring tool, 283.—Action of the piston, 283.— Rotation of the boring tool, 284.—Advance and withdrawal of the machine, 284.—Changes in detail constantly introduced, 285.— Nominal power exerted by each machine, 285.— Amount of power required to supply ditto with compressed air, 286.

Discussion.—Bartlett, T., 288.—Bateman, J. F., 317.—Bidder, G. P., 308. —Bramwell, F. J., 301.—Brassey, T., 295, 296.— Brereton, R. P., 296.— Brunlees, J., 319.—Cowper, E. A., 296.—Eckersley, W., 299.—Fell, J. B., 313.—Gregory, C. H., 300.—Harrison, W. C., 317.—Hawkshaw, J., 308.— Hopkins, E., 307.—Mallet, R., 297.— Neumann, G., 287.—Russell, J. S., 318.—Sheilds, F. W., 300.— Smith, C. H., 299.—Sopwith, T., Jun., 309, 319.—Sutherland, D. S., 291.

——Progress of works, probable cost and time of completion, xxix. 301.

Moorhouse, New Zealand, xxix. 106, 122. *Vide* PUBLIC WORKS.

TUNNER, P.

Iron and steel (Sandberg, C. P.), xxvii. 407.—Bessemer metal made at Neuberg, in Styria, 407.

TURNBULL, G.

Timber. Durability of different kinds

TYLER.

of sleepers on the East Indian railway, xxiv. 22.—Creosoting wood in India, 23.—Arracan oil as a substitute for creosote, 24.

TURNER, E. R. [Election, xxv. 65.]

TURNER, F. [Election, xxviii. 325.]

TURNER, F. T. [Election, xxv. 262.]

TURNER, G.

     Ships of war, xxi. 201.—Construction of a model ironclad frigate, 201.

TURNER, W. B. [Election, xxv. 508.]

TURTON, T. B. [Resignation, xxiv. 117.]

TUSON, J. F. [Election, xxvi. 79.]

TWEEDIE, W. [Admission, xxvii. 55.]

TWIGG, R. H. [Election, xxix. 98.]

TYER, E.

     Railway telegraphs, xxii. 196.—System of train-signalling, 196, 198.—Mr. Preece's paper on railway telegraphs, 196.—Mr. C. V. Walker's system in operation on the South Eastern railway, 196.—Semaphore electric telegraph for train-signals, 197.— Disc signals, 197.—Reply to objections raised against his instruments, 199.— Effects of atmospheric electricity on the wires, 199.—Expediency of only one line wire, 200.—Instruments being kept under lock and key, 200. —Electric signalling a great auxiliary to the efficient working of a railway, 201.—Colonel Yolland's report of an accident on the Greenwich railway, 201. — Resemblance between the needle system and the semaphore system, 202.—Proper evidence of efficiency of instruments, 202.

TYLER, H. W., late Captain, R.E. [Telford medal and premium, xxv. 164, 180; Associate of Council, xxvii. 122; Telford premium, 124, 142.]

     Bridge, Albert Edward, over the Severn, on the Coalbrookdale railway, xxvii. 110.—Use of steel for railway bridges, xxvi. 297.

     Bridges, suspension, xxvi. 297.—Steel ditto, 297.—Suspension bridges for railway purposes, 297.—Plans for stiffening ditto, 297.—Lambeth Road bridge, 298.—Inverted arch bridge, 298. — Requirements of a railway

TYLER.

suspension bridge, 298. — Form of girder suspension bridge, 299.

Girders, bowstring, strains on, xxvii. 448.

Permanent way, xxvii. 387.—Deterioration in the manufacture of iron rails, 387.—Failure of rails in the Penge tunnel, and on the Grand Trunk railway of Canada, 387.—Durability of rails in Canada, 388.—Tests for rails, 388.—Requirements of a good rail, 381.—Best form of rail, 389.— Quality of rails, 389.—Publication of the results of the wear of rails by different makers, 390.—Strains on rails under passing loads, 392.

Railway accidents, xxi. 383.—Porters frequently crushed between the buffers of railway carriages, 383.— Desirability of some better tribunal for deciding compensation cases arising from railway accidents, 409.— Colonel Yolland's report on the railway accident at Tottenham in 1860, 410.—Causes of accidents seldom involved in mystery, 410.—Percentage of accidents from various causes, 410.

Railway curves and inclines. "On the working of steep gradients and sharp curves on railways," xxvi. 310.—Remarks, 325.—M. Thouvenot's and Mr. Fairlie's locomotives for working severe gradients and sharp curves, 325, 391.—Pneumatic system of railway, 325.—Working the Navigation incline of the Taff Vale railway, 325. —Application of the sledge-break to the central rail in Fell's system, 366. —Grooved wheels for locomotive engines, 388.—Coefficient of adhesion, 388.—Effect of dust, 389.—Coefficient of adhesion on the Navigation incline of the Taff Vale railway, 389.— Question of gradients in crossing mountain passes, 390.—Cost of constructing railways across the Simplon and Lukmanier passes with different gradients, 390.—Passage of trains round curves, 390.—Mr. Fairlie's system and M. Thouvenot's system of

TYRRELL.

locomotives, 391.—Atmospheric and pneumatic systems as applicable to the working of steep gradients, 392.

Railway locomotives and rolling stock. Locomotive engines on the Giovi incline, xxvi. 72.—Adoption of bogie-trucks on American railways, xxviii. 411.—Universal adoption in America of cast-iron wheels for railway rolling stock, 413.—Rolling stock in the United States, 413, 414.—Wear and tear of wheels, 414.—Cost of carriage maintenance on Indian railways, 414. —Rolling stock with adjustable axles, 415.—Pullman's hotel cars, 415.

Railway telegraphs, xxii. 225.—Use of the 'train-staff' in working single lines of railway in England and Ireland, 225.—Working double lines of railway by telegraph, 225.

Railway trains, communication in, xxvi. 106.—Objects to be attained by establishing inter-communication in trains, 106.—Expediency of a means of inter-communication for express traffic on railways, 107.—Instances of a want of communication, 107.—Report of the sub-committee of general managers of railways on inter-communication in trains, 109.—Superiority of the voltaic current for ditto, 109.—Communication between passengers and engine-drivers, 110.— Means of circulation in trains, 110.— Sleeping accommodation in ditto, 111.

Railways. "On the Festiniog railway for passengers, as a 2-feet gauge, with sharp curves, and worked by locomotive engines," xxiv. 359.—Remarks, 367.—Narrow-gauge railways generally, 367.—Comparative cost of working the Festiniog railway by horses and by locomotive power, 367. —Saving effected by narrow-gauge light railways, xxvi. 72.—Talyllyn railway, 72.—Mont Cenis railway, 319.—Provisions against snow and level crossings on ditto, 393.

TYNDALL, R. [Election, xxx. 323.]

TYRRELL, A. W. [Admission, xxix. 98.]

U.

UNDER-DRAINAGE.

Under-drainage, on the discharge from, and its effect on the arterial channels and outfalls of the country (Denton, J. B.), xxi. 48. *Vide* also DRAINAGE OF LAND.

UNWIN, H. [Election, xxv. 65.]

UNWIN, W. C. [Election, xxvi. 242.]

　Fans, xxx. 305.—Influence of the form of the vanes of a fan on the pressure produced, 305.—Sources of loss in a fan or centrifugal pump with straight radial vanes, 305.—Advantages of large casing for rotary fans, 306.

　Materials, resistance of, xxix. 38.—Formulæ for the resistance of long columns, 38.—Elasticity, 39.—Tension and compression, 40.

UTLEY.

Ships of war, xxvi. 218.—Penetration of iron plates placed at an angle to the line of fire, 218.—Resistance of laminated targets, 219.

UPWARD, A.

　Gas, illuminating power of coal, xxviii. 461.—Jet photometer, 461.

URE, J. F.

　Canals, steam-power on, xxvi. 20.—Waves produced by passenger steamers on the river Clyde, 20, 21.—Scouring action of ditto, 20.—Limitation of the speed of vessels in canals, 21.

USILL, G. W. [Admission, xxviii. 98.]

UTLEY, S. [Election, xxiii. 320.]

V.

VALENTINE.

VALENTINE, A. [Election, xxiii. 320.]
VALENTINE, J. S.
  Coasts, &c. East coast of England, xxiii. 249.—Action of the sea on the coast between Wells and Lynn, 249.—Travel of the shingle on the eastern coast due to the tidal wave, 250.—Coast beyond Whitby the source of the shingle-beds between Hunstanton and Woolverton, 250, 251.—Reclamations from the sea between Wells and Hunstanton, 251.
  Railway stations, xxv. 286.—New Cambridge station, 286.—Abandonment of platforms at railway stations, 286.
VARDON, R. [Resignation, xxiii. 120.]
VARLEY, C. F. [Election, xxv. 65.]
  Telegraph cables, xxv. 34.—Insulating power of Hooper's electric cable, 34.—Galvanized iron coverings for submarine cables, 35.—Strength of galvanized iron wires, 35.—Repairing submarine cables in shallow waters, 35.—Submarine cables without a covering of iron wire, 38.—Methods adopted for testing the amount of leakage through the joints of the Persian Gulf and Atlantic telegraph cables, 41.—Insulation of wire covered with indiarubber by Hooper's process, 50.
  Telegraphic communication, xxv. 32.—Employment of European clerks for working telegraph lines in India, 32.—Necessity of having more than one line of telegraph between England and India, 32.—Excellent management of telegraphs in Germany and Russia, 33.—Desirability of opening a route to India through those countries, 33.—Improvement in the communication between Alexandria and England, 36.—Action of the British Government in granting permission to carry telegraphs across its territory,

VIADUCTS.

36.—Telegraphic communication between England and Constantinople and England and St. Petersburg, 36.—Importance of reducing the number of manual transmissions between London and Bombay, 37.—Continuation of the telegraph from India to Australia, 37, 38.—Quotation of a letter from T. A. Rochussen as to ditto, 37.—Land telegraph lines in India, 39.—Manufacture and testing of telegraph wires, 40.—Joints of ditto, 40.
VARLEY, S. A.
  Railway trains, communication in, xxvi. 97.—Mr. Martin's and Mr. Preece's electrical systems, 97.
VAUGHAN, J. [Memoir, xxviii. 622.]
VAUGHAN, T. [Election, xxiv. 184.]
VAUX, A. H. [Election, xxv. 262.]
  Rivers, freshwater floods of, xxvii. 265.—Flood in Beerbhoom, in 1866, 265.
VAWDREY, W. [Election, xxv. 352.]
VEITCH, D. D'A. W. [Admission, xxvii. 54.]
VENABLES, W. H. [Admission, xxvii. 54.]
Venice, Lagoon of, xxviii. 317.
VERDON, G. F. [Election, xxviii. 439.]
VERNON-HARCOURT, L. F. [Election, xxv. 65.]
VIADUCTS.
  "Description of the Loch Ken viaduct, Portpatrick railway." By E. L. I. Blyth, xxi. 258.—Size of the loch and extent of waterway, 258.—Glenlochar bridge, 258.—Girders spanning the waterway, 259.—Foundations and piers described, 259.—Sinking the tubes to the gravel foundation, 259.—Tubes filled with concrete at the base, and the piers completed with masonry, 261.—Dimensions of the girders, their weight and mode of connection, 261.—Tensile strains, 262.—Bow and string preferred to Warren girders, 263.—

o

VIADUCTS.

Girders built in position on the staging, 263. — Strength of girders tested, 263.—Cost of the viaduct and period occupied in its construction, 263.

Discussion.—Hemans, G. W., 265.

" The Hownes Gill viaduct on the Stockton and Darlington railway." By W. Cudworth, xxii. 44.—Description of the Hownes Gill, 44.—Traffic originally carried on in wagons over inclines, 44.—Original estimates for a viaduct, 45. — Description of the viaduct as finally carried out, 45, et seq.—Method of securing a firm foundation for the piers, 46.—Dimensions of the viaduct, 46.—Plan for diminishing vibration, 47.—The bricks used in construction, 47.—Tabular statement of the cost of the structure, 48. —Question of the relative cost of brick and iron viaducts, exemplified in the case of the Hownes Gill, compared with the Deepdale and the Beelah viaducts, 49.—Choice of materials, for the construction of viaducts, dependent on local and other circumstances, 50.—Estimates of the cost of a stone and of an iron viaduct at Hownes Gill, 51.

Discussion. — Barlow, W. H., 56.— Bidder, G. P., 52, 55.—Bouch, T., 52, 56.—Cudworth, W., 52, 57.—Fowler, J., 56.—Pole, W., 55.—Russell, J. S., 56.—Sheilds, F. W., 54, 55.

" On the reconstruction of the Dinting and the Mottram viaducts." By W. Fairbairn, xxii. 327.—Considerations in favour of wrought-iron girder-bridges where great width and span is required, 327.—Probability of the future use of steel for large bridges, 327.—Description of the viaducts as constructed of wood by the late Mr. Joseph Locke, 328. — Temporarily repaired by Mr. Jee, 328.—Description of the restored portion of the viaducts, 330. — No interruption to traffic during the progress of reconstruction, 330. — Suspension of the girders, 331.—Description of the ap-

VIADUCTS.

paratus for raising and lowering the girders, and account of the reconstruction of the viaducts, 332.

Discussion.— Bateman, J. F., 334. — Fairbairn, W., 334.—Hawkshaw, J., 335.

" The Craigillachie viaduct." By W. H. Mills, xxv. 229.—Position, 229.— Physical features of the river Spey, 229.—Dimensions of the viaduct and waterway, 230.—Bed of the river not suited for a timber-pile coffer-dam, 230.—Cast-iron cylinders sunk for the foundations of the piers, 230. — Pumping operations, 231. — Cylinders filled with concrete, 231.— The masonry of the piers, 231.—The girders, 232.—The cross-girders, 233. — Diaphragms for holding together the lattice girders laterally, 233.— Girders riveted together, 234.—Longitudinal timbers for carrying the rails, 234. — Holes for the rivets, 234. — Method of erecting the girders, 234. — Progress and execution of the works, 234.—Specification as to the tensile strength of the wrought iron, 235.—Results of the testing of the viaduct, 235.—Weight of iron in the different portions of the work, 235.— Cost of the structure, 236. — Engineers and contractors, 236.

" The Grand River viaduct, Mauritius railways." By W. Ridley, 237. —Position, 237.—Dimensions, 237.— The piers, 237. — Excavations for foundations for ditto, 237.—Pumping operations, 238.—Foundations, 239.— Method of lifting the iron cylinders, 241.—Ditto of filling the piers with concrete, 241.—The bedplates, 242. —Plan for erecting the piers originally intended, 242. — Arrangement for launching the girders, 243.—Progress of launching ditto, and final failure, 244, et seq.—Method of launching the girders ultimately carried out, 245.— Completion of the viaduct, 247.—Total weight of the superstructure and of the ironwork in the piers, 247.

Discussion.—Atkinson, W., 254, 258.—

VICKERS.

Berkley, G., 260.—Broad, R., 250.—Cubitt, J., 258.—Fowler, J., 261.—Fox, Sir C., 255, 258.—Freeman, J., 260.—Harrison, T. E., 258.—Hawkshaw, J., 256, 258.—Hemans, G. W., 248, 258.—Heppel, J. M., 249.—Longridge, J. A., 248, 249, 260.—Phipps, G. H., 250, 259.—Porter, J. H., 254.—Vignoles, C. B., 249.

Boyne viaduct, points of inflection of the, xxix. 75.

Vide also RAILWAY BRIDGES AND VIADUCTS.

VICKERS, A. [Election, xxvii. 320.]

VICKERS, G. N. [Election, xxiv. 511.]

VICTOR, H. E. [Election, xxvii. 55.]

VIDLER, M. [Election, xxviii. 216.]

VIEIRA, A. A. [Admission, xxvii. 55.]

VIGERS, R. [Election, xxix. 98.]

VIGNOLES, C. B. [Member of Council, xxi. 133; xxii. 112; xxiii. 112; xxiv. 106; xxv. 161; xxvi. 119; Vice-President, xxvii. 122; xxviii. 158; President, xxix. 208.]

Address on taking the chair for the first time after his election as President, xxix. 272. — Claims of senior Vice-Presidents waived in his favour, 272.—Progress of the Institution, 272.—Ancient sources of water supply, 274. — Indian tanks, 275.—Ancient canals of Egypt, China, and Spain, 275. — Embankments against floods, 276. — Canals of the middle ages in Holland and Italy, 276.—Engineering works undertaken by governments in early times, 276. — 'Chaussées' of France, 276. — Revival of 'the ancient laws and customs' by Charlemagne, 277.—Rochester bridge, 277. — Monastic order of bridge-builders, 277. — Maintenance of ways of communication, 278. — Canal engineering in France, 279.—Origin and establishment of the 'Corps des Ponts et Chaussées,' 279.—Various branches, 280.—Organization, 281.—The 'École des Ponts et Chaussées' and the 'École des Mines,' 282.—'Conducteurs des Travaux et Gardes-Mines,' 282.—Position of the officers

VIGNOLES.

of the École des Ponts et Chaussées,' 283. — Directory and 'Annales' of the 'Corps des Ponts et Chaussées,' 284. — Interference and control in matters of engineering by foreign governments, 284. — Leading principle of civil engineering in England, 285.—Rise of companies associated in devising improvements for local benefit, 285. — Canal engineering in England, 285. — Roads in England and in France, 286.—Roads in India, 286.—Amsterdam sea-canal, 287.—Tower subway, 288.—Bermuda dock, 290. — Engineering works of recent date in North Germany, 291. — Armour-plates and military engineering. 293. — Rifled ordnance, 295. — Blackfriars bridge and Holborn viaduct, 299.—Madrid waterworks, 300.—Atlantic railroad, 300.— Wire tramways, 300.—Mont Cenis tunnel, 301. — Mont Cenis railway, 301. — Suez canal, 303.—Introduction of gaslights into London, 304.—Navigation of the lower reaches of the Thames before the introduction of steamboats, 305.—Progress of the trade and population of Liverpool and Manchester, 306.—The Stockton and Darlington and the Liverpool and Manchester railways, 307. — The 'Rainhill experiments,' 310. — Dinner at Liverpool on the occasion, and toasts, 310.—Engineer and Railway Volunteer Staff Corps, 311.—The introduction of the railway system into France hindered by M. Thiers, 313.—Macadam's principle of constructing and repairing roads introduced into France by M. Le Grand, 314.—Mistakes of scientific men illustrated in the case of Dr. Lardner, 314. — The 'Irish Railway Commissioners,' 315. — Evil effects of not adopting their recommendations, 315. — French and English systems of railways contrasted, 316.—The Student Class, 316. — Comparison between English engineers and French engineers, 316.—Proper aims of civil engineers, 317. — Dr. Whewell on

VIGNOLES.

theoretical and practical work, 317.—Honourable ambition in the minds of engineers to have their names associated with works with which they have been connected, 318.

Armour-plates and military engineering, xxix. 293.

Artillery. Consumption of powder, xxvi. 201.—Rifled ordnance, xxix. 295.

Bridges and viaducts, xxv. 249.—Mode of launching the girders of the Grand River viaduct, Mauritius railways, 249.—Cast-iron bridges, xxvii. 112.—Bridge-building in the middle ages, xxix. 277.—Blackfriars new bridge, 299.

Bridges, suspension, xxvi. 270.—Strength of the platform of suspension bridges due to the stiffness given to the cross-girders, 270.—Suspension-rods, 270.—Equalization of the strains on each side of the top of the piers of suspension bridges, 271. — Back chains of ditto, 272.—Experiments on the links of the Kieff suspension bridge, xxx.274.

Canals, ancient and modern, xxix. 275, 279. — Amsterdam sea-canal, 287.—Suez canal, 303.

Canals, steam-power on, xxvi. 32, 33.—Advantage of vertical retaining-walls for canal banks, 33.

Cement, hydraulic, preparation of the clay for, xxv. 135.

Coast, &c. Arrangement and origin of the Chesil Bank, xxiii. 230, 254.

Concrete. Disintegration of concrete blocks, xxiv. 168.—Passing concrete through water, 170.—Preparation of blocks of concrete with salt-water, at Algiers and Marseilles, xxv. 135.

Docks, graving, xxv. 322. — Origin of the term 'camel' as applied to pontoons, 323.—'Bermuda' floating dock, xxix. 290.

Drainage of towns, xxiv. 346. — Great cost of the Paris sewers, 346.

Foundations of the suspension bridge at Kieff, in Russia, xxi. 479.—Antiquity of well-foundations in India, xxix. 402.

Gas, illuminating power of coal, xxviii. 465.—Use of coal-gas, under certain given conditions, as a standard of com-

VIGNOLES.

parison for testing the illuminating power of other gases, 465.

Iron, cast and wrought, application of, xxvii. 573.

Irrigation, antiquity of, xxvii. 525. — Its introduction into Spain, 525. — Irrigation works as commercial speculations, 525. — Irrigation in India, xxix. 275.

Lighthouses, Red Sea, xxiii. 26.—Use of timber piles for foundations of ditto, 26, 36.—Whether wrought-iron cylinders would have been preferable, 27.

Locomotive engines, disturbing forces of, xxii. 100. — Duplicate locomotive engines manufactured for the Tudela and Bilbao railway, 613.

Materials, durability of, xvii. 572.—Impregnation of timber by metallic agents as a preservative, 572.

Permanent way. Failure of turned double-headed rails, xxii. 30.—Imperfections in the permanent way the occasion of oscillations in locomotives, 100. — Maintenance and renewal of permanent way, xxv. 379.—Strength of iron and steel rails of different sections, 379.—Fracture of double-headed rails when turned, 380. — Complication introduced by the use of chairs, 380. — Fishing the rails, 380. — Improbability of reducing the cost of maintenance of permanent way, 381. —Bessemer rail, 396.—Specifications for iron rails, xxvii. 355.—Manufacture of rails from a homogeneous material, 356. — Substitution of iron for wooden sleepers, 572.

Public works in France, xxix. 278, et seq. —In England, 285, 304.—In India, 286, 287.—Table showing the facilities of internal communication in the United Kingdom, France, Prussia, Spain, and the United States of North America for the year 1868–69, 286.—Public works recently executed in North Germany, 291.

Railway curves, xxiii. 431. — Rule respecting reversed curves on the Continent, 431. — Super-elevation of the outer rail on a curve, 432.

VIGNOLES.

Railway locomotion. Adams's radial axle-boxes, xxiii. 430. — Combination of the radial axle with the single bogie, 430.—Friction of iron upon iron, xxvi. 354.—Amount of adhesion on railways deviating from the horizontal, 354.

Railway rolling stock, xxx. 194.— Analysis of railway statistics by Mr. R. P. Williams, 194, 213.—Train mileage, 204.

Railway station platforms, xxv. 280.

Railways, German system of construction, xxii. 27.—Perfection of German railway statistics, 28. — Comparative cost of railways in Germany and Great Britain, 29. — Santiago and Valparaiso railway, xxiii. 401.—Suitability of ironwork for railway structures in Chilé, 402. — Importance of obtaining statistics in regard to railways, xxv. 395. — Economical construction of railways in the colonies, xxix. 123. — Atlantic railway, 300.—Mont Cenis railway, 301.—Progress of railways in England, 306; in France, 313; in Ireland, 315.— Mileage of railways and turnpike roads in the United Kingdom, 371.— Causes that have enhanced the cost of railways, 371.—Working expenses of railways, 371.—Financial operations of railways, 372.—Great Indian Peninsula railway, 402.

Reclaiming land from the sea, xxi. 478. —Continuation of reclamation banks across creeks by sinking fascines in the breach, 478.—Ebb and flow of the water through openings in reclamation banks, xxiii. 181. — Closing breaches in ditto horizontally, 182.— Reclamations of land generally made gradually and in small enclosures, 183.

Rivers, freshwater floods of, xxvii. 242. —Formation of lakes to obviate the perils of floods in the rivers Saône and Loire, 242. — Embankment of torrential rivers, xxix. 125.

Rivers and estuaries, xxi. 295.—Failure of parallel piers in maintaining a good channel at the mouth of the

VOSS.

river Adour, 295. — Success of the works in Dublin bay, 295.—Changes resulting from sea-currents at the mouth of the Thames, xxiii. 231.— Ditto at the mouth of the Ganges, 231.—Formation of bars at the mouths of rivers, xxvi. 423.—Dredging operations at the bar of the river Tyne, 423. — Ditto at the mouth of the Liffey, 424. — Incompatibility of effective drainage with the perfection of navigation, as illustrated in the estuary of the Witham, xxviii. 81.

Roof. Tie of the St. Pancras station roof of the Midland railway, xxx. 105.

Steam navigation, xxix. 196.—Proportion between resistance and the power of overcoming resistance, 196.

Stoves, regenerative hot-blast, xxx. 321. —Superiority of Russian brick stoves to German iron ones, 321.

Students of the Institution of Civil Engineers, xxix. 316.

Subway, Tower, xxix. 288.

Tramways along suspended wire-ropes, xxix. 300.

Tunnel, Mont Cenis, xxix. 301.

Viaduct, Holborn, xxix. 299.

Water supply of Paris, xxv. 494.—Large amount of water used for ornamental purposes in continental cities, 494.— Water supplied by the Berlin Waterworks Company, xxvii. 37.—Madrid waterworks, xxix. 300.

Wells, machinery for boring, xxiii. 473. — Difference between the Chinese system and Fauvelle's system of well-boring, 473.—Fauvelle system, 473.— M. Kind's system of well-boring as carried out in Germany, 473.—System of boring in Paris, 473.—Shafts sunk for minerals in France and Germany, 474.—Economy and propriety of sinking wells by percussion, 474.—Resemblance of Mather's system of well-boring to the Chinese system, 477.

VIGNOLES, Henry. [Election, xxiii. 257.]

VIGNOLES, Hutton. [Auditor, xxix. 207.]

VIVIAN, G. W. [Election, xxvii. 553.]

VIVIAN, H. A. [Election, xxviii. 59.]

VOSS, H. [Election, xxiii. 151.]

W.

WADDINGTON.

WADDINGTON, J. [Election, xxii. 65.]

WADE, W. B. [Election, xxiv. 358.]

WAKE, H. H. [Election, xxx. 323.]

WALKER, C. V.

Railway telegraphs, xxii. 203.—System of telegraph signalling in operation on the South Eastern railway, 203.—Origin of the bell-signal system, 203.—Rise, progress, and cost of the bell system on the South Eastern railway, 204.—Bell-signals almost universally applicable, 205. — Arrangement of bells with balanced currents, 206.—Working of ditto, 207. — Form of semaphore, 208.—Superiority of the bell system to the index system, 208.—Efficient working of the bell system, 209.—Contradiction in the semaphore systems, 209. — Large amount of traffic worked over the South Eastern railway by the bell system, 210.

Railway trains, communication in, xxvi. 101.—System of electrical intercommunication in trains adopted on the South Eastern railway, 101.—Results of the working of ditto, 104.

WALKER, James. [Past-President, xxi. 172; Memoir, xxii. 1, 630.]

WALKER, James.

Rivers. Depth of sand-beds in some of the rivers in Madras, xxiv. 194.

Timber of the Madras Presidency, xxii. 256.—Native woods generally unfit for railway sleepers, 256.—Difficulty of thoroughly creosoting timber, 257.

WALKER, J. R. [Memoir, xxi. 567.]

WALKER, T. [Election, xxvii. 218.]

WALKER, T. A. [Election, xxvii. 398.]

WALL, P. W. [Election, xxiv. 458.]

WALLACE, D. [Admission, xxix. 98.]

WALLER, J. H. [Admission, xxvii. 180.]

WALLIS, G. A. [Election, xxv. 65.]

WALLIS, J. J. [Election, xxvii. 443.]

WALTON, J. B. [Election, xxvii. 55.]

WATER, FILTRATION OF.

WANKLYN, Professor J. A.

Water supply. Effects of filtration on water taken at Hampton, xxvii. 13.—Varying action of permanganate of potash on different forms of albumen, 13.

WARBURTON, R. [Admission, xxvii. 54.]

WARD, Lieutenant C. V.

Rivers and estuaries. Extracts from his report on the depth of water and on the tides of the Hooghly (Longridge, J. A.), xxi. 18.—The Mutla accessible to vessels during the S.W. monsoon, 30.

WARD, J. [Memoir, xxi. 567.]

WARDEN, W. M. [Election, xxii. 336.]

WARHAM, J. R. [Election, xxi. 492.]

WARING, A. J. [Admission, xxvii. 54.]

WARING, C. [Associate of Council, xxiii. 112.]

WARING, T. [Election, xxi. 345.]

WARREN, C., Lieutenant, R.E. [Election, xxv. 429.]

WARREN, J. N. [Memoir, xxi. 595.]

WASHINGTON, Admiral. [Memoir, xxiii. 512.]

WATER, FILTRATION OF.

" Experiments on the removal of organic and inorganic substances in water." By E. Byrne, xxvi. 544.—Pure water necessary for health, 544. — Preliminary considerations on the purifying effects of charcoal, 544.—Results of the examination of bog-water, 545.—Examination of the removing power of animal and vegetable charcoal, 547.—Experiments with animal charcoal, 549.—Ditto with wood charcoal, 552.—Ditto with peat charcoal, 553.—Ditto on animal charcoal with some well-water, treated with permanganate of potash, slightly in excess, previous to its passage through the charcoal, 553. — Results of experi-

WATER, FLOW OF.

ments show that charcoal has but small efficacy for purifying water, 555. — Water supply, 555. — SUPPLEMENT, xxvii. 1.—Experiments with magnetic carbide and silicated carbon filters, 4.—Feeble removing power of magnetic carbide, 4.—Resemblance of the action of silicated carbon to animal charcoal. 4.—Animal charcoal and silicated carbon quickly lose their power to remove organic matter, 5.—Filtration useless as a means of removing substances in solution, 5.—Danger of using water not naturally pure, 5.

Discussion.—Ansted, Prof. D. T., 24.— Austin, C. E., 46.—Bateman, J. F., 10, 38.—Byrne, E., 6, 7, 48.—Chadwick, E., 32.—Chapman, E. T., 14. —Cowper, E. A., 35.— Frankland, Dr. E., 8, 10, 18. — Gregory, C. H., 53. — Hawksley, T., 15, 19.— Heisch, C., 45. — Hemans, G. W., 31.—Letheby, Dr. H., 6, 7, 35.— Longridge, J. A., 41.—Olrick, L., 43. —Shield, H., 27.—Smee, A., 22.— Spencer, T., 10, 13.—Vignoles, C. B., 37.—Wanklyn, Prof. J. A., 13.— Webster, T., 42.

Vide also WATER SUPPLY.

WATER, FLOW OF.

" On the results of a series of observations on the flow of water off the ground in the Woodburn district, near Carrickfergus, Ireland; with rain-gauge registries in the same locality for a period of twelve months, ending 30th June, 1865." By R. Manning, xxv. 458.—Scheme for supplying Belfast with water from near Carrickfergus, 458.—Courses of the two branches of the Woodburn river, and extent of the rain-basin, 458. — Rain-gauges, 458. — Streamgauges, 458.—Formula for calculating the discharge of ditto, 459.—Extent of surface drained by each branch of the Woodburn river, 459. — Table No. 1: summary of the results of the rainfall on, and flow of water off, the Woodburn district, 460.—Facts collected from ditto, 459.—Ratio of the rainfall on the Carrickfergus mountains to that at Belfast, 460.—Proportion of rainfall available for water supply, 460.—Definition of the term 'evaporation,' 461.—Loss from evaporation dependent on the distribution of the rain throughout the year, 461.— Calculation of the mean loss of water from evaporation in the Woodburn district, 461.—Table No. 2, showing the calculated winter and summer rainfall, loss, and available water supply from the Woodburn district from 1851 to 1864, 462.—Years of maximum and minimum supply, also the years of maximum and minimum winter rain, 462.—Conclusions, 462. —Storage capacity for the maintenance of a constant supply measured by the longest period of defect of supply over demand, 462.— Table No. 3 : calculations of the particulars of the storage required for all quantities, from the mean annual supply down to that of the minimum year, 463.—Storage of the water supply yielded by the Woodburn district, 463. — Proper amount of storage as regards the economical supply from the Woodburn district, 464.—Lough Mourne, a natural reservoir of the maximum supply from ditto, 464.—Relative interests of water-companies and millowners to be considered, 464. — Question of waterpower, 464.—Proportion of the mean annual flow of the Woodburn river applicable to the supply of Woodlawn mills, 464.—Table No. 4, showing the results of observations as to ditto, 465. —Amount of water lost, 465.—Circumstances on which the available quantity of water depends, 465.— Appendix: discharge of the Woodburn rivers for nine months, from July 11, 1865, to March 31, 1866, 467. —Remarks on formulæ for the discharge over notches or weirs, 467.

Discussion. — Bateman, J. F., 472.— Beardmore, N., 474.—Cawley, C. E.,

WATERFALL.

477.—Fowler, J., 479.—Greaves, C., 476.—Homersham, S. C., 476.—Manning, R., 470, 476, 477.—Rawlinson, R., 476.—Scott, M., 477.

Vide also DRAINAGE OF LAND ; and RIVER THAMES.

WATERFALL, W. F. [Admission, xxvii. 54.]

WATER SUPPLY.

Madrid, xxix. 30.

Paris. "On the water supply of the city of Paris." By G. R. Burnell, xxv. 480.—Sources of information, 480.—Details of water supply to Paris in 1860, 480.—Supply to the population per head per day, 481.—Quality of the water, 481.—Capacity of the Paris basin for furnishing a water supply, 481.—Hardness of the water, 481.—Project of supply from the sources of the Somme Soude, 482.—Supply from other sources ultimately obtained, 482.—Yield of the water of the Dhuis and the Surmellin, 483.—Description of the aqueduct, 483.—Reservoirs at Menilmontant and Belleville, 483.—Supply of water from the Marne, 484.—Water to be obtained from Armentières, and course of the intended aqueduct, 484. — Period at which the waters from the different sources of supply will be available, 485.—Water supply from the Seine to be ultimately abandoned, 485.—Expected supply of water when all the works are completed, 485.—Waters of the Seine and of the Canal de l'Ourc to be used for fountains and street-washing, 486.—Pumps for raising the waters of the Seine, 486.—Revenue derived from filtered Seine water, 486.—Other aqueducts, 486.—Principle upon which the reservoirs of Passy and of Menilmontant are constructed, 487.—The Passy reservoirs, 487.—The reservoirs of Menilmontant, 488.—Ditto at Belleville, 488.—Water service, 488.—Total quantity of water distributed gratuitously in Paris per day, 489.—Constitution of "La Compagnie Générale des Eaux," 490.—Quantity of water supplied by

WAVES.

ditto, 490.—Income of ditto, 491.—Wholesale and retail price of filtered water supplied by ditto, 491.—Supply defective, particularly in the upper flats of houses, 491.—Sum paid to the engineering service, 492. — Faulty principle of the water supply, 492.

Discussion.—Atkinson W., 499.—Bateman, J. F., 500, 506.—Burnell, G. R., 506.—Clutterbuck, Rev. J. C., 496.—Fowler, J., 507.—Hawksley, T., 506.—Hemans, G. W., 494. — Homersham, S. C., 502, 506.—Jenkin, F., 505.—Lane, C. B., 505.—Murray, J., 498.—Rawlinson, R., 494.—Vignoles, C. B., 494.

Worcester, xxvii. 42.

Vide also ARTESIAN WELLS ; and WATER, FILTRATION OF.

Waterworks at Thames Ditton and Kingston, extracts from reports as to the performance of the pumping engines at the (Simpson, J.), xxiii. 70. *Vide* also STEAM-ENGINES.

WATSON, J. W. [Election, xxvi. 398.]

WATSON, R. [Election, xxviii. 59.]

WATSON, W.

London and Dublin communication. "On the communication between London and Dublin," xxii. 574.—Remarks, 597, 602.

Ships and steam-vessels. Vessels for the improved service between Kingstown and Holyhead, xxii. 597.—Cause of abandoning the superheating apparatus, 597.—Length of fast-going vessels, 602.—Skin resistance of ditto, 602.

Watt medals. *Vide* PREMIUMS AND PRIZES.

WATTS, T. R. [Admission, xxvii. 54.]

WAUGH, General Sir A.

Materials, decay of, in tropical climates, xxiv. 24.—Causes of decay of buildings in the tropics, 24.—Excellence of the bricks in ancient Indian buildings, 24.—Teak and Saul woods, 24.

WAUGH, H. [Election, xxvi. 477.]

Waves. 'Lead' of the sea, xxii. 443.—Motion of waves in a deep sea, 444.—Deadening effect of coral reefs on a rough sea, xxiii. 35.

WAWN.

WAWN, C. [Election, xxvii. 180.]

WEALLENS, W. [Memoir, xxii. 633.]

WEBB, E. B.

Irrigation enterprises, xxvii. 551.—
Quantity of water required for irrigation, 550.

Public works in Brazil, xxii. 413.—Destruction of a timber pile by 'teredo'
in the bay of Rio de Janeiro, 413.—
Rapid decay of sleepers of native
Brazilian timber, 413.—Use of iron
for telegraph posts on the Dom Pedro
Segundo railway in Brazil, 414.

Timber, Brazilian, xxii. 413.—Durability
of timber in various situations, xxvii.
574.

WEBB, F. C.

Surveying instruments. Notice of an
improved sextant, xxi. 540.

WEBB, F. W. [Election, xxiv. 511.]

Permanent way, maintenance and renewal of, xxv. 409.—Wear of steel
rails on the London and North
Western railway, 409.—Ramsbottom's
wrought-iron chairs and fishjoints on
ditto, 410.—Use of turned rails, 410.
—Welding steel rails, 426.

WEBB, J. S. [Admission, xxix. 98.]

WEBB, W. L. [Resignation, xxiii. 120.]

WEBSTER, T.

Low-water basin at Birkenhead, xxix. 7.
—Sluicing operations, 7, 17.—Geological character of the site, 17.

Railway accidents, xxi. 408.—Difficulties
in amending the present system of
inquiry, 408.

Rivers and estuaries, tidal levels of,
xxviii. 513.—Changes in the highwater and low-water levels in the
Nene and Ouze, 513.—Tide in the
Mersey, 514.

Steam-engines. General accuracy of
the results of the duty of the Cornish
engine as recorded by Cornish
engineers, xxiii. 83.—Introduction of
the Cornish system into London, 83.
—Use of steam expansively in the
Cornish engine, 83.

Timber, preservation of, xxiv. 36.—
Absorption of chemical preservatives
by soft woods, 36.

WHEELER.

Water supply of Worcester, xxvii. 42.—
Purification of water by natural processes, 42.

WEBSTER, W. [Election, xxviii. 59.]

WEEDON, F. M. [Election, xxiv. 257.]

Weight, per square foot, of a crowd of
men, xxii. 531, et seq.; xxvi. 281, 289.

WEILD, W. [Election, xxi. 492.]

Weirs, construction of, in India, xxvii.
457, et seq.—Weir across the Henares,
515.—Principal dimensions and circumstances of the most remarkable
weirs constructed in Spain, 552.—Vide
also IRRIGATION.

Wells, Artesian, on the machinery employed in sinking, on the Continent
(Burnell, G. R.), xxiii. 459. . Vide
also ARTESIAN WELLS.

Wells, on sinking, for the foundations of
the piers of the bridge over the river
Jumna, Delhi railway (Bell, I.),
xxviii. 325. Vide also FOUNDATIONS.

WENDEN, H. C. E. [Election, xxix. 98.]

WESLEY, M. E. [Election, xxv. 479.]

WEST, A. A. [Election, xxvi. 79.]

Rivers, freshwater floods of, xxvii. 264.
—Floods in the Sattara districts of the
Bombay presidency, 264.

WEST, T. E. [Admission, xxix. 322.]

WESTERN, C. R. [Admission, xxviii. 59.]

WHEATSTONE, A. [Admission, xxix. 98.]

WHEELER, W. H. [Election, xxvii. 55;
Telford premium, xxix. 211.]

River Witham. "Description of the
River Witham and its estuary, and of
the various works carried out in connection therewith, for the drainage of
the Fens, and the improvement of the
navigation," xxviii. 59. — Remarks,
104.—Effect of the Grand Sluice in
causing an accumulation of silt in the
river, 81, 83, 104.—Removal of silt by
freshes, 84.—Proper outfall, 111.

Rivers and estuaries. Condition of the
Nene, the Ouze, and the Welland,
xxviii. 83.—Sluices on the Fen rivers,
83.—Injurious effects of the internal
system of drainage in the Fens
introduced by Vermuyden, 105.—Eau
Brink cut, 106.—Antagonism of the
navigation and drainage interests in

WHEWELL.

the Fens, 106.—Action of saltwater in a river-channel, 108.—Deposit of silt at the extreme end of the tidal wave in the Fen rivers, 108.—Proper situations for sluices on rivers, 108.—Training the outfall of the Fen rivers, 109. —Silting-up of the Wash, 109.— Schemes for its reclamation, 110.— Tides of the Lynn and Boston deeps, 111.

WHEWELL, Rev. W. [Memoir, xxx. 426.]

WHITE, C. F. [Election, xxi. 492.]

WHITE, C. H. [Election, xxiii. 375.]

WHITE, G. F.
Cements. Manufacture of Portland cement of a high specific weight, xxv. 117, et seq.—Tests of Portland cement adopted by the engineers of the Ponts et Chaussées, 117, et seq.—Disadvantages likely to arise from the use of heavily-burnt cement, 119.—Requirements of the Metropolitan Board of Works and of the French engineers, 120.—Table of results of comparative experiments on Portland cement, 121. —Adaptation of different classes of cement to various sorts of work, 122.

WHITE, L.
Concrete blocks, chemical action of water on, xxiv. 169.

WHITE, R. [Election, xxix. 272.]

WHITE, R. O. [Election, xxii. 241.]

White ants, chloride of zinc used as an antidote against the ravages of, xxii. 496.—Gun-carriage destroyed by white ants, xxiii. 29.—Creosoted timber not liable to their attacks, xxv. 416. Vide also MATERIALS.

WHITEHEAD, A. [Election, xxi. 48.]

WHITFIELD, J. [Election, xxiii. 257.]
Public works in Pernambuco, xxii. 415. —Great variety of timber in Brazil, 415.—Durability of ironwork in hot climates, 416.

WHITING, J. E. [Election, xxv. 429.]
Bridges and viaducts. Effect of deepening continuous open girders over piers, xxvi. 306.

WHITMORE, W. R. [Decease, xxiii. 121.]

WHITWORTH, Sir J. [Member of Council,

WILLIAMS.

xxi. 133; xxii. 112; xxiii. 112; xxiv. 106.]

Whitworth scholarships, resolution of Council and of General Meeting as to foundation of, xxvii. 552.

WHITWORTH, W. S. [Election, xxiv. 184.]

WHYTE, H. F. [Election, xxix. 98.]

WICKENDEN, A. A. [Election, xxviii. 517.]

WICKES, H. W. [Election, xxv. 352.]

WIGHTMAN, A. [Memoir, xxv. 581.]

WIGRAM, C. [Election, xxx. 1.]
Steam navigation, xxix. 163.—Indicated H.P. obtained by steamers, 163, 167. —Results of voyages of the steamship 'Somersetshire,' 164.—Most suitable size of steam-vessels destined for long voyages, 165.—Effect of the Suez Canal on steam navigation, 166.

WILKINSON, A. A. [Election, xxiv. 62.]

WILKINSON, J. S. [Election, xxvii. 55.]

WILKS, C. [Election, xxix. 98.]

WILLIAMS, A.
Drainage of towns. "Description of the sewerage and drainage works of Newport, Monmouthshire," xxii. 273.— Remarks, 303.—Relative cost of brick and pipe sewers, 303.—Diminished percentage of deaths in Newport consequent on the carrying-out of the drainage-works, 303.

WILLIAMS, C. S. [Admission, xxvii. 54.]

WILLIAMS, C. W. [Memoir, xxviii. 627.]

WILLIAMS, E. [Election, xxvii. 580.]
Permanent way. Superiority of rails rolled from solid ingots, xxvii. 341.— Steel heads for iron rails, 341.— Durability of rails dependent on the capacity of the iron for welding, 342.— Tenders for the manufacture of rails, 342.

WILLIAMS, E. L.
Canals, steam-power on, xxvi. 16.— Results of steam-tugging on the river Severn, 16.

WILLIAMS, E. L., Jun.
Canals, steam-power on, xxvi. 23.— Steam tugs and barges on the river Weaver and on the Gloucester and Berkeley canal, 23.
Rivers and estuaries. Superiority of the system of training-walls to that of

WILLIAMS.

jetties in tidal rivers, xxiv. 77.—
Desirability of augmenting the
hydraulic mean depth, 77.—Velocity
of the tidal wave in the Severn, 77.—
Materials for training-walls, 78.—
Successful application of a fascine
embankment on the Severn at Tewkes-
bury, 78.—Improvement of the river
Weaver, xxvi. 23.

WILLIAMS, J. [Election, xxviii. 518.]

WILLIAMS, J. M., Captain, R.E. [Election,
xxiv. 144.]

WILLIAMS, R. H. [Election, xxx. 323.]
Lead ores, dressing, xxx. 131.—Dressing
tin ore, 131.—Williams's buddle, 132.

WILLIAMS, R. P. [Telford medal and
premium, xxvi. 121, 138.]
Coal-mining, xxviii. 146.—Use of gunpowder in the Rhondda valley district,
146.
Permanent way. "On the maintenance
and renewal of permanent way," xxv.
353.—Remarks, 375.—Deflections of
iron rails under strain, 375.—Of
steel rails, 376. — Strength of a
steel rail that had sustained a large
amount of traffic at Chalk Farm, 377.—
Sections of rails tested, 380.—Uniformity in keeping permanent-way
accounts, 426.—Comparative endurance of steel and iron rails on several
English railways, xxvii. 381.—Life of
steel rails, 382.—Manufacture of rails
from highly phosphorized Cleveland
iron, 382.—Present and future advantages to be derived from the substitution of steel for iron rails, 382.—New
arrangement of switches for railway
junctions, xxix. 23.—Permanent-way
valuations, xxx. 194.
Railway income and expenditure, xxix.
338. — Maintenance, renewal, and
working expenses, 338. — Improving
the value of railway property, 339.—
Fallacy of the train-mileage principle
in estimating the cost of working
expenditure on railways, 341.—Locomotive expenses per train mile and
per engine, 344.
Railway rolling stock. "The maintenance and renewal of railway rolling

WILSON.

stock," xxx. 136.—Remarks, 192.—
Relationship between locomotive
expenses and train mileage, 192.—
Comparison of railway expenses on
lines having different classes of traffic,
193. — Great Eastern railway train
mileage, 193.—Permanent-way valuations, 194. — Tables of locomotive
expenses on different railways prepared by Mr. Armstrong, 206.—
Existing anomalies connected with the
subject of train-mileage, 207.—Definition of the term 'mean money life' of
an engine, 208.—Importance of ascertaining the serviceable value of rolling
stock, 208.—Normal depreciation of
rolling stock, 209.—Comparison between the cost of current repairs and
the first cost of locomotives, 212.
Steel, strength of, in compression and
tension, xxvi. 295.

WILLIAMS, W. W., Jun. [Admission,
xxvii. 120.]

WILLIAMSON, Professor.
Stoves, Siemens-Cowper regenerative hot-
blast, xxx. 317.

WILLIS, E. R. [Election, xxiv. 511.]

WILLIS, Colonel P. W. [Decease, xxvi.
129.]

WILLMAN, C. [Election, xxix. 272.]

WILMOT, H. F. E. [Admission, xxvii.
54.]

WILSON, Alexander, General I. R. E.
[Memoir, xxx. 461.]

WILSON, Allan. [Election, xxvi. 310;
Telford premium, xxviii. 161, 178.]
Irrigation. "On irrigation in India,"
xxvii. 454.—Remarks, 546.—Small
works of irrigation in Southern India,
546.—Facilities for constructing artificial reservoirs in India, 546.—Irrigation in the Raichore Doab, 547.—
Irrigation works in India by private
companies, 547.

WILSON, A. F. [Election, xxix. 98.]

WILSON, Edward. [Election, xxv. 65.]

WILSON, Edward. [Election, xxix. 322.]

WILSON, George. [Election, xxii. 167.]

WILSON, George. [Election, xxiv. 257.]

WILSON, H. [Election, xxii. 241.]

WILSON, H. C. [Resignation, xxix. 217.]

WILSON.

WILSON, I. [Election, xxiv. 511.]

WILSON, J. W. [Election, xxviii. 232.]

WILSON, W. [Election, xxii. 604; Telford medal and premium, xxviii. 161, 178.]
Bridge, Victoria. "Description of the Victoria bridge, on the line of the Victoria station and Pimlico railway," xxvii. 55.—Remarks, 82.—Testing the new Victoria bridge, 82.—Victoria bridge built at different periods on different principles, 82.—Choice of wrought-iron for the Victoria bridge, 116.—Chief points of difference between the original Victoria bridge and the widening, 116.—Resistance to strains, 117.—Effect of loading, 118.—Expansion joint and segmental shoes, 119.— Relative cost of the Victoria bridge and the widening, 119.

WILTON, F. [Admission, xxvii. 180.]

WINBOLT, J. S. [Election, xxviii. 517.]

WINDHAM, F. W. S. [Admission xxvii. 54.]

WINGATE, R. [Election, xxv. 429.]

WINTERINGHAM, H. [Election, xxiii. 320.]

WITHERS, J. [Decease, xxii. 640.]

WOOD, A. H.
Gas, illuminating power of coal, xxviii. 465.—Want of uniformity in the rate of consumption of sperm-candles, 465. —Necessity for a better standard of comparison, 465.

WOOD, J. [Election, xxvii. 553.]

WOOD, J. T.
Public works in Brazil, xxii. 412.— Probable effect of the Recife and São Francisco railway, 412.—Labour question and extension of the railway system in Pernambuco, 412.

WOOD, N. [Decease, xxvi. 129.]

WOODBRIDGE, G. [Election, xxviii. 59.]

WOODHOUSE, J. T.
Coal-mining, xxviii. 127.—Machines for superseding the use of gunpowder, 127.
Railway locomotion. Speed of starting and stopping trains on the Midland railway, xxx. 206.

WOODIFIELD, M. [Election, xxiv. 358.]

WOODS, E. [Member of Council, xxix. 208.]
Bridges, iron-girder, principles of construction of, xxiv. 433.
Locomotive engines, xxiii. 400.—Engines employed on the steep inclines of the

WYTHES.

Copiapo Extension railway, 400.— Ditto on the Santiago and Valparaiso railway, 401.—Tank engine with a two-wheeled bogie-truck on the Coquimbo line, 401.—Consumption of coal and coke on the Chilian railways, 401.—Action of the 'Bissell truck' in passage round curves, 435.—Locomotives for light railways in Chilé, xxvi. 67.—Rolling stock on the Tongoi and Carrizal railways, Chilé, 67.— Results of working the Copiapo Extension railway by locomotive power, 352.

Permanent way, destruction of, owing to increased weight of rolling stock, xxvi. 68.—Additional strength of rails and fastenings demanded by government inspectors, 69.

Railway curves, super-elevation of the outer rail on, xxiii. 401.

Railways. Santiago and Valparaiso railway, xxiii. 399.—Destruction by a flood of a screw-pile bridge over the Viña del Mar river, 401—Rapidity with which the works of the Valparaiso railway were executed, 401. — Expediency of iron structures for the Chilian railways, 402.—Curves and gradients on ditto, 402.—Gauge of railways in India, xxiv. 379.—Railway in Chilé, 379.—Light railways, xxvi. 67.

WOODS, E. H. [Election, xxvi. 79.]

WOODS, W. H. [Election, xxv. 429.]

WOOLCOTT, G. [Election, xxv. 65.]

WRAGGE, E. [Election, xxix. 272.]

WRENCH, J. M. [Admission, xxix. 98.]

WRIGHT, A. P. [Admission, xxix. 322.]

WRIGHT, G. H. [Election, xxvii. 55.]

WRIGHT, J.
Concrete, use of, in large masses under water, xxii. 445.—Concrete sea-walls at Brighton, 446.
Foundations. Plenum process of sinking iron cylinders, xxvii. 308.

WRIGHTSON, T. [Election, xxix. 98.]

WYLIE, H. J. [Election, xxviii. 232.]

WYNDHAM, H. [Election, xxv. 262.]

WYNNE, F. G. [Admission, xxvii. 443.]

WYTHES, G. [Election, xxiv. 184.]

WYTHES, G. E. [Election, xxiv. 184.]

Y.

YARROW.

YARROW, A. F. [Election, xxix. 98.]

YOLLAND, W., Colonel, R.E.

Railway accidents, xxi. 396.—Comparative immunity, on the Great Northern railway, from accidents caused by the fractures of tires, 396.—Advantages of the suspended over the bracketed fish-joint, 397.—Analysis of the causes of all the accidents reported on by the Board of Trade inspectors in the years 1854 to 1861, 397.—Advantages of adopting an interval of space in preference to an interval of time between trains, 398.—Accidents from trains running off the line, 398 ; from fractured tires, 398 ; from fractured couplings, axles, wheels, and springs, 399.—Miscellaneous causes of accidents from trains running off the line, 399.—Immunity on broad-gauge railways from accidents having reference to the nature of the permanent way, 399.—Causes of trains leaving the line on narrow-gauge railways, 399.—Desirability of having two railway whistles of different tones, 400.—Policy of placing a break-van behind the engine and at the rear of every train, 400.—Introduction of distant signals, 401.—Recording the speed of trains in travelling, 401.—Use of continuous breaks, 401.—Break-power recommended by the German railway engineers for various gradients, 402. —Break-power used in France, 402.—Gradual introduction of continuous breaks on different lines, 402.—Readi-

YOUNGHUSBAND.

ness of railway companies to afford information to the Board of Trade inspectors when investigating accidents, 403.—Tuxford accident on the Great Northern railway, 403.—Accident at Hatfield, 403.—At Merton, in which Dr. Baly was killed, 404.—'Cant' of the rail at the spot, 405. —The accident due to the tightness of the gauge on the curve, 405.—Number of accidents from fractured tires in 1854 and in 1861, 413.—Continuous breaks, especially on subdivisions of trains, 413.

YOUNG, D. W. [Election, xxvii. 443.]

YOUNG, E. W.

Bridge, Victoria, Pimlico, xxvii. 105.—Reasons for the form of construction adopted in the widening of the bridge, 105.—Piers, 107.—Stability of ditto, 108.

Bridges, suspension, xxvi. 299.—Clifton suspension bridge, 299.—Various forms of suspension bridges, 300. — Compound cantilever truss-bridge, 300.

Girders, continuous, xxix. 38.

Materials, resistance of. xxix. 34.—Phenomena of materials under strain, 34.—Strains of the fibres of solids submitted to unequal flexure, 34.

YOUNG, J. [Election, xxiv. 358]

YOUNGHUSBAND, O. [Election, xxiv. 62.]

Railway rolling stock, xxviii. 433.—American locomotives and rolling stock, 433.—Cast-iron chilled wheels compared with wrought-iron wheels, 434, et seq.

Z.

ZINC.

Zinc, xxvii. 568.—Zinc roofs, 568.—Superiority of Belgian zinc to English zinc for sheathing vessels, 569.

——, chloride of, preservation of various

ZINC.

articles by immersion in, xxii. 495.
—Efficacy of Sir W. Burnett's process, 496.—*Vide* also MATERIALS.

LONDON :
PRINTED BY WILLIAM CLOWES AND SONS,
STAMFORD STREET AND CHARING CROSS.

Lightning Source UK Ltd.
Milton Keynes UK
UKHW020759200223
417314UK00006B/388